1977

This book may be kept

FOURTEEN DAYS

Psychologists
on Psychology

Psychologists on Psychology

David Cohen

Taplinger Publishing Company / New York

First published in the United States in 1977 by
TAPLINGER PUBLISHING CO., INC.
New York, New York

All rights reserved. Printed in the U.S.A.
Copyright © 1977 by David Cohen

Library of Congress Cataloging in Publication Data

Cohen, David, 1946—
Psychologists on psychology.

Bibliography: p.
CONTENTS: David McClelland. — Donald Broadbent. —
Noam Chomsky. [etc.]
1. Psychologists — Biography.   2. Psychology —
Methodology.   I. Title.
BF109.A1C63   1977   150'.92'2   76-11687
ISBN 0-8008-6557-X
ISBN 0-8008-6558-8 pbk.

Contents

Contents

Acknowledgments

I am grateful to all the psychologists interviewed who, often, not only gave me a good deal of their time but also made me feel very welcome. I am also grateful to the editors of the *New Scientist* and of *Psychologie*, Paris, for their permission to use some material which had first appeared in their publications.

Finally, without the help and support of Aileen Latourette and our son, Nicholas, I would never have managed to concentrate enough to get it all finished.

Introduction

The psychology of psychologists might seem to be an esoteric, even frivolous, subject. It should be an important one. Psychology has become a very influential profession. It has often been said that psychologists and psychoanalysts, especially, have become the priests of a godless age. By 1976, the membership of the British Psychological Society had risen to over 6,000. The American Psychological Association has grown so large that some of its members are wondering if it has not become too large to be useful. Its list of members has the weighty feel of the telephone directory. By 1976, the membership of the American Psychological Association had risen to over 42,000 members. These statistics can establish, at least, that there has been a tremendous growth in the number of people who earn a living by psychology. Psychologists often excuse the state of their discipline by saying that it is, after all, a very young subject. In years, it is. In terms of man-years devoted to it, it is not. In nearly all sciences, the total number of scientists currently at work easily outnumbers all those who have ever worked at the subject. Psychology looks younger than it is.

Though some philosophers, especially Berkeley, Hume and J. S. Mill, were interested in psychological problems, psychology did not begin to disentangle itself from philosophy until Wundt and William James set up their respective laboratories. Wundt founded his laboratory in Leipzig in 1879: and William James founded his at Harvard in 1879. At first, the United States absorbed a good deal of the influence of German psychology. It has been argued that one of the reasons why J. B. Watson obtained such a response for his approach, first set out in 'Psychology as the behaviourist views it' (1913), was that it was an all-American methodology. It freed American psychology from German tutelage. Although Watson had to leave Johns Hopkins in 1920 because of a scandal – he was having an affair with a research assistant and divorced his wife – after which he gave up academic psychology for the more hustling climes of Madison Avenue, behaviourism went from success to apparent success. By the end of the Second World War, it was the dominant school of psychology in almost all American universities.

In Britain the progress of psychology, and of behaviourism too, was less spectacular. In 1949, psychology was an unusual degree course for a British university to offer. As Broadbent explains (1961), Cambridge was one of the few places where you could read psychology. London, too, offered a psychology degree. Oxford only began to provide a degree with some psychology in it with the opening of the PPP school which offered those who wanted to vacillate between the arts and the sciences the chance to combine philosophy with psychology. Now, most British universities and polytechnics offer degree courses in psychology. The late sixties saw a great demand from students for them. Many of those interviewed in this book believe this was because the students thought that if they studied psychology they would find out about life, a most unfortunate misconception according to at least a number of leading psychologists, who are not quite sure how to define psychology but are sure that it is only remotely connected with life.

Although Germany had the very first psychological laboratory, interest in psychology on the Continent has been slow to awaken; or that, at least, is the impression that has usually been conveyed by American and British psychologists. But there is now a vigorous movement, especially in social psychology. In the interview with Professor Tajfel, one of the prime movers and organiser of the European Association of Social Psychologists, he talks a good deal about the way in which the European tradition in psychology has been ignored. There is also an interest in experimental psychology – especially at the popular level. Both France and Germany have glossy magazines on psychology. The French one, *Psychologie*, sells some 75,000 copies a month.

Psychology offers, in fact, a rather promising career. Psychologists have infiltrated widely. The psychologist is no mere doer of experiments: he, or she, is no mere purveyor of theories. He advises. He consults. As an adviser, he wields much influence, and, sometimes, power. He can go into industry, into personnel work, into clinical work, into education and into the civil service. Many professions now include some training in psychology. Nurses, social workers, teachers receive such training obviously enough. But even policemen, magistrates and stewardesses get some smattering of psychological insights to equip them better for their jobs.

All in all, there is much psychological activity. For all this activity, it can be argued that the corresponding growth in knowledge has been disappointing. Nehemiah Jordan in his book *Themes in Speculative Psychology* (1968) states:

> There can be no doubt about it, contemporary American scientific psychology is the sterilest of the sterile. Years of arduous labour and the assiduous enterprise of hundreds of professors and thousands of students has yielded precisely nothing . . . . In the fifty-three years that have passed since that 'momentous' occasion [J. B. Watson, 'Psychology as the behaviourist views it', 1913] can *one* positive contribution towards any increased knowledge of man be pointed to? None such can be found: no substantive contribution can be named. The canard that 'psychology is a new science' has long outlived its explanatory-away usefulness: the unpleasant and discouraging facts must be faced honestly.

Written in 1968, Nehemiah Jordan's book has slowly started to provoke such questions. It must be said, very clearly, however, that not all psychologists share his pessimism. Donald Broadbent in what is, for me, the best and most convincing statement of the modern behaviourist position, has declared both in *Behaviour* (1961) and in *In Defence of Empirical Psychology* (1974) his commitment to traditional experimental methods. Near the end of *Behaviour*, in a section titled 'The Endless Search'. Broadbent wrote (pp. 200–1):

> We end then upon a note of doubt, with no certainty about the beliefs which future psychologists will hold. This is as it should be. Nobody can grasp the nature of things from an armchair and until fresh experiments have been performed we do not know what their results will be. The confident dogmatisms about human nature which fall so readily from pulpits, newspapers' editorials and school prize givings are not for us. Rather we must be prepared to live with an incomplete knowledge of behaviour but with confidence in the power of objective methods to give us that knowledge some day. These methods have proved themselves even in the past fifty years. Looking back we can see them destroying one over simplification after another, forcing us to reject Pavlov's theory or Hull's and

3

bringing theoretical opponents together by the sheer weight of factual evidence. In this half century there has been recognisable progress in our understanding of behaviour . . . .

Neither Donald Broadbent nor Jordan are extreme advocates of their sort of position. It is surely striking, therefore, that fifty-three years for Jordan have brought us no new knowledge of 'Man', while fifty years for Broadbent have seen a great advance in our understanding of 'behaviour'.

There are, I want to argue, very few facts that are accepted as being important and true by all psychologists. Jordan, for example, does admit that we have understood some of the processes by which perception works. Others like Laing, Hudson and Chomsky would not deny that experimental psychologists have, indeed, established many facts about perception, nor would they deny that physiological psychologists like Jouvet have made interesting discoveries about the neurophysiology of dreaming. It is just that these subjects do not seem to them to actually touch the core of what psychology ought to be about. What is at issue is not facts, nor even what the facts mean, but what importance the particular facts have. There is disappointment with what psychology has achieved. In *The Cult of the Fact* (1972), something like an intellectual autobiography, Hudson wrote of his undergraduate work at Oxford (pp. 40–1):

> Any idea that we were there to uncover the mysteries of the human mind would have been greeted with embarrassment; the kind of embarrassment that hardens into derision, and eventually into contempt. Just as a man on a desert island was held to illuminate the moral order so a rat or a monkey or student pressing a bar was thought to illuminate the brain. However odd, even mildly bizarre, such an assumption can now be made to seem, it unquestionably exerted a powerful grip. And it did so for a reason that is essentially aesthetic. The belief that the truth can be laid bare by parsimonious means is inherently handsome. The conceit that this can be done by means that are trivial is perhaps inbred and even a little decadent, but attractive nonetheless.

In a later chapter, Hudson produces a damning summary (p. 111):

> The discipline's health is suspect: as Zangwill remarked, it has failed to produce a coherent body of scientific law; and its fruits,

unmistakably, have about them an air of triviality. Attempts to justify psychological research in terms of its social utility at present lead inexorably to bathos. There is little we have produced in the last fifty years that is, in any sense of that complex word, 'relevant'.

Hudson finishes this particular section of his indictment with this comparison: 'One might as well try to justify space exploration in terms of its technological "spin off", the non-stick frying pan' (ibid.).

So much for the consistent advances we have made in our understanding of Man and his behaviour, as Hudson sees it.

There are, crudely, two versions of the position that Hudson indicates and it is difficult sometimes to know where he or other critical psychologists are pitching their loyalty. The 'hard' position suggests that psychology has succeeded in finding out almost nothing, which implies that we should see a total change in the kind of psychology that is done. The 'soft' position is that certain sorts of psychological problems and approaches have been seriously under-represented. If we are to get a more relevant, a more nearly complete psychology, there must be work using these less experimental, less behaviouristic means.

On the other hand, Broadbent reveals in his interview that experimenters rarely disagree, unlike those who, with the best of intentions and worst of conceptions, confuse psychology with theology. And Broadbent is not alone in this view.

There are then psychologists who do not deny some value to experimental psychology as it has been practised but who have come to believe that its so-called 'objective' methods have really produced very little advance. They see the facts that have been established as being true, but often trivial. Jordan put this nicely when he wrote (1968, p. 2):

> It is not that facts are lacking; if anything we are overwhelmed with facts, we have far too many facts at our disposal. What seems to be needed are new ways of processing the facts, new ways of *thinking* about the facts, perhaps in conjunction with a revival of some of the older, neglected ways of thinking about psychological facts as well.

On the other hand, those psychologists who are committed to truly objective methods, as they see them, argue that without rigour it is impossible actually to establish any of the facts. The arguments that have revolved around Freud are interesting in this respect. Professor Eysenck has repeated, often, that Freud truly deserved the Goethe

Prize for Literature which he won in 1925. Freud was a great novelist. His connection with science has proved embarrassing – and has, in Eysenck's estimation, retarded the progress of psychology by some fifty years. Broadbent has proved no more charitable in his evaluation of Freud. After writing that objective methods are 'generally accepted', he asks 'accepted by whom?' His answer is telling (1961, p. 35):

> The answer to this question is, primarily, 'those people in the English-speaking countries who engage in pure academic research in psychology'. This immediately excludes large numbers of people who are regarded by the public as authorities on human nature. For example, it excludes many psychiatrists who are medical men concerned with the treatment of mental illness and rarely possess academic degrees in psychology. Whether university-trained or not, such men find themselves with urgent clinical problems on their hands and must solve them, using any means available. It is therefore usual to find that they rely on intuitive interpretations of their patients' difficulties, more than would be acceptable to academic students of human nature. Naturally one cannot wait for the results of objective experiments on conflicts of motives when one is faced with a patient threatening to commit suicide. Systems of treatment, and of theory, based on experience of the clinical situation have most recently been developed; of which there are various ones stemming from the psychoanalytic views of Freud. These approaches are of value in suggesting experiments as well as in their immediate practical application: but they cannot all be true, and it is often very difficult to decide exactly what observations would verify or disprove a particular theory. For these reasons, they have been viewed with considerable scepticism by psychologists in the ivory towers of the universities.

It is worth noting some of Broadbent's little put-downs of the unfortunate non-Anglo-Saxon who lacks a degree in academic psychology and perhaps, *horribile dictu*, has not been 'university-trained'. If he errs, is it surprising? He has been so disadvantaged. Eysenck went even farther than Broadbent. In a famous paper in 1952, he claimed to show that persons who underwent psychoanalytic treatment had less chance of recovering than if they did nothing at all. More people recovered spontaneously than were cured by psychoanalysis. The psychologists committed to objective and rigorous methods, as they see them, see no merit in more contemporary forms of humanist and radical psychology. Broadbent sees in these approaches nothing but confusion. Those who use them in psychology are really trying to do theology, to establish some world-view. What they are doing may possibly be important though, usually, he seems to be sure it is not. But it is not psychology and, as psychology, it is not true. Such would-be psychologists have great faith in their own intuitions. Intuition is much less hard work than experimentation. It is, alas, usually, wrong. And if you do not do experiments to check your intuitions, you can never tell. You remain, self-willed, in perpetual ignorance, granting yourself the delusion of special knowledge. You never can know, for Broadbent and those who think like him, unless you find out. Hence the insights of workers like Freud or Jung or, among those living, Laing, have no value because one does not know if they are true.

The situation has not altered much since the sixties. In fact, the divide has widened. Broadbent comments on this in *In Defence of Empirical Psychology* (1974). If empirical psychology were not under attack, it would hardly require defence, let alone on such a prestigious occasion as the William James Memorial Lectures in Harvard. On the other hand, more humanist psychologists like Hudson and Chomsky are appalled by the way in which behaviourism is now sweeping the United States with Skinner in its vanguard. In his interview, Chomsky provides some very interesting arguments for the success of Skinner's ideas.

In the preface to *The Structure of Scientific Revolutions* (1962) Thomas Kuhn writes that the final stage of the work developed while he spent a year as a visiting fellow at the Center for Advanced Studies in the Behavioral Sciences. He describes the contribution this made to this idea as follows (Preface, p. viii):

Once again I was able to give undivided attention to the problems discussed below. Even more important, spending the year in a community composed predominantly of social scientists confronted me with unanticipated problems about the differences between such communities and those of the natural scientists among whom I had been trained. Particularly, I was struck by the number and extent of overt disagreements between social scientists about the nature of legitimate scientific problems and methods. Both history and acquaintance made me doubt that the practitioners of the natural sciences possess permanent answers to such questions more than their colleagues in social science. Yet, somehow, the practice of

7

astronomy, physics, chemistry or biology normally fails to evoke the controversies over fundamentals that today often seem endemic among, say, psychologists and sociologists.

The situation has not become any less endemic since 1962. If anything, the battle between different schools of psychology has sharpened. Experimental psychologists like Broadbent and Miller are worried that the development of radical, humanist psychology will threaten methods of studying Man that were beginning to establish themselves. On the other hand, psychologists like Hudson see much of contemporary psychology as irrelevant while others view with alarm the actual success of neo-behaviourism with Skinner as 'a kind of demi-god' as McClelland calls him in his interview. (Incidentally, is one reason for the success of neo-behaviourism as Skinner advocates it that we feel machines are tractable? If only we were machines, we would be tractable. Things are so meek.) Since Kuhn wrote, however, there has been a whole series of books of meta-psychology, exploring not what psychology is so much as what psychology ought to be. I have already quoted from Broadbent's *In Defence of Empirical Psychology* (1974) and Jordan's *Themes in Speculative Psychology* (1968). Other works that have taken up this sort of problem include Skinner's *Beyond Freedom and Dignity* (1972), Chein's *The Science of Behaviour and the Image of Man* (1972), Hudson's *The Cult of the Fact* (1972) and *Human Beings* (1975), Taylor's *The Explanation of Behaviour* (1964) and Shotter's *Images of Man* (1975). Both Eysenck and Chomsky, from their very different points of view, have written about this problem in recent books. Chomsky's *Language and Mind* (1968) contains notable attacks on behaviourism. Eysenck, in a contribution to a very useful set of confrontations, *Explanation in the Behavioural Sciences* (1970a), also treated the subject of what psychology ought to do and how it should set about it. Since Kuhn, there have been no magical reconciliations. Theoretical opponents, to paraphrase Broadbent, have not been brought together by the sheer force of any theory or the weight of new ideas.

The reasons for this book, one hopes, are beginning to emerge. By talking to thirteen of the most influential psychologists in the world, many of whom, like Skinner and Chomsky, appear to have initiated new approaches, I have tried to look at the differences and the assumptions behind those differences in their approaches and beliefs. In a modest manner, I am also trying to understand them. This investigation is in no way scientific. I did not approach any psychologist armed with a questionnaire and attempt to conduct either a clinical or a survey interview. Nor did I attempt to collect sociological data on the backgrounds of psychologists, eminent or otherwise. There were a number of reasons for this. First, and perhaps foremost, I felt that psychologists, expert in the manipulation of tests, could very easily manipulate any tests I might have to give whatever impression they wished to give. Second, there would be issues of confidentiality raised. One could hardly publish results that showed Professor So-and-So's neuroticism score, say, was X. I feared that any such attempt might make the psychologists involved, many of whom are public figures as well as eminences within their own profession, clam up. Third, although I touch on both the motivations and satisfactions of the psychologists involved, my main aim was to tease out the differences in their various approaches to Man and, in Chein's phrase, to the image of Man. I chose the psychologists to reflect a wide range of approaches to the discipline.

One of the original aims of the book was to try and see if there was any link between the theories advocated by a particular psychologist and his own personality and motivations. This has only very partially proved possible. Few of the psychologists were very forthcoming when it came to discussing their own motivations, not so much because of reticence as because of the fact, it seemed to me, that it was an odd question for them. As we shall see during the interviews, many psychologists took up the career by accident. But the personality of psychologists is, I want to argue, a very important area to investigate; for a psychologist is in a curious relation to his subject who, to be candid, ought usually to be referred to as the object of the experiment. The 'subjects', so called, are persons. So is the psychologist a person. The nature of the experiment and of the hypothesis a psychologist postulates usually implies a great deal about his image of Man. A psychologist's personality must be reflected in some way in the manner in which he treats of Man.

More generally, too, it is interesting how little the psychology of psychologists has been studied. A cynic might be forgiven for thinking they have preferred to avoid the subject. Only two serious investigations seem to have been carried out – and both of these were as part of larger investigations. Anne Roe (1953) published a series of monographs on the personalities of eminent scientists and, in the course of these, she discussed the personality of psychologists. At Harvard, under McClelland, a certain amount of research has been done into the personality of psychologists under the heading of work into the power motive. Apart from a few scattered papers, including some ideas on the subject by Hudson (1972), this appears to be the sum total of research into the problem.

In her series of studies on eminent scientists, Roe found some very interesting differences between biologists, physicists and psychologists. Biologists and physicists tended to be rather isolated during their childhood. Many theoretical physicists suffered from some serious disease so that they were left in bed, and to their own devices, for long periods. About a quarter of the biologists she interviewed had lost either their mother or their father before they were ten. So as they grew up, biologists and physicists both tended to lay less stress on personal relations. Though many still respected their parents, few stayed or felt very close to them. One biologist told Roe, 'My ties aren't that close.'

Psychologists, on the other hand, reacted to the difficulties of childhood quite differently. They did not absorb themselves in some intellectual pursuit which allowed them to withdraw from personal relationships. It is, in fact, telling both how late most psychologists came to psychology and how often the personal influence of some teacher seems to have been vital in deciding them to become psychologists. Though many of the men Roe interviewed were in their forties and fifties, they still spoke with quite marked hostility of their parents. Many had been afraid of their fathers. One told Roe, 'I was always in conflict with my mother,' another said, 'I think family discipline was very strict', while a third admitted that he 'hated father overtly'. Twenty years after these conflicts, they were still reacting with guilt and violence about their childhood and youth. Many also admitted to Roe that they were conscious of being superior to others from their youth on.

Roe's ideas – which I did not pursue in clinical detail in these interviews for the reasons mentioned above – suggest that while psychologists value human relationships very highly, they may not be very good at them.

Professor David McClelland, who did most of the original work on the achievement motive, believes that psychologists have a high need for power. In a paper on 'The two faces of power' (1973a), McClelland argues that the essence of the need for power is to want to have 'a strong impact on others'. This need could express itself in two ways. It was found that students who had a high need for power tended to hold more offices in student bodies and also tended to drink more heavily. It was not the same students who did both. As McClelland summed it up:

'Men whose power thoughts centered on having impact for the sake of others tended to hold office, whereas those whose thoughts centered on personal dominance tended to drink heavily, or to "act out" in college by attempting more sexual conquests or driving powerful cars' (1973a, p. 305).

McClelland argues that psychologists do have a very high need for power. In the paper, he explains how when he and certain colleagues were involved in a project to develop achievement motivation among Indian businessmen, observers began to wonder if they were 'psychological Machiavellians' who were interfering with other people's lives by foisting achievement motivation on a people who managed perfectly well without it. Imperialism of the mind is the ultimate imperialism. McClelland confesses that none of them thought they were exercising power in this way but the fact remains that they did act as leaders. As they tried to make the businessmen feel strong, competent and effective, they had to behave throughout as 'effective socialised leaders'. McClelland goes farther and notes a paradox that the effect of being exposed to leadership, even to charisma, is not to make an individual feel submissive to the Great Leader but to inspire him to be a leader himself. In their modest way, the psychologists were levers who succeeded in making the Indian businessmen leaders.

McClelland believes that psychologists have this high need for power. He thinks this is true of himself and that it was one of the things that drew him to psychology. He may not have been aware of it at the time, of course. In spite of being exposed to the accusation that he is, now, a conscious psychological Machiavelli, McClelland has continued running workshops in which he tries to raise the achievement motivation of entrepreneurs, and would-be entrepreneurs, from the Third World or from disadvantaged ethnic groups. There is still a certain ambivalence about admitting one enjoys even the unselfish use of power. When I asked McClelland what he got out of working as a psychologist and doing research, he mentioned fun as his main reward while being able to do something for people from time to time was a second, secondary motive.

In the interviews that follow, psychologists do often reveal themselves to be combative and to seek both to influence and, occasionally, to control people. The reader will be able to judge the extent to which this bears McClelland out.

One of the interesting points to emerge from the work on the power motive is the extent to which this makes psychologists seek arguments. They tend to become emotional and highly involved with their disagreements. They may, even, go farther than this and seek, in effect, to parody the position their opponents hold in order to have the joy of demolishing it. In this context, Eysenck is worth recalling. He took delight, it seems to me, in his constant attacks on Freud and psychoanalysis. And then what is one to make of this attack by Professor Isidor Chein on the blindness of the behaviourists? He seizes on a paper by Ludwig Immergluck (1964) who claims that the experience of freedom is a distorted perception, even an inevitable illusion [as far as one's own self goes] and that it implies a view of the nature of Man that will make science impossible. Chein writes (1972, p. 18):

> Similarly on Immergluck's premisses we can, at most, only have the *illusion* of prediction because 'predicting' in normal usage implies forward-looking (that is, intentional) behaviour. Thus Immergluck's paper moved me to write the following somewhat satirical passage:
>
> Since the illusion is so potent, it seems to me that unless new conditioning processes intervene, the Immerglucks are doomed to continued unresolved conflict (a term he does not perceive as inconsistent with his premisses) between their philosophical premisses and their phenomenological experience. As I view the historical scene, it seems to me that more and more psychologists are becoming conditioned to respond to unresolved conflicts by introducing conditioning programmes that have the consequence of resolving conflicts. . . . Moreover because of the great potency of the illusion. . . . it seems only a matter of time before the Immerglucks will be subjected to conditioning programmes designed to extinguish the response 'Dangerous for Science' and to substitute for it the response 'How Wonderful for Science' to stimuli implying mental human freedom. The Immerglucks will be then be happy (a mentalistic term that I use to cover up my ignorance of the real stimuli and responses involved in happiness – unless, of course, the neurosurgeons and psychiatrists are stimulated by the noises that generate an illusion of anguish to beat the psychologists to the gun by lobotomising and/or tranquillising them first.

Chein charges that psychology has not changed much. Oblivious of reality and real life, behaviourists have made psychology into a game with its own complex rules only remotely connected with reality.

It should not be imagined that psychologists who veer to positions

12

like Skinner or Miller or Broadbent are defenceless. Skinner rounds on the 'mentalists' as if mentalism were a kind of disease. It is not clear whether those who suffer from it are more to be condemned or pitied because of their pathetic need for self, and self-importance, that makes them believe they consciously run their lives. On Skinner's own premisses, they surely need pity. Their environments must have made them the vainglorious beings they are.

It seems reasonably clear from many remarks made by psychologists that they enjoy these arguments. This has a number of consequences. First, it makes one wonder if they do not prefer often to extend arguments rather than do original work. In his interview, McClelland makes some telling points about this. Secondly, this desire and, also, skill in argument leads psychologists often to attribute positions that are far too extreme – not to say untenable – to their opponents. The exposure that certain psychologists like Skinner and Laing have received from the media has helped in this, for the media like to present a simple version of a man's ideas in which Skinner stands for this and Laing for that, their complexities reduced for the sake of convenience and mass consumption. In the chapters on Skinner, Laing and Eysenck, especially, I have tried to look at the way they have been reported. But the main point here is to ask whether it is not possible that one of the factors that perpetuates the fundamentally different approaches to psychology is that psychologists enjoy the idea of the argumentative battle these differences make possible. They generally, therefore, cling to their own theories with great conviction and rectitude and blind themselves to the other's point of view.

There is, it seems to me, a tendency among psychologists to seek to polarise the subject so that if you adopt one view – let us say a behaviourist one – it follows that you argue, not that your approach is a valid approach to psychology, but that it is the only approach to psychology. Psychologists often try to claim that their ways of tackling the problems are the only legitimate methods and, however well-intentioned or clever what their ideological opponents are doing might be, it is clearly not psychology.

Psychologists seem to be constantly embroiled in disputes that are aimed at defining what psychology should be about.

How difficult it is to define what psychology really should be about only becomes clear when you try to do it. The argument advanced by Skinner, that psychology is the science of human behaviour, is rejected by many; for we do not just live in our conscious and external actions. In a paper in which he criticised a romantic approach to the

13

study of personality, Holt (1962) wrote: 'In science, when we say we understand something, we mean that we can predict and control it.' This is, of course, the precise aim of psychologists like Skinner. Holt contrasts this scientific sense of understanding with the romantic sense in which to understand is to identify, to feel absorbed by, to enjoy or suffer, empathy with a particular personality. Many psychologists feel that if psychology is to be defined as the study of human behaviour, it will confine itself merely to predicting and controlling how people behave in very artificial situations.

On the other hand, definitions of psychology which involve less prediction and more understanding are usually, if not always, unacceptable to those who argue like Skinner and Holt.

In an important passage in his interview, Professor Hudson touches on this point when he argues that one might often think different psychologists were working in quite different disciplines. They do not share the same assumptions, the same language, the same idea of 'what counts as a decent piece of research'. Lacking such communal criteria, are they doing the same kind of thing? Furthermore – and I must confess that writing this introduction after having spoken to all the psychologists I tend to share Hudson's view – no one school is willing to allow the other a right to exist as psychologists. The one great exception to this appears to be the ethologists: everyone seems to think that ethology should flourish and will come up with the answers to many problems. That ethologists should be given such due by nearly all psychologists (Skinner is far less friendly) reflects, perhaps, the insecurity of psychology as well as the merits of ethology.

In other words, much of the quarrel between psychologists revolves not round what psychology is but round what psychology ought to be. And, as I have tried to suggest, the position a person adopts here must have curious implications for himself for he must, in some way, live with himself as the kind of being his psychological work sees Man as.

And this set of controversies has not been helped by the fact that very little contemporary philosophy of science seems to touch on this problem. However, it does seem clear that the two key modern works of the philosophy of science, Popper's *The Logic of Scientific Discovery* (1972; original German edition, 1934) and Kuhn's *The Structure of Scientific Revolutions* (1962), have little to say about psychology. In Popper, I can find only one mention of psychology as opposed to the psychology of knowledge. On page 82, Popper warns the sociologist and psychologist not to succumb to new conventionalist' stratagems, arguing that it is not possible to divide

14

systems of theories into falsifiable and non-falsifiable ones. For his part, Kuhn explains that he has developed his ideas from the history of the natural sciences. In a later essay. 'Problems, aims and responsibilities in science' (1963), Popper repeated his main argument that falsifiability is the criterion by which to judge the reality of a theory. He wrote: 'Testing a theory means trying to find its weak spots: it means trying to refute it. And a theory is testable only if it is refutable' (1963). His ground seems to have shifted little.

There have, of course, been other philosophers of science, and some have addressed themselves specifically to psychological problems or, at least, to problems which appear to be psychological from the standpoint of philosophy. My contention is that these philosophical problems usually have little relevance to psychology. To take an example: the opening debate of the confrontation in *Explanation in the Behavioural Sciences* (Borger and Cioffi, 1970) was between two distinguished philosophers, Stephen Toulmin and R. S. Peters. Their argument centres on whether reasons can be causes. Their method of argument was, essentially, the analysis of the uses of language when we talk about reasons and causes. Psychologists may be interested in this debate as a debate but it does nothing to clarify the practice of psychology. No amount of linguistic analysis will convince a psychologist who is a determinist that if I say I am going to do X because of Y and I then do X, that the cause of my doing it was the reason Y that I gave if Y is a feeling or a mental state. This, obviously, is only one example. A further example is Charles Taylor, in his book *The Explanation of Behaviour* (1964). In 1970, in the confrontations, Taylor repeated many of his arguments of that book. Taylor, first, accepts the present state of confusion. He writes (Borger and Cioffi, 1970, p. 54):

> The search for a conceptual framework, for a concept of the 'normal' course, is no less vital in the sciences of behaviour than it is in the physical sciences. Only in the former field it seems to have met with success. One can describe the state of disarray and contention in which we find the sciences of man as arising from deep disagreements over the conceptual frameworks which are appropriate. Each of the above fields is the scene of several rival 'approaches', no one of which seems to be able to establish itself to the satisfaction of all workers in the field as the definitive framework.

Then Taylor sets out to attack in detail what he calls the behaviourist approach (ibid., pp. 61–2):

Introduction

The behaviourist view of science is a kind of closed circle, a self-induced illusion of necessity. For there is no self-evidence to the proposition that the mental is the unobservable. In a perfectly valid sense, I can be said to observe another man's anger, sadness, his eagerness to please, his sense of his own dignity, uncertainty, love for a girl or whatever. I can find out these things about another sometimes by just observing him in the common sense of that term, sometimes by listening to what he says. But, in this latter case, I am not learning of some dubious and uncheckable 'introspection' on his part. For what people say about themselves is never in principle and rarely in practice uncheckable.

Taylor appears to be making his case against one particular, and extreme, form of behaviourism, which, at times, he seems to suggest is the whole of modern academic psychology. This is an assumption that appears wrong.

There are a number of issues, it seems to me, that Taylor develops in such a way as to polarise and confuse what it is that actually has happened, and what is happening, in psychology.

First, he claims that the mental is the unobservable. When many psychologists claim this, they place quite a narrow restriction on the 'mental'. They claim that mental states cannot be directly observed. For example, the only way I can know that you intend to do X is if you say so. You may be lying; you may be deceiving yourself. Many behaviourists like Broadbent are quite willing to listen to a person who says this but they would not be willing to count it as the only evidence about the fact. For example, if a person who says he intends to go to New York is observed to be making arrangements such as packing, buying a plane ticket and so forth, it may be concluded that what he said was his intention is, indeed, his intention: on the other hand, if he says that he intends going to New York and is not, for years afterwards, observed to be making the slightest attempt to budge himself out of Streatham, we may decide that it was never really his intention in the first place. A behaviourist would not necessarily quarrel with the fact that you can be said to observe a person's intentions. But what is their importance? In his interview, Skinner declares that he does not doubt people have feelings, and actually, admits to having feelings himself. What he denies is that these feelings matter as causes of behaviour. Taylor simply avoids the issues by depicting behaviourists as people who do not think you can observe a man being sad, a man being angry and so on. It is the meaning you put on these observations which matters. And it is because the behaviourists place little meaning on

16

them, in the end, that they do not bother to carry the observations out.

It is interesting that some of the states Taylor claims he can observe in a commonsensical manner but that behaviourists deny can be tested are being tested, in fact, by psychological tests which are in current use by psychologists who claim much more sympathy with behaviourism than with competing points of view. Eysenck's work on dimension of neuroticism and extraversion-introversion would tell one a good deal about a person's tendency to be sad and his tendency to be uncertain. Eysenck relies on people filling in, honestly and accurately, questionnaires about their feelings. Academic psychologists, misguided beings according to Taylor, have actually devised self-report tests and questionnaires that try to give an idea of a person's self-esteem and self-image which are close enough to his sense of his own dignity. There is little to suggest that many of the psychologists who use these tests would accept that they are teleologists which Taylor seems to offer them as their only option if they are not his kind of behaviourists.

Lastly, and perhaps most important, Taylor appears to ignore completely various new approaches to experimental psychology which have been espoused by behaviourists. Broadbent and Miller have both made much use of the computer analogy and are on record as denying the simple behaviourism of the twenties. That was a necessary phase out of which psychology has moved. Eysenck, who would certainly line up with the behaviourists against the teleologists, equally has spent much of his time criticising the more simplistic models of behaviourism. There are undoubtedly many psychologists, even Skinner himself, who do still practise something like the form of behaviourism Taylor derides. But they do not comprise the whole of behaviourism. Taylor's book has been one of the most direct philosophical contributions to psychology. It is a real pity that its treatment of what actually goes on, or went on in the sixties, in psychology, seems to be so caricatured.

One other major philosopher of science, Michael Polanyi, has touched on psychological problems. But Polanyi, though he rehearses some arguments very pertinent to psychological methodology, offers more psychological than methodological insights. It is worth quoting one, at length, since it offers a vision of a potential psychology quite different from that Taylor accepts. Polanyi writes (1971, p. 160):

> All human thought comes into existence by grasping the meaning
> and mastering the use of language. Little of our mind lives in the
> natural body: a truly human intellect dwells in us only when our lips
> shape words and our eyes read print.

Tacit knowing now appears as an act of indwelling by which we gain access to new meaning. When exercising a skill, we literally dwell in the innumerable muscular acts which contribute to its purpose, a purpose which constitutes their joint meaning. Therefore, since all understanding is tacit knowing, all understanding is achieved by indwelling. The idea developed by Dilthey and Lipps, that we can know human beings and works of art only by indwelling, can thus be justified. But we see now also that these authors were mistaken in distinguishing indwelling from observation as practised in the natural sciences. The difference is only a matter of degree: indwelling is less deep when observing a star than when understanding men or works of art. The theory of tacit knowing establishes a continuous transition from the natural sciences to the study of the humanities. It bridges the gap between the 'I- It' and the 'I- Thou' by rooting them both in the subject's 'I- Me' awareness of his own body, which represents the highest degree of indwelling.

Polanyi suggests a much more wholistic approach. But though he has influenced some scientists who are looking at psychological problems, like Sir Alister Hardy, who is studying religious experiences, Polanyi has had little impact on the mainstream of psychological controversies.

Two recent studies by Mahoney (1976) have examined how psychologists reason. One experiment tested the reasoning skills of fifteen psychologists, fifteen scientists and fifteen conservative Protestant ministers. There were few differences between the ministers and the psychologists. In a second study, Mahoney asked seventy-five behavioural psychologists to review manuscripts on a controversial subject in psychology. The introduction and experimental procedures were identical in each manuscript but referees were given different results and discussion sections. In one group, results were 'positive' in that they supported the referees' known point of view. In another group, the results went against the referees' viewpoints. Additional groups were handed ambiguous results followed by discussions that either supported or went against their own previously taken positions. Mahoney expected these rational psychologists to evaluate the manuscripts purely in terms of logic and evidence. Ambiguous manuscripts should get less support. Mahoney concluded: 'our scientific reviewers tended to recommend the article only when it reported evidence that supported their positions. When the data contradicted their position opinions, they criticised the article's method and interpretation, and they urged it be not published.' Psychologists are less objective than they like to think.

If philosophers seem either to have neglected or caricatured

18

psychology, it is not surprising that almost none of the psychologists I interviewed mentioned a philosopher as having had any influence on them. There are two exceptions. R. D. Laing cites Sartre as a major influence. Liam Hudson, who said that he preferred philosophy to psychology at Oxford, mentions William Kneale, a logician, and Brian Farrell, a philosopher, as major influences. But they were personal influences much more than ideological influences. Kneale was an influence through his kindness; Farrell through his combativeness.

This philosophical lack is, it seems to me, particularly serious for a subject whose practitioners come from such a range of earlier studies. They need a conceptual framework as they usually become psychologists only after they are twenty when they have absorbed many different frameworks. Many of them took first and even second degrees in other fields, many had wanted to be something else. Skinner wanted to be a writer; Festinger wanted to be a chess player; Eysenck wanted to be a physicist; Hudson would have liked to be a philosopher. Others started out, and have remained, experts in other fields but find themselves embattled in psychology. Chomsky was, and is, a linguist; many psychologists wish he had remained that. Jouvet was, and is, a doctor and neurophysiologist; Laing was, and is, a doctor and psychiatrist; Leupold-Löwenthal was, and is, a doctor. The generation of psychologists who have now reached positions of importance and influence often took up psychology by accident. Only in the last twenty years has psychology become a career as physics, chemistry, biology and other subjects have been much longer. Many of the psychologists who now control and direct research, who allocate funds, stumbled into psychology with all kinds of previously acquired conceptual frameworks. Professor Tajfel, for example, did not actually get a degree in psychology till he was thirty-five. All this argues the importance of looking at the backgrounds of psychologists and of attempting to tease out their assumptions to understand the way they do psychology a little better. This very diversity also makes it important to try and establish, at least, the problems that a philosophy of psychological methods should look at. As I have tried to suggest, philosophers have been of little help. Physics is more prestigious, after all. By temperament, psychologists seem to wish to polarise the issues for the thrill of polarisation almost. One interviewee, for example, asked how many psychologists had given me a hard time – only to be expected from such a set of 'individualistic bastards'. After the interviews, encumbered with a few less preconceptions but a few more obsessions, I shall return to some of these points.

1
David McClelland

David McClelland made his reputation through his studies of achievement motivation. Since 1948, McClelland has examined why and how people are economically successful. It is important to make clear that 'achievement' and 'achievement motivation' have a limited meaning for McClelland. He has studied economic achievement mainly among businessmen and in entrepreneurial situations. We normally use the word 'achieve' to cover a multitude of successes. You can achieve success as a writer, an admiral, a doctor, an engineer or, even, as a psychologist. McClelland now wishes that he had chosen a more precise, if drabber, name for it like 'a need for economic efficiency'.

McClelland came to the study of achievement motivation through, it seems, a series of accidents. As a student, McClelland nearly became a German scholar. He came from a family of academics and, as he was an able student, the question was not whether he would become an academic but which field he would go into. He went to university. He became disenchanted with German as it seemed to consist mostly of grammar. One of his teachers introduced him to psychology and it excited him. As a graduate student, McClelland studied under John McCue and also under the almost legendary Clark Hull. Clark Hull decided to become a psychologist when he was in hospital with polio at the age of twenty-four. By the 1930s, he was probably the most influential psychologist in the USA. He was a behaviourist; he attempted to construct a definitive theory of human motivation on the basis of what rewards made rats learn to run down mazes and make visual discriminations. Hull had been much influenced by Spinoza, another marvellous spinner of systems as intricate as spiders' webs but rather less real. McClelland says that Hull taught him to care about the details of science, about precision, about experimental design and about checking the minutiae of results. If it had not been for the war, it

20

would seem, McClelland might never have broadened his horizons. But during the war McClelland went to work at Brynmawr College as a substitute for a social psychologist, Donald Mackinnon. Knowing no social psychology, McClelland had to learn the field from scratch in order to teach it.

This crash course in social and also abnormal psychology made McClelland feel that it was unlikely that the understanding of human motivation would come about by studying the effects of hunger, thirst, sex and sleep deprivation in the rat. At the time when McClelland saw this, it required a rather independent frame of mind to be critical of behaviourism. Hull was the master; Skinner was about to come into favour with the publication of *Walden Two* (1948) and *Science and Human Behaviour* (1953). Of course, McClelland's background in the humanities and, especially, his interest in literature made it likely that he would find the behaviourist view rather too narrow. It is curious, of course, that McClelland mentions no hopes of becoming a writer, as do both Skinner and Miller. McClelland has maintained his interest in literature. The most engaging of his books is probably *The Roots of Consciousness* (1964), a collection of essays which range from technical comparisons of German and American elites to an analysis of the life and work of André Gide.

Convinced it was impossible to find an explanation of human motives through experiments with rats in very artificial situations, McClelland turned to research using fantasy. It is telling, of course, that an American Protestant psychologist like McClelland should turn to the study of economic success. First, McClelland devised a means of using fantasy to measure the extent of a person's 'achievement motivation'. Again, I remind readers that his use of the word 'achievement' is technical: it is best expressed as achieving economic success and efficiency. Typically, a person who is high on achievement motivation will be concerned to achieve good cost-benefit ratios. The actual means McClelland used to tease out this motivation seem very odd. In a typical experiment, McClelland gave subjects pictures and asked them to devise a story based on them. For instance: 'A boy about eighteen years old is sitting at this desk in an occupied classroom. A book lies open before him but he is not looking at it. The boy rests his forehead on one hand as he gazes pensively out toward the viewer.' This generated some very different stories. Compare: (1) 'He is trying to reconcile the philosophies of Descartes and Thomas Aquinas – and at his tender age of eighteen. He has read several books on philosophy and feels the weight of the world on his shoulders'; and (2) 'He will leave

21

home but will only meet further disillusionment away from home.'

The first story is high in achievement motivation. Effort, work and purpose are revealed. It is active. The second story is passive. There is neither effort nor purpose in it. McClelland showed that scores of achievement motivation obtained in such studies correlated well with the choice of career of individuals and with the degree of business success they achieved. Those high in achievement motivation made successful businessmen.

By the early 1950s, however, many psychologists felt that McClelland's scores were too unreliable. His results did not repeat as neatly as they should. He then developed two powerful ideas. The first looked at the causes at the roots of achievement motivation. He suggested that children developed a high need to achieve if they were expected to be independent at an early age. A study by a student of his, Winterbottom (1953), compared the achievement motivation scores of boys aged eight to ten. Boys who were high in achievement motivation were expected by their parents to know their way round the city, to be successful in competition and to try new things for themselves when they were much younger. McClelland became convinced that a cluster of personality traits that involved independence, aspiration and self-reliance was essential for the development of high achievement motivation. He could not prove the cause and effect relationship very easily but he seems to have felt sufficiently sure of his ground to embark on what Roger Brown, who is a caustic critic of much contemporary psychology, calls 'one of the more audacious investigations in the history of the social sciences'.

The background to McClelland's thesis was religious. Max Weber, the sociologist, argued that the Reformation which saw the birth of the Protestant work ethic led to capitalism. In 1904, Weber thought both that Protestant countries like Britain and Sweden were more developed economically than Catholic ones and that Protestant workers toiled harder. Weber was particularly struck, it appears, by the hard work of Protestant shop girls. Weber's impressions were no scientific proof. McClelland both tested some of Weber's ideas empirically and extended them. First, he established that Protestant countries were more developed economically. As an index of economic development, McClelland chose kilowatt hours of electricity consumed per capita. All his countries were in temperate zones. He found striking differences between Protestant and Catholic countries – differences of the sort suggested by Weber. McClelland turned to psychology again. He argued that Protestant parents trained their children to be more independent and more in control of their environment. Calvinists, especially, believed that you either were one of the elect and saved or you were not. Nothing you did would make you a candidate for election. People were thus forced to try and prove to themselves that they were of the elect. The only way to do this was to achieve success. This led to the emphasis on independence in the young which, in turn, produced children high in achievement motivation who became entrepreneurs. It is a grand thesis.

McClelland believes this grand thesis hangs together not just because of his studies with successful individuals but also because of his analysis of achievement motivation in cultures. He extended the measurement of achievement motivation to literature. He could measure the texts of the key works of fiction, and especially children's books, for the images linked to achievement motivation. He could then see how levels of motivation correlated with economic development. McClelland found that they correlated very well. One impressive finding was that the amount of achievement motivation in Greek literature rose some hundred years before a major expansion of Greek trade in antiquity as measured by where archaeologists have unearthed Greek goods. In the interview, McClelland comments on how well this thesis, grand as it is, has stood the test of time. In 1961 he published *The Achieving Society*, his major book that drew together all these strands from the individual's childhood and motives to the cultural ethos and linked those to the economic effects.

In McClelland, you expect to meet someone very American. In the 1950s business was the American career *par excellence*. Few questioned its value. One can argue that McClelland and Skinner reveal the twin obsessions of the modern American male—at least, among the unpoor, unblack, unyoung: how to succeed in business and how to remedy failure. Skinner, with behaviour modification techniques, offers us a technology that leads to human redemption. Those who seem to have failed will be saved by being changed. McClelland studies, of course, those who have less trouble succeeding. It is fitting that they should both be professors at Harvard.

McClelland seems at first rather bland, though tall, elegant and moustachioed. His office is modern and dull. He has not bothered to impose his personality on it. But he soon sheds this rather conventional image in two ways. He has a cutting and critical humour. He is not in love with modern America and is willing to criticise it more than one might expect. Then, he is very open up to a certain point. And, as it was the first time I had interviewed him, it would have been unreasonable to expect there not to be limits of frankness. He was quite willing to go into his reasons for doing the work he was doing. He talks about his research with a certain distance, as if to say 'I will coolly and rationally discuss my maybe less cool and less rational motives for doing what I do.' But, he did it.

Religion is important in understanding McClelland. He believes many psychologists turn to psychology in order to get away from a very fundamentalist religious upbringing. He stresses he is a non-conformist from a long line of dissenters. His mother's ancestors were Huguenots and radical Presbyterians from Scotland. His mother was brought up as a Covenanter, a radical form of Presbyterianism. His father was a Methodist minister. He has himself become a convinced Quaker whose approach to religion is 'primarily mystical'. In 'Psychoanalysis and the Jewish mystical tradition' (in McClelland, 1964) he argued that psychoanalysis was so popular because it offered a form of secular religion offering comfort to man in his state of existential anxiety. McClelland enjoys theological concepts. He concluded the paper with these playful and appealing thoughts:

Has the Christian Church become so petrified, so insensitive to the needs of our times that a new religious movement has arisen out of Judaism, opposed to orthodoxy and spread by secularised Jews? Certainly, psychoanalysis has all of these characteristics. It is essentially individualistic, mystical and opposed to religious orthodoxy . . . Would it not be the supreme irony of history if God had again chosen his People to produce a new religious revolt against orthodoxy, only this time of Christian making?

McClelland likes to juggle with ideas. In an introduction to a study of attitudes to death which he called, playfully, 'The Harlequin Complex', he wrote (1964): 'It should be stated at the outset that the chapter is an imaginative tour de force, an adventure that I enjoyed writing more than anything else included in the book. But even in my wildest flights of fancy, I trust my loyalty to the scientific tradition of Professor Hull is still discernible.' In 1957 McClelland wrote a short comparison of the careers of Freud and Hull. Sharing his own playful mood, one might compare the influence of Freud on him as that of the id encouraging him to dally with deep, powerful, wild ideas, while Hull is the scientific super-ego. In much of McClelland's work, there is this tension. Like Hudson, McClelland enjoys the imaginative part of science and, even, that curious zone where the act of writing itself

24

creates insights. 'Fun', he told me, 'is one of the greatest rewards I get from doing research.' But he has to keep his imagination on a leash.

Beyond fun, McClelland sees his main motivation in religion. It is again useful to look at his study of the careers of Freud and Hull. He outlined some parallels between them. Freud was brought up in a home that was fairly traditionally Jewish. But it was not oppressively traditional. There was room for free thinking. Similarly, Hull was of a family of Protestant free-thinkers. In McClelland's own case, his father was a methodist minister. McClelland wanted to have scientific arguments to hammer his father with. He suffered then from the youthful illusion that you win arguments with facts. He smiles and admits that he is wiser now. McClelland, then, is sure that religion and reaction against religion helped make him a psychologist.

As a psychologist, McClelland has also formally studied the motivation of psychologists and other scientists. The main bulk of his work has aimed to try to see what motivates creative physical scientists. Some of the findings are, McClelland argues, relevant to psychology. Psychologists have a need for power rather than for economic efficiency. McClelland differentiates between a need for power and a need for economic efficiency. The power motive involves a desire to stand out, a need to make an impact and a need to make one's influence felt. Money matters less: economic success is, perhaps, too crude. Physical scientists want to know how things tick. Psychologists are even more ambitious. Not satisfied with understanding things, they want to know how people tick. Some go so far as to construct elaborate models and theories of how Man works. What could be more god-like? McClelland harps, interestingly, on the fact that Freud had a 'Messiah' complex. He had a longing to declare himself and be seen as the Messiah. In some ways, of course, Freud was a secular Messiah offering a new Bible. Freud would always experience a terrible nervousness when he went to Rome. In Jewish tradition, the Messiah will declare himself in Rome. He could not face up to being in the city and the tensions that would create. To know how people work is a supreme expression of power.

McClelland has revealed a need for this kind of power in much of his own work. One of the most interesting projects here is his comparison of German and American elites (1964). At sixteen, McClelland fell in love with Germany and German literature. He had a Swiss tutor, a lady who had improbably escaped from her last post as governess to the children of the last Czar of Russia. She found herself in central Illinois. McClelland was easily carried away by German romantic idealism.

Then 'came the shock of Hitler and the Nazi period punctuated by a lifelong friendship formed in a Quaker work camp with a man who turned out to be the son of Konrad Adenauer'. During the war McClelland believed that the most detached social scientists could not examine the German character without bias. He thought it important to use psychology to achieve a better understanding. 'I felt that I must do the best I could as a psychologist contrasting it with the American character to highlight the virtues and defects of each,' he wrote. Such a study reveals that McClelland thinks it is important that psychology should look at those attitudes which mean something. Too much research is trivial.

McClelland has also used his work on achievement to criticise the educational system. To lay stress on nothing but academic excellence, to rely on nothing but educational tests, seems to him rather foolishly narrow. Education may be excluding some of the most dynamic and creative young people in a society from the best education. McClelland said:

> Academic excellence is a wonderful thing. As a teacher, I much prefer to have conscientious people in my classes who do what they are told, read their assignments and turn in interesting papers on time. I am annoyed by the boy in the back of the room who comes late to class, never participates in the discussion and appears to be listening only half-heartedly to the pearls of wisdom I am dropping before him, and I will certainly give him a low grade – but is that all there is to education?'

McClelland believes not. He believes, too, that many psychological discoveries have been badly used in education. For twenty years, he has been an opponent of too dogmatic a use of tests in selecting children for higher education. Recently, he contributed a critique of the whole testing movement to the *American Psychologist* (1973b). This quotation shows, I think, how he feels that it is not enough for the psychologist to know, he must also try to use his knowledge to benefit people. He wrote:

> suppose you are a ghetto resident in the Roxbury section of Boston. To qualify for being a policeman, you have to take a three hour general intelligence test in which you must know the meaning of words like 'quell' or 'pyromaniac' or 'lexicon'. If you do not know 1 enough of these words or cannot play analogy games with them,

then you do not qualify and must be satisfied with some job as being a janitor for which an intelligence test is not yet required by the Massachusetts Civil Service Commission. You, not unreasonably, feel angry, upset, unsuccessful. Because you do not know them you are considered to have low intelligence and since you consequently have to take a low status job and are unhappy, you contribute to the celebrated correlations of low intelligence with low occupational status and poor adjustment. Psychologists should be ashamed of themselves for promoting a view of general intelligence that has encouraged such a testing programme.

Most psychologists, of course, believe that since they are scientists they are above, or below, shame. Scientists do not deal in moral or political values. Skinner argues that it is not his fault if techniques of behaviour modification fall into the wrong hands. He could not refuse to discover them because of the moral dangers they might cause. Critics of Skinner point to the reaction of eminent physicists to the discovery of the atomic bomb. Many of the physicists came to regret the discovery. Skinner would adapt Oscar Wilde and say: 'There is no such thing as a moral or immoral experiment – just good or bad science.' McClelland makes out the contrary case and is not above using a personal example to bludgeon the psychologists into a little shame. He added in his *American Psychologist* article (1973b):

> I was recently in Jamaica where all around me poor people were speaking an English that was almost entirely incomprehensible to me. If I insisted, they would speak patiently like to a slow-witted child. I have wondered how well I would do in Jamaican society if this kind of English were standard among the rich and powerful (which, by the way, it is not).

Of course not, for the rich and powerful Jamaicans were well trained by the British before they left. As for McClelland, he has not been content merely to criticise the others. He has been working with blacks and Puerto Ricans, using his discoveries in the field of achievement motivation to train them to become better entrepreneurs. This is an important field both within the States and for help to the Third World. It is better a man teach a man to become an efficient farmer than to dole out some wheat to him so that he may just survive: it is better yet to enable him to use the entrepreneurial spirit to build himself and his society up. Some will, of course, criticise this kind of work as redolent of a neo-colonial attitude. We no longer use gunboats to have our way, we use the imperialism of the mind. McClelland, nevertheless, feels convinced that it is an important and worthy practical application.

In McClelland's case, the psychologist emerges as both something of an idealist and a politician. After telling me that he got fun out of research, he added 'I also like the idea that I might be helping other people.' Psychology offers a possibility of power, power to do good. McClelland takes failure to make an impact with wry grace. In his paper in the *American Psychologist* he noted that all his arguments and eloquence over twenty years had not had the least effect on the educational testing movement which has indeed, thrived.

Not surprisingly, McClelland's ideas about why he became a psychologist fit in well with his own recent work on the power motive.

Why did you become a psychologist?
It's a long time ago and I have to think back. I was, first of all I think it's relevant, the son of an academic. My father was a college president and I grew up in an academic atmosphere. My uncle was also a university professor. Growing up in a college, as I was good at studies, I never really thought of any other kind of career. The only issue was, what would it be in? I was very good at languages so that my early training was in classics – Greek, Latin, German and French, I knew before I went to university. And when I did go, I was half planning to go into German. But I found German was rather dull as it was mostly grammar. I was very good at German grammar. Then, in my second year, I had a teacher who really turned me on to psychology. A very striking person who hit me right. Well, obviously, that's no answer. I was responding to him because I was pre-set to do, because of certain ideas I must have had already.

In a general way, too, I would say that my father was also a Methodist minister. And a lot of psychologists in my generation actually were the sons of ministers who were rebelling against the church but who, also, had become tremendously interested in psychological things because they were so involved in religion, like seeking reasons for doing things.

That's interesting because psychologists have generally been so hostile to any approaches that had a hint of religion in them. Jung was castigated for that, certainly. Do you think that kind of religious background is linked to the hostility?

Definitely. You'll find when you talk to Skinner that this is one of his main motivations. As he's written in his autobiography, he was so opposed to the doctrinaire fundamentalist religion he was exposed to when he was growing up. On the other hand, if you look at his psychology, it nearly is a religion of some kind when he writes about utopias, for instance. I think there is something religious in the way he writes though, of course, not at all believing in God. But there is the idea that there is a moral law which in his case gets converted into the law of science. I think our attitude to law came from religion to some extent and, also, our attitude to human betterment. Basically, I suppose we were interested in being scientists though I used to say it appealed to me to think I could perhaps convince my father who was very hard to convince of anything. We used to argue all the time, we delighted in arguing and I thought that maybe, if I had a fact or two, I could persuade him. Of course, facts didn't persuade him but that was my idea. If I could establish something scientifically I could prove my point and win the argument. I've long since learned you don't win arguments with facts.

What was your early work in?
Learning theory. The psychologist I worked with, John McCue, was a learning theorist, human learning not animal learning. He was in the old Ebbinghaus tradition, which has continued on in this country, though not very strongly. We did memory, psychology of memory and learning lists of nonsense syllables. I spent my early years as a graduate running experiments of that kind and then I went to Yale where I was a student of Clark Hull's. And that was all learning theory.

I think that that was no accident. As I've pointed out elsewhere, it is no accident that learning theory should be the psychology *par excellence* of America. It's because Americans are so much interested in adaptation to a strange environment. Having come from Europe, many of them being the children of immigrants, the whole thing they wanted to know and understand about was the process of adjustment.

What were the major influences on you when you started?
I think the learning psychologists - McCue, Hull - had a tremendous intellectual influence on me in the sense of training me to discipline and science. I could have been a humanist or something. But I was really interested in care and systematic observation and

29

checking, the whole science game. I got turned on to that. The other influences really came from my education which was very broad and wide, from my family background, from teachers I had in languages before I went to college. At college, I had a sociology teacher, a German refugee, who got me started in the field of sociology. The influences were more personal rather than books, though I must have read many, many books.

Anne Roe, in her studies of psychologists, suggested that though they cared very much about human relations, they were rather bad at them. That suggests perhaps that, being desperate for human relations but bad at them, they chose to become experts in that field. I know it's a rude question, but was that at all involved in your case?
No, I'm trying to be accurate about it. I was not a very social person but I never thought of psychology as in any way facilitating that. I wasn't very social in the sense that I didn't think I needed it, more like Roe's biologists. I wasn't interested. I would say with me it was more a matter of power motivation.

Did your work in experimental human psychology lead fairly directly to studying achievement?
No, that was a lot later on. I think that maybe some of the same ideas and the same reasons were involved for my getting interested in achievement much later. But I had gone through an earlier transformation in the war years, as happened to so many people due to the dislocation. I was sort of forced into another set and setting, quite different from my graduate training. I happened to be in Philadelphia. I wasn't drafted because I was a conscientious objector and to avoid being sent to a camp for conscientious objectors I did work in Philadelphia which meant I did a fill-in job for Donald Mackinnon who taught personality and abnormal psychology at Brynmawr College. He was called away to the war and I was a substitute for him.

The result was that I had to teach two courses I had absolutely no training for. That forced me to learn a whole new field of psychology, personality and abnormal. I found I was really tremendously interested in that but I was really self-taught. Then, I got interested in motivation after that. People have, of course, often argued, since it turned out that way, that though I certainly didn't know it then, it was all pre-set or predetermined as the achievement motive was a key part of the Protestant Ethic and I was of liberal

Protestant background. I was bound to end up interested in that. I
can really say that that was not at all in my mind when I started. I
didn't discover the connection, even, for six years.

*Has any work been done relating the personality of scientists not to
whether they achieve or not but to the kinds of fields they go into?*
There's some of Hudson's work. I looked at the problem too a little
but there is no systematic evidence, for instance, about what kind of
person is attracted by behaviourism.

What about in your own case?
I think of it as fairly accidental. I feel I strayed into achievement
motivation accidentally. I wanted to raise some money for research.
There was a cocktail party and someone said he had some money for
research in the Navy. I said I wasn't really interested in the colour of
flares at sea and he said, 'Oh, ask me for some money for something
you are interested in.' I had a student, Atkinson, and he was
interested in the achievement problem. I had many other good
students but he had six months off before he went to graduate
school and he needed some money so I applied for some money and
got it to work in this rather than on twelve other things. And once I
had the money, I found I could keep the money coming by sticking
with it. So that's the way I feel it was determined: externally
determined rather than internally determined. But you could say
that what kept the money going was that I was good at it and that I
was good at it because of some internal determinants. I really
understood the syndrome. Many of us [psychologists] feel accident
played a great part. If I hadn't been good at it, however, I couldn't
have got the next grant because I would have done lousy research.

*And, logically, I suppose other psychologists of liberal Protestant
background didn't become interested in achievement?*
Yes.

*How well do you feel the work on achievement has stood the test of
the twenty years or so since it first appeared?*
Extremely well. I started in 1947 just after the war. My primary
interest at that time was to get a good measure of human motivation.
Most motivation work was being run on rats and on hunger and
thirst. I really thought that those motives were not the key ones for
adults and that we needed some measure other than self-report

measures which were so open to bias and to social desirability sets. So I developed the measure.

Basically, the problem that psychologists had with the measure then, and that they still have now, is that it is so unreliable. One of the fundamental things you learn in psychology is that if you take a measure, you ought to be able to rely on it. If you take the same person and measure him on it again, you ought to get the same number on the second occasion. Unfortunately, with this measure, which is based on fantasy, you don't get the same number the second time round. That really upsets many psychologists very much and, therefore, they have never really in my opinion accepted it. The reason you don't get the same number the second time is very simple but no amount of explaining it will help. The explanation is that the measuring device says, 'Be creative.' That means to people you don't tell the same story twice. If you take a personality test, the set is to be consistent. You're crazy if you answer it differently this time from the way you answered it last time. So you get a high degree of consistency in the way people report. As a result, I've been forced to fall back on the fact that, even though the measure is quite unreliable in the normal sense, it gives quite enough indication in groups of other things that a person will do. So at least it is theoretically useful, if not practically useful.

And, presumably, it is possible that achievement motivation fluctuates?

It does fluctuate, sure. As a matter of fact, we get greater consistency over ten years than over three weeks. By ten years, people have forgotten what story they wrote ten years ago. I would say that there are many psychologists who are very unhappy with the measure. They think it very unreliable and inconsistent. On the other hand, the pattern of results hangs together rather amazingly well. I traced it not only through individuals but also through cultures. The theoretical pattern holds together very well. We have measured the motivational pattern of societies and the dominant motive-orientation of societies through coding popular literature. We worked out the whole scheme in *The Achieving Society* of how people with high achievement motivation make better businessmen. Businessmen who are more successful, in fact, have higher achievement motivation and, if you have a lot of them, the country develops and you can tell that from how oriented the literature is. So it's more the whole pattern that falls together rather than any link in the chain. I think that's stood up amazingly well.

The chief criticisms that have been made of the argument of *The Achieving Society* have been from other disciplines. They say it's too psychologically oriented and I ignore historical conditions which change achievement motivation. I don't happen to think that I do. They also felt there might be other variables that really account for the change – social conditions, for instance. The studies in *The Achieving Society* didn't use multivariate analysis, for example, as much as we should have. It was single-variate analysis. They said that if you really searched systematically for other variables, you would find that it was population decrease or something like that which happened to be associated with *nAch* which happened to be related to economic growth. Actually, a sociologist named Southwood has now checked out the multivariate argument and if you correct for all the variables that are connected with *nAch* and economic growth, the relationship still holds up.

Are you using this knowledge practically?
Yes, we're now largely involved in putting it to work. We're using our knowledge of achievement motivation to train minority business entrepreneurs all over the country. And we find then that when we train them in this way, they make better businessmen. They make more profits, create greater growth and so on.

The achievement motive really does hone in on economic achievement as opposed to any other achievement?
Yes – and that's the curse of the name. I have often wished I'd called this motive something else because, in the English language, it's perfectly proper to use the word 'achievement' in a very general sense. You use it for generals, you use it for opera singers. It turns out the particular thing we were measuring and happened to give the label to has to do with efficiency. I often wish I'd called it the need for efficiency. Then, there wouldn't have been all this problem. But no matter how many times I say that one should pay attention to what these people are really like rather than to the word 'achievement', there's a lot in a word. As soon as I say that what I'm measuring is a concern for cost-benefit analysis, for efficiency, for input-output ratios and things like that, they say, 'Well, that's a economics.' And then they realise that's why it's connected. I'm now looking into the power motive which is quite different. But, you see the linguistic confusion that started because I used the word achievement.

David McClelland

You said that you are now training people to develop achievement motivation. How are you doing this?

What we did was to look at all the literature on psychotherapy. We looked at anybody who claimed that he knew how to change people. That included people like St Ignatius of Loyola. The Jesuits apparently knew how to change people even if the psychoanalysts didn't. At that time, everyone was quoting Eysenck that psychoanalysis didn't work and was very expensive. We felt that Communist Party cells, the Jesuits, the Mormons might know more about training and changing people than psychoanalysis did. They succeeded where psychoanalysts didn't. We borrowed every principle we could. We devised a training programme that is based on four major types of input.

The basic approach is a little Skinnerian, in a sense. We knew a lot about the way a person with high achievement motivation acted and thought. We knew precisely how he thought because we developed this object coding system. So we taught people to think like that and we even taught them to act like that. We said, 'Do you want to be a successful businessman? Here's precisely the way to behave, here's what you have to do!' We taught them how to think and act by using models and feedback. That was the first part. We gave them the model.

The second main input was self-study. Where do you stand with respect to this model? And we put them through a lot of games and exercises so that they could observe themselves in a competitive situation, in an achieving situation. The third step is goal setting and planning. Do you want to be like that? What difference would it make in your life? How would it affect your relationship to your wife, to your kids? How would it affect your job? You may have to change your job because you're not really in a job that demands entrepreneurial or achievement-oriented behaviour. The fourth step which we sometimes use, and sometimes don't, is the building up of a network of interpersonal supports. All the successful change groups we ran into created a new identity. The Jesuits put a robe on you, a new robe, and it said, 'Now you're a Jesuit.' That also keeps reminding you you've changed in certain ways. We felt that a lot of group work, follow-up work, checking up, was desirable. Basically, it was all very short-term and straightforward, very different from the long-term, subtle suggestive approach of psychoanalysis or non-directive therapy. Straight out.

Have you been able to trace why certain people are more achievement-minded?

We've found that certain sub-groups teach this naturally to their kids. All over the world, we kept on running into minorities, usually minority groups, who were very good at business. When we checked out, we found they were bringing up their kids that way, the way we were trying to bring them up artificially. All over the world, such people pop up. For instance, when I was living in Ethiopia, I ran across a tribe called the Garagi. The Garagi had never had any contact with the West but they had developed high achievement motivation on their own. They're not the dominant tribe. Emperor Haile Selassie belonged to the Amhara tribe and they are high in power motivation. The Garagi are high in achievement and they learn this in connection with their system of agriculture which is very different from that of the Amhara who are cattle-breeders. The Garagi grow *aniset* which is a kind of plant that takes eight years before you get anything out of it. They have to tend it for eight years. That means long-term planning.

And getting used to delayed goals?
Yes.

You have also tried to establish a historical connection between achievement orientation and economic growth. I remember a finding of yours that linked the achievement motive in Greek literature with the upsurge of Greek trade.

The upsurge in achievement motivation in Greek literature preceded by some hundred years the great expansion in Greek trade. We did the same kind of thing with the history of England and Spain in the Middle Ages. We've done a lot of history. Generally speaking, achievement motivation goes up before a time of economic rise and declines before economic fall.

So, presumably, some nations have done well in achievement motivation recently, Japan, for instance, while Britain must have done miserably.

I don't know the answer for Japan. Our figures for Japan are, I think, unreliable. Our big comparative data in 1950 are from children's stories read in the public schools. The problem with the 1950 Japanese stories is that they were all written by Americans during the American occupation under MacArthur. I have never known how much to believe them.

The British case is quite straightforward. They were fairly high in achievement motivation in 1925 and very low by 1950, along with Sweden and some others. So, I predicted that England was going to have a hard time, that is that its rate of growth was going to slow down. It certainly has. We don't know exactly why it goes up and down but we do know that it fluctuates.

Could it be something as simple as action/reaction? People react to achieving times by being less achieving and vice versa.

The trouble is that there are gaps that are hard to explain. We've done England from 1400. There's a little gap in the nineteenth century but we picked it up again in 1920 through to 1960. Twice in English history, there was a big burst of achievement motivation. The first time was round the reign of the first Elizabeth, in Shakespeare's time. Then, there was another burst in the mid-eighteenth century which preceded the big Industrial Revolution. So, there was a fair gap in between. There seems to be nothing automatic about it. We're sure of that. There was a big rise in achievement motivation in the US between 1860 and 1900. Then it tailed off till the Second World War. After the war, unaccountably, it started to rise again. We haven't found any regularities yet. I used to think it had something to do with religion. I think it still does remotely, though I wouldn't call it religion. Achievement motivation seems to follow a period of idealism.

Because idealism makes people forget economics for a while, maybe?

I don't know why. It was originally connected with the Protestant reform which was a wave of idealism against the Establishment. That's the most consistent thing. It seems to follow a period of rebellion, of striking out against the Establishment. You could say that if England wanted a wave of achievement motivation, it should have had more rebellion against the Establishment. It really didn't have much compared to us. The university kids were nowhere near rebelling the way they did here or in France. Achievement motivation in France is much higher than in England, in fact. It also went up in the communist countries, in the primary communist countries, Russia and China. But not in the satellite countries like Poland, Hungary and Bulgaria; they all stayed low. I think they weren't rebelling, they weren't at the centre of the rebellion against the Establishment. The communist countries did have rebellions, after all, and they were followed by higher achievement motivation.

Yes, and the period in English history that preceded Elizabeth I was very turbulent.
Very turbulent, yes.

Your work clearly offends against behaviourist tenets. Do you think that behaviourism is sterile and dead now?
It's very much alive and enjoying a revival. Ten to fifteen years ago, it was dying down, It had fallen out of fashion when the culture and personality people came in and that, obviously, is the school to which I belong. I thought 'Thank God' and then, all of a sudden, it came back with a bang, with behaviour modification, with Skinner becoming a kind of demi-god. Young people are pouring into it. You have to explain that in terms of the social psychology of social psychologists, of the ethos of the whole time. I have a theory that I haven't checked out that it has to do with motivational patterns in society. It's not just a question of economic growth but of what kind of ideological currents attract people in psychology. It's clear that behaviourism has been very lively, very lively for the past ten years. It appeals to the American genius. It's very simple-minded, not intellectual at all. You have just a few simple sovereign principles and the rest is practical engineering. It has a kind of engineering quality.

Is there much hostility between behaviourists and non-behaviourists?
Very much. They never even talk because they have all the answers so that it isn't worth talking about anything. Everything else is epiphenomenal and 'soft'. They don't believe in statistics, they don't believe in any of the things that the others think are all-important. There is certainly a lot of non-communication between the two.

Why do you think psychologists are driven to such hostility?
It's their power orientation. They love to argue. They hate to be wrong. Power contributes to science but it also makes people in science terribly argumentative.

Isn't another point that many psychologists take physics as their

David McClelland

model and worship it?
There is some of that but I think that was truer ten years ago than it
is now. I think it's more that they want to be right and will go to any
ends to prove it. The great thing in psychology is that there is a
temptation to get drawn into endless arguments so that you waste
time you should be spending doing research. As Thorndike said, he
would rather spend the time it took to reply to an attack doing
another piece of research.

*Does the attention that psychology now gets from the media make
psychologists even more argumentative?*
Somewhat – because they get paid for it. But they always did it. If
you go back to the old days in the animal literature, you find this
great controversy in the early forties between Spence and David
Krechevsky, who is now David Krech, on whether rats formed
hypotheses. The journals were filled with it. Reputations were made
and fell. PhDs were written. Who remembers it now? Because they
were so interested in proving they were right, they lost track of
whether the issue was important and, in fact, whether it could be
resolved at all because many can't be; 'It all depends' was the answer.
Take place learning versus response learning. It all depends on
whether animals can see or not. If they can see, they do place
learning. If they are fairly blind, like albino rats, they have to rely on
response learning. There is far too much controversy that isn't
productive at all.

*Has the work you've been doing on creativity in scientists shown any
reasons why this might be?*
I did some work on that field a while ago but not lately. I looked at
the motivational patterns of creative physical scientists. Then I
stopped work on it but I'm coming back to it. I discovered then they
tended to be rather power oriented. I'm working on the power
motive now. It's very clear that the power motive is associated with
eminence in fields where achievement motive doesn't apply. Success
in other roles, politicians for example, and teachers, are high in
power motivation, not achievement motivation. Teachers like to
influence people.
    I simply reported my work on creative scientists. I didn't go into it
very much. I had a feeling there was a lot of aggression in physical
scientists that was kept under control. They were very nervous about
expressing aggression but it was sublimated into some desire to tear

38

the world apart and see what made it tick, which is what physical science is all about. This sort of motivation — and I'm leaving aside the ability factor but there are a lot of people with ability who don't become outstandingly creative — appears to be connected with some kind of aggression.

Even in scientists who were pacifists?
Oh, often. Historically, in terms of their drives, scientists are notorious. I'm not talking here about theoretical physicists but about experimental physicists and chemists. Biologists already shade off a bit. But physical scientists tend to be very inhibited socially. They tend not to date much, they tend not to be very active sexually as if there's a lot of libido that's squeezed off there and redirected into science. A kind of passion, if you like. A Freudian would say that it can't be expressed socially and that it has to go into another channel. All I can say is that, factually, it seems to be true that your scientists are quite inhibited. In terms of Hudson's work, they're odd. They're diverger-convergers. The convergers are very inhibited and the divergers very released. Scientists seem to be very inhibited in some areas but very released in others.

I think Hudson also found that in periods where sciences were undergoing major changes, creative scientists often had very high rates of divorce and breakdowns so that maybe they also get destructive release that way?
Maybe.

Am I right in thinking that psychologists have been very little studied themselves?
Well, we've studied them. They're very high in power motivation both here and in England. But, in general, you're right, they have been little studied.

Could you explain some of the ways in which you've tapped the power motive?
The theoretical framework is basically Freud's except that we are looking at the power motive rather than at libido. If you have someone who is basically at stage one, oral development, though there will be signs of other levels of behaviour, he will in response to a questionnaire or an interview reveal that he has far more admired characters, far more people who he's been inspired by. If you take a

39

person at the third stage, the phallic stage, then his need for power should express itself in far more competitive activities like sports and arguing. This is the empirical work. The theoretical framework is Freudian.

Do you feel that much psychology is simply telling people very obvious things they have known all the while?
No, it's telling you a lot of things that no one cares about, very technical things that involve minor variations, minor readings. American social psychology is primarily experimental. There is some academic attitude work but even that is primarily experimental. You ask, 'What kind of thing can you do to change somebody?' Now, to do experiments you have to make settings on many variables. American social psychology has gone over to multivariate design using analysis of variance, analysis of co-variance. The amount of changes you can make on some of these variables, whether they're individual difference variables or style of influence variables, seem to me – and I'm not a social psychologist – to be infinite and infinitely boring. Infinitely boring because, in the end, it doesn't add up to anything except another article that another person who's interested in that very specialised field is going to read. How it boils down to some overall picture is something that we seem totally incapable of doing.

The British social psychologists, like Argyle, at least try to pool results in book form to show how all the results fit together and how they are significant as in the case of human interaction. But American social psychologists seem to get into some controversy as to whether this finding disproves dissonance theory. You have a hundred articles to prove or disprove dissonance theory. I find it rather nit-picking. It's very hard to get a general picture.

Do you think psychology has reached a stage where it can usefully put forward large general theories? Donald Broadbent in England has argued that psychology should concentrate on the art of the possible. We should add small bits now and, one day, when we are long dead, someone will put together a theory of Man.
I know. That's the defence psychologists always use. It used to be the plea that every young psychologist made at the end of his research article. 'Of course, this is the first brick of a magnificent edifice. More research needs to be done'! The thing is, you hope

someone will come along and put a brick somewhere near your brick - on top of it. In point of fact, if you look at the history of psychology, nobody puts a brick on top of their own brick. They make their own brick-pile. You want someone to come along and see how these things are all connected.

Many of these people have physics as their model. Somehow, they think Einstein will come along. I think psychology is much closer to biology which isn't surprising since you're dealing with a biological organism. I'm not for grand theories but I think what people should do is concentrate on content areas. I'm one of the few psychologists to have done that.

What exactly do you mean?
Psychologists are always trying to get maximum generalisation. Skinner is the perfect typical example of that. It's very clear what he set out to do, that is to find a few sovereign principles of learning that would apply to paramecia as well as to man. He was really carried away by it. And it is a kind of glorious thing. The law of reinforcement works, it works across all species with certain well-defined limits.

The biologist, on the other hand, says I'm going to find out how the liver works. That's enough. I don't have to find out the principles of the body. I said I was going to learn about achievement motivation, about how it affects individuals, about how it affects history. And I stuck to that long enough to sort of do it. That's not nearly so general, you might say, as Skinner. I have nothing to say about paramecia. They can't talk and my measure depends on talking. I can't say anything about rats. Tough. I limited myself to human beings. Some psychologists try to get a broad band across species. I think there are limited generalisations you can make.

But do you think people are seduced by wanting to make greater generalisations than the evidence warrants?
If you look at people who are doing attitude work, for instance, you find they don't care what attitude they study. Any attitude is as good as any other because they want a theory that cuts across all attitudes. I keep saying, why don't you study the attitudes that are really important in life? They say they can't decide what is really important. I don't think they've really confronted that problem. Cattell tried to. He tried to deal with what the main

41

dimensions of mind are. Eysenck did the same thing using factor analysis. I don't happen to think that's the way to do it but I find that they saw the problem the way I do.

Do you think it is possible for psychology to have an Einstein? It seems there might be too much information for one man to master and systematise!
Einstein didn't know everything. He knew enough about the areas he was working in to make some generalisations. But it certainly isn't possible for a psychologist to be an expert in sensory physiology all the way to the stuff that I do, motivational research. Those days are gone. There is a great deal of specialisation.

Too much?
It's inevitable. You have to become good enough to do your thing really well. If you are a liver man, you might say it would be interesting to know more about the brain but that isn't really possible. So, I guess, I am a kind of Broadbent man – except that I would think you can carve out somewhat bigger areas. That's a matter of judgment.

Is one of the problems that psychology deals with subjects that are full of unscientific stuff, people are making value judgments, people are making decisions that aren't so rational? And this is opposed to what we've learned are scientific phenomena which should be null, neutral?
No doubt. There are two problems here that are related. There is no doubt that passions run high over certain things like the race and heredity issue. In a sense, passion is OK. It requires passion to get interested enough in a subject to work really hard at it. On the other hand, it leads to an awful waste of time and a terrible amount of spilled ink, going over and over the same ground. Particularly if the media pick the arguments up and get serious people involved.

From my point of view, the other main problem in psychology is that we use the English language. Everyone is a psychologist because he uses the English language. And when I say 'achievement motivation', everyone assumes they know what I mean by that. If I said 'zygote' or something like that, nobody would assume he knew what it was and he would look it up and understand the technical meaning, especially before he used it. But I find that even psychologists sometimes don't take the trouble to find out what I mean by the terms because they are so sure they know since they also use English. That's a terrible problem of communication.

But there is a danger, too, isn't there, of psychologists inventing technical terms which are just jargon masquerading as new concepts?
Sure.

So, some scepticism is called for?
That's the other danger – that psychologists write fancy words. I am a measurement man. My meaning of achievement need, *nAch*, is what it measures, what its correlates are in action and in thought. It's true that psychologists often use vague references.

Do you think it will ever be possible to define what a person is by correlating his scores on various dimensions of personality?
That depends on what you mean by define. I suppose that the goal of psychology involves the game of parsimony which is predicting the most things a person will do under various circumstances with the least number of measures. Unfortunately, we have a plethora of measures. The problem is what is the minimum number you need to say anything about the guy. And when I say 'say anything', that means predict what he will do.

But does that depend on personality? Argyle and Brian Little at Oxford have been looking at the way situations affect the way we behave. And very often, they argue, it is the situation that determines it.
That's one of those things that's kind of boring. It takes up endless pages, like heredity and environment, which is more important? Everybody keeps putting up straw men and then the other people rush and say it isn't really all heredity, it's some environment and then the other side rush back. Well, now people are saying that it's useless to talk about dimensions of personality because it doesn't account for the variance across situations and the situations account for it all. Anybody who knows anything at all about it knows that it depends on the trait you are measuring. It depends what you're trying to predict, as Argyle has shown. In some traits, there's a lot of individual difference stability; in some traits,

it depends on the environment.

As always with these arguments, they derive from the personal experiences of the people involved. Michel worked for years with delayed rewards. Would you rather have a small candy bar now or a large one later? He found very little individual consistency in that situation. It depends whether the guy trusts the guy who's making the offer to give a lolly next week, it depends on the wrapper, it depends on the size of the lolly. But if you're talking about the sort of traits that Vernon and Allport were working with forty to fifty years ago – gestural expansiveness, for instance, doesn't depend much on the situation at all. Length of stride or whether you gesture out or gesture in is highly individual and idiosyncratic and doesn't depend on anything else much. It all depends. They should stop arguing what is, essentially, a nonsense issue and get on with their work.

One of the accusations that some European social psychologists have made against American social psychology is that it seems to have been obsessed by some very specific American issues, problems of race and marketing especially. Do you feel there is justice in that?
I would accuse it of many things but not of that. I wouldn't have said that. There is interest, of course, in race but if you take any issue of a journal, the *Journal of Personality and Social Psychology*, a rough guess would be that only two or three articles out of twenty have to do with race. And the rest would have to do with small groups. There seems to be much more focus on that. There seems much more work on dissonance theory, attribution theory, attitude theory, and none of these have to do with race or with application.

But I think many Europeans feel that all the work on attitude is about persuading people to buy things.
I never thought of that. You mean that might be some hidden reason why psychologists do it? They certainly never talk about it. In fact, the only person I've ever come across who tried to make use of attitude change findings for marketing was a Uruguayan who's written quite a good book about it. You would have to say it's an unconscious motive. Most social psychologists would be horrified at the accusation they had anything to do with business. That's very low status. They look down on applied research. I happen to believe in applied research because I think it keeps you

honest, it keeps you working on things that are important instead
of on trivial things.

*If it isn't too grand a question, how would you hope that your
work would be integrated into a whole psychology, a grand theory of
Man?*
I've always resisted trying to answer that question. When Sid Koch
got together his books on theories of psychology, I refused to
participate because I felt it would take much energy away from
finding out more about the concrete things I was interested in. I
can't really answer that. I guess, in a general way, that I have tried
to make Americans less action orientated in their psychology. I
think that as a people we tend to believe only in actions, choices.
That's what behaviourism really means, though technically it
doesn't. A thought is a behaviour in some sense. But Americans
have always resisted thought as anything important. It becomes
all-important, and I fall under this, too, only if it predicts action.
But surely, from the point of view of a thorough-going
psychology, I would want to see a psychology of the contents of
thought to be included.

2
Donald Broadbent

Many of the psychologists I interviewed took up their careers by accident. Some others became disenchanted with what they had started out as. They found out they did not want to, or could not, be physicists like Eysenck or writers like Skinner. Many also chose psychology because it allowed them to work on a variety of problems. Neal Miller and Liam Hudson both emphasised how important it was to find a field in which they could express themselves. Hudson's phrase that it was 'when I found I could *utter* myself' that he became an enthusiastic psychologist seems to me particularly graphic. Donald Broadbent is the only psychologist among those interviewed who decided to take up psychology as a career because he felt he ought to as a moral or civic duty. When he came out of the RAF at the end of the Second World War, it seemed to him that there was a need for psychologists to help resolve those problems like relations between people, relations between societies and relations between men and the machines and technology we have managed to create. It seemed to him that we understood the world and things much better than we understood men – and that was a dangerous imbalance.

Other psychologists do, of course, refer to the fact that it pleases them if their work turns out to be useful to the community or other people, but this is, nearly always, an afterthought or an after-motive. It is the happy consequence of work which was done because it was compelling in itself. Eysenck put it neatly when he explained that he felt obliged to do some work that was useful to society to repay it for the chance (and money) it gave him to 'pursue his fancies'. His fancies were what really mattered. Psychologists do not seem to be ruled by altruism or, for which I suppose we should be grateful, to manifest the belief that with their theories they have found the way to save the world. Even Skinner, who is often cast as being ambitious in this regard, stops short of that.

Donald Broadbent was Director of the Medical Research Council Applied Psychology Unit in Cambridge from 1958 to 1974, when he moved to Oxford in order to concentrate on research. For years, he explained to me, he had to squeeze in his own research three afternoons a week between actually running the Unit. Until his move to Oxford, Broadbent had spent all his academic career in Cambridge. When he came out of the RAF at the end of the Second World War, he studied psychology in Cambridge. He believed that he would go into industrial psychology, a supremely useful field. But the opportunity came along to do some research on the effects of noise for the navy. The noises that had to be used were too loud for the navy laboratories to bear. So Broadbent did the research at the Applied Psychology Unit going some miles out of Cambridge to a deserted hangar to run his subjects who performed certain tasks while shrill white noise screamed at them in the middle of the countryside. Broadbent stayed at the Unit and, in 1958, he became its Director.

His ideas about the kind of work that is actually useful would strike many people as over modest. He tells the story of a Viscount airliner which crashed at Prestwick in Scotland. The pilot said he was at 14,500 feet and requested permission to land. The airport gave it. He started to descend. He called again at 12,500 feet and at 10,500 feet. Shortly after that, the airliner struck the ground. The inquiry that followed showed the pilot had always believed his plane to be 10,000 feet higher than it was. He had misread his altimeter. The traditional view, Broadbent explains, is that this was the pilot's fault. He made the wrong choice, the wrong decision, and he had to bear the responsibility, in this case the terrible responsibility, for his error. In the crash, many people died.

Broadbent does not think this traditional view is just or realistic. He asks you to imagine the altimeter. It is designed like a clock face, with numbers from 0 to 9 on it. It has three pointers on it. The longest points to the height in hundreds of feet: the middle one to height in thousands of feet: the shortest to height in units of 10,000 feet. Each pointer moves constantly round the scale. The smallest (indicating 10,000 feet) pointer will be nearly opposite the number 1 when the largest middle one will be indicating 9. That should be read as 9,000 feet but it can be easily read as 19,000 feet. Experiments have shown that the relative length of the pointers makes the smallest one – the 10,000 feet one – the easiest to misread. In everyday life, we often read a pointer that is nearly on a digit as if it were on that digit. If something is pointed just a fraction off 2, we take it as reading 2. In this case, the pilot seems to have done the same thing and read 10,000 feet when they just were not there. Broadbent thinks that you cannot blame the pilot for the design of the altimeter that made it so possible for him to be so wrong.

Broadbent is very concerned about moral problems but his point is not only that we should be fair to the pilot in such a case. There is the even more vital matter of saving lives. His idea of psychology being useful very much involves discovering what is wrong with the design of such a device. Why does it not allow us to perceive easily what we need to perceive and how can it be altered to fit us better? The experimental work that showed such altimeters to be dangerous had been done around 1948, ten years before that crash. It took another seven years before the United Kingdom Altimeter Committee recommended an alternative instrument and, as of 1970, there was no legislation to prohibit the use of multi-pointer displays on altimeters.

Broadbent supposes that one of the reasons why it took so long to effect any change, even though experimental evidence and the evidence of accidents was so clear, was that many psychologists of his generation seem reluctant to break their silence. They keep a low profile. They do their work. No one is really attuned to applying their work, a trend which he admits is less to be seen in the USA than in Britain. The notion that the psychologists can do something very practical to help the community – and he excludes clinical psychologists – is only very slowly gaining ground. He is worried now that the development of a more humanistic psychology, which may be well-intentioned, but is vague, intuitive and unexperimental, will lose psychology the little ground that it has gained with difficulty over twenty-five to thirty years.

If all this led you to expect a dour, hard man, you would be wrong. Broadbent can be very funny. He has a round, moon face and he positively twinkles when he makes a joke or cutting aside, and these seem to be usually plentiful when you talk to him. Our discussion was peppered with laughs. As fits a moral person, some of Broadbent's best jokes are those told against himself or, at least, against the position that he is arguing for.

He is a genuinely modest man. He often refers to the fact that his theoretical opponents are more intelligent than he is. He smiled when he asked who else I was interviewing and suggested that the American psychologists were rather more distinguished. It isn't false modesty because Broadbent believes – that curiously traditional British belief – that intelligence and cleverness by themselves may well betray you.

If you know you are so intelligent, you do not feel the need to bother to check if your answers are right. In other words, you believe your intuitions are correct. You eschew experimenting to make sure they are. Broadbent has noticed that most of the times when he has felt intuitively sure about something he has been wrong about it. In this he reminds one of Eysenck, who told me he was usually amazed when something he predicted turned out to be true. Broadbent has written of the 'harsh stubborness of data', a stubbornness that will tame the most intuitive who bother to gather it. Experience has taught him to be wary of intuition – his own and that of others. He allows a few exceptions to this rule, the most interesting being William James and his old teacher, Sir Frederick Bartlett. But Bartlett, at least, was a convinced experimentalist and James was a pioneer.

Broadbent's own work has depended almost entirely on experiments. In his early work, he explored two particular ways in which the brain coped with information. He looked at the effects of loud noises on relatively complex performances. He found that noise tended to affect them badly, as industrial psychologists had argued but had never shown to the satisfaction of their more academic colleagues. He also looked at the way the brain deals with information coming from a number of sources. What will happen if you are trying to listen to two messages at once: what will you retain and how can you construct a model of what must be happening inside the brain at that time? As he explains in the interview, Broadbent was very much influenced by the model of a communication channel like a telephone system. It offered a language, therefore, for studying what went on inside the brain independent of any psychological work, for you could do experiments that required people to process 'information' or 'messages' in tricky or difficult ways and, from the results, you could begin to develop an idea of what the brain was capable of doing. You could start to work out a functional map of the brain.

Also, as Broadbent explains in the interview, he found this model of the brain as a telephone system to be much more important than its later development into the model of the brain as a computer. It was only as computers became more flexible in the sixties that they became conceptually important for psychologists or, at any rate, for him. What was crucial was the notion of the brain as an information processing system which could only handle a certain amount of information at a certain speed. Conceiving of a brain as a limited channel was, in fact, the key idea which gave psychologists like him a language which they could use for talking about what went on inside

49

the brain without having to talk physiologically. Broadbent has written two complex technical books, *Perception and Communication* 1958, and *Decision and Stress* (1971), in which he looks at the way the brain does cope with information and the practical ways in which these findings can be applied. He is proud of having done work which, for instance, allows postmen to pace the rate at which they sort letters – the self-pacing makes them far more efficient. It is work less dramatic, perhaps, than that involved with the altimeters, but it also contributes. It, too, is useful.

Given Broadbent's attitudes, it is not surprising that he should be a behaviourist. He has also written two of the most lucid and persuasive arguments for what one might call an evolved behaviourism instead of old-time behaviourism. These books are *Behaviour*, published in 1961, and *In Defence of Empirical Psychology*, published in 1974. *Behaviour* is meant to be a popular introduction which summarises what the behaviourist approach has enabled us to learn about Man in the last fifty years. *In Defence of Empirical Psychology* contains the William James Memorial Lectures which Broadbent was invited to deliver at Harvard in 1972. It also contains some more recent papers, including an appendix of Broadbent's thoughts on Chomsky. The audience here is presumed more knowledgeable than that for *Behaviour*. But that is not the only thing that accounts for a certain difference of tone between the two books. In between, thirteen years had elapsed. In Broadbent's opinion, the position of psychology in 1971 was worse than it was in 1961. By the early sixties, psychology was beginning to be accepted as a serious scientific study. It had long ceased to have any connection with philosophy: it was beginning to be clear that psychologists did not just have to cure neurotics but that there was a lot less glamorous but more exact psychological work going on. As Broadbent charitably observes, if a man is threatening to commit suicide, you do what you think is best, you take a gamble irrespective of whether your theory is complete. In *Behaviour* (p. 201), Broadbent wrote:

Nobody can grasp the nature of things from an armchair, and until fresh experiments have been performed we do not know what their results will be. The confident dogmatisms about human nature which fall so readily from pulpits, newspapers' editorials and school prize givings are not for us. Rather we must be prepared to live with an incomplete knowledge of behaviour but with confidence in the power of objective methods to give us that knowledge some day.

These methods have proved themselves even in the past fifty years.

And they have proved themselves because there has been a steady and sure growth of knowledge , according to Broadbent. We know more than J. B. Watson did. This accumulation of knowledge depends on using public and objective methods. A scientist working on memory in California must be able to verify and go beyond the work of a scientist working in Hamburg. This will only be possible if both work in a way that makes it quite clear what they mean by their data. You have to rely on what you can observe. You cannot, as psychologists thought before Watson, rely on introspections for if one man says he had an 'image of blue' when you showed him a picture of the sea to make him think about the sea, you really have no means of knowing what he means by this. If another person says he had an image of pink with a tendency to think of one that was blue, does this mean he was conscious of the same things or not? Introspective psychology degenerated, not into squabbles about the meaning of particular experiments and how to interpret them, but into quarrels about what the actual results of the experiments were. To attempt to understand the mind by introspection is grandiose and impossible. If Broadbent uses behaviourism, he does not ignore what goes on in the mind and is, indeed, trying to work out models of how it copes with information. But these models are based on observing how the brain deals with information that is put in and what action it takes in response to it. Broadbent believes now, too, that psychologists who had been influenced by early behaviourism were too ready to see the brain as a passive channel through which information passed or where it decayed. They did not realise how the brain might actively transform and use the information it received. But introspective psychology would never have enabled you to find out that.

Allied to Broadbent's behaviourism is his conviction that it is no good setting off to do research on topics which are fascinating but for which the techniques do not yet exist. He quoted to me the phrase 'the art of the soluble' from Sir Peter Medawar's book and he intimated that he felt many psychologists were trying, worthily, to do the impossible; and were doing it badly. At this stage, psychology has to advance its knowledge slowly, brick by brick. In this interview, however, Broadbent makes a distinction between work that he believes is conceptually possible – such as work on family relations for which useful tools like the Kelly Grid Repertory Test exist – and work that he believes is waiting for a good idea and a revolutionary idea before it can be taken further, such as work on psychopathic personalities. He does seem to feel, however, that even research on family relations is not very promising at present due to a lack of good social-psychological ideas.

What worries Broadbent now is the resurgence of humanistic and radical psychology, which is more prevalent in the USA. 'But then everything is more prevalent in the States', he adds. For him, the *bête noire* of humanistic psychology appears to be Chomsky. Broadbent grants that Chomsky is a genius as a linguist, and he speaks and has written of the achievements of transformational grammar as being on a par with those of Euclid. He says that the comparison is deliberate for Euclid's theorems are theoretical. They are not reflected in reality. Two explorers who set off from the equator in parallel lines in order to avoid each other for ever would get a nasty shock when they ran into each other at the north pole. Similarly, Chomsky appals him when he starts arguing that there is a psychological reality implied by his linguistics; in other words, that we can only learn to speak as fast as we do if we presume there is some innate, very specific schema that is triggered in a child who is normal by listening to others talk and beginning to talk with them. At the back of *In Defence of Empirical Psychology*, Broadbent includes an appendix in which he refers doubters to passages in Chomsky where this is argued. Chomsky is certainly not reticent in arguing these claims himself.

Worse, too, than Chomsky, there are many psychologists – whose intellects, Broadbent does not praise – who are doing very sloppy work relying on their insight which they themselves praise. Broadbent has the greatest doubts about the value of insight. Unless there is the painful business of checking those insights, you can never find out if they are wrong. And he sees a mad rush by students into psychology who think it will tell them something about life. That, he points out, is the very last reason for going into psychology. It will tell you awfully little about Life with a capital L.

But one of the reasons why Broadbent is such an effective advocate of behaviourism is that he does not seem to feel that by understanding people, you reduce them. It is clear that Skinner feels freedom and dignity to be dangerous illusions and, also, that in the last analysis, he feels one must sacrifice individual human values to the good of the race. Broadbent, who is much concerned with moral issues, talks at length about the fact that understanding a person does not reduce him. Psychology is not a threat to morality nor to responsibility in the grander sense of the word. That is why he hopes to see a psychology of ethics grow which explains how people make ethical decisions.

In the actual work that he does, Broadbent does not deny the usefulness of hunches but, as he puts it:

'Hunch is essential and never to be trusted. All new ideas come from hunch, and there is nowhere else they could come from, but on the other hand most ideas are false and you need to try them out empirically before you know which are true and which are false. I would not describe this attitude as ambivalent but rather as discriminating. After all, I think highly of a bicycle as a mean device for transportation but not as a thing to sleep on.'

Broadbent continues by saying that butter is excellent but only as a thing to eat, not for painting a house. But he is firm that he is not ambivalent or uncertain about the value of hunches, nor about their limitations.

When I asked Broadbent about the kind of pleasure that he got from research, he too hedged a little. He told me:

'It is in principle impossible to answer perfectly, because one can only communicate feelings that are common to people at both ends of the communication by indicating the situation in which you get it. It is pretty clear that there are marked individual differences in this particular experience. The nearest I can get is to say that it is certainly the experience I would prefer to any other I have met in any situation whatever. And that it is similar in kind, but more intense, to the feelings I get in religious or in certain aesthetic situations. That is, I get a similar but less complete feeling from Bach but not from Shostakovich or from Eliot but not from Hopkins. In both cases I am fond of the second name mentioned, but what I get from them is something different.'

Why did you become a psychologist?
Briefly, because I started as a natural scientist, became dissatisfied and bored and felt an imbalance in the way knowledge was developing and became aware of another field which seemed to be more relevant. To expand on that – the great thing was having a break between school and university. If I had gone straight to university I would have become a conventional natural scientist. When I went into the RAF in the war, I knew I was bored with it. The break gave me the chance, on the one hand, to see what was wrong with some techniques we were using and, also, to see what air force

53

psychologists were doing. Thirdly, it also happened that I did my training in the USA where I discovered there was another field – psychology, which was quite respectable.

How long were you in the RAF?
I enlisted in 1943 and when the A-bomb was dropped, I was learning to fly. As this was funded by Lend Lease, we were all stopped training and, rather unwisely, they decided to make us redundant. Either you became a career air force officer or you re-mustered to some ground job. So I went into personnel selection in the RAF which gave me another chance to see psychology in action. We were the vocational guidance service, advising what people should do in civilian life, testing, IQ testing, using various specific ability tests and so on. Then I came out. Mercifully, I was already going to Cambridge which was one of the few places where, at the time, you could get a psychology degree. So, all these things having converged, I came back to read psychology.

And what did you actually start working on after you had graduated?
I graduated in 1949 and, at the time, there was a job going as a member of this Unit working for the navy on the effects of noise. This struck me as very close to my orientation. I was looking for a job in industrial psychology basically – I never thought I would end up in a university. But, when the job was going, I seized on the chance. It then transpired that the navy laboratory where I was supposed to do the work was rather disturbed by the prospect of all the loud noises being made. So it was felt that I had better stay here in Cambridge and work at this Unit . . . and I've been here ever since.

Who were the major influences on you?
Sir Frederick Bartlett. Bartlett was a really great man in the Edwardian tradition and dominated work in the whole field of British psychology at the time. I think he was probably much better in lectures than on paper. Only one of his books, *Remembering* (1932), is thought much of now. However, he was a tremendous inspirational figure and he dominated anyone who came into contact with him. Of course, my basic attitudes are his. He believed in the importance of the study of real-life situations and in getting at psychological problems from a study of what is going on in real life. And he also believed in rather complex processes inside a person

which could not be described in introspective language. Bartlett was lacking a language, actually, until shortly before the time when I went through as an undergraduate but he had met Kenneth Craik who was the great innovative person who was killed in an accident about the time I was learning to fly in the USA. I never knew him but his influence was very alive. Craik was, to my mind, the real creator of cybernetics, which most people think of as the work of Norbert Wiener. He was knocked off a bicycle in King's Parade and was run over. He died very young.

Professor McClelland believes that many psychologists went into the field as a reaction to a very religious, fundamentalist upbringing they wanted to get away from. Was that true in your case?
It would be about the opposite. I think you have got a cultural difference here. I've noticed that American psychologists frequently show the pattern you describe. In the USA, there are rather more dominant anti-intellectual religious movements and they react against this very vigorously. Not just McClelland, but other people show a degree of venom towards religion that surprises me. I'm rather the other way around. During my adolescence, the brightest people I knew were religious. I have always regarded the obligation of the religious person to be as clever as he can be. I view psychology as a means of implementing my religion.

That sounds rather paradoxical. Could you explain it a little more?
I suppose, broadly speaking, that my general philosophical standpoint is that of the Church of England. That means it's rather eclectic and pragmatic. But it involves fairly tight formal ways of life and moral obligations. One of them is to do the best that you can for the community as a whole. If you look around, as I did in the war, and see the many problems of our understanding human nature, problems of relations between states, mental illness, problems of relationships between human beings and technology, then you should go where the need is and not go where, as my advisers very properly urged me to go, into the chemical industry because that was a good career. The need then was for psychologists. It still is. And that's why I went into it.

You feel it is necessary for psychology to be useful and practical?
Very much so. The theory is only important because it produces bigger, better practical effects.

55

Donald Broadbent

I read once in a book of yours that a friend had said that the job you would have best fitted in history would have been as scientific adviser to Oliver Cromwell. Do you think that was a fair judgment?

I think it is an apt description. It was quite genuinely coined by someone else. I think it has real advantages. It has some of my characteristics. I liked it, too, because there are clearly implicit self-criticisms. And though, of course no modern man could be in this position, I wonder sometimes about my ancestors in the Welsh hills and I wonder what life would have been like if I had been born then and been like that but I wouldn't have been like I am, of course. Nevertheless, the cultural tradition is recognisable. If you want to be negative, I belong to a strain that is anxiety-driven, other-directed, sometimes ruthless, and I think this is a good way to be. [He laughs.]

And how did your work for the navy develop?

It was a hard slog. The position then was that most laboratory experiments had failed to show any effect of noise on people. But industrial experience was that reducing noise was a good thing. It was asserted by various influential reviewers that the effects found in industry were pure suggestion. The navy wasn't convinced. Nor was Bartlett. They felt there still might be something in it because the psychological tests used in the lab were rather simple-minded, reaction times, reversible perspective and so on. The Cambridge lab, following Bartlett and Craik, had been studying more complex functions like flying aeroplanes. [He laughs.] Tests of these more complex functions might be more sensitive to noise. It was necessary to use rather long tests like vigilance tasks. I spent the first year piloting a new kind of vigilance task where, first, the equipment turned out to be unsatisfactory. Then we had to get a noise room established, and it was only after two to three years that we got a group of subjects through where we got effects.

Then, the then Director [Norman Mackworth] felt progress was rather slow and he gave me another problem – that of speech communication in complex nets which was involved in air traffic control so I also started a line on that which was held up by equipment again. I was able to get hold of a primitive form of wire recorder and then one of the early tape recorders. We began to do more elaborate things with tape recorders. About three years after I began, I started to get a proper vein of experiments on listening in these complex situations. All the time the noise experiments were going on. It was very slow.

What exactly did you do in the noise experiments?
Typically, one would require a subject to work for one and a half hours on each of five days. It had to be done outside Cambridge because of the noise. We went out to an old airfield miles out, so no one was with me. I used to pray the subject would come up on the bus. I would run him on the various tests with different levels of noise. Then, we'd come back together and that would be all for that day. We would come back the next day. It would take four months to do a group of subjects.

But the experiments on listening worked relatively quickly. They provided a quicker turnaround. After about three to four years, I got a number of results on speech which provided evidence of limited capacity in people's ability to speak and listen at the same time. The first publication of papers began in about 1952, and then in 1953 and 1954. By that stage, the work began to look very reasonable. The first years were very worrying.

On the basis of these experiments, did you begin to build up a picture of how we operate faced with such complex situations? With lots of information coming in?
I spent a long time standing in air traffic control towers being as inconspicuous as possible, watching what people were doing. Now, if one thinks back to the theoretical ideas current at the time – which is very difficult, the world has moved on and, you know, I can't quite think how I used to think and I'm sure it would be quite strange to you . . . . But what was really manifest was that what I was seeing was inconsistent with the theoretical points of view around in academic literature. They were out in a different dimension. You'd see a man sitting with four loudspeakers – the RAF had then just introduced jet fighters – and he'd have several sections of these coming down back to the airfield. He would identify which direction they were coming in from, give them courses to steer and bring them out eventually in a position to land. It was obvious you could not treat what he was doing as a Stimulus-Response system. What happened to one stimulus depend on what had happened in the whole situation and on what seemed to be about to happen. It just was not this simple Stimulus-Response system. The whole problem seemed to be one that most psychology of the time hadn't even recognised.

Donald Broadbent

To find something on a complex situation like this you had to go back to William James and his chapters on attention. And you could recognise often enough things he was seeing. I was seeing them in there. The problem was, what was causing the air traffic controllers problems and what could I do about it?

Before you go on to that, could I just ask you if you found this natural history stage of observations very valuable?
Yes. What we did then, what we still do, was to watch the situation, to get out of it the key parts that made the problem and to reconstruct these in the laboratory and design and experiment. You can't usually get data out of the raw situation because there are too many accidental features in it. Perhaps this controller smokes too much, perhaps this controller had a bad night, perhaps he doesn't hear a message from a particular pilot as he had a row with him yesterday. There's no way of telling. If you remove the accidental features, you can get it into a laboratory. Then you can get the speakers arranged much the same, using tape recorders, you can control what the messages are and you can put through large numbers of people. There aren't accidental features or they cancel out. And then you can show there are limits to the amount of information you can get through the man and what the nature of the limits are.

And what did you discover these to be?
I found that Man is not limited in the number of tasks he can do at the same time, but cannot handle more than a certain amount of information in the technical sense of that word. That is, he can do several things at once if events in each of them are fairly probable, but he cannot handle two very improbable stimuli at the same time, in order to avoid overloading of the central sensory input. That is, they may listen only to words coming from a certain spatial position, or read words printed in certain coloured ink, and will know very little about other events while they are doing this. A third important point is that this selective filtering of the intake of information occurs *after* a short-term memory, which will hold everything that has happened for a brief period. This buffer store allows a momentary peak of incoming information to be handled, by selecting part of it first and understanding that, before going back to a memory of the other signal and dealing with it later.

58

Donald Broadbent

Is your quarrel, then, with psychologists who want to pursue idiosyncratic lines, studying individuals in real-life situations, not that you shouldn't do observations but that you cannot distil these observations in any very useful way?

Well, you can observe. All my experience is that observation in real-life situations may be mistaken and, if you impose some explanation on it, your first theoretical guess is almost always wrong or it's wrong fifty per cent of the time, something like that. The only way you can attach any reliability to it is to say that if the theoretical explanation is right, then if you alter the situation in this way, then something will happen – and see if it happens. This is enormously difficult to do in any concrete situation. The point about an idiosyncratic approach isn't quite the same issue. I'm concerned with functions that are common to a large number of people. I was then. I'm much more able now to be concerned with individual differences. I would now argue on the basis of all I've learned in the last twenty-five years that various functions, common to all people, can be operated and combined in different sequences and assemblies of sequences so that what will happen in any person can be unique. One must expect individual persons to be studied idiosyncratically and I would have thought it entirely proper if it was, for some reason, worth one's effort to try and analyse what was happening in one particular case rather than what all people do in situations. On the other hand, as a matter of taking decisions about where to apply one's effort, you can see there is a case for using my method. If I find a function common to ninety per cent of people then by making use of that knowledge I can improve the lot of many people. Where if I put great effort into one individual, I may not help him much and I certainly won't help the next man or anyone else.

In reading you, I was struck by a quote in which you spoke of the harsh stubbornness of data. Are you satisfied that by taking the experimental approach you do, you are not closing yourself to some kinds of data, observations in some areas Hudson, for instance, would think relevant? Shouldn't one struggle with it even though it is difficult raw data and can't be reduced to experiments that are elegant?

If it were really true that you couldn't reduce data into experiments, I should feel I was deceiving myself by thinking I was getting anywhere. I do believe that by struggling with it, you can get things into repeatable, objective form. It isn't worth anything until you've done that. When I say that, of course, it is a slight over-statement. If,

59

as I have done, you watch an industrial worker or an air traffic controller and you get a hunch that way, that may argue for doing an experiment of this kind or that. The kind of observation you do is always determined by the theoretical framework existing. There's no question about that. But until you've made a check on the observation, you can make no check on the theoretical framework. If you are, say, struggling with an immensely difficult, rich set of data that is quasi-clinical and then sit down and say, 'I'm not going to reduce it to experiment', it's not merely, I would say, in principle that I rule out that kind of thing but I also think this chap is deceiving himself. This chap has a fifty per cent chance of being wrong. It is not possible for all psychoanalysts to be right, for instance, for they contradict each other. You must have some way of deciding between them.

But surely experimental psychologists also disagree amongst themselves?
Experimenters don't disagree all that much.

And you would say it's a self-delusion . . .?
It's a self-delusion to believe you can look at all these messy, important data and get the right answer by thinking! Eysenck phrases it rather nicely by saying he is completely lacking intuition, insight into human problems. I can only speak from my own experience. I can get enormously confident about an idea and I'm often wrong when I check. If you don't check, you never find this out. [He laughs.]

Do you suspect that many of those who argue for a more humanistic psychology don't want to check because they suspect that they might be wrong?
No question about that. To analyse the motives of people who disagree with me is always a great temptation for me. [He laughs.] But working it out at this intuitive level and being subjective, to do precisely what I've been criticising – I would say there are some people who possess genuine insight into situations and are right. And they, because they can make personal and private checks, know that they are right and are impatient. There are others who are wrong because they just don't understand the situation but they have the same internal experience. They believe they are right. There are some who are reluctant to check because they know they're right,

anyway, and so why waste time, and there are others who have a sneaking suspicion they are wrong anyway and don't want to find out. But you can see the temptation. If you're sure you're right, why do the checking? I, of course, check because I've had so many experiences of being wrong.

Is that why you favour an approach that you describe as Bayesian in In Defence of Empirical Psychology, *an approach in which one keeps a number of alternative theories in mind?*
Yes, it's inevitable that if one views different kinds of minds, you meet alternative strategies which are gambles about the most effective view of looking at the world. People who have one style will argue for the merits of their style . . . I'm speaking at this intuitive level I've been criticising . . . and they will argue for the merits of that style rather than some other style. I think through this objective technique of describing what goes on inside people, I can make some sort of statement as to where the intuitive chap does well. To take an example I mention at the beginning of *In Defence*. Take the problems raised by immigration into New York where events, as Daniel Schon pointed out, were developing so quickly that if you waited until you had all the facts, the problem was also there and worse. Therefore, to sit back and collect facts is too slow an approach. To check every alternative until you are certain can be too slow in dealing with real-life problems. It's guaranteed to fail. The chap who reacts quickly to his first guess may be wrong but, in many situations, any action is better than no action. And he may be right. This means that, if you're advising the armed forces as we are, you often get people of different temperaments at different sides of the table. You have the chap trained and temperamentally inclined to be decisive, to take the reasonable interpretation and act on it and, on the other side, you have the psychologist trained to look for the possible error, to do another experiment, to do another control and never to say anything until he's sure. And of these two, one is supposed to be advising the other. The danger is that they will be completely out of communication. In my experience, since they're both highly intelligent, they have enough intelligence to understand the difficulty. But I would not argue the fighter pilot is an inferior type to the research scientist. However, having said all that [he laughs] I think it is extremely dangerous simply to adopt the intuitive approach and neglect alternative explanations.

Donald Broadbent

As your work developed in the fifties did you find the analogy of the brain as a computer to be very useful?

Not at that time as a computer. It's difficult for me to think back to the theoretical ideas of that time and almost impossible for you. Let me start with a concrete instance. Someone else here was studying a new spelling alphabet for use internationally in the air. In the war, if we wanted to say A B C D, we said Able Baker Charlie Dog. That was used jointly with the US. The trouble is that this was not very natural or easy for the Latins to speak properly. The French didn't like it much and the Spaniards liked it less. By the 1950s there was a big international study to produce something equally good for Anglo-Saxons and Latins so they produced the Alpha Bravo Coco Delta which we still use. During the experimental work that led up to this, various alphabets were tried and I remember that people came out from looking at the results white and shaking because they had found the word VICTOR in one alphabet was more intelligible than the word VICTOR in another one. In other words, the intelligibility of that word was not decided by the stimulus, by the word itself, but also by what else was in the list. In the alphabet in which it was less intelligible the word for letter N was NECTAR so when they had heard 'ectar' . . . they didn't know if it was VICTOR or NECTAR. But in the list where VICTOR was more intelligible, the word N was a monosyllable . . . I can't remember what. But if they heard 'ectar' they knew it was VICTOR so that word became more intelligible. This would be completely taken for granted nowadays. It was surprising then. During the late forties, we had Claude Shannon's great analysis of the concept of information and this began to percolate into psychology in Britain, especially through Edward Hick (1952) who wrote a paper (that circulated in manuscript when I was an undergraduate but which was finally published in the early fifties) on reaction times and the amount of information in the stimulus in the technical sense. He showed a plausible relation. Now we are more sophisticated but it was still an enormous contribution. We began to see that you could discover what went on inside a man in the same terms that you could discover what went on inside a telephone system. Shannon discovered what went on in the phone system without considering it it was using a wire or going by radio or whether it was an FM or AM system, which was very important. Till Shannon produced his work, I believe nobody was quite sure that it might not be possible to get more information through the same bandwidth by some new radio system. It was Shannon's demonstration that there was a theoretical upper limit to capacity that convinced them. If you could discuss the information limits regardless of the physical nature of the communication channel then we could discuss information in the brain without discussing what neurons it travelled in or whether it went by electrical stimulation or chemical changes. We had a language to talk about what happened inside a man which was not a mentalistic introspective language, which was not hypothetical neurophysiology and which wasn't simply a description of the visible behaviour, the stimulus and the response. Now, everywhere around us, these were the only languages that were available. Bartlett's problem was that he knew from his psychological insight, from results of his experiments and just because he understood people, that there were things going on inside them which we could now describe by analogy with information retrieval systems and computers. But Bartlett had no language for it. Now, Shannon's work and the whole approach of telephone engineers gave us that language. At that time, computers didn't seem to us more than a subdivision of this. Then, of course, computers were also rigidly programmed to perform a predicted sequence of operations. Although they were information-processing machines, they were less interesting for our purposes than telephone systems.

What was limited then, as part of our own approach, especially in the US, was the view of the phone channel as a passive channel with things pushed in at one end and emerging at the other. I think American psychologists, in the Watsonian tradition, tended to take up information theory and treat it in the same way. You push in information at one end and it comes out at the other. In Britain, we were never quite as naive because of Bartlett's skill concept and Craik's manuscripts to guide us. But there was still a tendency in that direction. Now, computers come in later as a major influence in the sixties rather than the fifties. When computer programmes began to get more complicated and show conditional branches and loops and recursive processes so that the chap who programmed the system no longer knew what the machine was doing it became interesting. The crux as to whether it reacted to a stimulus or not depended on what was going on inside it, not how much it could deal with in a certain time.

But, for an older chap like me, the key concept was the shift to information processing – not neural processes.

Does that mean that you tend to agree with Skinner on the

Donald Broadbent

uselessness of physiology, for psychologists at least?
   No – briefly. But can I counter that? What specifically are you
   thinking of? Skinner isn't interested in physiology himself. But
   surely he allows other people to be?

*As I understand it, he wrote as far back as 1938 that psychologists
who were relying on physiologists were wasting their time. There was
no need to be interested in what went on inside the head or the
organism. What matters was what went in and what went out as
behaviour.*
   I certainly couldn't agree with that. That's not quite true. It is true
   that, as psychologists, all we know about what goes on inside and in
   the head is derived from what we see go in and out. There is no other
   way we can get knowledge about it but that does not mean that the
   work itself is all in the insertion and extraction, that that's all I'm
   interested in. I'm interested in what does happen in between, but I
   have to infer that from what goes in and out.

*I think, if I may clarify what I think Skinner thinks at least, that he
believes it is the link between what goes in and what comes out that is
important, not any model of what might go on in between. Secondly,
Skinner seems to claim that physiologists have not learned anything of
any use to psychology which seems rather sweeping.*
   That is sweeping. If he really goes as far as that – he sometimes uses
   phrases one could force that way but I'm cautious about that – I
   often find that . . . if I can define my attitude rather than knock
   other people's . . . it's obvious that ultimately we must understand
   the physiology of the brain. There are many things for which the
   crucial explanation will be physiological. For instance, as a matter of
   research strategy, I would guess that biochemical approaches to
   schizophrenia would be a better bet than the psychological one. I
   might be wrong. And I also think that when we do understand
   physiological mechanisms, it puts desirable limits on the kind of
   psychology one can suppose is going on. On the other hand there are
   two arguments that make me do very little physiological
   psychology – in fact, none. One is that I think it important at an
   early stage in understanding a system to find out what it does rather
   than to look at its internal mechanism that produces the results.
   With any complex machinery, if you look at it analytically, you
   can't work out what it's doing. It's very difficult to work from the
   analysis of each part of a complex machine to see what its total

function is, to work back to that. Physiologists will say that about neuro-anatomy. They will say when we know a certain inhibition exists or a pathway, then people will look through a microscope and see it. But they didn't see it before and they see what the physiology declares must be there. You have to show a physiological relationship and then you can find an anatomical relationship between this complicated tangle of fibres. Similarly, I think there is a danger, if you look at a physiological function, of misunderstanding what its psychological function is. There are examples that leap naturally to my mind in the mechanisms of hearing. There are a number of cases where people have looked at the physiological nature of the system and misunderstood what it was doing. Helmholtz likened the structure of the basilar membrane to the wires in the back of a piano: long at one end and short at the other. When you sing into a piano with a damper pedal off, it sings at you. So he thought the basilar membrane was a series of resonators and he was wrong. In fact, there is a complex analysis of complex waves going in the basilar membrane but it is not like a set of piano wires. And you only find this out when you start doing behavioural experiments or simple anatomical ones like cutting the basilar membrane and showing it is not under the tension it ought to be. I think looking at a mechanism can frequently mislead one as to what it is doing.

So, psychology should precede physiology?
Yes. It will also be left as a subject when physiology is totally understood.

Are you worried by the emergence of humanistic psychology that suggests our approach should be more intuitive and less scientific or rigorous?
Yes, I am worried by that. I think this is a confusion of purpose, or categories. As I was saying, for certain problems, the conduct of a military operation or making love, some styles of mind and behaviour are more appropriate than the pure scientific approach. And it is sufficiently clear and obvious that people have a need for . . . well . . . information about when they need to adopt such kinds of attitudes and what these attitudes should be. [Pause.] Sorry, but this is hard to formulate . . . . The sort of thing I'm saying is, old-style language, we have no machinery of agreed morality in our society and everybody is wandering around looking for

something to believe in. And some of them are coming into psychology and saying, 'Oh, let's not do psychology, let's do theology; let's adopt some world-view as being the content of psychology.' And this, I think, is a confusion. Psychology is one subject: world-views are another. The difficulty arises now from a lack of an agreed world-view. That's why people are doing this kind of thing in psychology.

Do you think that, apart from the lack of an agreed world-view, there is also the lack of a language for work on complicated real-life situations, say, the family, marriage, divorce. There seems to be a danger of work in these areas being just superior journalism or surveys: in seventeen divorces out of a hundred in Aberdeen, we found . . . . Can you see a language emerging that allows one to tackle such problems?
I think we have the language already. I don't think there's any difficulty in discovering, discussing these problems either in information-processing language that I use or personal constructs. There are vocabularies in sociology and social psychology. The plain fact is that what is wrong in these areas is not a lack of language but a lack of ideas. [Pause.] By ideas, I mean what relationships it might be interesting to observe or might be valuable to change by action. I think this is rather sad. I'm rather prepared to agree that there should be more people working on family relations – parent/child as well as husband/wife, and why confine it to the traditional nuclear family? But there are some factors that push people against doing it. It's their judgment that they are, right or wrong, unlikely to come up with anything useful and it is better to have a high probability of finding something that is less valuable than have a high probability of finding out something more valuable. I don't think there is the kind of conceptual problem you mentioned.

So, in a way, it's a decision about how to allocate resources?
My reasons for the kind of work I do are pragmatic. Not theoretical. It is a decision about allocation of time and effort. I think what many young people don't see when they start in research is that you need a research strategy . . . it is like that of an industrial manager or the Chancellor of the Exchequer. It's a matter of buying information by spending time and using equipment. Although in one sense you can go about it any way you like because the logic of Nature remains the same, in practice any of us is incredibly limited. You're not going to find out much in forty years and the whole community

can't spare many people for this sort of thing. You have to use the most effective tactic. When I started it seemed the obvious thing in terms of return to look at functions common to most people.

Rather than look at individuals in depth?
Yes, I don't feel that differences between individuals are conceptually trivial or anything like that. I'm merely saying they don't repay investigation all that much. At the time, Eysenck was establishing his dimensions of personality which was certainly a major contribution, so I was by no means clearly right.

So, in a way, the tendency not to do social psychology is a social psychological fact itself.
Yes, that's one of the things. There are system constraints in all these problems. If you look at the whole society of academic psychology, there are few professors or senior staff in social psychology. They may approve it but they don't know much about it. They may have a lecturer or other staff member who knows about it and who is overloaded with teaching so that undergraduates don't see a large amount of valuable social psychology research being done. Resources are limited. Students tend to be biased towards the things they see working well around them. There's a flywheel effect. They tend to go into work on what people are working on. Once they have graduated, if they work on marriage relations, it could take, say, five to six years to get results that are convincing and important. It can't be done in the confine of a PhD thesis. So you don't do it till after you have your doctorate then, you've got to find six years, you need a tenured position. So you do something that will produce answers quickly.

And by the time you have the answers you're set along a particular line of research?
Certainly. And, of course, that other line will have its own merits. It's not a case of marital relations being the only interesting problem in psychology. [He laughs.] It's easy to go off on other turns. There's no conceptual problem as such. It's partly a sociological problem, partly a calculational problem and partly the lack of ideas is the only blunt way to put it. What do we do about it? I don't know.

I find it interesting you say there is no conceptual problem. I've usually understood you to argue differently that one should do what it is possible to do and the constraints of what can be done in these fields are pretty severe so that even if you get some great driving idea like Laing and Cooper, you won't be able to follow it through, you'll get lost.

Yes. (There are cases where I would take the position you outlined.) That's exactly the thing that gets you into unproductive positions. Driving ideas are usually fatal. The interesting thing is that you took marital relations and I think there are techniques you could apply, but no one is doing it.

Where could one apply that position of yours that I outlined?

I think I took the problem of psychopathic personality, a much more difficult problem. There, my judgment is that we have to do a holding operation till someone has a very good idea whereas the family structure thing is very ripe. Hudson thinks so and is working on it. More resources are needed but there isn't a conceptual difficulty about that. There are problems in social psychology where there are conceptual difficulties.

I can only put this question in a vague way. But have you through your work formed an idea of what Man is, what it is to be human?

No, I know what you mean and I think my instant reaction is, in the sense I think you mean, no. What I am asserting is a belief in a way, not a belief in a vision, so to speak. I'm saying I think if you check ideas I think it is possible to find out their truth. I think you on the other hand are seeking a general picture of the nature of Man, then to be filled in in detail. Admittedly, I think there are some things about people I would regard as well-established. It is obvious, for instance, that to the same extent that our anatomy has analogies with any other mechanical system, so our brain has analogies to a computer. There are storage processes, transmissions and transformations going on. But that isn't saying very much because the question is, what's the programme? Because there are many programmes run on computers which are not analogues to things men do. Very few, hardly any, are [laughs], in fact.

Do you think it will be possible to describe Man as a very complicated mechanical system and to be able to specify what the word 'complicated' means in detail?

I would believe that.

And once you've specified that, that's all we are – no more.
I would object to the 'all' or 'no more'. People are what they are and
their value depends on that. If you develop a greater understanding
of that, I don't think you change their value. I don't think you can
then imply that there might be something that might have been
better that we might have been. Here we're getting into the crux of
it. Therefore I take a certain tactic in my thinking. I do not know
exactly what you mean by 'could be more than' a 'very complicated
mechanical system'. I try to find out what you mean by putting
parallels with other analogies or by saying if you believe this, how
would you react to this situation? I'm trying to get more insight into
what you mean by this phrase. I don't fully understand it.

*I think what I'm trying to get at, which is vague, is that if you
describe that mechanical system, does it limit Man, once and for all, to
being that system. There's the end of it. Any abilities that are spiritual
or random or that survive could not be admitted. Since you hold a
Church of England position, maybe your conception of a mechanical
system is much less limited than mine?*
Than your conception of a mechanical system? I think that's
interesting – what's going on in your mind is that when I talk about a
mechanical system you think of a clock of a typewriter, whereas I
think of something immensely more elaborate than that. And I
would certainly agree that people are not clocks or typewriters. If we
pursue the specific issue of what it means to talk of survival after
death, I'd remind you that as an Anglican, I am only required to
believe in the resurrection of the body, not the immortality of the
soul. I don't fully understand and no one has understood what does
lie behind the various discussions of immortality that philosphers
have had through the ages. I would prefer to change the basis of
discussion and take the computer analogy . . . .
In computers, we have a quite clear separation of problems of the
hardware of the machine and the problem of particular operations
and performances on it. The same machine can run different
programmes. The same general programme can be run on different
machines. They are, of course, constrained by one another. There
are many programmes that we can't run here because our computer
is too small or the speed is too slow. Or, if you pull the plug out, the
whole thing will stop in mid-programme. But I interpret what
worries most people in asking this kind of question is, if you plot
every localisation and the connection of every neuron in the brain,

have you really completely understood that man? The answer is 'No' because if you go down to the computer and plot the layout of every connection, you have not understood the computer because that depends on what programmes are running.

The problem of the human situation is, of course, different from that of the computer. You walk in one day and you put in Fortran. You switch off at the end of the day and the next day you put in something quite different. Human beings aren't like that. Nevertheless, they are more analogous to the mechanism that's never switched off, when you put in an executive programme early in life and, therefore, any information you put in gets gripped and handled in set ways, and the computer may, and indeed should, reject what you put in sometimes. Nevertheless it is possible that the system can be swung over to a new mode of operation. Most of the problems that our conscious thinking is concerned with in ordinary life are rather of that kind – spiritual problems. Should one repent of what one has been doing? Should one have a change of heart? Whether we should be less selfish. More sacrificing. Whether you have been unjust! These are all software problems that don't affect the interconnections of the neurons and they are the problems that interest most people. But I will meet you and say, if we're going to talk ordinary language, that the spirit is more important than the flesh. On the other hand, if we stick to ordinary language, we're not going to get much further than that, or farther than people have got for thousands of years. We at least can discuss what it means to have change of heart: does it mean changing the people you admire, as many social psychologists imply, or does it mean changing the style of your thinking, or is it adequate to keep the same general processes of thought while changing the content? There's a crack in *In Defence of Empirical Psychology* about communists and fascists and how they are rapidly converted back and forth. The chap who claims to be converted is just using different slogans in the same way. I think these operations can be analysed.

Would you like to see a psychology that concerns itself with ethical problems?

I'd like to see a psychology of ethics. That's not quite the same thing. An ethical problem is like the exercises theological seminaries set. 'A has confessed to planning to commit a future crime. Does B have an obligation to reveal this confession? Discuss.' That's an ethical problem. You can distinguish between logic and deductive processes and scientific information on one hand and the gods that these are serving on the other. You can say what is, but not what ought to be. Psychology is at the 'is' end of it. You must distinguish what is from what ought to be. But there's no use saying people ought to float two feet in the air. I'd like to see a psychology of ethics, that is, a psychology of what the processes are that result in ethical decisions.

Do you suggest that this would be – I'm asking for intuitions again – a model similar to the one on how we take perceptual decisions?

Yes, I do. If you ask me for an intuition, the kind of rough scheme that I have at the back of my mind in thinking about people is analogues to the general problem-solving programme of Newell and Simon. As you will know, if you have a programme trying to solve problems of a certain category, it's a good idea to have heuristics which improve its chance of doing well. If it's a chess-playing programme, avoid the next move that will lose your queen. It won't immediately lose the game, but it's not a very good idea. It's improbable you'll win if you make a move like that. Stronger and weaker heuristics are stacked up once again above the other. If we think of people, I would say that they have similar levels of heuristics. You start with things that are heuristics of the philosophy of life – I would say religion. Lower down, you have other moral principles that are derived from philosophy of life and that are obeyed as long as they don't conflict with it. Then, there are, lower down, political attitudes and so on. Now if we had a real understanding of how ethical decisions are arrived at, it would involve knowing how the system goes up through these various principles till it knows – 'Ah, this is an ethical decision.' Go to the top. 'I must stop.' 'There are higher things.' Once you get there, there may be a balance between ethical principles on the same level, where you get similar factors as with perception.

3
Noam Chomsky

Noam Chomsky became a psychologist out of necessity. He did not choose to become a psychologist; he did not train to become one. He found his work in linguistics was making a psychologist out of him. It took him into the field. Many psychologists who are very impressed by Chomsky's linguistic work say they regret the fact that he dabbles in psychology. He does not know the subject. Two ironies can be found in this. First, Chomsky argues that many of these psychologists, obsessed with the desire to be scientists, are no better than pseudo-scientists, breeders of a dogma whose origins they barely understand. Secondly, Chomsky himself does not regard himself as a professional linguist. As he points out in the interview, he does not know many of the things a linguist should. His work is the product of working in a number of disciplines. Until 1957, when he published *Syntactic Structures*, his first book, and a book that radically changed linguistics, he was having difficulty in getting his papers published and even in getting a job.

Chomsky very nearly dropped out of college in 1948. After two years at the University of Pennsylvania, he had lost all his proper Jewish enthusiasm for academic work. He had decided to go to Israel and seek out a radical Arab/Jewish working-class movement. Since the age of eleven, he had been interested in radical politics. If such an idealistic Arab/Jewish movement did not exist he might well create it. At this moment of disillusion with all things academic, he met Zellig Harris, professor of linguistics at Pennsylvania. They met because they shared radical political interests. But Chomsky liked Harris, and Harris not only shared radical views but turned Chomsky to the study of linguistics. It was the first event at university that fired Chomsky and one wonders how much it was the subject and how much it was Harris himself.

When Chomsky met him, Harris had just finished writing his

Structural Linguistics (1949). Harris was trying to achieve an empirical and almost behaviourist linguistics. He was trying to formulate principles of phonological and syntactic analysis of language without any reference to meaning. Until 1955, Chomsky worked very hard and loyally, it would seem, to make Harris's system work. He tried to refine it; he tried to formalise it. It was a long time – and, I suspect, a measure of Harris's influence over Chomsky – before he threw it over and developed his own account of a generative grammar. He had been toying with that as a kind of hobby, a task of lesser importance at first than making Harris's system work.

Chomsky was well qualified to try to formalise Harris's work. After Pennsylvania, he worked under the philosopher, Nelson Goodman. Goodman recommended him for a junior fellowship in the Society of Fellows at Harvard. There, Chomsky pursued a wide range of studies. He studied mathematics, formal logic and algebra. He liked working with symbolism. This mathematical influence on Chomsky was important for his work: I suspect it is also important in defining the attitudes of psychologists to his work. For four years, there was no pressure on Chomsky to specialise in any particular branch of a particular subject to 'deserve' his fellowship. Chomsky believes he was very lucky. In the early fifties, too, it was not yet necessary for American academics to publish or be damned to dull jobs. Chomsky says that he found this freedom and lack of pressure very helpful. He seems rather to dread to think what might have happened if he had been forced into a conventional postgraduate career where the PhD thesis is all. Hudson, who enjoyed a similar privileged period at Cambridge, found this to be a period of 'wasteful fallowness' during which he drifted and lazed to no particular purpose: Chomsky, on the other hand, believes it was the freedom to pursue odd topics like formal logic that allowed him to play around with the ideas that led to *Syntactic Structures*.

Chomsky is now professor of modern languages at MIT. He looks rather younger than his forty-six years. He gives an impression of youth. He is rather bouncy and informal. He speaks very quickly and in long sentences that sometimes become too involved, so that he has to scrap them and start again. His written, revised work, of course, is very precise but it is curious to note that a man who has changed our attitude to how we analyse language and sentences should get himself embedded in his own sentences. I have preserved some of this in the interview. He is clearly very practised at interviews. He helped check my tape-recorder and facilitated matters by holding the mike –

73

something most European psychologists would never dream of doing. Chomsky has described himself as having grown up in the radical Jewish community in New York. His family background, however, was also interesting. Chomsky's father was a Hebrew scholar of some distinction. From an early age, Chomsky picked up a body of informal knowledge about the structure and history of the Semitic languages. As he explains in the interview, he had some idea of what linguistics might be about historically, studying how a word had evolved so that, at a particular time, it had a particular meaning. The task of the linguist was to explain why it had come to have this meaning at this time. In itself, this seems to be a slightly richer definition of linguistics than that which was current in 1948. Interestingly, Chomsky did some of his early work in modern Hebrew and some of his own work on a generative grammar was also first done in Hebrew,

Chomsky made his initial contributions in linguistics. He developed a theory of language in which there are three key parts. There is the 'surface structure' of the language which corresponds to the actual sentences that we hear. There is the 'deep structure' which is composed of meanings. For example, the surface structure 'a wise man is honest' emerges from the deep structure 'a man who is wise is honest.' The actual sentence emerges by a series of transformations. Chomsky himself described his theory as follows in a contribution to a symposium on *Explanation in the Behavioural Sciences* (1970, p. 429):

> The general framework that seems most appropriate for the study of problems of language and mind was developed as part of the rationalist psychology of the seventeenth and eighteenth centuries, and then largely forgotten as attention shifted to different matters. According to this traditional conception, a system of propositions expressing the meaning of a sentence is produced in the mind as the sentence is realised as a physical signal, the two being related by certain formal operations which, in current terminology, we may call *grammatical transformations*. Continuing with current terminology, we can thus distinguish the surface structure of the sentence, its organisation into categories and phrases as a physical signal, from the underlying deep structure, also a system of categories and phrases but with a more abstract character. Thus, the surface structure of the sentence 'a wise man is honest' might analyse it into the subject 'a wise man' and the predicate 'is honest'. The deep structure, however, will be rather different. It will, in particular, extract from the complex idea that constitutes the

74

subject of the surface structure an underlying proposition with the subject 'man' and the predicate 'be wise'. In fact, the deep structure, in the traditional view, is a system of two propositions neither of which is asserted but which interrelate in such a way as to express the meaning of the sentence 'a wise man is honest'. We might represent the deep structure, in this simple case, by the formula (1) and the surface structure by the formula (2) where paired brackets labelled with the symbol A bound a phrase of the category A. (1) $(_S (_{NP} a$ man$(_S (_{NP}$ man$)_{NP} (_{VP}$ is wise$)_{VP})_S)_{NP} (_{VP}$ is honest$)_{VP})_S$ (2) $(_S (_{NP}$ a wise man$)_{NP} (_{VP}$ is honest$)_{VP})_S$.

If we understand the relation 'subject of' to hold between a phrase of the category noun phrase (NP) and the sentence (S) that directly dominates it, and the relation 'predicate of' to hold between a phrase of the category verb phrase (VP) and the sentence that directly dominates it, then the structures (1) and (2) specify the grammatical functions of subject and predicate in the intended way. The grammatical functions of the deep structure (1) play a role in determining the meaning of the sentence. The phrase structure indicated in (2) on the other hand, is closely related to its phonetic shape.

Chomsky has analysed the necessary constituents of the deep structure and the transformations through which this deep structure is turned into the surface structure we recognise and use as sentences. He has, of course, extended his theory from this point into the implications for our knowledge of man that comes from the fact that our knowledge of language is based upon this deep structure, a structure that we cannot guess or divine just from speaking, and upon the necessary transformations.

A few facts about Chomsky's theory should be noted. First, it is very formal and technical, and depends a great deal on symbolism and being able to manipulate symbols. Much of the information we have about psychologists suggests that this form is one which they do not like and have not mastered. Among our psychologists, we have a number who wanted to become physicists or dabbled in physics but did not become physicists. An interest in symbolism seems to run counter to an interest in people. It is arguable that just as psychologists are suspicious of the kind of literary and poetic elements in the work of a man like Laing, they are suspicious of Chomsky's work. But there is an important difference. It is relatively easy for a man who wants to be scientific to dismiss Laing as a poet, a dabbler in things scientific that he does not

Noam Chomsky

really understand. The reaction of conventional psychiatry to much of Laing's work has been to ignore it, even though it has useful insights. Chomsky is a different proposition. For Chomsky has been trained in the tools of science. He holds a chair in an institution that is devoted to much hard science. And, even more than any splendour of his status, he deploys his arguments with all the rigour and hallmarks of science. In fact, he condemns most psychologists for being pseudo-scientists. He presents a different problem.

Moreover, Chomsky did not first secure a base in linguistics and then extend himself into psychology. As a graduate at Harvard, he read Skinner's *Science and Human Behaviour* in manuscript. It was being passed around the campus. He found it empty then, he claims. Only two years after *Syntactic Structures* appeared, Chomsky wrote his long hostile review of Skinner's *Verbal Behaviour*. Already, Chomsky was arguing that you could not account for the way children learn language on any behaviourist model. Children did not learn the habit of saying particular words, phrases or sentences: it was not a question of language being reinforced by parental attention. The essential point is that our use of language is creative. Nearly every sentence that is spoken has not been spoken by the speaker before or listened to by the listener before. Yet the speaker can speak it; the listener can understand it. Any model of language learning, a phrase that Chomsky prefers to Skinner's bleak 'verbal behaviour', must be able to explain this fact. From early in his work, then, Chomsky saw the psychological implications of his work in linguistics.

In two later books. *Cartesian Linguistics* (1966) and *Language and Mind* (1968), Chomsky has taken his ideas much further. He has reintroduced the mind, that empiricist bogey, into psychology. Chomsky makes the case that we have failed to understand some of the more valuable points rationalist philosophers made in the seventeenth and eighteenth centuries. The doctrine of innate ideas was demolished by Locke and Berkeley. Locke attacked the doctrine, for example, on the grounds that if a child were brought up listening to no speech, he would not speak. But no one, Chomsky points out, or at least no philosopher of any consequence, ever held this form of the doctrine of innate ideas. It was always held that the conditions in the environment had to be right to allow the innate ideas to mature and become manifest. Chomsky believes that language learning depends on innate biological schemata whose sole purpose is to allow the child to learn language. The schematism is such that it allows the child to sift the external evidence he gets from listening to other people's speech. He quickly learns between the ages of one and four years to extract the very complex rules of grammar needed for speech. Chomsky argues that if one listens to children learning to speak one can see them trying out various rules. By the time the child is five, certainly, his speech is very close to that of an adult. He has mastered an infinite repertoire for he can now generate and understand an infinite amount of new sentences. Such novelty is not accounted for on a behaviourist model. Nor, according to Chomsky, is the fact that children in all known cultures learn to speak. To speak is human. It helps, of course, if the child is encouraged in talking but it does not really matter. Children who are exposed to speech learn to speak. Being encouraged, coached, rewarded, makes only a marginal difference to the ease with which they speak. But, however much you speak to an ape, it will only grunt back. This emphasis on the innate schemata that are essential for language learning goes against the spirit of much American psychology which is based on actions rather than thoughts.

Chomsky has expanded the role of 'innate ideas' as being essential for language. He argues that thinking and the use of our imagination may also well depend on biological schemata that are innate. To think, to be imaginative, may also be part of our biological specialisation. Chomsky wrote: 'The notion that there may be innate principles of mind that makes possible the acquisition of knowledge and belief, and, on the other hand, determine and limit its scope suggests nothing that should surprise a biologist, so far as I can see'. (1968). Perhaps not. It holds plenty of surprises, though, for what Chomsky calls a 'pseudo-scientist'. This creature, the typical American behavioural psychologist, is so steeped in superstition that he has decided learning is acquired in certain dogma-decreed ways. It is acquired mainly by association, trial-and-error learning and reinforcement. He does not seek to prove these hypotheses because he regards them as necessary truths. Chomsky appears to such a creature as a latter-day Kant, a heretic. Chomsky, for his part, argues that the trouble with such psychology is that it has all the hallmarks of medieval thinking – and that Skinner has replaced Aquinas. Having denounced their point of view as better fitted to a theological debate, it is curious that Chomsky should himself argue that they are superstitious and mystical, terms well-fitted to theological debate. It recalls the emphasis of David McClelland on religion and psychology.

Chomsky argues that the empirical tradition in psychology has prevented the development of a serious scientific attitude. People may acquire knowledge in more ways than behaviourists and learning

Noam Chomsky

theorists dream of. They may have organised within the mind schemata
that allow them to sift and fit in evidence from the external world in
particular ways. To refuse to tackle such questions, to beg such
questions, is the sign of an unscientific attitude.

In the interview, Chomsky expands on his critique of behaviourism.
One point however that he barely touches on is introspection. It is
important because behaviourists have always attacked those who
sought to reintroduce the mind into psychology on the grounds that
they want to return to the chaos which introspection produced in
psychology in the early 1900s. Chomsky is hostile to introspection.
There may be innate principles of mind. There is no reason to suppose
that we can, by thinking about how we think, discover these principles.
That was a rationalist doctrine, of course. They did believe that by
scrupulous introspection, they could unearth the principles of mind. It
was not, incidentally, just the rationalists who indulged in such fancies.
David Hume's *The Treatise of Mind*, one of the gospels of the empirical
tradition, contains no experiment but plenty of introspection. Like
Descartes, Hume believed he could define the universal mind out of the
workings of his own. Chomsky holds no such illusion. He makes that
very plain in some of his writings. It is important because it secures him
from a valid attack by behaviourists. It is also important because of
knowing how one will attack the problem of studying these schemata
of thinking and imagination.

Chomsky, personally, is also interesting because science is not his
only major interest. He remains torn between research and radical
politics. He describes himself as 'schizophrenic': and he has been in that
state for a long while. Visiting his office at MIT is bizarre. For MIT
seems a temple of hard, aggressive science. You wander through
corridors with signs that warn of danger. Notices suggest you are not far
from work on radioactivity or war programmes. Chomsky's office is
decorated with revolutionary posters. Since 1965, he has been one of
the most persistent critics of US foreign policy, especially in Vietnam.
He encouraged draft dodgers and risked prison by refusing to pay half
his taxes as a protest against the Vietnam war. He published articles in
journals like *Ramparts* and the *New York Review of Books* in which he
criticised the war and American scientists' role in making the war
possible. Science should be more moral. Chomsky became a hero of the
left. He remains that and an acute political critic. When, in 1969, he
came to lecture in Oxford, over a thousand students and dons attended
his lectures. He is both an intellectual giant and a true radical. He has
been involved in radical politics since the age of fourteen. It is not

78

something he came to when it became fashionable.

In terms of McClelland's ideas about the way psychologists are motivated by power, Chomsky fits. He has never given up his radical political activities which are, explicitly, about power. His psychological work, too, has made him a critic of behaviourism. There, he is not just an academic critic. He is afraid of the social consequences of behaviourism. He sees it as an ideology that is very well tailored to American society. He is very careful, in the interview, to distinguish between what Skinner may hope his work will do and the way Skinner's work is being used; for he is not always, of course, responsible for the way it is applied. The battle between Chomsky and Skinner is, now, somewhat legendary and it is interesting to see, in both interviews, the rather different ways in which they express hostility to one another. Skinner says that Chomsky is emotional and cannot bear the idea that he, Skinner, is right. He is at a loss to explain why Chomsky reacts so violently to anything he writes. Chomsky's attack is less personal, more subtle. Skinner is articulating ideas which are either empty or are only popular because they are useful to American society.

Chomsky admits that there is little that is 'unconventional' to say about what he likes and dislikes in research. He told me:

'Of course it is always exciting to pursue an interesting idea and to find out it works. My main frustration, I guess, is that I never seem to have the time to follow up in detail since some other demand intervenes. Hence, often, the satisfaction is vicarious, in that it is a matter of seeing how students follow up and work out a half-baked but intriguing idea, or, often, to see how someone I do not or barely know comes up with something that provides real illumination into problems that interest me. As for frustrations, when research doesn't go, it is annoying, naturally, but there generally are enough promising lines of investigation open at any one time that I find it easy to simply abandon (I hope, temporarily) a line of inquiry that seems to be getting nowhere hoping it will fall into place later on, on the basis of some new insight or understanding. Hence that kind of failure is not much a source of frustration. Much more frustrating is the discovery that an idea that seemed really nice (or a principle that suggested something deep) doesn't work out (or is false), i.e. that the world is less elegant than one might have hoped. Again, there always seem to be enough intriguing alternatives to compensate.'

Three interesting points, it seems to me, come out. Like many psychologists, Chomsky has to do research by proxy. One begins to wonder if there are not two main kinds of psychologists – those who produce the ideas necessary to create studies and experiments and those who follow this work and carry the experiments out. Secondly, Chomsky does not get stymied if lines of research fail to work out. He plays with other possibilities at the same time as he pursues one major one. This keeps him from being frustrated. The most interesting point is, it seems to me, the third one that what is frustrating is not a personal failure but the discovery that the world is not as 'elegant' as 'one might have hoped'. A lover of symbolism must love elegance. This phrase, I suspect, differentiates Chomsky from many psychologists who are both confused and fascinated by gathering inelegant data and seeing if it will vaguely fit some theory. It is ironic, though, that another psychologist who seems to have loved elegance and was deeply influenced by the rationalist Spinoza's *Ethics* was Clark Hull, the architect of that pseudo-scientific behaviourism Chomsky belabours. This love of elegance, of course, accords well with his training in mathematics and logic. But can it fit in with a much less exact science? Chomsky would say that without a formal system, you could make little sense of all these heaps of observations.

Could I ask you one or two things about your career before you became a linguist? You have often spoken about the rules of rational science and it strikes me as strange that one of the most humanist of contemporary workers in psychology should be at MIT. Were you trained as a scientist?

No, I had no scientific training to speak of other than what I learned at school. The reason I'm at MIT is very simple. The work I was doing as a graduate student was considered too esoteric and too outlandish that it didn't belong to any recognised field. I didn't get much work published and I certainly had no job offers when I finished graduate school at Harvard. The reason I'm at MIT is, first, that I had a very close friend here, Maurice Halle – who is a real professional linguist in the sense in which I'm not – who was interested in what I was doing and tried to arrange a niche into which I could fit. The second reason is that the research lab of electronics was, at that stage, a pretty wide-open institution. It had all sorts of strange things going on – neurophysiology, automata theory, communications theory. Gary Weissner who was then head of it felt they could tolerate another strange creature so that they could see what was coming from any of this stuff. That's why I'm here,

What was your early training in?
Well, my undergraduate work was in linguistics at the University of
Pennsylvania with Zellig Harris. Then, I did a year or two at Penn of
graduate work with Harris and Nelson Goodman who was a
philosopher. Goodman nominated me for the graduate fellowship in
an organisation called the Society of Fellows at Harvard, which is a
small graduate research institute where they give you three years. I
got one of those and I stayed four years. I got a renewal. I was doing
mostly my own work on linguistic theory and also studying
philosophy, logic and mathematics. It was really a marvellous
structure to do graduate research. There were no formal conditions.
I could study anything I wanted. I could spend as much time on my
own work as I wanted and take it in any direction I wanted. I didn't
have, fortunately for me, the structure of a graduate programme
imposed on me. I did what I felt like. The result was that the
work I did did not belong to any recognised field, so I was not
professionally qualified when I finished in any field. I mean I'm not
really a professional linguist. There are a lot of things a linguist ought
to know which I don't know and I'm not interested in. I'm not
criticising anyone for not offering me a job as a linguist. They were
perfectly within their rights. But it had the advantage that I could go
my own way. It worked pretty well. It's a good system but it carries
the risk that you won't be employed or published. The major work
that I did in this field was a very extensive book completed in 1955,
which still isn't published.

*What were the early influences on you or were you going your own
way so much that there weren't any major influences?*
Can I give you my version of that? Which I'm not sure is accurate.
What I'm aware of, certainly, was . . . in the first place there were
negative and positive influences. Harris was an enormous influence
in that I tried very hard for many years to make his kind of system
work the kind of way he believed it could work. Nelson Goodman
who was a philosopher who didn't know Harris but who worked
along the same lines was, intellectually, rather similar to him too. He
was interested in developing constructional systems. I was a student
of his at a time when he wrote a really important book called *The
Structure of Experience* which was an effort to build up in quite a
systematic way an account of the nature of our organisation of our

experiences on the basis of primary, primitive perceptions of qualities. I was very much influenced by a lot of the methods that he developed. Ultimately, I came to believe this was the wrong approach but the experience of trying to work through it, with it, was extremely valuable and I'm sure carried into a lot of work I've done in another way.

At the same time, it was very helpful to have studied modern logic, mostly at Harris's suggestion and, again at Harris's suggestion, modern mathematics and mathematical logic, the foundations of algebra. I don't know that I derived some specific conclusion but it was a way of thinking I found congenial and which could be easily put to use in my own interest. Somebody like Quine, too, at Harvard had a very great influence on how I came to think, though in the end I came to disagree sharply with him about many things.

My original work in generative grammar was influenced as much as anything by the knowledge I picked up as a child about Semitic grammar. My father was a Semitic scholar. I knew as a kid just something about the history of the Semitic languages and when I came to do my own work in generative grammar, I sort of carried over one very important principle of historical, traditional grammar, namely, that one is trying to give an explanation for a particular stage of the language on the basis of a layering with historically successive things that have taken place. That's to say, we know certain things about biblical Hebrew and we might try to explain why the language is that way by assuming a series of changes, successive particular changes till it ended up that way. Well, that kind of model is very easy to transfer to an explanatory theory of the stage of the language. And that seems as much of an influence as any.

Professor McClelland believes that many of the people who went into psychology did so in reaction to a very strict religious upbringing. Was that so in your case?

No, quite the contrary in fact. I was very much involved in radical politics. Involved is a funny word. I was never part of an organised movement. I was very much a loner in that respect. That was my main interest in life by the time I was thirteen or so. I had convinced myself that all of the organised movements, namely, the Communist Party, the Trotskyites, were quite reactionary basically. And, at a kind of fourteen-year-old level, I had worked myself in to a left-wing Marxist of Marxist-anarchist position which was critical of any authoritarian tendency and regarded them as, basically,

reactionaries of some sort who had taken on a kind of socialist
terminology. And I had no particular place to go with this belief till I
met Harris. And I met him . . . he was a very acute social critic. He's
never written about it but a lot of people have been influenced by
him politically. Surprising people, who passed through his influence
at some formative stage in their lives. And I was one.

I met him at a time when I was planning to drop out of college,
which seemed a stupid waste of time. I had no interest in anything I
was doing in college. I was planning at that point – it was 1947 – to
go off to the Middle East and to work on an Arab/Jewish
working-class movement of a sort that I dreamed at that time,
whether it existed or not, and I'd live in a kibbutz which,
incidentally, I later did. Though I had entered college with a great
deal of enthusiasm, by the time I'd had two years, I'd had all the
enthusiasm knocked out of me. Every course I took convinced me it
was completely boring, and not for me. It wasn't till I met Harris that
I found anything intellectually stimulating, though my contact with
him was originally through radical politics. So that's the actual
background. I mean there may be subtler things . . . .

More unconscious ones?
That was the conscious background.

How did you come to be interested in psychology?
Well, I think it would be more accurate to say that I became
interested in linguistics and came to feel that what I was doing in
linguistics was psychology by any rational definition of the field.
There is a tendency to define psychology in what strikes me as a
curious and, basically, unscientific way, as having to do only with
behaviour or only with processing of information or only with
certain low-level types of interaction with the environment or
whatever, and to exclude from psychology the study of what I call
competence. And this is what just seems to me to leave a discipline
that has no rationale. That is, I would assume that if psychology is to
be a comprehensive and, in any sense, deep investigation of its
subject matter, it would also have to take into account in a
fundamental way an investigation of what kinds of cognitive
structures an organism – that is a human in this case – acquires and
comes to use. And language is one of those. So I would assume that
by being a linguist I am automatically a psychologist.

83

Noam Chomsky

At what point when you were doing your linguistic work did you feel that what you were doing was, by any other name, psychology?
Almost at the very beginning, when I was a graduate student, as far back as I can remember. I came here to Harvard in 1950 as a graduate student. That was shortly after Skinner's William James Lectures had been delivered. They were being passed around in manuscript and hadn't yet appeared as a book. I had friends who were students of his. The whole thing was in the air and rather influential at the time. And it struck me at once as a curious sort of mysticism, for just the reasons I mentioned. It was very foreign to the spirit of the sciences and rather empty when you looked at it. I couldn't understand the interest and why anyone would conceive of psychology, of putting psychology in that weird straitjacket instead of using the standard approach of the sciences. It always seemed to me obvious that investigating cognitive structures, whether they have been acquired by the organism, and investigating language must be psychology. If psychology is going to have any hope of coming to terms with its subject matter, it's going to have to deal with this central problem.

How did your early work develop?
How much detail do you want me to go into?

As much as you need.
I worked first as a student of Harris's at the University of Pennsylvania. In fact, my introduction to linguistics was in my sophomore year. I happened to meet Harris through common political connections but I got interested in his work and I liked him a lot. I read his book *Structural Linguistics* which was then in manuscript and that was my introduction to the field. I then took some of his courses, and he suggested that I did some work on a language I knew. I picked modern Hebrew which I knew quite well. I tried for a while to use the methods of linguistics on Hebrew but it was just very clear that it was unilluminating and it wasn't getting anywhere and then I sort of abandoned it and said, 'What would be the rational way of approaching this question?' And I saw that the only rational way to approach it would be to try and construct a generative grammar: that is, a system of rules that would characterise the infinite class of structures of the sense of the language and give a base for interpreting them. So, I dropped all that and just went on with that. I didn't regard that as linguistics, I just

84

regarded that as my private hobby. In fact, for a number of years, I was leading a schizophrenic existence until about 1953. I was working along two lines. On the one hand, I was trying to sharpen and clarify the methods of structural linguistics which is an inductive approach in some ways like behavioural psychology. It was alleged that one could arrive at a class of observations which would characterise the language. I was completely convinced that must be possible and, therefore, worked very hard at it. I thought the reasons it was obviously failing had to do with the lack of formality of the methods – or, some gap. At the same time, I was working, first in Hebrew and then in English, on the problems of generative grammar.

I was following these two quite independent lines of work. One an effort to refine the methods of structural linguistics more or less along the lines of Harris and, secondly, my own private interest in generative grammar. It became obvious to me at some point, partly because of the results I was obtaining and partly because of the prodding of a few friends, that there was a good reason why the effort to refine the methods of structural linguistics wasn't working – namely, that it was intrinsically the wrong approach. There was no reason to expect an inductive step-by-step procedure, no matter how sharpened and refined, to give an, or the, enlightening, or true, grammar of the language, the one that is acquired by the person who has learned the language. Because there is no reason to accept the *a priori* assumption that that's how it's done by the organism. In fact, there's another good reason why the other approach I was taking was, in fact, giving rather interesting results, explanations of complicated phenomena – namely, that they did reflect the way the system came into existence and was used.

Did you do this in parallel? I mean did you begin describing the rules of generative grammar and becoming aware that this could reflect the way language was actually learned at the same time? One frequent criticism of you is that, though you are a fantastic linguist and these may be the rules, there is no reason to suppose these are actually, psychologically, physiologically, coded in that way.

The question is whether I took a realist interpretation of the system of grammar and did I assume it reflected the structure of the organism. And the answer is that, at first, it did not. I assumed, I took for granted, the approach to structural linguistics which was close in spirit to much of behaviourist psychology – namely, that I

Noam Chomsky

took for granted that the way the system really works is that people apply these inductive procedures and by applying them to the data they experience, they arrive at systems of classification which are their grammar. But, gradually, it became obvious there were fundamental difficulties in working out these inductive approaches. It also became obvious that the other approach, that didn't raise any questions about how these principles were developed but simply investigated their consequences, was leading to what I thought were some pretty dramatic successes. It gradually dawned on me that it was wholly unscientific to take the realist approach with respect to *a priori* assumptions that were involved in the behavioural approach and to refuse to take the realist assumptions for a system that seemed to be working and giving, approximately, a satisfactory explanatory theory. Once that realisation dawned, it was an elementary step and a correct step to abandon the *a priori* commitment to data-processing, inductive procedures as simply a metaphysics that could be thrown out of the window. It seemed unreasonable to accept it. And reasonable to assume that, if a system of principles seemed to be giving insight, explanations and predictions and so on, to take a reasonable approach and postulate, yes, this does reflect the structure of the organism.

Now, in this case, as we don't know anything about how such structures might be represented neurologically – but that's beside the point. If a scientist were unable to break into a machine that he was investigating, he wouldn't hesitate for a moment to postulate that the structure of the machine was in accord with the principles of organisation that he'd postulated, if these principles, in fact, meet conditions of providing insight, explanation and so on.

Well, let me make this clear. In investigating the adult organism, one is only determining the steady state, the final state that is achieved at the point at which further acquisition of language is either marginal or non-existent. The analogy I mentioned before I meant to be taken pretty seriously. [The analogy mentioned here was developed early on in the interview as it happened. As I have edited it, the analogy is developed later on pages 92-4.] There is, in the case of language learning, a radical change through one period of life, and then you reach a pretty much steady state. You may learn new words but nothing fundamental changes. In studying the adult's speech we're trying to find something out about the steady state. That does not tell us anything in itself about how the steady state is achieved. If all we knew were adults, the null hypothesis might be that adults were born speaking English. If a Martian scientist were to come here, that might be his first assumption. It might be a reasonable assumption. Why assume that the system has evolved or even changes through time? Of course, we know that that's not true because people aren't born speaking English. So, by an investigation of the range of the evidence, by looking at the similarities of final states achieved by speakers of the same language, by investigation of the similarities of the final states achieved by speakers of different languages, by studies of different languages, we can begin to make some pretty plausible suggestions about what must have been the initial state that made it possible to acquire those particular systems. For instance, if we discover that, then in the case of English grammar, some very abstract principle is operating.

And if those conditions are well confirmed – they do explain things – then we have to face the question of how do the conditions of knowledge of those principles arise? On the basis of what sort of evidence does the organism determine that those principles are to be operative. And, in fact, in many cases, there is no evidence to the language learner, or marginal evidence at the most, that these are the operative principles. Nevertheless, they are applied at once – and uniformly. Given that kind of observation, it would be most rational to postulate that they are part of an original schematism that the organism simply brings to bear on the acquisition of these systems. This is the approach. If it were not human beings that were involved, if it were some other organism, that would be taken without question. No one would dream of showing that a bird learns to fly through association. You just assume that the kind of complex structure is simply in the nature of the organism and has developed through evolution – not through learning. In the case of humans, their special characteristic, I suppose, is a certain type of intellectual structure. I see no reason to take a different approach to the study in the case of humans, or a machine, for that matter.

Your schematism still has to be triggered. How do you relate the role of the environment? Is it just negative so that if certain things don't happen, then your innate capacity, your schematism, just withers away?

Well, I don't believe there's enough evidence to answer that question. The possibility you suggest does exist. In fact, it is known, I believe, that's the way some intrinsic structures do seem to operate. Deprivation experiments seem to show that some of the highly organised perceptual structures do wither away if they're not set into operation at a certain early stage. It's quite conceivable that the same is true of the special structures that determine the nature of language system and systems of thought, representation, of symbolisation and so on. But, of course, we have no really serious evidence for that. We don't do deprivation experiments on humans, obviously. There are a few examples that have been discovered of children who were apparently subjected to very serious sensory deprivation. And some of these have been investigated, but they don't give very sharp evidence. That's certainly plausible. But, I mean, there's no doubt there are effects of the environment, of experience, on the language you learn. That's certainly true. How extensive that influence is is an open question. How much evidence does a child have to have to acquire a language? Well – remarkably little. Very complicated structures are set into motion in very specific, highly articulated ways on the basis of very rudimentary evidence. And, what's more, it's done uniformly by all children. This indicates that there are very specialised, highly developed schemata that are presupposed in the acquisition of knowledge. It does even more than that. It directs us to what some of these principles might be.

How do you deal with the study that shows if you read to a child for thirty minutes each day his vocabulary, his verbal skill is improved? Are your schemata the basic element on which almost Skinnerian principles act?

Well, I don't know there's any reason to assume there's any role for Skinnerian principles in particular. There is learning, undoubtedly, but there's no reason to suppose it's based on those principles. I'm quite sure that if you pay a lot of attention to a child, you can increase its vocabulary and its linguistic skill, quite substantially.

But, still looking at it from the Martian point of view, from the outside, I think that a scientist would be very much struck by how minute are the differences between individuals who are given radically different training and treatment as compared with the enormous similarities. I mean a child who has just picked language up off the streets, to whom no one pays much attention, still has acquired an extensive, complex, intricate system. He may not be using the same vocabulary as a child who's been force-fed but, still, there is no child, apart from one who is severely disabled, who fails to acquire an enormously rich linguistic system – very much like that of anyone else. For this reason, I would assume that special training procedures like reading don't really affect the acquisition of the basic structure of the language. They may add some frills.

How do you deal with the Pygmalion situation? Did Eliza in My Fair Lady *pick up an entirely new set of rules?*
Well, the Pygmalion situation is a bit different. It doesn't have anything to do with the acquisition of language really. It has to do with the acquisition of a certain system of cultural snobbery. That is, Eliza, before they got hold of her, was still speaking as rich and as complicated a language as she did after the transformation. It was a different one. It wasn't the language of the British upper classes. It was rather the language she had acquired in her natural fashion. So, I think, there are no reasons to assume there is a difference in the richness or expressive power between the language of, say, upper-class snobbish and the language of the streets. Obviously, they have their differences. But, just in so far as we know, there are no differences between the languages of so-called primitive societies and those of, say, technological situation societies, apart from the kinds of things they talk about. There are probably forms of cultural richness in, say, Australian bush society reflected in their use of language that we don't bother with. And, conversely.

But these are refinements to the basic structure for the acquisition of language?
Well, you can train people to speak with a British accent like you can train people to distinguish different kinds of wine or to behave with the proper manners at an academic dinner or something of that sort. However, I don't think that that kind of training ought to be confused with the acquisition of fundamental human traits such as the ability to eat, take in cultural patterns or the ability to acquire the very complex and not yet fully understood system of cultural patterns that anyone who grows up in a society internalises and puts to use.

Is language the most fundamental, most basic of all our higher-level skills?
Well, it's often been speculated and I think it's a reasonable speculation. But we have to be very careful about it because the difficulty is that the question has often been raised by psychologists and by philosophers as to whether these linguistic abilities are a

89

unique faculty of mind, let's say, to use some old-fashioned terminology, or, whether they're simply a reflection of much more general capacities. We will only have an answer to that when other areas of intellectual achievement are investigated in much the same way as language. If, for example, people learn a great many things other than language: they learn something of, they develop a theory about, the physical world, they develop a theory of social relations, they develop the ability to analyse personality structures on the basis of a very small amount of evidence once again. All sorts of systems are developed by human beings in the course of their normal growth and maturation. If other systems are investigated, if grammars of them are constructed, we will then be able to ask the question if they have the same or analogous properties to those of the faculty of mind. Frankly, I don't see any reason to suppose that they do. It would be surprising if they did, but that's an open question.

You have been credited with reintroducing the mind, or innate abilities and capacities into philosophy and psychology. Do you really feel that the work you have been doing bears any relation to that long tradition of rationalism, Leibniz and Spinoza, for instance?
I think it bears a very close relationship. I think so and I've tried to show in a number of books that there is a close relation and, further, that the classical tradition has been misunderstood. People paid attention to certain parts of it and omitted consideration of other parts of it. For example, there's a good deal of attention now to the classical rationalist theory of innate ideas as a contribution to the foundations of necessary knowledge and necessary truths. And that's certainly one part of it. But there's another part which I find much more interesting, personally, and on which I've focused. That was the attempt to develop a rationalist psychology which had nothing to do with necessary truths, but which had simply to do with organising principles in perception which had to do with a basic schematic framework that is an essential part of mind, that determines the preconditions for experiences and determines the system of knowledge that's acquired on the basis of experience. That's a point of view more naturally associated with Kant. But one finds a lot of interesting things in the seventeenth century, in Descartes, in Cudworth, in the minor Cartesians and, in particular, in the grammarians who developed under their influence. In fact, there are great similarities between many of the things they were

attempting to do and many of the things I am trying.

There are also quite a number of differences for, I think, Descartes and Leibniz seem to have taken for granted that the contents of the mind were in principle open to introspection, that is, if you thought hard you could find, introspect into, the principles by which you're functioning mentally. That assumption was quite common to classical rationalism and empiricism. It was everybody's assumption. And that assumption is very implausible because there's no reason to believe it to be true. There's no reason to believe that by mere introspection you can discover the principles of the operation of the mind. Why should that be the case? They had a reason. They didn't just arbitrarily make it up. We can discover what their reason was but we don't have to accept their reason. Similarly, they, Descartes, had an argument favouring dualism, for thinking that mind was a substance not reducible to physics and chemistry. Nevertheless, we don't have to accept that argument. There are flaws in it. There are other ways of looking at the matter. His concept of physics was far too narrow. Everybody knows that now.

So, we're not forced to follow a Cartesian line of reasoning that leads to dualism and, similarly, Descartes's argument in favour of the necessity of the phenomena of Nature has enormous logical flaws in it. It's based on the assumption – he thought he'd proved it but it's clearly unproven – that there is a God who cannot deceive us. Well, OK, that's a pretty bad argument. In that respect, it'd be absurd to try to pursue classical rational framework as it saw itself. Still, I think there are many striking and interesting respects in which these developments were important precursors and suggest what ought to be undertaken.

What are the necessary preconditions of experience that you see other than language?

Well, I think it's hard to be specific because no other domain of human intelligence, to our knowledge, has been studied in a similar manner. It's just obvious or superficial thinking, in the view of our experience, they interact. With people, in the main we're putting to use a system of very complicated beliefs. I don't know what the system is. We have to try and find out what the system is. It seems to me clear, qualitatively, the situation is not so very different from the one sketched in the analogy earlier. We find different people, say you or I, are employing very similar patterns of beliefs. That's why we can communicate, why we can predict one another's behaviour

Noam Chomsky

intuitively, why we know the way we will behave in the physical environment around is more or less fixed. We have acquired quite complicated systems of belief which is a matter which we can't introspect into. We can't find out what they are like by thinking about them. However we acquired them, they are quite comparable. There is a great deal of shared belief in the fact that we have very little evidence for the system or of the structure of these systems which must be similar and also innately ridiculous. I don't see how we can go beyond that except by carrying out an inquiry and investigation comparable and analogous in many ways to the one which has been carried out into language and trying to make explicit just what those systems are and how they are put into action. In doing that, we may find principles quite analogous to the principles that appear to govern our linguistic behaviour.

Do you think that one of the reasons why psychologists have so stubbornly refused to go into this kind of area of the mind for so long is that they didn't feel they were able to do it in a serious, sound way?
Well, I think there are a lot of historical reasons why psychology took the turn it did, some no doubt valid at the time. Objections to rather empty introspection, objections to rather empty mentalistic approaches, for example. I think there are really much deeper reasons. I think one has to go into why the study of humans since the origins of British empiricism has been so remarkably remote from the mainstream of science.

There are certain dogmatic elements in association and empiricist psychology which mark it as extremely hostile to the spirit of the sciences. For instance, that certain modes of learning must be postulated without any investigation of whether such postulations, such modes of learning, will, in fact, account for the systems of belief that are, in fact, acquired. This is a remarkably unscientific approach. I mean this is the approach one would expect from some branch of theology, quite distinct from the approach of the sciences. I think the tendency of much of modern psychology to pursue a line of approach that is remarkable in its hostility to the scientific method is, perhaps, an outgrowth of that in part.

That is strange. Many psychologists say that it is precisely because they are so enamoured of the scientific method that they have to leave out the sort of work you are interested in.
Let's forget about studying humans. Suppose we were to become

92

interested in some organism or machine. Suppose some machine is placed in front of us. We find lots of examples of it and, for some reason, we're interested in discovering how it works. Here is a problem of science, of engineering almost.

The natural approach any scientist would take – we assume we have evidence this machine changes through time and that it interacts with its environment and that, in certain respects, it's acting differently from the way it did at the beginning. Suppose we discover that much to be the case and suppose the scientist is interested in the questions what is the nature of the machine, how is it changing through time, how are other machines like it? The way that any scientist would approach this question would be to try and characterise two basic states of the machine, its initial state and its final state. Let's add one assumption – that, at a certain point, the modifications in the way the machine acts are marginal as compared with the changes that have taken place up to that point. It's kind of hit a steady state, in which slight modifications take place. Given such a wealth of qualitative observations, what the scientist would attempt to do is to characterise by any complex of inquiries he could try the steady state of the machine and he would search for uniformities among these machines in the kind of final states that they achieved. He would also try to characterise their initial stages. Then, having developed some form of hypothesis about the final state of the machine, he would try to ask himself a developmental question. He would say: 'What must I presuppose about the initial state, given my knowledge of the interaction with the environment the machine has undergone, given a hypothesis about the final state, given its adequacy and given whatever experiments I've been able to conduct and given my observations of interaction. What must I postulate about the initial state to be able to account for these changes?'

And these second-order postulations about the initial state of the machine would be the theory of learning for this machine. Now, if you then went on to discover that there are great similarities between the machines as to their final states, that would be evidence as to what the possible initial states would be. So you would proceed.

Suppose, on the other hand, some sort of pseudo-scientist were to approach the same qualitative observations but were to approach them as follows: 'Look, I don't care what the final state is, I'm not even going to look at that. I'm just going to postulate *a priori* that the modes by which this machine interacts with the environment are such and such. It forms associations, it generalises in terms of certain physical dimensions which I specify. It constructs probabilistic habit structures.' I mean this sort of pseudo-scientist picks out a number of such techniques and whatever they are says, 'I simply postulate that these are the ways in which the machine interacts with the environment.' And suppose we get him to abandon entirely the question of whether by postulating these properties he could explain the final state of the machine which he would consign to some kind of mysticism, and suppose he were simply to conduct experiments on the ways in which these *a priori* procedures could be made use of by the device – no doubt he could make up a subject. It could be that the methods he picks actually have virtually nothing to do with the way the machine interacts with the environment. Nevertheless, he could evolve a long subject, have many PhD theses and so on investigating this *a priori* selection of principles by which one supposes learning takes place.

Now, I find this view characteristic of psychology. Psychology through British empiricism and modern behaviourism has never seen an effort to show that the methods of learning which are postulated do, in fact, succeed and did succeed in attaining the final state which is postulated as being true of the machine. To carry out the scientific approach one would try to determine the systems of belief, the cognitive structures, the competence or whatever that the organism has, in fact, attained. It's precisely this problem that, traditionally, large domains of psychology have excised as being outside their concerns. These branches of psychology are theological about it, almost.

What do you say to the psychologist who says there just are not the techniques to cope with such problems? That psychology is the art of the possible and that all we can now do is to build up little bricks here and there? Then, someday in the future, an Einstein will come along and give us a more total, rounded psychology?

First of all, it's not correct. There are many things we can discover about the systems of knowledge and belief that a person has. And then, I think that investigating it would give us a lot of insight into the system, into what may be the modes of coming to terms with the environment. But if someone were to take the position you attributed to Broadbent I would consider it pointless but not irrational. But, on the other hand, I don't think that is the position psychologists are taking very often. They're not saying, 'Look, it's premature to discuss this, to study the adequacy of the methods that we postulate *a priori.*' It's not that. What we're saying is that psychology is defined by the investigation of these methods. Psychology is defined by the study of S–R connections, by habit structures, by stimulus sampling theory and so on.

Ever since your work became so influential, there's been a tendency to try and construct a grammar of non-linguistic kinds of human interaction. Is it likely that the model of language will turn out not to be a unique model?

Well, it depends. I think myself – and this is speculating – we don't have the results or the knowledge at this point. But I think it's very likely that the grammar of the system of language does reflect a special faculty of the mind. I think it would be surprising if there were very striking or strong analogies between our innate capacities to acquire linguistic systems and our innate capacities to acquire an understanding of social reality or the physical world. There's no particular reason why they should be modelled on the same set of principles. But, at a certain high enough level of abstraction, the systems will of course observe similar principles and be in some way interrelated. However, I think I wouldn't suggest if someone is interested in social interaction that they should try to apply the model of transformational grammar. But what I'd do is to approach the problem in the same manner which is borrowed from the physical sciences – namely, to ask, what is the system, what is the system of belief that governs the behaviour we are observing? Let us discover the competence that underlies the behaviour of a person in a social situation if that is the topic. And having developed an understanding of that competence, that internal system of beliefs and knowledge, then we have first to ask the question, what is it that's learned? Let us discover as scientifically as we can what we can about the system that's been acquired and call it the grammar, if you like it. Then, having, to the extent that we can, answered that question, we can sensibly raise the question of learning for the first time. The question of learning is the question of how that postulated system arises. On the basis of interaction with the environment, the question about learning can't be asked except to the extent that we already have some picture, some postulate, some concept as to the acquiring of the system. So, in this respect, I would think that any approach to psychology ought to follow the model of linguistics or, I

95

Noam Chomsky

hasten to say, it's not the model of linguistics but the model of any rational endeavour. And the fact that psychologists regard that as strange and curious is just a comment on how remote that kind of psychology is from rational endeavour and from the sciences in particular.

Do you think that stems from the American preference for studying actions rather than thought?

Well, now you've raised the question of why behaviourist psychology has such an enormous vogue, particularly in the United States. And I'm not sure what the answer to that is. I think, in part, it had to do with the very erroneous idea that by keeping close to observation of data, to manipulation, it was somehow being scientific. That belief is a grotesque caricature and distortion of science but there's no doubt that many people did have that belief. I suppose, if you want to go deeper into the question, one would have to give a sociological analysis of the use of American psychology for manipulation, for advertising, for control. A large part of the vogue for behaviourist psychology has to do with its ideological role. Behaviourist psychology is pretty empty as a intellectual pursuit, in my opinion. But it does have an important ideological role. For example, it's considered not nice to treat human beings by the techniques of the police state. It's not nice to coerce people or to control them or to train machine guns on them. But, on the other hand, if you have a mass of people you want to control and you can claim you are not doing anything ugly like that but just applying the methods of science which, as everyone knows, are neutral and good and benevolent and achieve the same result, that's much more palatable. Much more acceptable. So one finds, let's say, in total institutions, in institutions in which masses of people are placed subject to external controls, like prisons, schools and mental hospitals, not quite even that behaviourist psychology is in vogue but that it provides support. It may even sharpen and refine the methods which are known intuitively to anyone who has to control masses of people. It provides a kind of palatable ideology for the application of these techniques of coercion.

Skinner, in fact, says that one of the reasons why he feels badly misunderstood is that people think he advocates greater controls. What he's been trying to do is to show people the way they were and could be controlled so they could guard against it. Is that fair do you think? Or

96

does it go against the whole trend of his thought as you see it?
I think one has to distinguish what Skinner himself may be trying to
do from something quite different – namely, the question of why it
has such appeal. These may be very different things. As to what he
may be trying to do, I can't say. I don't have any idea of what he's
trying to do. I've looked at his work pretty carefully and I have
never been able to discover or tried to impute to him any motives
in particular. I don't know what they might be. It seems to me
that when he gets away from the investigation of partial
reinforcement – when he does things like one finds in *Beyond
Freedom and Dignity* – it's basically trivial and wouldn't be taken
seriously by anyone if it weren't for the fact that it fills a certain role
for those who are accepting the system. Now, the role it fills for
them may be very different from anything he intended. So, my point
is when one gives anything like a close analysis to the system Skinner
proposes – and I'm not talking now of his detailed studies of
conditioning and reinforcement, they are what they are, but I am
talking about what he calls his extrapolations in which he's showing
people how they are controlled, what the system of controls is and
trying to build up a social philosophy – well, that second Skinner, as
far as I can see, is almost entirely empty. You cannot find a
substantive thesis that's even worth discussing, let alone refuting.
And therefore no serious person would pay the slightest attention to
it on the basis of its actual intellectual content. Yet people do pay
enormous attention to it and it's enormously influential. The
reasons may have nothing to do with content or with what Skinner's
intentions may be, which I know nothing about. All I'm saying is
that the appeal and the acceptance has to do with other matters:
namely, that the system, though quite vacuous, does provide a kind
of aura of acceptability for techniques of control and coercion that
are very naturally sought in situations where people have to be
controlled, coerced and guided. Now I'm not imputing to Skinner
that intent. That's my point.

How does your concept of competence work?
Well, I used the word 'competence' because I didn't want to get into
pointless arguments with philosophers about whether one should
call unconscious true belief knowledge. A lot of people don't like to
use the word 'knowledge' where the beliefs are unconscious. OK. I
think it's a kind of pointless argument but I didn't feel like getting
into it so I invented a technical term, but it turns out, as usual, to be

97

more misleading than the original. By competence, I just mean that system of internal principles and structures that we use for our behaviour. I would be perfectly happy with the term knowledge. What I mean by competence is our knowledge of language but my only hesitancy is that the knowledge here is plainly unconscious. We don't have, we couldn't have, conscious knowledge of these principles. I find it difficult to say we know the principles. By competence, I just mean that system of knowledge that we put to use. There's no principle of competence. I think, if I use those machines I was talking about, I would have no hesitancy in assigning to those machines a system of competence, namely, a system of organisation and principles and structures and interaction that I am led to postulate can effectively explain what they do – the characterisation of their mental states, if you like. The characterisation of the steady state achieved by these machines would be what I'd call their competence.

Do your views about Man hint at some kind of sympathy with a man like Laing who sees many mystical elements in Man, that are maybe too random to be encompassed by a finite science?
I would look at it differently, I think. I would just take it for granted that a human being is a biological organism like any other. It's a biological organism with a very unique intellectual capacity that we are only barely beginning to understand. I think our intellectual capacities are very highly structured. They are our biological specialisation. These biological structures enable us to construct extremely rich, very penetrating systems, scientific theories if you like. Some of them are common sense. Some of them are articulated, which allows us to understand things rather deeply far beyond any evidence that's available to us. However, these same principles which give such enormous range to our system of understanding also limit its scope. These two facts are very closely linked together. Any sort of principles that enable you to construct a rich theory on the basis of limited data, also is likely to limit the class of possible theories that you can attain. Now it may very well be that among the theories we are able to attain by our biological endowment there is included the theory of mind, or it may be among the theories that we are not able to attain is included the theory of mind. In that case, it will appear that human beings have mystical, unintelligible properties because we as biological organisms will not have within our range (which is obviously a finite range) the theory which would,

in fact, explain it. There's nothing inconsistent about that. We are
biological organisms. We are capable of constructing certain systems
and understanding certain scientific theories. It's an open question
whether those scientific theories happen to include the true theory
of some domain that happens to interest us. It may or it may not. If
it does not, that domain will appear to be mystical. It will only be a
higher organism or a differently endowed organism that will
understand it. But I think that's about all that can be said.

*So you think it is finite? Professor Jouvet told me that he thought
psychology is so finite it's about reached the end of the road.
Presumably you see a time when it will have reached the end of the
road.*
I think human intelligence will reach the end of the road except for
details. We'll always be able to learn more details, more specific
facts. I think it's quite possible that, at some point, we will have
exhausted our intellectual capacities in some domain. And, I
suppose, at every stage of history that seemed to have happened, it
turned out to be false. I think one could build a kind of case, a mildly
persuasive case, that we have reached a stage not in psychology but
in many other domains. A very striking fact about twentieth-century
modernism is the move in one area after another, in art, in poetry, in
music, in certain parts of science, into a kind of unintelligibility. I
think there's probably no period in this brief history of Western
civilisation in which the creative achievements of artists were so
remote from the common consciousness and understanding of
non-artists. I think it's conceivable that this does indicate a reaching
the limit or approaching the limit in certain domains of intellectual
and creative achievement.

Is that true of psychology?
Frankly I don't think it's in any sense true of psychology.
Psychology has barely come into existence. It's just barely beginning
to ask some of the questions that might lead to a future science. But
someday it will happen – precisely because we are biological
organisms with fixed capacities that provide both the range and,
ultimately, the limit of our understanding.

*Finally, may I ask you how your work is developing now? You seem
to have been very active politically lately. Is that correct?*
For the last ten years I have been very heavily engaged in political

activities connected with Vietnam, with US foreign policy, with civil liberty issues. I've tried to maintain throughout this an ongoing commitment to both areas and, of course, both have suffered. But I've recently completed a long study on the conditions of these rules and I've got other work on these lines going. But it's a rather schizophrenic existence again.

4
H. J. Eysenck

H. J. Eysenck provokes and, to a certain extent, seems to relish controversy. When I was a student, comfortably before the race, IQ and heredity debate became such a sharp issue, Eysenck already seemed to pose an ideological problem. You were for him or you were against him. Most of the psychologists who taught me personality theory were against him. They singled out his famous attack on psychoanalysis in the *Journal of Consulting Psychology* (1952) as an example of narrow vision and doubtful data. Personality theory should be sensitive and, whatever the merits of that paper, it was not sensitive. He was said to court publicity, that heinous academic sin, the art being, of course, to get publicity without courting it. He was said to be a very cold man and, it was implied, this coldness prevented him from understanding more wholistic, sensitive approaches to the study of personality.

To meet, Eysenck is a courteous, friendly but distant man. He talks about his work, he talks about his ideas, he talks about his critics. But he talks little about himself. When, in this interview, I asked him about his feelings when research went well, there was, it seemed to me, a flicker of surprise, as if it was odd to be asked so directly personal a question. When Eysenck speaks critically of others and responds to criticisms of himself, he can adopt a tone of amused but condescending reasonableness. It seems so clear to him now, that you cannot defend psychoanalysis as a scientific enterprise that he is a little bewildered by those who cling so stubbornly to it. At a point in this interview, when he explains that it was a psychoanalyst, Alexander Herzberg, who first gave him the idea for behaviour therapy, he said it seemed so odd to him that Herzberg and other analysts, who used some techniques very like those of behaviour therapy, to speed up analysis, did not ask if it wasn't these tasks they set patients which healed – and not analysis itself. Eysenck seemed startled when I suggested that maybe these

101

H. J. Eysenck

analysts who had devoted their lives to this practice of analysis just could not ask themselves that question. He admitted it as a possibility though, it appeared, not one which had occurred to him before.

Since Eysenck is an excellent controversialist and can turn in a much better wounding phrase, a neater intellectual insult, than most, such a reasonableness can be infuriating. He admits he enjoys opposing other people's ideas. Eysenck gives the impression, as he did to me when I pressed him about the value of some work on creativity by Wallach and Kogan, of not being willing to see much merit in apparently objective criticism that goes radically against his argument.

Eysenck likes to explain the hostility he arouses in different terms, or at least he did, until the race controversy became so acid and made him, as he says ironically, 'one of the devils' of our times. As a personality theorist who believes in rigorous scientific methods, he steps on two sets of toes. He steps on the toes of most experimental psychologists who blithely perform experiments on perception, memory, verbal skills, learning, whatever you care to name, without ever considering whether personality might affect the results. Eysenck quotes an instance of this attitude: is performance on a simple crossing-out task better in the morning or the afternoon? If you do not consider personality, you get total balance, each time being as good as the other. The effects cancel out if personality is not examined. Mice as well as men show the effects of personality. Eysenck refers to a study in which the effects of alcoholic fumes on six different strains of mice were studied. Two strains improved their performance; two strains declined; and two strains behaved just the same. But this emphasis on personality and individual differences is most upsetting to experimental psychologists who are out to encode the laws of human behaviour. All humans should, to make their task more convenient, behave in the same ways. Eysenck has suggested that there are individual differences in susceptibility to conditioning and that these depend on personality. This is a very difficult idea for psychologists who believe in the omni-competence of conditioning. They do not like the notion that some people may be more readily conditioned.

And, so Eysenck believes, if he has offended these psychologists in their simplicity, he has offended the romantic personality theorists in their sensitivity. Personality is, for him, a matter of data, statistics and factor analysis. It is a matter of questionnaires and samples and performing complex operations on the data. He has little truck with the approach that sets out to understand, in some grandiose sense, the personality of other people. Psychoanalysis offends him because of

102

that. And so do many more contemporary personality theorists like Kelly or Laing or Hudson. They lack rigour. As he insists on rigour, he suggests they depict him as insensitive or superficial, or plain wrong.

A good example of Eysenck's skill as a controversialist and his dislike of what he defines as unscientific approaches to personality theory may be found in a confrontation he had with Don Bannister (1970) in which they debated explanation in personality. In his reply, Eysenck begins: 'Bannister's commentary on my paper shows his usual sparkling coruscating style but is rather spoilt by a certain crash bang wallop attitude which relies on assertion rather than argument.'

And when Bannister does not merely assert, he 'resorts to innuendo to cover a failure to look at the literature or to give a true impression of its contents'. Having pointed out the 'monumental error' of his innuendo, Eysenck then allows himself his own assertion that: 'Trait theory seems to rouse Bannister's ire though why he should feel that way about a theory he seems to consider defunct is not clear. Perhaps he objects to the fact that it refuses to lie down and seems to go on to bigger and better triumphs.' Eysenck then accuses Bannister of being 'philosophical' and rounds off his attack by commenting that one of Bannister's central criticisms is put in words that sound splendid. Abstractions often do. 'The words are there to be read but the sentence as such carries no meaning at all.' Bannister, in the terms of the confrontation, did not get a right of reply to Eysenck's reply.

I have quoted from this confrontation because it seems important to realise how savage Eysenck can be in debate. Much of his work, on behaviour therapy, on IQ and on race, has provoked just these kinds of controversial debate. Eysenck believes that people do not want to find out the truth in a reasonable way. They prefer to think they know it all or to guess or to just go on as they always have done. They do not have a scientific attitude.

Eysenck himself, as he explains in the interview, wanted to be a physicist. When he had to leave Germany because of Hitler, he came to the University of London. A series of accidents forced him into psychology. He says that one of the main thrusts of his work is to make psychologists realise that unless they adopt the model of the natural sciences in trying to understand people, the whole enterprise is doomed. The truth may be difficult and uncomfortable as in the case of race, IQ and heredity but you must discover what it is before you can take sensible remedial action. You must be willing to face it. Eysenck is severe about this. People, and many of his fellow psychologists, seem willing to avoid the truth, they even seem willing to avoid the risk of

103

finding it out. They claim the best of motives, of course, for these attitudes which Eysenck condemns. In the race issue, Eysenck goes farther. He claims that he has had the support in private of many geneticists who are simply frightened of speaking out in public. Jensen has been reviled: he has been reviled for supporting Jensen. Eysenck is very careful to point out that he has no sympathy with the views of Shockley who wants to see the so-called inferior stock, as Shockley sees it, sterilised. Eysenck condemns that. But the fact remains that unless you avoid the evidence, heredity and race affect intelligence to a great extent. Eysenck feels bitter about the way he has been treated for expressing this simple and well-supported fact. He resents the fact that he can no longer address students. And it is his opinion that the one duty a scientist owes society is for him to speak the truth. That is the bargain he makes when he receives public money to allow him 'to pursue his fancies'. Eysenck is, again, severe about his refusal to break such a bargain.

There is, it seems, a very delicate borderline here. On the one hand, there is some truth, it seems to me, in the fact that race and intelligence arguments makes psychologists feel uncomfortable. It would be simpler if a little tinkering with the environment and more well-funded programmes like Head Start could remedy the fact that American blacks do less well, it seems, than American whites on IQ tests. It would be comforting if the centuries in which the whites maltreated American blacks led only to such superficial differences and effects that environmental engineering could soon make us all equal and blessed and guiltless. That such feelings have been involved in the race debate is beyond question. But not all criticisms of Jensen's and Eysenck's position come down to that. In Jensen – and Eysenck defends him to the hilt – there is a certain tendency to cast himself as Galileo persecuted þy the orthodox, the devout, the misguided who hold transient power. I must confess to ending a review of Jensen's *Genetics and Education* by saying: 'Was he so stupid as not to know he was handling dynamite? Did he proceed to such incautious conclusions from his data with no political axe to grind. Perhaps. Scientists are often political infants. It seems to me, though, that Jensen presents his conclusions more forcefully than he ought' (1972).

But Eysenck seems to go too far, to press his controversialist instincts too hard and too rigidly, in insisting that all, apart from technical criticisms, are either ignorant or self-deluded. And that seems a characteristic, that also manifests itself in his earlier controversies over psychoanalysis.

Eysenck also, of course, arouses envy. He is a prolific psychologist. He is a very successful popular writer and he seems to enjoy writing for a non-professional audience. His books have covered a wide variety of themes: *Dimensions of Personality* (1947), *The Scientific Study of Personality* (1953), *The Structure of Human Personality* (1953), *Crime and Personality* (1965) and *The Biological Basis of Personality* (1967).

The two areas in which he has done, it seems to me, his most original work are behaviour therapy which derives its techniques from learning theory and the mapping of the three dimensions of personality, *extraversion – introversion, neuroticism* and *psychoticism*. As Eysenck concedes in the interview, the dimensions used have been toyed with and put forward since the time of Galen in the second century AD. Various psychologists like Kretschmer and Jung refined them out of their own experience. But Eysenck sees the particular merit of his own dimensions as being their rigour. They come out of studies involving large samples, questionnaires, and sophisticated analysis. The dimensions make connections between various kinds of traits of behaviour or personality and, which is very crucial for Eysenck, they allow predictions to be made and promote not just psychological research but research in other scientific disciplines. 'Most psychological problems transcend psychology', as Eysenck has put it. As his own volume *The Biological Basis of Personality* explains, he is very much in favour of this transcendence. In his confrontation with Bannister, Eysenck argued against the notion of a 'pure' psychology which could work in isolation and contemplate none but psychological problems. He wrote (1970a, p. 406):

Genetics, physiology, neurology, anatomy and biochemistry are all implicated in our attempt to account for individual differences in neuroticism and extraversion. It will be clear that this is not the end of the chain, however, and much further research will be required in these various fields . . . . The referral of the problem to physiologists and others will undoubtedly offend some psychologists, particularly those with a firm belief in the 'empty organism', but to most people it will simply serve as a reminder of the obvious fact that the distinctions between psychology, physiology, genetics and other biological specialities are man-made to serve administrative and other practical purposes, but have no counterpart in nature. It may be convenient to cut the cloth in this way but to make a suit it has to be sewn together again.

This attitude would, of course, lead Eysenck to see the problem of race and intelligence as one that involved both psychology and genetics and, also, as one that could only be seriously discussed by those with the proper grounding in both disciplines.

The difficulty, too, that such an attitude poses is a practical one. It is almost impossible now for one person actually to master more than one field, given the enormous explosion of scientific manpower and publications. Psychologists often accuse Jensen of not being able to master the psychological literature round the IQ test. In principle, of course, Eysenck seems very sensible and moderate in advocating a kind of integration of psychology, physiology, genetics and biochemistry. In the far future, accounts of human behaviour will be framed at all these levels and the arguments against it are usually defensive. It cannot be done, now or yet. Skinner is, of course, particularly convinced of the uselessness of physiology for psychology. But less visionary psychologists too, like Broadbent, see little point in actually doing any physiological psychology themselves. Again, one can see Eysenck holding a position which strikes him as being utterly reasonable but which arouses the hostility of many psychologists. In his reply in that confrontation, Bannister argued that the psychological problems must be faced in their own terms, not in physiological ones, and that translating problems from one discipline to another was no help. It is, I find, difficult to quarrel with the outlines of Eysenck's position on the integration of work in psychology and physiology. How he has applied this, in some areas, is a different matter.

As a would-be physicist and a psychologist who was trained by Sir Cyril Burt, probably the most mathematically inclined British psychologist of the first part of the century, it is not surprising that Eysenck should have such a strong view about the need for psychology to be scientific. But he does criticise psychologists for the way they interpret this need. He believes they have an idealised notion of how the physical sciences work. He has described the discovery of the planet Neptune as it happened as 'a mixture of genuine deduction from established scientific law, chance, error, luck and farce'. The discovery depended on the fact that at the time the astronomers looked for it, it was in a part of its orbit where the quite erroneous calculations predicted it would be. But, as the textbooks usually describe the discovery, it was a model of logical scientific deduction after the orbit of Uranus turned out to have perturbations in it. And it is textbooks and popularisations that psychologists read if they read anything at all about the physical sciences. They have, he claims, a starry-eyed view of the way the physical sciences achieved what they did. As the actual research went on, it was less exact, less inhuman.

Eysenck, also rather surprisingly, derides the mania for prediction. He certainly thinks that prediction is important. But very often an experiment in which the predictions fail does not mean that work in that field is useless or that the theory on which the predictions were based is to be abandoned. Eysenck points out that Newton himself had failures of deduction and, in places, found it necessary to invoke the interference of God in order to rescue his theory. He doubts that such a plea would carry much weight with the editor of the *Journal of Experimental Psychology* if a major prediction in a study had failed to materialise. But, in their wish to have strong theories that look like those of the physical sciences which they do not comprehend, psychologists can tend to put too much insistence on the extent to which their work should be experimentally rigorous. They can throw out good new ideas. And Eysenck, as he comments in the interview, finds a sad lack of important new ideas among young psychologists. They do know the techniques; but they do not find the problems.

And, as Eysenck believes in the need for psychology, physiology and other biological sciences to co-operate in the strongest ways possible, he thinks that the borderlines between these disciplines can be especially fruitful in ideas which one cannot often hope to be particularly strong but which, with patience and with work, can yield valuable results. Psychologists who want that gloss of rigour tend to avoid precisely such areas. It is curious that Hudson, one of Eysenck's fiercest and most telling critics over race, should be thinking along not dissimilar lines.

I have stressed some of the details of Eysenck's work because, like Skinner and Laing, he seems to suffer from the danger that besets all those psychologists who have become contemporary figures outside psychology, that is, of having his work oversimplified. He now seems to personify a certain attitude, even to many psychologists. I think this is unfair. One may object to Eysenck on race (strenuously) and Eysenck on psychoanalysis (less strenuously perhaps) but still see in his work on personality traits a very major contribution.

As Eysenck explains, he became a psychologist by accident and many of the turns his career took were by accident. He became a clinical psychologist because he needed a job during the war when he was considered an enemy alien, and, despite many attempts, would not be accepted by the armed forces. Nevertheless, some of his remarks in the interview suggest he gets more than accidental pleasure from his

107

work. He has always felt obliged to do some work which would be useful rather than interesting to himself. Behaviour therapy is for him the chief example of that. He did the work in order to repay his debt to a society that gave him the time and money to 'pursue his fancies'. He stresses that it is a personal opinion that some of his work should go to repay society: he is not laying down rules for all psychologists. But the phrase 'pursue his fancies' does suggest more of a curiosity about human behaviour than he ever explicitly admits to. It is also interesting that he should admit great surprise when any of his predictions do happen to work out. But, as he points out, he makes no claim to insight. Like Broadbent, he suspects those who rely on their self-declared insight. At precisely the intuitive level that he would condemn, this seems to fit in with one of the remarks in the interview when he explains that when his research goes well, he feels, most sensually, like the cat who has had the cream and, less sensually, as he does when he listens to Brahms' Violin Concerto and knows 'this is good'. He is a severe judge of himself, but is not above liking it when that judgment he can make is a good one.

Why did you become a psychologist?
It was an accident really. I had really always been interested in becoming a research physicist. When I had to leave Germany, I tried to get into the University of London and I was told I would have to sit an examination. The subjects it was easiest for me to do were Latin, French, German, English and maths and when I presented myself to register for the physics courses, I was told I had taken the wrong subjects for that. The University of London was terribly bureaucratic in these things and I wouldn't be able to attend the physics courses. I asked what I could do about it. They said I could come back next year and present the right subjects. But I didn't have the money to do that, so I asked if there wasn't any scientific subject that I could take. 'Yes,' they said, 'psychology'. And I said, 'What on earth is psychology?' I'd never heard of it. So I became a psychologist. It took me a long time to get over the shock.

In much of your work you criticise the unscientific approach of much psychology. Would you have preferred to deal with the certainties of physics?
In many ways, yes, I would have preferred that. On the other hand, I think that my particular gifts are more needed, shall we say, in psychology than in physics. There are a lot of very good physicists

but few psychologists who have the proper scientific background. In psychology, one finds that one has to spend half one's time making it clear to people that problems should be attacked in a scientific manner rather than in a political, social or philosophical or existential manner or whatever. And that is very time consuming.

Professor David McClelland told me that he thinks many psychologists turned to psychology in reaction to a very fundamental religious upbringing. Did you have such an upbringing?
No. Religion was not much mentioned. My father was a Lutheran but pretty sceptical about it. My mother was a Catholic who never did much about it. My grandmother, who was the person who really brought me up, later became a very devout Catholic and died in a concentration camp which shows, of course, how strong religious feelings can be. But that was not true of the way I was brought up.

Were there any major influences on you as you worked towards becoming a psychologist?
Cyril Burt was my professor. He was a very important influence. I think he was probably the most intelligent person I ever met – very knowledgeable. I was very fortunate to be in his department because it was the only department that really laid stress on the mathematics, statistics and psychometrics that were needed for a scientific approach. Burt had a great influence. People say that I am just his pupil and so go on with the same kind of stuff. But this is quite untrue. My natural reaction to anybody is to try and oppose it, to find the weaknesses in it. It is because I couldn't find the weaknesses in it, in his general theory – I found many weaknesses in particular but the general teaching he gave is, I think, pretty invulnerable – that I took it over. Not because I was his student, but in spite of being his student.

Spearman was another influence. I met him at some lectures. I found his book *The Abilities of Man* (1927) just the kind of think I was looking for, the application of proper scientific methods to psychological material. The other person was Pavlov whom I never met, of course, but who showed me there is a way to attack these problems biologically. Neither Burt nor Spearman was very biologically oriented. I found Pavlov's approach refreshing. It was these two general directions – the psychometric and the biological – that were the most important.

What was your early work in?

I did quite a lot of things at the beginning on different lines. I did
some work on the effects of hypnosis. The problem that interested
me was this. People had claimed, and there seemed to be
experimental evidence, that under hypnosis people can do things
way above what they can do usually. Perception was said to be
better. People could do muscular work better and for longer. I found
that all hypnosis could abolish was pain and the sense of pain. So,
you could abolish the sense of pain, the sense of muscular fatigue
and get people to carry on longer. But the hypnotised subjects did no
better than a well-motivated, non-hypnotised one on a whole set of
tasks.

You were also interested in aesthetics, weren't you?

Yes, especially the degree to which people agree in their assessment
of the beauty and attractiveness of certain things. I made some
statistical investigations and I found out that you can get a more
precise judgment by asking more people. If you ask one person to
rank a hundred pictures in terms of which is more beautiful he won't
be very accurate. But if you ask a hundred people, then their average
order of rank of beauty will be very similar to that of another group
of a hundred people. And I devised a formula which indicates how
many judges you need to produce agreement between groups of
judges. I was also interested in the sense-of-humour idea. You know
how all nationalities – the French, the British, the German, the
Americans – boast of their own particular sense of humour, as
something very special. Well, I discovered that this very national
view just didn't stand up.

*Does this early work you did bear any relation to the work you later
did on personality and IQ or was it just a question of using similar
techniques again?*

I did things that interested me. It didn't concern my later work
because that also came about by accident.

*How did you, from studying aesthetics, hypnosis and humour, get
into the field of clinical psychology?*

I was an enemy alien here and no one wanted to give me a job or take
me into the army, though I tried very hard. Then I was appointed
research psychologist at Mill Hill Emergency Hospital. It was highly
fortuitous. A friend of mine, Philip Vernon, recommended me and I

was accepted. I had no particular interest in mental abnormality or personality. I was more inclined, in fact, to psychometrics and learning theory, in the experimental study of various things rather than in such a nebulous area but . . . one has to live and I made a living by going into psychiatry.

Was your paper in 1952 in which you argued against the efficacy of psychotherapy and, particularly, psychoanalysis, your first controversial one?

Yes, my previous papers were quite well received, I think. But as they weren't controversial, there was nothing in them to really excite people.

But when I came into this field of mental abnormality, I found a large number of things wrong in it. I have already mentioned the unreliability of diagnoses. When I looked into treatment I found there was no evidence for the efficacy of treatment either. In the war, I got a job at a psychiatric clinic dealing with people who had war neuroses. One of the things that needed doing was to prepare tests that would distinguish between different diagnostic categories. So, it was important to know how reliably these diagnostic categories were assessed by the psychiatrists. So, I went to the head of the Unit and asked to check what the diagnoses had been for patients who had been treated by different doctors at different times. I wanted to compare these. He took me aside in a fatherly fashion and asked if there weren't any more important things to do or that I wanted to do. I said there were other things, of course, but I thought that this was important. Everything possible was done to discourage, and even stop, me. When I looked into treatment I found there was no evidence for the efficacy of treatment either. This was just accepted on personal hearsay, on what people believed or had been taught – but not on any evidence. And when I looked at the kinds of test that were used to assess psychiatric patients' state of mind, like Rorschach tests and projection tests, I found there was no evidence you could do anything with such tests. I took a sample of fifty highly neurotic patients and fifty normals who were alike in terms of age, sex, class and so on. They were all given a Rorschach test by one expert and then their Rorschachs were sent to another expert. All I asked him to do was to sort them out into which had been done by normals and which by neurotic patients. I found that he could do no better than chance. The same went for another Rorschach expert. Now, if you can't even find out from such a test whether a person is severely neurotic or normal, what can you do with it? That was very controversial then, but it is widely recognised now.

Then Professor Aubrey Lewis, chief professor of psychiatry at the Maudsley, wanted to start a profession of clinical psychology in this country and wanted me to do it. So, I went to the USA to see what American practices were like and I became very disenchanted. I had to decide what needed to be done and it seemed to me that one needed to have a proper clinical psychology based, not on psychoanalysis, but on experimental psychology which would give us a proper system of diagnosis, a proper system of mental assessment, a proper system of therapy. The first stage was to write a series of critical papers like the 1952 one. At the same time, I was working towards the more positive aspects, creating a set of tests that could be used for personality assessment in psychiatric testing and developing adequate methods of treatment which I called behaviour therapy. All this, of course, took a few years. In 1959, I started writing about behaviour therapy referring back to material collected in the past. In our practice at the Maudsley, I got colleagues who were in daily contact with patients to try out these new methods.

You know, of course, that there have been a number of criticisms of your 1952 paper such as that spontaneous remission is a myth you invented and that the statistics you based your case on came from life insurance companies. Did you ever feel you had to modify your conclusions?

If you look at the criticisms, I think you will find that most of them, a dozen or so, didn't criticise what I said at all but what they might have liked me to have said. What I said in that paper was that there was no evidence that psychotherapy of any kind produced any effects greater than those of spontaneous remission. What they criticised was a statement I never made, namely, that psychoanalysis and psychotherapy were ineffective. I never said that. You can't demonstrate a negative. I never claimed that. But the evidence for efficacy is poor, the statistics are poor and the descriptions are insufficient. One would not normally deal with evidence of that kind but as it was all the evidence there was, it didn't prove anything whatsoever. Most of the criticisms rather viciously attacked the material I had collected but I said I was aware of its insufficiency but it was all there. So that if you accept these criticisms, my general

conclusion still stands, there isn't anything like evidence
of the effects of psychotherapy because the evidence is not
sufficient.

And what about spontaneous remission? Is that a myth?
As regards the question of spontaneous remission, one or two people
have credited me with creating a myth which is without any truth.
The evidence for it is now much better than in 1952. It has been
reviewed by S. Rachman in his book on the effects of psychotherapy
where he comes to the conclusion, after very carefully looking at the
evidence, that my original conclusions both as to the effect of
psychotherapy and to the existence of spontaneous remission
cannot be modified. Later evidence supports what I argued. So, I
would say, it is still true and better supported now.

*Why do you think that psychology is so unscientific in its general
approach?*
There are a number of reasons. In the first place, people have always
been interested in psychological problems, problems of motivation,
problems of attitude, problems of changing people's behaviour and,
round all these problems, a number of disciplines have grown up.
Penologists, educationalists, psychiatrists, who all, without any
scientific background, have accumulated what they consider to be
expertise. So they think they know the answers where, in fact, they
know nothing at all. So, they vehemently oppose anyone who wishes
to study the subject on a scientific basis. Take what I described
happened to me when I was a raw young experimental psychologist
who wanted to look at diagnostic consistency. After that and my
1952 paper, people were terribly upset and I was practically shunned
and exorcised in psychiatric and clinical circles. Now the message has
got through and many will accept my criticisms as true statements of
fact. Many people even want to do something about it. And there are
now experiments that show that behaviour therapy does better than
spontaneous remission or psychotherapy. So, there has been a
change.
    But, in education for instance, there has not been much of a
change. You still get these silly swings from one enthusiasm to
another, without any demonstration that what you're doing now is
any better than what you did before. Often, people don't even try to
document what they are doing so that later it might be possible to
say if it was or wasn't effective. People seem to be afraid to put their

ideas to the test. And that, of course, is just what the scientist wants to do.

When you work as a scientist on a problem, do you use your intuition or do you proceed in a very mechanical way, step by step?
It's a difficult question to answer because I'm not sure what you mean by intuition or how one would recognise it. I would put it this way. That one of the traits in my make-up that has helped me to do work in science is an ability to recognise important problems. I take in what many people just let go as unimportant or irrelevant. I've been working for about twenty years on reminiscence, which is a very intriguing phenomenon in which a person's ability to perform a certain type of task when he is learning it, gets much better during a period of rest when he isn't learning. Now there are many theories for that. I got interested in it. What interested me was not this jump in the ability to perform the task but rather that, once the jump had occurred and one had recorded the performance of a subject, they suddenly went down again. Whereas if they had gone on without any pause they would have gone up, improving surely and sharply. Most people simply dismissed this by saying, 'Oh well, they were getting tired or it was inhibition', which doesn't make any sense since, after a period of rest, they should have been getting rested, not tired. I felt that unless you could give an account of this particular failure in theoretical terms, you would not have a proper theory of reminiscence. Well, I'm just publishing a book which gives our theory of reminiscence and which also accounts for this downswing. I'm sure that I could not have gotten on to the theory if I had not taken account of the downswing. That was the important factor.

And isolating it was crucial?
Seeing it as the important point in the whole structure. There are many points associated with reminiscence, the slow growth with massed trials, the sudden jump when you have rested, the warm-up phenomenon after the rest. It was the downswing which everyone disregarded which turned out to be the important thing. You could call it intuition that led to that. I don't know what it is. I couldn't have said at the time why it was important or why I felt it was important. It simply seemed to be the one thing that didn't make any sense. You could account for all the others by a number of theories. This you could not account for, so it seemed to me

114

obviously the thing to go for. If you could account for that then you probably would have something like the true theory.

Do you feel that this ability to isolate is a very key one – especially with so much information and experimentation being produced now?
I think it is. We have over two hundred PhD students here. The thing that impresses me even about the very bright ones is that they're very good at applying the methods they have learned. Many of them know more statistics than I do and many of them are very good at manipulating apparatus and writing programmes for the computer. The thing they fall down on is looking for the right question to ask. They go for the things that are popular and are considered interesting but that are really of no importance at all. The same is true of most of the papers that I read in the journals. In ten years' time no one will remember them because they are not addressing themselves to important questions.

But can you define what it is that makes you see a problem as important?
I try to define it in seminars and I try to do it by giving students examples, by telling them what kind of thing to look out for. It's really the unexpected, the odd, that you can't explain within a framework easily. For instance, I got started in behaviour therapy in that way. I was not concerned with that problem at all. I had just finished my degree and I met a German psychiatrist, Alexander Herzberg, who was writing a book on active psychotherapy. He was Freudian, very Freudian. But he was impressed with the fact that Freudian analysis was slow and he wanted to speed it up because that was the only way to make it accessible to many people. What he did was set his patients tasks. For instance, if someone was homebound and afraid to go out, he would give treatment as an analyst and say then, 'Go to the door and look out, then go two steps to the right, two steps to the left and then back again.' Next time, it would be five steps. And so on. And he found when he did this that his patients did get better much more quickly than before. He allowed me to sit in at meetings which he had with other refugee German psychiatrists who discussed their cases. They all agreed it was a useful method. The thing that occurred to me immediately was that there was no evidence that psychoanalysis played any part at all in this. Was it not possible that the tasks by themselves produced the improvement? There was evidence that analysis helped. You could account for the

115

H. J. Eysenck

improvement in learning theory terms through extinction. So that
was the beginning of my notion of behaviour therapy. It was typical
that none of the others saw in this anything, except a slightly useful
adjunct to analysis, whereas it was important because here you had a
comparison of psychoanalysis with tasks and psychoanalysis
without tasks. It was much better with the tasks and there was no
evidence it was any use without the tasks.

*But, of course, you could allow yourself to see that. You were not
committed to psychoanalysis.*
No - and that reason is, of course, very important. These people had
spent their lives training and working in it. It was their livelihood. I
can see that.

How did you become interested in problems of personality?
I had been interested in personality from the time I came into the
psychometric field. It seemed obvious that it was a central area and it
raised a number of problems. For instance, are the differences
between normal and neurotic people differences of category, are
they different in some fundamental way or are they simply
differences of degree so that neurotics are simply more neurotic,
farther along a dimension which 'normals' also share. I became
interested in the statistical aspects of the problem.

*And did the idea for your dimension of extraversion - intraversion
also come by isolating a particular problem as important?*
It's a theory that goes back a long way to Galen and Hippocrates and
the theory of the humours. In various ways, quite a large number of
people have put it forward. I was impressed with many of them,
particularly the work of Heymans, a Dutch philosopher who did
some original work in 1909, with Gross, a Viennese psychiatrist, and
Kretschmer. All those seemed to have something true to say but
none of them used a method which could prove it. Consequently,
you had a great variety of people saying something similar but you
could not make a choice between them because there was no
evidence. They were just saying it. From very good observation, no
doubt, but you could not do it much with it. Similarly with Jung,
who relied on very good observation but had no idea of the
implications of some of the things that he was saying. For instance,
he said that at one end hysterics are inclined to be psychotics and
also that extreme introverts were inclined to be psychotics. But that

116

immediately implied a second dimension where the extremes are
identical in some sense, a dimension different from neurotic. It was
the kind of thing that is akin to the cycloid or schizoid put forward
by Kretschmer. If at both extremes there were psychotic groups,
then that implied there must be another dimension where these
groups would find themselves at the same end. You had to turn the
graphs round, so to speak. So I set about investigating the dimension
of this field.

*Do you believe that the dimensions of personality you have
postulated are enough?*
I have no doubt there are more dimensions. It's just the very
elementary beginning. We are working on psychoticism, the third
dimension which I proposed in 1952. I think these dimensions are, if
not unique, at least different from other dimensions that have been
put forward because they are so closely linked with physiological
systems. Neuroticism is linked with the reticular formation and
psychoticism with the androgen/oestrogen balance and endocrine
balance but I'm sure that these three dimensions are not enough to
encompass the whole of personality. I've never suggested this and I
wouldn't believe it for a moment.

*Is it difficult to explore personality from this point of view? You
said once that you were left in the middle between the S-R
psychologists, who ignored what goes on inside the organisms, and the
murky depths of psychoanalysis, as you might call them. Do you still
feel that?*
Very much so. On the one hand, you have experimental
psychologists who go about their tasks in what they think is a
functional way, and who traditionally look at what goes into the
organism – the stimulus – and at what goes out – the response –
without paying any attention to the actual organism. And on the
other hand, you have the so-called 'depth' psychoanalysts who devote
all their attention to the personality but do so in a completely
unscientific way. Take for example the way that alcohol affects
performance.

In some people, it makes a difference: in others, it doesn't. When
you average the whole, you must have a hypothesis that links the
experiment with personality. And you must bear in mind the nature
of the organism in any experiment. Without that, the whole thing is
meaningless. Another example is the mouse because mice, too, have

117

personality. Suppose you ask the question 'Is the activity of the mouse affected by alcoholic fumes?' It sounds a reasonable question but it is meaningless unless you specify what kind of mouse. This experiment has been done on six strains of mice. For two strains, it didn't make any difference. For two strains, it made them more active. For two strains, it made them much less active. How will you average out these results? They become meaningless.

Surely this raises a very difficult problem in psychology in general. If you have only a vast range of individual differences, how can you ever arrive at general laws? Will you not be left with laws about individual cases?

I think you could make the same point about physics. There are now over ninety-two elements. Really, what it amounts to is that you can have a general law but you must recognise there are different types. The problem is not insoluble but it must be recognised. Psychology, experimental psychology, has not recognised it in the past but it is beginning to recognise it now. Kenneth Spence was one of the few psychologists to work along these lines but, outside this department, no one else is doing much. So I feel that, though I am an experimental psychologist, I look at it in a rather different way from most. I insist that we must introduce the organism into the general picture. On the other hand, I disagree completely with the usual personality theorists like the existentialists because they try to create a personality psychology that is not based on scientific evidence and that again is wrong. What we have to do is to look again at the concepts of experimental psychology and use these concepts as parameters to study individual differences in; for instance, one could do this with reactive inhibition, a leading concept in Hullian theory. What I have been trying to do is to combine personality and experimental psychology, which means sitting between two stools, which means you tend to get clobbered by both sides. But things are looking up. People are beginning to recognise the need for approaching problems this way.

You have been one of the great popularisers of IQ. Do you feel that all the work done on creativity and divergent thinking requires you to modify your view of IQ as the only reliable measure of intellectual capacity?

First, the work on creativity is very bad psychometrically. The division between convergent and divergent thinking was originally postulated by Woodworth, just after I was born, in fact. And then Spearman also postulated a factor of fluency that was measured by precisely the kind of divergent tests that are now becoming so popular. You show a picture of a tree and put a cross under it. Then you ask people to make a list of all the possible things that could be under it. Exactly the same sort of test is being used now to measure divergent ability. But you achieve the same kind of results by suggesting that it is a composite of intelligence and personality. Extraverts of equal intelligence as introverts will tend to give more suggestions because they're less afraid of making fools of themselves. The introverts tend to censor themselves. They have as many ideas but they tend to keep the bad ones to themselves. Further, the whole work on creativity is bad in two ways. In the first place, there is no criterion. No one takes really creative writers, mathematicians or scientists and compares them on these tests with uncreative ones. These tests are called 'creativity' tests simply because the investigator chose to do so. And so it begs the whole question, of course. In the second place, and this is much more serious, the hypothesis that this is separate from intelligence is testable. If you take a number of these creativity tests and you correlate performances on them with performances on a number of IQ tests, it has been shown that the creativity tests do not correlate well with one another and that, in fact, there is more correlation between IQ and creativity tests than between the creativity tests themselves.

So IQ accounts for the results on creativity. I believed Wallach and Kogan (1965) had overcome this and shown high correlations between creativity tests independent of IQ?
Wallach and Kogan are in a quite different category to Guilford and Hudson. They were among the first to criticise the deficiencies in the earlier work and to point out what I had pointed out. What I think is interesting is that the effect they demonstrate is valuable largely for the measurement of personality. I don't think Wallach and Kogan demonstrate that these are creativity tests in any way.

So what do you think Wallach and Kogan are tapping?
I think they are tapping personality differences, stylistic differences rather than ability differences. I'm looking forward to seeing this research extended.

H. J. Eysenck

So, you still feel that IQ is the only reliable guide to measure of general intelligence?
Essentially, what I think is that the theory put foward by Burt in 1910 is right. Burt argued one was dealing with a hierarchical system at the top of which you have general intelligence and this comes into every intellectual activity. Below that, you have a number of specific factors, numerical, verbal, visual and so on, which involve general intelligence and a specific ability. This view goes beyond Spearman and is in line with Thurstone's later view. I know of no evidence to contradict it. Guilford's structure of the intellect model suffers from very grave psychometric defects. He uses a theory of rotation that begs the question. Most psychometricians of any standing feel he errs very badly in not having a general factor of intelligence and he doesn't have one because he couldn't have one due to the exigencies of his method of rotation.

So, presumably, if you are satisfied with the status of IQ, it suggests that you still uphold the arguments put forward by Jensen and yourself on the grounds of race and IQ. That argument can't be criticised because IQ is not a good measure?
I think that criticisms of that sort are quite beside the point. They rest on a misunderstanding and the evidence doesn't bear those criticisms out.

You sound as if some criticisms are justified?
Oh yes - and I have criticised it myself. I think we are working now on attempts to improve on Jensen's work. What we are trying to do now is to improve his analysis, which is very fundamental. What people correlate are test scores on, say, a hundred items. You can get two people who both score fifty but when you look at the answer sheet, you see they have answered questions very differently. The point is that we usually simply count the number of correct responses, but people differ in the amount of time they spend on a problem. Some will never leave a problem undone. Some will quite happily move on. The whole behaviour is entirely different and to regard their scores as identical just because they both got the same number right is wrong. And, particularly, because it can be shown that the kinds of error you make correlate with personality. I think it is very important to take each item as the thing to be analysed. There are other points, such as how long does it take to get to a solution. We have found that you can analyse scores on IQ tests into three

independent components – first, speed of mental function, second, error-checking mechanism and third persistence and continuance. I think it is very important to find in which of these three – it may be only one, it may be all three – there are racial differences or class differences; and how these differences are related to achievement. I think Jensen's model has to be criticised but at a serious, professional level and not at the level that people write at in popular journals where they are often inaccurate and demonstrate nothing except that they don't know what they are talking about.

The body of Jensen's work holds, in your opinion?
What I'm suggesting is that there is a pattern. Just as the concept of the atom was once thought to require an indivisible atom and, later, the atom was split, so with IQ. Spearman and Burt thought the general factor of intelligence was unsplittable but we have shown that IQ can be split into these three components. More possibly, later.

If IQ is so effective, would you not expect to find some physiological differences between high and low IQ scorers?
Yes, and we have found some basis in evoked potential of the EEG in which we have shown there are marked differences between the latencies of those evoked potentials. Basically, the quicker the response, the higher the IQ. The greater the amplitude of the evoked potential, also, the higher the IQ. There are quite high correlations between IQ and evoked potentials, correlations of about 0.6. We have also done work on evoked potentials in twins. In identical twins, we have shown that evoked potential patterns are almost the same. In other words, they are highly hereditable. All these lines of work go to show that IQ is still a very valuable concept which has by no means been disproved.

As far as race and IQ go, do you not feel concerned that Jensen's work and your work may be used for political ends and that its conclusions ought to have been more cautiously put forward?
In the first place, I think from the scientific point of view you cannot fault Jensen. I know him very well. He spent two years here. He picked up his interest in the intelligence here and he is really very knowledgeable and scholarly. I don't think you will find anything to criticise in his factual statements. I think you want to read the fine print. He does not assert that American Negroes are inferior in IQ. He

sums up the evidence that it is quite likely to be so. It is put that way – and not that it has been definitely established, and I think I would go along with that. That is my view especially in the light of some research that has not been published yet but which is difficult to account for in any but a hereditary way. Suppose you take a Negro boy and a white boy of superior IQ, say 120. You then test their siblings. The IQ measures of the siblings will regress to the mean but the interesting thing is that the white siblings will regress to the white mean and the black siblings will regress to the black mean. You cannot account in environmental terms for any differences in IQ, as the high IQ Negro boy has the same environment as his siblings and the high IQ white boy has the same environment as his siblings so the differences in regression to the mean must be due to genetic differences between the two. Heredity segregates the genes of the parents and re-combines them so you expect to get wide variations between siblings, which you get. Jensen's results are quite in accord with genetic principles but not with environmental ones.

Do you regret now having become involved in the controversy about race?
In one sense, I very much regret it because one doesn't like to be painted as a sort of devil. Furthermore, it's made it impossible to talk to students on anything. On the other hand, I feel it as a sort of duty. Society is setting aside large sums of money for universitites and scientists and laboratories. It has a right to expect one thing from scientists and that is the truth. That is why they are there. If you say, 'Well, I know the truth but I won't tell because it may be to my disadvantage', you are really breaking that bargain that you have with people as a whole. I feel scientists have no right to do that. If I happen to know more than anyone else on an interesting subject – and this subject is both interesting and important – then I must say what I know and to hell with the consequences.

And do you feel you have not been fairly treated?
I know I haven't been. [He smiles.] There are so many things that happened that are clearly to a pattern. Most of the people who have written and complained are, unfortunately, those who know nothing about the subject. I have not had one biologist in this field, a geneticist or a psychologist with expertise, who has pointed out a single error. Those people who pretend to find these errors are journalists, if you'll forgive my saying so, and people in greatly

different fields. It's very bad. Even some scientific journals, so called, have adopted a policy of hostility and suppression. The *New Scientist*, for instance, had a review of Jensen's book by Stephen Rose who wrote a stinking review, irrelevant and inaccurate. I wrote a brief letter pointing this out. Rose and other people replied, all in a hostile manner. I thought by the law of averages some letters should be on my side. Then, I got a letter from Eliot Slater, one of the elder statesmen in this field, who said he had written a letter to the *New Scientist* in my defence but that this had not been published. Practically every geneticist I know is on my side though many are afraid to say so.

Do you feel psychologists have a duty, then, to do work that is useful to society?
No. I don't think that one should ever prescribe for other people what they should do or shouldn't do. I think that many psychologists are interested in pure science and the best of luck to them. It's an important thing for people to do. I'm glad people are doing it. I have a kind of . . . I'm not sure what . . . a sense of duty to repay society in some degree for the leisure it gives one and the chance to pursue one's fancies and so I feel that some of the work I do should be useful, at least. It would go a little way to repay society, which was why I worked in behaviour therapy, though it didn't wildly fascinate me, but it was useful. I don't think everyone else should feel that way. It's just a personal feeling.

You seem to be very insistent on a scientific approach to psychology and I wondered if you had been impressed at all by any of the work like Rhine's ESP work and Gauquelin's on astrology that suggests there may be more to Man than scientists have traditionally allowed?
I have looked at the studies Gauquelin has done and was very impressed in the sense that they indubitably show some relation. They were checked by the Belgian Academy of Sciences who were pretty hostile and came to the same conclusion. The results that showed the saturnine temperament indicates scientists are in agreement with what psychologists have said for a long time. I find it very difficult to make anything of this. On the other hand, it would be unscientific to reject it out of hand. I hope Gauquelin will continue with it and I hope he will do it on an experimental basis using personality inventories. Most people working in the field have found scientists are introverted so possibly introverted people will

show the same kind of horoscope. ESP I am even more impressed with – particularly recent work like that of Schmidt using decay of radioactive material and recording by computer right and wrong choices so that there is no possibility of error. I am also impressed with the work on animals.

My own interest is that I suggested years ago on theoretical grounds that you would expect extraverts to be better at this than introverts. This is precisely what happens. Extraverts show ESP and introverts show negative ESP. But, again, there is no theoretical framework into which one can fit these things and my feeling is that the people who work in it are so much obsessed by the need to prove there is such a thing, they don't care about the kind of investigation that a normal scientist or a normal psychologist would do. Take a simple instance. They have never shown the reliability of an ESP score and that's the first thing one would do with a score on a normal psychological test. The distribution of ESP in a normal population, no one has ever bothered with. I think that that's a mistake. And, as long as people go on like that, simply trying to show there is such a thing, which will never convince those people who don't want to believe it, we won't get much farther.

Do you think it will be accepted in the end, as a sound body of knowledge, so that forty years from now, it will seem strange it was ever excluded? Rhine has been doing the work for forty years now and we still treat it as something a bit sensational.

I should imagine it will be in due course. In a way, it's rather like Mendel. His work was not accepted because it didn't fit into any theoretical framework. Biologists and botanists weren't interested. It may be similar. After all, forty years is not such an awfully long time. It took Newton forty years to be accepted by the French physicists. In the purview of science, it's not all that long when you bear in mind how unlikely it is in terms of current forms of scientific thinking. If Schmidt is right and people are able to predict this radioactive decay, it throws out immediately Heisenberg's indeterminacy principle and all sorts of ideas physicists place great stock on, so naturally they wouldn't want to believe it.

How does it feel when some research that you have been doing works out well?

You feel like the cat who got the cream. It's very difficult to describe. It's a general pervasive feeling of goodness. You feel very

124

pleased with all things. I, at least, always feel somewhat astonished that something I predicted came off. I always feel it's so unlikely that, when it does, it deserves a celebration. Yes, you feel pleased with yourself, pleased with nature, pleased with the world. It's a feeling, perhaps, like you get when you listen to Brahms' Violin Concerto. You know this really is good and that life is worth living and so on.

5
Leon Festinger

Very few psychologists change their interests radically in mid-career. Psychologists who have made a reputation or even a discovery cannot easily switch their interest. For example, Skinner has refined the theory and potential applications of operant conditioning since the thirties: most of Hudson's work still stems from his early work on the differences between arts and science specialists. Jouvet has continued to look at various aspects of dreams: McClelland still works on achievement motivation though he is also, these days, interested in the power motive. Eysenck changed his interests to some extent when he took a job as a clinical psychologist but, as he explained, it was a question of earning a living during the war. Psychologists seem to prefer to develop their first interest or, perhaps, the first interest that brought them recognition. One cannot be expected when one is a professor to drop all this expertise, slowly and expensively acquired, so as to do, say, physiological psychology – a fascinating subject, no doubt, but one of which one is totally ignorant. The whole organisation of science militates against such restlessness. One's work must progress but the progress should be within one's own domain.

Leon Festinger has broken this rule. He became interested in science while he was at school in New York. When he went to the City College of New York, he took physics courses. He found them excruciatingly dull. Worse, it appeared, to go by the teaching, that there was no room left for any new discoveries in physics. All the physics there was to be discovered had been discovered. There could be no fun and no future in physics. He switched to chemistry which he found to be even more boring. In something like desperation, he then switched to psychology. He confesses, and is a little vague about this in the interview, that he found the psychology courses to be almost as boring but by then he had committed himself. He had also grasped that there was plenty of scope for new discoveries in psychology.

Festinger trained as a social psychologist. He went out to Iowa to do graduate work on levels of aspiration under Kurt Lewin who was a major influence in shaping the thinking of many American social psychologists in the forties. It was later, in the fifties, while Festinger was professor at the University of Minnesota that he started work on the theory that made him famous, the theory of cognitive dissonance. From 1957 when he started work on the theory, Festinger created almost a new discipline. Then, as he explains in the interview, he decided that he could have no new ideas. Research ceased to be fun and had become frustrating as his mind seemed only to be able to repeat ideas he had had before. Both for his own sake, and for the sake of the theory, he decided to stop working on it. He abandoned social psychology and cognitive dissonance theory altogether and he is now working on the relationship between eye-movements and perception. It took him a number of years, being a graduate student on a professor's salary, to learn the new background, the new techniques that he needed. He was fortunate that at the New School of Social Research in New York he could be afforded this renewal. The only alternative was, he told me grimly, to start becoming an administrator which he disliked and was bad at. To remain creative, he had just needed a drastic change.

Festinger talks a little brusquely and distantly about himself. As cognitive dissonance became an important theory, he must have given many interviews and his answers to questions often have a *déjà* spoken feeling. He is a small man, rather trim, who takes an obvious pleasure in being scathing. He does, from time to time, include himself among the objects or subjects it is fit to be scathing about. He wonders if he felt so forced to make the radical change that he made because he was either so restless or so egotistical he needed to make new discoveries.

His original motive for sticking to psychology also offers some clue. As he says in the interview, he graduated during the Depression. It was impossible to do what he really would have liked to do, play chess, for a living. He was often remiss in his studies because he haunted chess clubs. He was, and he is, fascinated by games. He would have been quite content to play chess for his living. He seeks and, therefore, finds, in psychology, a similar quality of the game. Science is a game. It has, for him, strict logical rules. But his reasons for sticking to those rules aren't puritanical: without rules, you can't have a game: without rules, anything that might be like a game cannot be fun.

In the interview, Festinger explains how he arrived at the theory of cognitive dissonance by studying a collection of rumours gathered in India after a terrible tremor had been felt. People were afraid. They had

127

exhibited plenty of fear during the tremor. They now needed to justify their display of fear and one of the ways of doing it was to invent and circulate rumours of worse yet to come. The rumours did not, as was to be expected from the literature, reduce their anxiety about another set of tremors. That was not their psychological function at all. The rumours came into existence to justify the fear people had shown.

From this base, Festinger developed a whole theory in which he argued that dissonance is a state in which a person holds two cognitions or thoughts or beliefs which are inconsistent or do not hold together; for example, I may believe that smoking is bad for my health yet I persist in buying cigarettes. Just as Freud had Man acting to reduce psychic and libidinal tension, Festinger argued that Man acts to reduce dissonance because it is a state of tension. In the presentation of his theory in 1957 in *Theory of Cognitive Dissonance*, Festinger stated this idea in a set of formal propositions.

He wrote: 'two elements are in a dissonant relation if, considering these two alone, the obverse of one statement would follow from the other. To state it a bit more formally, x and y are dissonant if not-x follows from y' (1957, p. 5).

Festinger cited various examples of dissonant situations. If a person who was already in debt went out to buy a new car, the 'corresponding cognitive elements' would be dissonant. If a person gave ten cents to a beggar who, it was suspected, did not really need such bounty, there would be dissonance though of a relatively weak sort. A much stronger form of dissonance would affect a lazy student. Festinger wrote there would be dissonance, 'If a student does not study for a very important examination, knowing that his present fund of knowledge is probably inadequate for the examination'.

In these circumstances, Festinger felt able to propose two general, but formal, hypotheses (p. 2):

1. The existence of dissonance, being psychologically uncomfortable, will motivate the person to try and reduce the dissonance and achieve consonance.
2. When dissonance is present, in addition to trying to reduce it, the person will actively avoid situations and information which would [be] likely [to] increase the dissonance.

Festinger's theory led to a great deal of research. But there are a number of difficulties it raises. First, he seems to imply that there is a logical question whether or not two cognitions are dissonant. X and y are dissonant, if not-x follows from y. Let us take the case of the indebted person who buys a car. If x is buying a car and y is being in debt, in what sense can it be said that not-x *follows* from y? It is certainly not in a logical sense. We may feel it is imprudent for a person in debt to buy a new car, but it is not defying the laws of logic. We presume, therefore, that it is a question of psycho-logic. For a sensible person who is in debt will not go out and buy a new car. Or, at least, the kind of person whom Festinger takes as being sensible. The car-buyer may feel that he can get away with both: the student who does not bother to study may not care whether he passes what Festinger calls 'the very important examination'. It may be an examination that is very important to Academe, to the student's parents or for his prospects, but it may matter not at all to the student. What Festinger seems to do is to depict certain situations as, *ipso facto*, creating dissonance. They may not for all people. One man's dissonance may be another man's delight. In the interview, Festinger touches on this point but dismisses it. It was one of a number of *ad hoc* criticisms.

But the fact remains that, in the very complex experimental situations that were set up, subjects were often not asked if they had experienced dissonance. Consider an experiment by Festinger and Carlsmith (1959). Students who volunteered to take part in an experiment to measure motor performance spent an hour in a boring and fatiguing session. At the end, the experimenter thanked subjects and asked for their help in preparing for the next experiment. Subjects were given the impression that, for experimental purposes, it was necessary to persuade the next lot of subjects that the task they were about to perform was not boring or fatiguing but lots of fun. Some subjects were offered one dollar for taking part in this deception; other subjects were offered twenty dollars. Festinger argued that the subjects who were only being paid one dollar would tend, when interviewed after deceiving the next subjects, to rate the experiment itself as having been less boring and fatiguing. They would have less justification, nineteen dollars less to be precise, for lying, so they would reduce dissonance created by having lied about what fun it was, by deciding the experiment had not been so bad after all. They did, in fact, change their opinion of the experiment much more than the group that were paid twenty dollars for the deception. Chapanis and Chapanis (1964), whose criticisms Festinger pays much attention to demolishing, doubt the task was as dull as it was rated, ask why subjects were not asked if lying created dissonance, and suggest that the group who got twenty dollars were incredulous and suspicious. In a quite different series of criticisms, Bem (1967) suggested that subjects did not have to change their internal awarenesses. If I know that I am being paid so much money just to say I liked 'x' then I discount that opinion of mine just as an external observer would. It is not a matter of an internal reduction of stress, but of doing a specific paid job.

It is impossible to actually judge dissonance theory, of course, as an introduction to an interview with Festinger. But it is noteworthy that he rebuts all these criticisms out of hand. He also denies that the amount of deception subjects were asked to suffer helped corrupt the whole situation. It was never the case that they did not make the experiments real. Festinger also denies that the subjects, exasperated by the whole procedure, actually felt no dissonance at all. It has been argued that instead of feeling bad because they had been forced to lie for one dollar, the typical subject would say to himself, 'I am doing this to finish this and get it over so it doesn't matter', or, 'I am doing this for the progress of science.' In either case, the whole premiss that dissonance existed would be weakened disastrously. Festinger dismisses these criticisms. Subjects were involved in the experiments. They did not do what they thought the experimenters expected of them. They did not feel they were being tricked by the whole business and, therefore, failed to involve themselves. Festinger and his colleagues never believed – and they still do not believe, Festinger emphasises – that they failed to make their experiments real situations in which real dissonance was created.

In the interview, Festinger reserves especial scorn for two critics of his theory, Chapanis and Chapanis. In 1964, Chapanis and Chapanis wrote a review, scathing in itself, of the achievements of cognitive dissonance theory. They concluded as follows (1964, p. 22): 'The magical appeal of Festinger's theory arises from its extreme simplicity both in formulation and in application. But, in our review, we have seen that this simplicity was generally deceptive.'

It often depended on assuming that the experimental situation was such that it created dissonance and on interpreting the results in, they claimed, favourable ways. Chapanis and Chapanis were not content to leave it at that. They added (ibid.):

In general, a cognitive dissonance interpretation of a social situation means that the relevant social factors can be condensed into two simple statements. To be sure, Festinger does not say formally that a dissonance theory interpretation works only for two discrepant statements but it is precisely because in practice he does so limit it that the theory has had so much acceptance. Which brings us now to the crux of the matter: is it really possible to reduce the essentials of a complex social situation to just two phrases? Reluctantly, we must say 'no'. To condense most complex social situations into two, and only two, simple statements represents so great a level of abstraction that the model no longer bears any reasonable resemblance to reality.

I have quoted at some length from this critique because, in the interview, Festinger savages the authors with great skill. A number of things are interesting about this. Festinger feels strongly about the theory although he has left it behind in terms of his career. Second, he does not reply to the last point which seems a crucial one and is linked, not logically but in a general direction, with criticisms that argue that the situations in the cognitive dissonance experiments may not have been real enough. They may have been real enough for the psychologists: they were not real enough for the students. Psychologists who ask their subjects if the experiment seemed real to them may, after all, be like playwrights who come on stage, to no tumultuous applause, and inquire of the audience if the play was good. Some will hoot derisively: but most of us, meekish and well-mannered, will be too embarrassed to say 'no'. Psychologists rarely see themselves as actors, let alone as being dependent in an experiment. This point, it seems to me, Festinger fails to answer in the middle of his most convincing scathing. Again, it is interesting to see that he is fully willing to accept and praise critics who modify and criticise within the general scope of the theory. But those who are out to destroy it can only expect to be destroyed themselves.

Festinger's defence is also interesting because a glance at some of the key experiments between 1967 and 1972 suggests that cognitive dissonance theory has become much less powerful or, at least, less wide-ranging. There is also a major problem as to how long dissonance reduction lasts. Just after you have decided you will buy a Ford, you have a surge of dissonance. The post-decisional regret is greatest immediately after a decision. So that dissonance reduction may only last for a little while. It has been argued also that the salience of the decision may lessen with time as other factors, seeking new information, getting new social support, come into play. As well as this factor, Rosenberg (1965) repeated the dissonance experiment getting subjects to lie for twenty dollars or one dollar. He, however, elicited the co-operation of the subjects before they knew they were to be paid. He found that, in this condition, those who were paid twenty dollars rated the experiment as best. Rosenberg saw this as a simple matter of reinforcement. For twenty dollars, I will lie more (even to myself) than for one dollar.

Such findings do not, of course, prove dissonance theory wrong. But from being a very powerful theory, its range might be thought to have been considerably lessened. Festinger believes firmly it has stood the test of time and flays his critics.

Festinger would be quite scathing with these criticisms. He touches in the interview on the idea that behaviourists failed to read his book as it deals with cognitions rather than actions but believes this view to be wrong: he is still wryly convinced they did not read his book.

In a sense, of course, by treating of Festinger's old work rather than his new work, I am being rather unfair in these criticisms in so far as they may bear on his attitudes. One of his reasons for leaving the field was that he found it impossible to get new ideas which, he felt, did neither him nor the field any good. What is striking is his willingness from his new position to lash into his old critics.

Why did you become a psychologist?
I went to college fascinated by science. I'm sure that I had at that time some obscure concept of science but I knew that I liked it. I started off by taking physics courses. They were incredibly dull. I'm sure they were fascinating at other places but at CCNY [City College of New York] they were boring. After two introductory courses, I came away with the idea that physics was a science in which there were no questions left. So I switched and started taking chemistry courses. That was even worse.

Part of the problem may have been that I wasn't doing much work in my first two years. I was mainly inhabiting chess clubs and playing chess. But then I went through a period of going to the library and taking books out in various sciences and I remember very clearly the book that influenced me the most. It was an early book of Clark Hull's called *Hypnosis and Suggestibility* which was a beautiful series of studies in which he took what is still an obscure phenomenon and examined it. The impression I was left with was that here was a field that was scientific and still had questions to be answered. So I switched to psychology.

That was better than physics?
Introductory psychology was also very boring but by then I had kind of committed myself.

What were the major influences on you apart from Hull's work?
I suppose the major influence was Max Hertzmann who was a
teacher professor at CCNY. Then, I became intrigued with the work
of Kurt Lewin and I started doing work on levels of aspiration. That
was as an undergraduate and, as a result of that, I went out to do
graduate work with Lewin in Iowa.

What was your graduate work in?
Everyone nearly always repeats a study they've done or an
experiment they've done. And I did my master's thesis on levels of
aspiration. Having repeated that I was free to move to other things.

*David McClelland has suggested that one of the major motivations
that psychologists of your generation had was to get away from a
religious background, to rebel against very strict ideas. Was that true of
you?*
Everyone projects their own problems but the answer is no. I don't
think I have any religious hang-ups. I grew up in a totally atheist
home and I have always been an atheist. I don't think there is a God
and, even if there were one, on the basis of the available evidence, I
would have to reject the hypothesis. If you are trying to ask what I
think my motivations were . . .

Yes.
Well, I love games. I think I could have been very happy being a chess
player or dealing with some other kind of games. But I grew up in the
Depression. It didn't seem one could survive on chess, and science is
also a game. You have very strict ground rules in science and your
ideas have to check out with the empirical world. That's very tough
and also very fascinating.

*Was it this love of games and complex games like chess that led you
to study thinking?*
I connect my motivation for doing science with my fascination with
games. But that's mainly because I look at my reactions when I'm
doing science and for me, the only interesting thing is to have some
idea, some concept, and to see if it works, and if it doesn't work, to
amend it so that it does work. And what does working mean? It
means seeing if it checks out. Do you play chess?

No, very badly.
It's just like chess or the Japanese game of Go. You have to have a conception and if that conception is valid, it works. If it isn't valid, it's a shambles.

But surely one of the points about social science research is that it is so complex that you rarely get the elegant solutions, the yes or no, of games?
I'm not sure you always get an elegant yes or no in games. Someone wins, someone loses, that's true. But the analysis is not that clear. Science is, in a sense, a less restricted field but, ultimately, it has the same ground rules. I don't know if I'm communicating.

Oh yes.
It applies to more complex matters.

How did you come to study cognitive dissonance?
I really stated that in the preface to the *Theory of Cognitive Dissonance* but nobody believes it because I am always asked it again. So, either nobody believes it or nobody reads the preface. The answer is in terms of precipitating conditions. And, maybe, people who are concerned with deeper levels of explanation want a deeper kind of explanation but I'm not sure I can give you that. I'm certainly not aware of one.

I was engaged in going through the literature on rumour and I came across a study by an Indian named Singh who had collected thousands of rumours that were circulating widely after disasters. Thirty-five thousand rumours he collected were from an area that felt a tremor and a shock that was very prolonged but where there was no destruction. About ninety per cent of the rumours collected were predicting even worse disaster. On the surface, it seems implausible that people would circulate anxiety-provoking rumours. For a rumour to be accepted by people, the rumour-monger must be motivated to communicate and the people must be motivated to believe. I searched to know why people should be interested in believing that tomorrow there will be a horrible flood that will wipe us all out.

These people were very much frightened by the shock. The shock stops but the fear doesn't subside. They come out from where they have been hiding. They have been through a great deal but they see that nothing has happened. They feel so frightened, though, that they become very interested in providing themselves with some context that will justify their fear. And, if that is true, you will see why they were eager to believe the anxiety-provoking rumours. They weren't anxiety-provoking, they were fear-justifying. And from that idea came the idea of cognitive dissonance.

You did some research on a sect that believed the world was going to come to an end, didn't you?
That book was called *When Prophecy Fails*, written with Stanley Schachter and H. W. Riecken.

I found it amusing. Was it hard to do?
Yes, very difficult. By the time it was finished, we were all exhausted.

Did they ever realise you were not true converts?
Later.

Could you say what you did find out happened when prophecy failed?
We have a group who believed the world was going to end on a specific date. I think it was 21 December of that year. They would be picked up at a specific time by flying saucers and be taken to a planet. When the flood had subsided, they would be returned. And they would be very important people, of course. They had spent a lot of time making arrangements and establishing procedures. They had received all kinds of communications and indications. Someone was supposed to arrive on the night of the 20th to take them to the flying saucers. They were all sitting around, waiting, and, of course, nobody came. And, after four to six hours of turmoil and desperation, they reached the conclusion that God had saved the world because they had sat up all night praying. And then, they did the same thing you find in any historical movement of millennia. They went out proselytising very very hard. In other words, if you exist in a strong state of dissonance and you can't change either cognitions really, one of the things that you can do is to get some social support which helps to reduce the dissonance. [The cognitions being 'that the world would end on 21 December' and the obvious fact 'that the world didn't end on 21 December'. Belief in the first is too strong to allow it to be dismissed. So the mind seeks, in effect, some kind of compromise. As there is no logical compromise,

135

adherents of millennial movements seek converts instead. Author's note.] Because if everyone agrees with you, then you can't but be right.

Was this study an important cornerstone of the development of the theory?

The basic theoretical premisses were all developed. We did the study because of the theory. You easily and quickly come up with many theoretical questions. How would people react if they had very strong dissonance and if the cognitions involved were absolutely unchangeable. You start trying to think of things in real life that could approximate to the theoretical issue. We wanted one kind of issue that people have a belief in that cannot change because they are so committed to it that changing it would be psychologically ruinous. And, at the same time, we wanted clear disproof of that belief. So we started digging up the literature about millennial movements. We happened to hear about this group so we plunged right in.

Were you surprised by the fact that they went out so aggressively seeking converts?

No, we weren't surprised. We were surprised by a later study that two of my students, Masha Brady and Jane Allen, did. They studied a similar situation that occurred. A group from a town in Ohio moved to Arizona. And they had made a specific date prediction for a nuclear holocaust. They had invested all their money digging shelters. Then, something like five days before the holocaust was due, they went down into the shelters and stayed there. Masha Brady and Jane Allen went down there. They couldn't get as close contact with this group as we had had with the 21 December group. But they collected a lot of information and waited till they came up from the shelters after forty-one days. They came up with a new prediction for a holocaust. It was to be when an iceberg appeared in the southern waters. But they had a deeper conviction than before about the things that they knew. They had spent forty days and nights waiting and praying. But, also, there was absolutely no inclination to go out and proselytise and gain new adherents.

Could you explain why?

I think I know the reason, yes. Every historical movement, and the group we studied initially, were subject to enormous ridicule in the press and among neighbours. This group in Arizona predicting the nuclear holocaust were not the subject of ridicule. Lots of people were building nuclear shelters. This reaction of increased proselytising may be primarily due to the ridicule.

If you are subjected to ridicule, it makes you more defensive?
Perhaps you only get proselytising if the outside world has been previously ridiculing you. The ridicule adds to the dissonance and getting new adherents has a bigger impact. Perhaps, if the outside world has not been ridiculing you, there are means for reducing the dissonance which could have a chance to take place. But this we never followed up.

Why did you feel it was valuable and necessary to set out the theory originally in such a strict formal way, with propositions and corollaries?
I'm having trouble following you.

It was very formally stated, wasn't it?
If you are going to state any theory, you have to accept the only kind of theory that is going to live for a very long time is one that can't be tested. If it's testable, it's going to be questioned. If it isn't even testable, it isn't even any fun. If the theory isn't testable, you can't distinguish between concepts and garbage. It's only if it's testable in the empirical world that it has some meaning. Or, let's say, that it follows the rules of the game. And to make it testable, you have to make it as specific as you possibly can. You want to eliminate as many ambiguities as you possibly can and, unfortunately, the theory of dissonanace has lots of vaguenesses. But I tried to make it as specific as I possibly could.

Do you feel it has stood the test of time well?
Some people would argue with it but I think it has.

There have been many criticisms of it, the most vituperative, I suppose, being Chapanis and Chapanis.
Yes – but that's garbage.

Why is it garbage?
It offers nothing constructive. It goes through an attack on each experiment and each experiment is being attacked on totally different grounds and on an *ad hoc* basis. If you are going to change

your *ad hoc*ness every time, you can destroy Newtonian mechanics. The point is that there is a theory that does explain certain phenomena. It explains diverse phenomena. If you think that theory is wrong, you propose an alternative theory or you produce data that directly contradict the theory. But Chapanis and Chapanis is an emotional expression – it's not a scientific attack.

You don't think they showed up any internal inconsistencies within the theory?
No, no, I don't think so. I don't know if you've read it recently.

Within the last year, again.
They take an experiment and say that maybe what was happening was this and let's label this A. Then they take a second experiment and say that maybe what was happening was this but, now, they no longer appeal to A but to B. Then, they take a third experiment and this time, they don't appeal to either A or to B but to C. What is it doing? It's like you telling me that if you drop something it falls with a constant acceleration and I say 'Well, maybe it's someone pushing it down.' It's got nothing to do with gravity, it's some invisible being pushing it down. And then, I say from this thing I can also predict the orbits of the planets in motion and you say, 'No, that's absolutely different.' The motion of the planets is totally different. You're not saying anything constructive, you're simply saying, 'I don't believe, I don't believe, I don't believe.'

It seems that the theory did generate quite a lot of hostility. Is that true? It seems to have been one of the few American theories to centre on thought rather than action.
Oh, it did create hostility. I'm not sure it was because it dealt with thinking processes. My guess is that quite a few people were hostile to it because the image of Man that was portrayed of the human organism was not very idealistic. Solomon Asch, in a review, essentially said, 'It offends me.' He ended the review by saying, as the Scottish verdict gives, 'not proven'. Which is a strange kind of thing because, if you take Scottish verdict, there is the implication that there are two alternatives, guilty or not guilty. Those concepts don't apply to science.

Just why do you think the image portrayed is not very idealistic?
Many people like to look at Man as a rational being, a rational

138

organism with humanity. That word stems from Man, after all. Now, dissonance theory certainly contains the idea that people are willing to delude themselves and to twist facts. It's not a picture of a rational Man.

Are there certain criticisms that you have found helpful?
Oh, there have been criticisms that were very helpful. Relatively early on, a number of people did experiments and found that one of the predictions was quite wrong, that people would avoid dissonance-increasing information. It was a constructive criticism to know people didn't avoid potentially dissonance-increasing information. What I regard as constructive criticism are data that mean you have to change your theory or even, in some ways, discard it. Cohen and Brehm have made many criticisms about the importance of commitment and choice. Zimbardo (1969) did the same kind of thing in his book. What is constructive criticism is criticism that improves the theory because it allows you to handle the material better or to account for it better.

Unlike Chapanis and Chapanis?
That is emotional nonsense under the guise of precision. I once had a lovely session with her but she was afraid to discuss it.

Apart from the criticisms of the substance of the experiments, there have been criticisms of the amount of manipulation and deception that some of the experiments involved, such as making people think that they were involved in experiments about motor performance, say. But often in fact, the only point was to force them to deceive others – which led, in turn, to people being so cynical they didn't believe the situation in the lab anyway.
That's a totally different problem. That's not to do with the validity of the theory or the validity of the results. It's an ethical problem.

But surely it does have to do with the validity of the results if people aren't convinced by the situation you created for the experiment?
But if the criticism is that, as a result of the situations we used, we made subjects unusable for other experiments . . .

Yes, but also that you made them unusable really for your own purposes.
Within the same experiment?

Not necessarily within the same experiment but as a process of time, so that by 1963/4 subjects had become so cynical about being manipulated that you couldn't trust the results.

First, I think it's nonsense and untrue. And, secondly, if you know how to do experiments, you work at them. The aim of an experiment is to reproduce, under controlled conditions a real-life situation. The things that are being affected are real to them and they are being affected as a person. Certainly, you must spend time to find out how to do that, so that it is a real realisation of your theory. Too often people in the social sciences don't do that and they turn out terrible experiments. It would be like someone in physics or in experimental psychology working with apparatus that didn't function properly. In terms of the experiments that we did, that students of mine did, do I think that they created real situations in which people reacted validly? There's no question.

Is there any question about the ethics of the methods you had to use?

I'm happy to discuss it but it's a different question.

I realise that, but having got your rejection of the first part of that critique I'd like to know if you reject the second.

Oh yes, there are ethical problems. To my mind, no society can function with an absolute ethic. There are conditions under which murder is sanctioned, like war, or when it is considered official justice. There isn't anything that cannot be affected by circumstances so that something which is considered bad becomes OK. And usually the circumstances when it's all right are circumstances when some other matter outweighs it. There is no absolute ethic. You have to weigh things. Not all of our values are internally consistent. Some are contradictory.

Now, it's unethical to deceive someone if there is no important societal value to be gained. So first, yes, it is unethical. But if there are important societal values to be gained, under which I would include gaining important new knowledge, then that outweighs the problem of deceiving though one always ought to, and we always did, accept the real responsibility after the experiment of explaining why we had to do it and trying to overcome that feeling of having been deceived. Which meant talking and talking and talking. We frequently ran a one-hour experiment and spent two hours talking about it. The problem of ethics is a very difficult one. Someone might maintain that the most unethical kind of experiment involving human beings is an experiment which is totally trivial. The subject coming to the lab might get hit by a car crossing the street and that kind of risk isn't worth it for something totally trivial.

You make it sound as if there are a lot of trivial experiments.
There certainly are. The journals are full of them.

Did you see your theory as a general theory? It seems to have interesting parallels with Freud – you have to reduce psychic tensions – and with Cannon suggesting that just as the body needs homeostasis the mind also needs to reach a point of balance.
I would say that it was limited. I wouldn't see it as a very general theory. And I don't think it's similar to Freud at all, though there are some things that Freud said that are very similar in various places about people having to justify fears.

I meant homeostatic in general.
It's very easy to say that it is another homeostatic theory. You have two hundred theories you can label homeostatic. Things aren't that simple. If you're asking me do I think there is any *Zeitgeist* or philosophy underlying assumptions about homeostatic processes in human beings – then to some extent, yes. To some extent, some things have to be.

I wanted to ask if you saw your theory as contributing to this philosophy.
No, I didn't. I intended it as an explanation, what I considered an explanation, of a broad range of psychological phenomena and of some social phenomena. But, with respect to the totality of human behaviour, very narrow.

Isidor Chein in his book The Science of Behaviour and the Image of Man *argues the theory doesn't allow you to deal with the fact that in most situations dissonance does not arise until a subject has been 'tricked' and, also, that a state of being without dissonance does not necessarily make for being happy.*
That's correct, it doesn't cover that.

It was never meant to be within the scope of theory?
It never addressed itself to that. It is an open question. I don't

141

remember if I ever said anything about that. It's certainly an open question if one totally eliminated dissonance, if one eliminated frustration which is different from dissonance, if one totally satisfied all one's needs, which is again different from having no frustration, whether that would be a happy person or someone who was comatose. That is an open question.

Another point that has often been raised is that your own pre-eminent position in cognitive dissonance meant that often if someone wanted to decide if there was dissonance, the answer was: 'Ask Leon.'

I think Eliot Aronson wrote that and, in a sense, he was correct. It was a valid criticism of the areas of vagueness and the areas of incompleteness so that predictions from the theory were not very clear. He said it very cutely. If there was uncertainty whether there was dissonance or not, he said, 'Ask Leon.' I would have hoped that by now more precision would have been put into it so that's unnecessary.

And, anyway, you have now moved out of the field.
Correct.

Why?
I was convinced that if the theory was going to be improved and if new specificity was going to be added, it was best. I'm not sure this has generality but the people least able to improve on ideas are the ones who had them in the first place. I just kept having the same ideas over and over again.

It's quite rare though for a psychologist to change fields as abruptly as you did.
I don't know. I suppose it is. Maybe I am more restless and egotistical. I am filled with ideas now. Research and science is a joy again. Instead of being frustrated.

How did you come to choose to study visual perception?
It's a long, long story made up of lots of little digressions. That explains why I was seduced. I was very frustrated because I wasn't having any new ideas and I wanted to do something new for the last ten years.

Leon Festinger

Was it difficult to make the change?
It took time. But I loved it. For a number of years, it was like being a graduate student again on a professor's salary. Which can't be bad. And I certainly had a lot of help from people in the field who enabled me to learn what I had to.

The move also meant you avoided becoming an administrator?
I don't enjoy administration very much and I'm not very good at it.

What is your new work in?
Right now, it's on the effect of the relationship between eye-movements and perception.

You said earlier that you doubted behaviourists read your book on cognitive dissonance.
They may have.

Do you think we are seeing a behaviourist revival?
It depends what you mean by behaviourist. Except for a few pockets of phenomenalism, all psychology has been behaviourist since the 1920s. I don't think Watson did anything but recognise a trend. Even the Gestalt psychologists were behaviouristic. We can look at observable things. If you don't look at observable things, the whole basis of science is cut off from under you. The problem that I see is the extent to which science tries to build inferences about non-observable things on the basis of observable things. And behaviourism in psychology has come to mean that all you can do is look at the observable thing and write it down. Perhaps Skinner is the last gasp of behaviourism. Although, personally, I think Skinner makes huge inferences about what goes on inside. It's ridiculous that he makes a fetish of talking only about observable facts. It's only to the extent that you can make bridges between facts and facts that you can build up a science. If you want to make a distinction between people who just want to record facts and those who want to explain them, well, this is a distinction that exists in all sciences.

And behaviourism seems to deny the usefulness of fieldwork, of seeing what happens rather than manipulating it. Have you found fieldwork useful?
In a laboratory experiment, you only get out what you put into it. If you also bring things into the field, you permit all sorts of things to

143

hit you. You can see that some of the theoretical statements are incomplete. It's a rich source for generating new ideas and when you have generated them, you have to check them out in the lab.

6
Liam Hudson

Liam Hudson is a very likeable psychologist. He has an engaging smile and he seems ready to be very open and frank without waxing pretentious about how vital it is for you and he to relate, interrelate and communicate.

Hudson is a tall, rather loping man. He is in his forties but looks much younger. He has the well-kept youth of some athletes and admits that in his youth he was something of a hearty sporting creature. He is a little shy. He used to peer round you in quite an intense way. But he told me when I spoke to him this time that he had discovered how to look people in the eyes. This was a major discovery in his life.

He is not at all self-important. He tends to deprecate himself in conversation. He used a curious turn of phrase when talking of those people who had been major influences on him. Describing one of his tutors at Oxford, William Kneale, the philosopher, he said that Kneale had once been 'kind' to him. He praised Hudson. Deprecatingly, Hudson added that he didn't think he had ever recovered from this praise. It was said in jest but it fitted the first impression one has of Hudson. People who are 'nice' like it if others are 'kind' to them.

The facts of Hudson's career – and, indeed, the implication of much of his own work – suggest that there is rather more to him than niceness, shyness and a touch of self-deprecation. Hudson's father was a commercial traveller who went into management. His mother did some school teaching. But apart from a great-aunt who had gone to Somerville College in the distant past, Hudson was the first member of his family to go to university. Many psychologists come, by contrast, from very academic backgrounds. Such a departure from family tradition suggests a kind of toughness that is not immediately apparent when you meet him. Moreover, Hudson did not have a particularly brilliant record at school. He was more interested in sport and people.

Hudson went to Oxford in 1950. He read psychology and philosophy. He loved the philosophy part of the course although he was not particularly good at it. He was much less at home with the psychology. At that time, Oxford psychology was dominated by behaviourist learning theory. In his book *The Cult of the Fact* Hudson analysed in some detail the way he reacted to what now seems to him to be a trivial approach to the study of Man. He admits that he got the impression with men like Deutsch and Sutherland of tremendous intellectual energy of 'fine minds at play', if you like. But he seems to have thought the fine minds should have been at work. It seems rather as if he felt privileged to rub intellects with the great but found out they were only really interested in using their minds to solve crosswords.

Hudson got a respectable degree and moved to Cambridge as a graduate student. He then spent what he describes as five rather 'wasteful' years in 'fallowness'. He worked in the laboratory of Oliver Zangwill who turned him to an interest in specialisation in the arts and sciences. But although Hudson was to make his major contributions in this precise field, it didn't particularly move him for years. He dabbled in it. He picked up what he thought of, and still thinks of, as rather boring research techniques. But he often spent months doing nothing at all. It was not until 1962 that he started to do any serious work.

From 1962, however, he produced a steady stream of quite important papers and books. They dealt, initially, with research on creativity and its relationship to specialisation in the arts and sciences. When, in 1946, J. P. Guilford began to criticise IQ tests, he set in motion a very influential theme in psychology, especially in the USA. The war had seen an upsurge in intelligence testing. Some people now wondered if you could completely predict a person's abilities and success on the strength of his IQ results. Guilford argued, and showed, that where IQ tests examined a person's capacity to converge on one correct answer, some tasks, especially creative tasks, required a different kind of skill or wit. The distinction between convergers and divergers was born. The converger scored more highly on IQ tests than on open-ended tests: the diverger did the opposite. It was argued that the diverger was more creative. In *Contrary Imaginations* (1966), Hudson looked at this argument. He found that in very bright schoolchildren, at least, you could relate convergence and divergence in this way. Some very creative science specialists were terribly convergent. A boy who had devised a computer to play the Chinese matchstick game, for example, only scored 1 in one test of divergence. Asked how many uses he could think of for a blanket, he replied with a simple 'On bed'. Yet he was clearly creative. Arts specialists, on the other hand, were very good at divergence tests, even though they might not turn out to be particularly creative.

In *Frames of Mind* (1968), Hudson elaborated this difference. He is now working on a more general theory of personality that stems from this work. He came to see both convergent and divergent thinking as different ways of coping with stress.

In *Human Beings* (1975) Hudson developed this argument and pleaded for a much fuller psychology that could begin to make connections between different parts of an individual's life. He has also become a philosopher of psychology. In *The Cult of the Fact*, a book that was partly intellectual autobiography and partly polemic, Hudson looked at what behaviourism had done to psychology. He claims that psychologists have been obsessed with being respectable scientists. They have become slaves to statistics. They have refused to look at the way people live and have preferred to do trivial, but seemingly meticulous, experiments on very artificial situations. Like Neal Miller, Hudson would like to see more studies of normal people but he is not interested in studying the super-normal, those who have adjusted magnificently to life so that the rest of us can derive lessons from their psyches. Hudson has no such messianic motives. He is just obsessively interested in people. It was this that made him turn to psychology.

Hudson recalls that when he was sixteen, he kept a journal in which he recorded sporting news, what he ate and whom he had talked to. If he had only exchanged a few words with Smith, he noted down that he had talked with Smith. He has, like Skinner and Miller, a great delight in writing. He writes poetry and says that he would love to write a novel. He feels that this combination of an interest in people and a love for words were crucial in his decision to become a psychologist.

There is another element, too, he seems to think. In his teens, he steeped himself in various kinds of philosophy. He read a lot of Zen. He wanted to 'be wise'. Perhaps that was one of the reasons why he enjoyed philosophy so much at Oxford. It easily lulls one into thinking one is wise. In the interview, Hudson talks of the combination of motives which, he thinks, made it very likely from the age of sixteen that he would end up as a psychologist.

But if he had the motivation from the age of sixteen – or if convenient hindsight allows us to find it there then – he seems to have lacked the will to do much about it. He did get his degree and his doctorate. But his heart was not in it. Hudson was fired by what seems self-indulgence. He liked to see his name in print. He describes graphically how it felt when he first saw an article of his published. It seems to have converted him to becoming a psychologist seriously. There were two other important elements. First, the research he was doing seemed to work. He was getting good results. Second, he re-married. He thinks there was a tremendous release of energy from the break-up of his first marriage. The energy found its way into his writing. And once he had seen his name in print in a learned journal, he really wanted to publish a book. Once he had published a book, and a successful book at that, he was incorrigibly hooked. He wanted to write more books.

If this sounds a little frivolous, he does add in the interview that it is through writing that the psychology falls into place. It is as if the setting up of the experiment, the research, the analysis of results are just preludes to the consummatory act of writing which is what makes it happen. Hudson seemed, at first, to differ in this from most psychologists. Rewriting this passage now, after many other interviews, I am much less sure. Many psychologists would disagree. Seeing psychology as science, they would stress that writing up the results is not where the real work lies. Setting up the hypotheses, analysing the results are the heart of the matter. But some other psychologists were equally willing to talk about the role the literary imagination plays in their work. Physical scientists certainly seem to work in different ways. The French mathematician, Poincaré, described in a famous paper how he had been struggling with Fuchsian functions for many weeks. He had decided to go mountaineering to get the problem out of his mind. He woke up one morning in the mountains with the problem entirely solved. It only remained to write out the actual functions which required nothing more than high mathematical competence. Poincaré's description echoes one by Mozart of how he heard a whole symphony at once. It then only remained to score it. Again, this required high musical skill. But the process of writing it out, and scoring it, was not the process that involved his imagination. To those who are critical of Hudson's position, it does seem that this is precisely what is wrong with his psychology. He is too interested in imaginative writing instead of hard-core science.

There seems to be also an element in Hudson's motivation that is less apparent. Doing psychology successfully does give one a kind of power. He enjoys, for instance, the wheedling that is involved in getting committees to give you money to do research. He enjoys the sense of understanding, of fit, that comes if a piece of research goes well. He explained how he was once sitting in his office in Cambridge when he realised he was getting a pattern of positive results out. He was so exhilarated that he rang eight people to tell them about it. He only recognised that this enthusiasm might bore others when the eighth person told him that he had already telephoned him a while ago to tell him of his good news. Unlike many psychologists, he does not seem reticent about it nor about how he expresses this good feeling. He does not feel obliged to cloak it.

In academic terms, Hudson has been very successful. He became a fellow of King's College, Cambridge, in 1966. Two years later, he became professor of educational sciences at Edinburgh. He has expanded some of his research interests although he has less time to pursue his own research himself. To some extent, and he stresses that it is only to an extent, others do his research and, in the process, it becomes less research.

One of the areas into which he has expanded his research illustrates neatly how simple-minded most of our ideas are about who creates and does a particular piece of research. In 1973, Hudson's department published an occasional paper by Mark Austin. In the paper, Austin looked at whether convergers or divergers were better at remembering their dreams. According to Hudson, the point is important. If Freud is right about repression and we do suppress part even of our dreams because they would be too shocking, too difficult to cope with, we would expect there to be a pattern in the way that people forget their dreams. Obviously, such a problem is a methodological nightmare for how can you tell that a person has forgotten a dream. The best you can do is to see whether he or she has remembered a dream less often than others. This is what Austin did. He divided his subjects into convergers and divergers. He argued – and one senses, of course, that it was Hudson who did the suggesting – that convergers should remember their dreams less often and less vividly than divergers. A traditional dreaming experiment was devised. Convergers and divergers were both woken up during periods of REM (rapid eye movement) sleep which is, usually, taken as an external sign that dreaming is taking place. Convergers remembered dreams much less well than divergers. The actual figures were as follows: convergers recalled what they had been dreaming of on 5 per cent of occasions only; divergers recalled on 95 per cent of occasions.

It is not unusual that Austin, a graduate student in Hudson's department, should have proved Hudson's point. What is strange is that

Hudson reveals in the interview that the idea of looking at dreams like this was given to him by Oliver Zangwill, whose graduate student Hudson himself had been. Scientists are really not like authors: they are often possessive of their research but it is harder perhaps, to justify possessiveness.

Hudson freely admits to loving an argument. One of his delights as an undergraduate was to spend two hours a week arguing with Brian Farrell who lectures in philosophical psychology at Oxford. Farrell's 'combative' style of tutorials was just what Hudson liked. As Hudson appears to be a shy and gentle man, it is a little startling to find he took such pleasure in, admittedly academic, rows.

Hudson has often argued the case for a more 'relevant' psychology. When he wrote *The Cult of the Fact*, this appeared closer than it is perhaps now, since behaviourism is enjoying a revival in the States. In *Human Beings* Hudson re-states these arguments, and suggests some possibilities for new work. Hudson stresses we need to use psychology also to make sense of individual biographies: for example, the willingness of a scientist to revolutionise his field is mirrored by a willingness to break personal relationships. It all shows his pleasure in argument, as McClelland might argue; on the other hand, the points are important and do have to be argued. The second way in which Hudson, it seems to me, betrays a desire for a certain kind of power is in his wish to be 'wise'. Wisdom is knowledge: it is also the power to teach, to persuade, to be an influence. Hudson has never shirked controversy even though he dislikes being critical. We talked about a particularly acid notice he had given to a book by Fox and Tiger. Fittingly, their book was on animal behaviour. But Hudson claimed, at least, that he took no pleasure in slating them. He was rather glad that he would be out of the country when the review would appear. He does not shirk controversy, surely, because he wants to have the power of influencing people to his view of what psychology should be like. It is interesting that Hudson, who is neither a geneticist nor a psychologist particularly concerned with race, should have become involved with the whole Jensen thesis. Hudson became one of the most dynamic critics of Jensen in Britain. He had no need to become involved in the controversy. This is not to suggest he was wrong to become involved: nor is it to suggest his criticisms were misplaced. It is just an illustration of how he does like combative controversy.

Hudson's description of his work raises very intriguing questions about the use of the imagination in psychology and the way that this differs from the way natural scientists use their imagination. Hudson remains a very self-aware psychologist. He is only in the middle of his career. It will be interesting to see if he does concentrate now on his own research or turns more to administration which, one senses, he seems to enjoy. In this, Hudson reminds one of McClelland's emphasis that psychologists are high in power motivation, liking to have both an impact and an influence on what people do.

Why did you become a psychologist?
When I was sixteen I was doing very badly as a history specialist, catastrophically badly, and I was struck with the desire to study psychology, to think wise thoughts. And I think the thoughts I thought of as psychology were really philosophy. I think it was philosophy I had in mind.

Many psychologists seem to have gone into the field as a result of accidents. Was that true in your case?
It was heavily overdetermined in my case. I think you could have looked at me at fifteen or sixteen and seen four or five over-riding reasons why I would end up as a psychologist.

Which were?
A preoccupation with people. I was looking recently at a journal I kept when I was fifteen, a very intimate, heart-felt journal. It has only three things in it – an account of the sports I played, which were almost endless, the amount of food I'd eaten and the people I'd spoken to by name. I spoke to Smith, I spoke to Jones, I met Brown. I think that kind of personal interest has obviously stayed with me. An interest at a distance – I'd been excessively shy when much younger, shy and rather solitary. And I was also very preoccupied with wisdom. I read the *Prophet* and the popularised versions of Zen when I was seventeen or eighteen. I was largely illiterate, and just thumbed my way through. Also I was brought up unconventionally. Long-haired and scruffy, and without much in the way of the social graces. Set down in a London suburb like that, we felt a bit outlandish, but confident in ourselves too.

What happened when you went to Oxford?
I gravitated naturally into philosophy rather than psychology. Psychology struck me as trivial – ridiculous, in fact. Philosophy seemed marvellous.

*And was that true of the psychology there at the time, was it
trivial?*

The Oxford department was dominated by behaviourists, learning
theorists like Deutsch and Sutherland. And I thought the work
they were doing was intellectually impressive. The sense of fine
minds at play was strong. But its relevance to the human lot was
pretty slender. Sutherland's work was an elegant analysis of how
the octopus tells a triangle from a square. Fine in a physiology
lab, but not what psychologists should be up to, in my view anyway.

Did you work at psychology while you were at Oxford?

Not much. I did enough to scrape by, but I took no real interest,
actually. I was interested in the philosophy very much. I loved it. I
was no good at it [he laughs] I ought to say that. But I loved it.
Up to that stage I'd done no academic work at all. I was an
athlete, a hearty. The world of words came alive for me at Oxford.
It clicked.

Which philosophers were a major influence on you?

One who was extraordinarily kind to me was William Kneale who
was my tutor - the biggest influence through being kind. He once
praised me. I don't think I've ever got over it. And the other
person who was a powerful influence was Brian Farrell. He was so
combative, and I found that exciting. Naturally, I wanted to do
battle with him. We had a row for two hours each week. I loved it.
[He laughs.]

*What other influences were there on the development of your
ideas?*

Well, the psychoanalytic tradition, obviously - though held at a
respectful distance. I've not had much to do with analysis at first
hand. Jock Sutherland is the analyst I know best and respect most.
Laing's work made a deep impression - *The Divided Self*. Also
Norman Brown's books. I find that privately I often talk in a way
that assumes a psychoanalytic frame of reference, but I'm rather
timid in what I write. For the rest it's novels - Angus Wilson,
Doris Lessing. The professional literature hardly at all. Almost
always, there's more excitement for me in talking to people
outside academic psychology. Psychiatrists and anthropologists -

historians too. And certain sorts of philosopher. The heartland of my own subject always seems so musty and only half alive.

McClelland believes that one of the reasons people go into psychology is as a reaction against a very fundamentalist religious upbringing. Was that true of you?
No, I was brought up somewhere between agnosticism and atheism. I was twelve – no that's a lie, I was ten – before I discovered what a church was for. Since then I have had little or no interest in religion apart from one or two soft moments. It hasn't been an issue. My father is now more religious. My mother not. There was no religious training at home, and the moral line taken was always liberal.

Was your Father an academic?
No, not at all. My father made a living as a commercial traveller and then went into management. My mother did some school teaching – she teaches painting particularly. Just recently, I discovered that I'm not, as I always believed, the first person from my family to go to university. There was a great-aunt who went to Somerville, years back. [He laughs.] But basically it's not an academic family.

How did your career develop after you left Oxford?
Well, I survived the course and I got a tolerable degree and I got a grant. But I could only get a grant to do research in psychology. You couldn't get a grant for philosophy unless you were terribly good and I certainly was nowhere near that. So I went to Cambridge and did research there for many years.

Were you doing your own research, pursuing your own ideas?
Well, I was. But to start with, it wasn't research I was interested in. It was a problem I had fallen into. I had discovered I was much better at spatial reasoning than I was at verbal reasoning and I thought I'd do a project on that. And I related it to the arts and sciences because Professor Oldfield suggested I ought to. But I didn't have my heart in research for the first five years. It seemed peripheral to my life. I was stumbling by.

Liam Hudson

What wasn't peripheral? I mean what was your 'inner life' about in those five years?
My inner life! Oh! It was quite thriving. I got married. I was married at the end of my first year as an undergraduate. I was very interested in painting, and very interested in being married too, actually. Very.

How did you get your heart into your research?
I struck some super results through attempting to use Getzels' and Jackson's material, and found that I'd fallen into the midst of something exciting. But what really got me going was seeing my stuff in print. Actually to see it written up in *The Times* and *Newsweek*. And, even more so, the thing that got me really hooked was publishing a book. That did the trick. There was no going back.

Intrinsic motivation?
[He laughs.] I'm now hooked like . . . well, there's nothing else like it.

What exactly were the results that got you started in this way?
You know that Getzels and Jackson had contrasted high IQ and high creative children. I found that this was confounded with specialization in the arts and sciences. I was the first person to find that. Pure luck. From that, quite an exciting line of argument follows.

And it was that line of argument that led you towards Contrary Imaginations *and the ideas in that?*
Yes. I'd been fumbling around in a dispirited way till then. I'd done enough to get a PhD, but it was a bad PhD. My heart wasn't in it - candidly. I would spend months doing no work at all, lying fallow and not enjoying it.

What was your PhD thesis?
It was on arts and science specialisation. It grew out of intelligence testing. Terribly dull . . . but I've glossed over something which *is* important to me. It's that when I was twenty-nine, rising thirty, I found quite suddenly that I could write psychology fluently, write it with jokes. It was like writing anything else - say, film reviews. It was prose I actually enjoyed. It wasn't full of all these 'it

154

appears to be the case that'. It was saying what I wanted it to say. And that sprang directly from a change in my personal life – the end of one marriage and the beginning of another. There was a release in that. And that's been the most important reward to me – to have been able to utter myself freely. Like my interest in people, I think there may be something compensatory about it. At school I was a backward reader – also left handed. And to this day I find I cross something of a gulf in trying to express myself. It's fluent enough when it comes, often quite vivid. But patterns of words come from a part of my mind I have little conscious access to. They seem to appear by some sleight of hand, and the most vivid spring out unbidden.

Was the freedom you had as a research student important in helping you settle your ideas. Was it creative?
It was wasteful in the sense that I progressed very slowly. I would have liked to work a great deal quicker, but I enjoy working on my own, under my own steam. I don't like being influenced – I don't like my elbow being tugged towards what I should do.

Was the work on arts and science specialisation the first piece of research you really had your heart in?
No. I did that right from the beginning, and it didn't pick up till I got this cross-connection with the American work. It was alive as soon as I could write about it quite honestly. As soon as I could utter myself on to paper, saying what I wanted to say, with turns of phrase that I liked and with chatty footnotes, I was in business.

Did you ever want to be a novelist if you place so much emphasis on the actual writing process?
I'd love to write a novel. I write poetry.

Skinner, of course, wanted to write
I know – and he writes very well.

And Neal Miller, too.
Yes.

You don't, as some psychologists seem to have, ever had a desire to be a physicist?
Not at all. I would rather be twenty things. I would rather be a

155

carpenter. I'd rather paint. I'd rather be a novelist. I'd rather sell
carpets . . . anything. Physics doesn't particularly interest me.

Do you think that the research you did and published in Contrary
Imaginations *has withstood the test of ten years as it is now?*
Oh yes, very much so. I think what's wrong with it as a piece of
research is that it's sociologically illiterate. You know, I had no
sense of the surrounding culture when I wrote it up. I was a
psychologist in the pejorative sense of the word. I just thought
about people and what happened in their heads. And so in that
sense it's less good than it might be.

The other thing that is wrong with it is that it's based on
samples and excludes the study of individuals. I think that that's a
fault. But it's definitely stood the test. There's no doubt in my
mind about that.

*Do you think that's actually led to changes in educational
practice?*
Well, Her Majesty's Inspectors tell me 'yes' – the friendly ones at
least. They say it's an important book because it helped change
the climate within which educational issues were discussed. And I
think that's true, probably I think at the level of testing
techniques it has nothing much to offer. It is only really
interesting at the level of the broad conceptual preoccupations it
expressed.

*But isn't that precisely why many psychologists resist your kind of
approach? It is broad and conceptual rather than a new set of
experimental results.*
Yes, I think that's probably true. Although almost all of the stuff I
do has a data base, and some of it is very cut-and-dried. For
instance the work on dream recall. That is precise work. It's a tight
piece of design, and one of the nicest things to flow out of *Contrary
Imaginations*. It worked beautifully, everything according to
prediction. I find that if you want to think at all adventurously,
you've got to be more fussy about your data base, not less.
Whereas if you're impersonating a physical scientist, people feel
safe with you, and they'll swallow almost anything you offer at
the level of research technique, however sloppy.

Liam Hudson

Has that dream work been taken any farther than the Occasional Paper you published?
No, that's as far as it's gone, but there is another project on dream content that's coming along in an exploratory way.

Jouvet has been studying his own dreams, you know, and he's found that quite often he cannot remember what a person is saying when he can recognise the person and, on the other hand, when he can get precisely what a person is saying he can't recognise them. There seems to be a sort of physiological repression as he sees it, because there is no contact between the left and right hemisphere in dreaming in, at least, the cat.
Yes, very interesting . . . my efforts to read and write feel rather like that. Whilst on laterality, could I mention another important influence on my life?

Of course.
Oliver Zangwill. He is the kind of person who leaves you alone to get on with your own thing. He produces surreptitious support, and once every eighteen months or so, very surreptitiously, gives you an extraordinarily good idea. And I have had, I think, five absolutely stunningly good ideas from him which he's subsequently disowned. Really marvellous ideas. And I've also had from him the sense of complete freedom from modishness that he conveys. You know he does not do modish research, and he's not taken up with saying all the OK things at conferences. He makes a report on two cases he's looked at, or five cases he's looked at, and if he's not sure that the interpretation is sound, he says so.

And is it your belief that research now is too modish and that psychology should begin to attack problems that are often not attempted, perhaps because they are felt to be too complicated, beyond the range of what can be done now?
Very much so. We should get back to the approach to psychology – to be catholic – that Galton had, that Rivers had, that Binet had, that Freud had. Looking at people. Be as orderly as you know how, get orderly data, argue in an orderly way, interpret it in an orderly way. But do not feel you are doing a quasi-physical science.

Is the model of the physical sciences one that has been . . .
It's been disastrous.

157

Liam Hudson

Why did it gain so much weight among psychologists?
It's a case of academic insecurity. I think they've had a desperate
need for any habit of mind, any frame of reference, which makes
them seem academically respectable.

So that its value is that it makes them look scientific?
And, academically speaking, there's no money in the arts. The big
money is with the physical sciences. In terms of politics, that's the
bandwagon you want to ride.

What fields do you think psychologists should be looking at?
I think we should be looking at the way people think, and the way
in which they run their personal lives. Quite simply, I think we
should look at what matters to people in life, and illuminate that.
And, eventually, help refine it too. That seems to me precisely
what the founding fathers like William James were writing about.
We've slipped away, and I think we should get back to it. In that
sense, my position is a conservative one - positively reactionary, in
fact.

*Would you object to a study of, say, ten or twelve people which
was almost like a series of long interviews?*
I'd say the sample was rather large but, otherwise, excellent.

*Why do you think there is so much objection to doing that sort of
work?*
It's this preoccupation with looking like science - failing to realise
that most of science has been based on the particular study of the
particular. Really revolutionary science, that is. And the most
influential psychology has been based on tiny samples - like Freud
and Piaget. Skinner himself uses tiny numbers. I would like us to
go back to the idea of building up our samples from individual
studies, one at a time - to understanding the integration of forces
within each individual life, because what can be said about large
numbers of people, considered as a whole, is usually rather trivial.

*So the most interesting things are those we can tease out of the
individual?*
There are bound to be principles of organisation that make us
seem so variegated. It's not random at all. But you won't find
these principles by looking at a hundred people and seeing what
they have in common.

Liam Hudson

What are the processes of integration?
That's what we don't yet know. We're trying to find out.

In your work, are you trying to integrate the evidence from Kagan on impulsivity, and from Witkin on field independence? They seem to be touching something like divergence, a construct, something in common to all three concepts?
Yes, I would quite like to attempt an integration of that sort, although not at the statistical level, because what happens when you try to integrate personality dimensions statistically is that you find they go together – sort of. [He laughs.] You have correlations of the order of 0.4 between five measures of personality. Well, so what? It seems to me that you have to produce an integration of a conceptual kind rather than a statistical kind. You have to think of a series of lawful relationships that could exist between those variables – that they are alternative reactions, say, to the same basic stress. But working out the intercorrelations won't lead you to that. You will have to look at lives one at a time and see how these cognate variables lock together to form a coherent pattern. No one is going to be consistent, we know that. But what are the laws covering the consistent inconsistencies?

Can you see anyone attempting that?
I have been thinking in a general way about the concepts of boundary maintenance and the management of impulse. That's the sort of language one wants to use. But that's at a very general level. If you try to knit together impulsivity with divergence and field dependence, you have got to argue in considerable detail, and that we can't yet do.

Do you think that kind of detail possible?
Yes, of course, it'll happen.

Has anyone done the crucial test of giving all the tests to one group and seeing how they do?
We've just done it in Edinburgh and Sam Messick has done it at ETS, but what do you do with the results? What our bloke did was to intercorrelate. Well, you know, you stare at the intercorrelations and you don't know what to say about them. What Messick is going to do is an analysis of variance, I think. But what do you do with that? It doesn't tell you much.

159

Couldn't you do individual profiles?
Of course you can. But then you have to find some sort of model
which would help you to make sense of them. That means you
have to think, and people are unwilling to do that. We've got to
the position where you do an experiment and, somehow, the
statistics are expected to look after themselves. [He laughs.] Yet
it's at that point – after the experiment and before the
analysis – that you have to start thinking really hard. Terribly
difficult, you see.

*Presumably, you will never get such neat intercorrelations that
everyone who does well on Task A does badly on B?*
Never, it's never like that. The porridge is what makes it
interesting. We know it's a porridge by just looking round the
world. People don't run true to type.

*And, after staring at them lengthily, what did the intercorrelations
in the Edinburgh study show?*
Nothing. That's it. Nothing. In fact, the various dimensions don't
go together very strongly. They do a bit. So what? That doesn't
tell you anything much.

*The last time we talked, you said you were hoping to work on
developing a more global theory of personality? Has that come
together?*
Yes, it has. In the book I'm just finishing, I've gathered together
material from all over the place, and I'm trying to get it into a
reasonably coherent shape. And running through it there are
some interpretative threads that I think are substantially right.
These are the ideas about boundary states and the management of
impulse. They are powerful ideas at the interpretative stage of an
argument, but in detailed application they're still vague.

Could you indicate what some of these ideas are?
Would you let me hedge? I find it almost impossible to talk about
schemes like these until they're sorted out on paper, safely in a
book. Broadly it's a balancing act – a sort of synthesis. I've tried
to stitch three sorts of psychological argument together into a
lump. Argument about evidence and inference. What it is for one
person to make sense of the life of another. Also the
techniques – the knacks of actually doing research. Argument

160

about what people themselves are like. How they grow up, and the kinds of people they are. How they are. How they get on together. And argument about the conceptual implications, the philosophy. Freedom and determinism, concepts like identity and authenticity, and the whole business of the tension between freedom and discipline, and what flows from that tension. There's a lot of art in an effort like that, because you've got to balance all sorts of materials against each other. It's an error not to theorise and it's an error to theorise too explicitly, in case you squeeze the life out of what you're trying to say. Perhaps it's quaint to say so, but ideas do seem to have an interior life rather in the way that people do. If you discipline them too tightly or too soon they're not worth knowing.

Do you think it would be interesting to take people who were normal, apparently very normal?
Very much so. Why not? I think too much of psychology is based on people who are freaks.

Is it hard to get funds to study ordinary people?
Almost impossible to get large sums for detailed work. You know, you can study a hundred thousand normal citizens on a wretched questionnaire for some government agency. But if you say that you want to find out something by looking at people one at a time, you have great difficulties. So what you have to do, which is very sordid, is to say the first and do the second. [He laughs.] One's led to do it all the time.

Have there been any studies along these individualistic lines you've been describing?
Outside psychoanalytic circles, no, not many.

But there have always been said to be very big problems with this kind of study?
I think the big methodological problems lie in the interpretation of large samples. It's such a hazardous process and saying anything, especially about correlations, and correlational data, is very risky because when you've calculated correlations you really have no idea, psychologically speaking, of what you have at the other end. Say you have a network of intercorrelations – it doesn't follow in the least that these relationships are relevant to the life

of any particular individual. The absence of a correlation, likewise, doesn't mean that the variables don't interact within a life.

And presumably, given large samples, you are likely to get some correlations?

Yes, and it's become so sophisticated. Now it's not factor analysis but cluster analysis. You feel you're part of science and you're doing your bit. You know, it's one of those awful boxes we've climbed into and can't climb out of again. There's no need to climb into complex statistical analysis, except that you get money for it. Money can be got for any crazy thing using statistics at the moment.

You're obviously very harsh about the over-use of statistics. Do you feel there is anything useful at all that can be got from statistical, correlational data?

Yes, certainly. I do a lot of head-counting myself and enjoy it. Often there's a problem, or a part of a problem, that you can get at with a sample. My worry is really about the seductive power of statistics. They're a delight to do, but they lull you into the crassest assumptions. If you keep them humble, and you're wholly in charge of them, numbers can be quite useful. God help you, though, when you get into the hands of someone who likes playing number games he doesn't quite understand. You end up with a pile of print-out and nothing to show. Or rather, something on which you can place no intellectually honest interpretation.

And why is the attitude of grant-givers so blindly in favour of the statistical approach?

I don't know. I think it's a form of fear. If you don't concern yourself with the glamour of computing, you have to think what the research is about. That's harder, and people prefer to avoid it.

Do you feel that psychology should be useful, if I can move on a bit?

No, I think it should be – I don't know how you avoid the word – relevant. I think it ought to be relevant to people. It should bear on those aspects of life that perfectly ordinary people see as important. I think it should tell us something about our lives, and clarify them.

Is that why you got involved in the race controversy?
No, I got caught up in that completely by accident, actually. I've
always been touchy about class discrimination, very touchy, and
that generalised to racial discrimination. I'm very touchy about
that, too. Anyway, how did I get involved? Oh yes, I'd been
reading Jensen's piece about racial differences in IQ, and picked
up the Money reference about Turner's Syndrome, which I
thought was jolly interesting. And I had one of those moments
you have every ten years, when you go back to a source and you
find it's been misrepresented. Drastically and systematically
misrepresented. It's intriguing, the whole process of unwitting
misrepresentation. And also, at the same time, I felt a very
considerable irritation towards Jensen himself. He is, I think,
exactly the kind of person who shouldn't be in that kind of
research, someone without the necessary capability. Very
dangerous indeed.

*He did present himself as something of a martyr to the left in his
subsequent book.*
Oh that's nonsense. He strings the references together, but he
doesn't understand the logical implications, nor the ideological
implications either. Some people in that field are intellectually
competent, but it attracts a lot of fools too, it really does.

What is your position on the race issue now?
Well, the research is irrelevant to the problems. I don't think any
of the research that's been done at the moment tells us how better
to educate blacks or whites. I don't think it tells us anything about
the allocation of resources to educating blacks or whites. I don't
think it tells us anything about the impact of racial prejudice in
society at large. The research we have just does not bear on these
issues. I'm not talking about dramatic impact, I'm trying to speak
about logic. If you demonstrate that blacks are worse at every
conceivable test under the sun than whites, it seems to me you've
learned nothing about what to do. Very useful for racial
propaganda but otherwise useless. And to demonstrate that it's
genetically determined is . . . well, the whole heritability research
is misconceived.

Why's that?
Because the people doing it seem unable to grasp that fiddling

around with heritability equations is going to tell you nothing about whether you can teach black children more than you now teach them. To say that intelligence is inherited is to say nothing about what shapes the expression of that intelligence can take.

If I can move on more to how you do your work rather than what it is. Do you use hunches and intuition in your research?
Yes. Very much. Often vicarious hunches. The stuff about sleep and dreaming Oliver Zangwill put me on to. The idea of looking at old demographic data like *Who's Who* is another of Oliver Zangwill's ideas too. But interpreting that has been a very intuitive business too. I think one plays one's hunches all the time. If you have any intelligence you do – they're better than one's literal-minded reasoning, as a source of good ideas anyway.

When you start a research project, do you make your mind especially receptive to hunches?
No, I sit around bored or irritated until something hits me – frustrated, fed up with the research you've been doing, fed up with the techniques or people you've been doing it with, and then something strikes you. Usually a conversation starts it or someone new you meet. It doesn't have to be much, just a detail that sets you going.

How important is it to have a mastery of technique to convert these hunches into experiments or experimental situations?
It's vital. For me. Because all the work I do that I like depends on the crystallising of hunches. I'll have a hunch, a luminous hunch, and find a way of exploring it that's orderly and systematic.

How does that part, getting an orderly way of exploring it, work?
I think that, at that point, one draws very much on those first five dreary years when you pick up a lot of skills that in themselves are really quite dead. But they do sharpen you up. Fretting about, oh, what the fallacies of factor analysis are. I know what they are. I can deploy them for myself. So I find that burdensome training useful after all.

So the notion that you can be a psychologist simply through your ideas doesn't hold? Ideas are not enough?
Oh, I think it can hold, actually. I was watching the molecular

biologists on the tele last night, Crick and Watson. Two tremendously bright people who walked in at the door and said, 'What's this?' Basically, they took other people's results, and they rattled them together. You could do the same in psychology. So easily. But I think the aesthetic satisfaction of doing that would be rather different. The translation of an intuition into some quite tight form – that's the part of psychology that's so aesthetically satisfactory.

So there are two steps. The initial satisfaction of saying, 'Well, maybe this is the case,' and then working out a tight way to test it?
You have a hunch and then you find a way of operationalising it. Then you have all the scaffolding – tests, tapes, histograms and so on. I don't think there's much elegance about it, just comforting hard work. Yet it's oddly necessary, aesthetically, because without it the next stage always seems to fall flat. It's the detailed structure of the evidence that forces you on to new ground, imaginatively. Without it, you relapse all the time into platitude. Then, once again there's the excitement of translating back from the literal facts into interpretative prose. Illuminating, intuitive prose. That again is the exciting part.

At that stage do you again in some way make yourself receptive to ideas or allow your imagination free rein? I find, often, that when I write something it becomes more than I started out with.
I rewrite absolutely everything. I do, in practice, at least nine or ten drafts. The first things I do are always ridiculous. They don't come to life until I redraft them many times. For instance, I've just written what I think will be an eighty thousand word book, and I will have written well over a million words to get that. There's something immensely punishing about the process. But in it there's the subtle gratification that, a very long long way down the path, you're back in the land of the luminous ideas where you began. You're back, but your ideas have a shape, and you're in less of a daze.

Do you know when that is happening?
You can feel it. It's gorgeous. A lovely feeling.

As you move on to write new books, do you feel quite dissociated from your earlier books?
Oh no. I forget what's in them, but I'm not dissociated from them.

Every now and again I flip through looking for a reference or an idea, and I find a joke I like. Even a bit of purple prose that I like too. There are one or two parts I feel quite proud to have written, actually quite pleased. And surprised. In any case, the main line of my work has followed the one path, with only the occasional deviations. It's not as though I have skipped from one topic to another. Lively books and more plodding books seem to alternate, I've noticed that. *Contrary Imaginations* was quite sprightly, *Frames of Mind* was a bit plodding. *The Cult* was lively, and now this one is a bit of a worthy plod, too.

Because you run a department, is your way of doing research less personal now? You mentioned that the dream research was done by someone else.

Yes. I had a very privileged life in Cambridge in the sense that I had nothing to do except research. And I loved it. Now I spend a lot of my time organising the research work of other people and that's much less gratifying. Most people don't actually enjoy research. They do it because it's a living or part of a career. So there are times when you deal with people who are rather miserable. And a lot of people, even people who are highly intelligent, can be terribly stupid about research. And there are all those sad research projects that just don't work.

Do you have to spend much of your time getting the money for other people's research?

I've spent quite a lot of my time doing that. I quite enjoy it.

Do you feel it cuts you off from the chance of doing the research you want to do?

I wouldn't do it if I thought it did that. Very recently, I started to climb out of a rut because I realised I was doing research that civil servants or grant-givers or people on committees thought was worth doing. They give you enormous sums of money to do something they think is worthwhile. And because one likes the money or the prestige or the posts, you do it. And it's a waste of time because good research follows from much more private intuition. A large number of people pick up the idea of what a respectable piece of research looks like from the literature, from journals, and then try to produce something that looks like a journal article. I think David McClelland is right. They are scared of taking any risk, making any judgment, saying that it's this way or that, imposing themselves on the situation in any way. And that makes for terrible research. Inductive research. Some of my most sophisticated young sociologists and anthropologists fall into this. They are so worried at the thought of making pre-emptive judgments that they end up, often, mindlessly recording everything in sight, and hoping that some telling conclusion will emerge of its own accord. It doesn't, and they're landed with the same platitudes that they had when they began.

When a piece of research goes well, your own research, what kind of pleasure do you get out of it?
Some of the most exciting times I've ever had, I think, have been when a pattern falls out of a tightly wrought set of results. I remember once getting a result I've never really quite understood. But it came out with incredible clarity. I remember sitting in my room in Cambridge struggling with the data – and I realised, suddenly, I had a pattern. It was a very paradoxical one, but quite consistent. I rang up eight people in a row to tell them. [He laughs.] In the end I was so excited I rang the same person twice. Oh tremendous, tremendous pleasure.

Is it also an aesthetic pleasure?
Oh yes, almost wholly aesthetic. There's the excitement and a sense of relief that there is order after all. It isn't all porridge. It's a wonderful feeling. Can I say a bit more about that?
In my days as a full-time research person I used to spend seventy to eighty days analysing and writing up for every day I collected evidence. And I'm convinced that I spent far too much time collecting evidence and not enough time analysing, not enough thinking. It seems to me you can't be a good psychologist unless you spend a great deal of time thinking and writing. Writing is when you come to roost. Anyone who simply scratches out their results and cobbles up a story is, I think, selling themselves short. It seems to me that it is in the process of writing about psychology, when you actually have your finger on the typewriter, that the action really begins.

But doesn't it have dangers? As you write, you may bias your conclusion, putting too much emphasis on one thing or . . .
Can't see how it can be any other way. It's all to do with

167

imaginative interpretation and recreation. That's what psychology
is about.

*But isn't that precisely where someone like Broadbent takes issue
with you?*
No, he does exactly the same himself. Massive selection of
evidence, massive . . . it's an imaginative achievement. The whole
business of the promotion of cybernetic imagery is an imaginative
feat just like writing a novel. When psychology hasn't passed
through this imaginative phase, it's bad psychology, and it's not
worth doing.

*Are you optimistic now about the way psychology will develop in
the next ten years, do you see the kind of views you're advocating
establishing themselves?*
I think there are signs. There are large numbers of people looking
round at the moment at the absurd things that have been done,
and are being done. I think the ground does begin to shift, and we
may well be less smug over the next ten years. But we will not do
anything unless we can evolve a good paradigm of research. We do
need to develop better styles of research. I think we shall get back
to doing detailed work on individuals, not as the exclusive way of
doing research, but as a good way.

*And work by interviewing someone, by talking and giving them
tests, also?*
Why not? There's nothing wrong with talk.

*I have noticed, of course, among the psychologists I've spoken to,
very great differences in approach. Sometimes you might find it hard
to believe they are involved in the same discipline.*
No, you barely would. In fact, candidly, they often aren't. The
latent metaphorical systems are different, the language is different,
all the assumptions are different, and what counts as a decent
piece of research is different. If you haven't got any of those
criteria in common, you're not in the same subject and it seems to
me you haven't got any one subject, you've got lots. And,
certainly, they don't have the same conceptual apparatus – they
don't use the same system of ideas.

168

And does that leave you at all optimistic?
Five or six years ago, I thought the whole thing was hopeless. I
think now that the psychology being done in most academic
departments is so manifestly unproductive, even in its own terms,
that some shift is bound to occur.

7
Michel Jouvet

The buildings of the Faculty of Medicine of the University of Lyon are sombre, impressive and old. Inside, they remind one of a cavernous railway station where people bustle, like desperate Kafkaesque characters in perpetual search of the platforms. You walk through wide corridors: you hear the echo of your own, and others', footsteps. The walls are going brown. You go past small doors on which someone, long ago to judge by the graphics, printed headings like Musée d'Anatomie or Histochimie. A smell of specimens, preserved in their proper fluids, pervades the place. A map is supposed to direct you to all the departments but there are too many corridors and staircases and doors.

It all seems a proper setting for a French professor. The buildings encouraged me to think I was in for having my stereotype confirmed. But one staircase up, the whole atmosphere changes. Modern lettering tells one this is the department of experimental medicine which is headed by Professor Michel Jouvet. There is a bright carpet, on the walls there are bright posters showing off flowers, animals and even a nude. The transition from the gloom of the corridors seems quite dramatic.

Jouvet himself is in his forties. He is rather elegant and he enjoys a certain worldly air. The last time we met he told me he had been delighted with his latest trip to the East which had included crossing Java by train. He smokes Havana cigars when he can and, as often as possible, cigars from Davidoff. He likes good food, fittingly enough for a Frenchman. But he also takes delight in irony and humour, qualities which he attributes in flattering excess to the British. He enjoys a cutting remark. He told me that he had caused consternation among American colleagues because he told them he had never written a book. He even can turn such ironies against himself. He became a professor young, he points out, by French standards, only because of a timely death. There is also, in Jouvet, a certain love of the exotic. On his desk there is a rather macabre sculpture of stuffed animals, a snake in the jaws of a lizard. The exotic strain in Jouvet is not something he talks much about but it seems connected with a certain intensity he feels, especially about doing research.

In 1900, Freud wrote to his friend Fliess that he wondered if future generations would set up a plaque at his country house, Belle Vue. To spare future generations the effort, Freud wrote the inscription he would deem fit. 'Here, in 1895, the secret of dreams was revealed to Dr Sigmund Freud,' he suggested. Jouvet is no Freudian and emphasises that he has never seen any way of testing Freud's ideas. He has, however, found, if not the secret, at least the neurophysiological origin of dreams in the brain. In a series of experiments from 1956 on, he localised the critical structures in the brain stem that triggered sleep and dreaming. It was this work that caused him to become a professor so early. Jouvet is continuing this work because he is now trying to wrest the secret of dreams. He would not put it so grandly though.

After the war, Jouvet studied in Lyon to become a doctor. There was nowhere else available, he explained, and Lyon had a good medical school. He specialised in surgery and worked for a while as a neurosurgeon. He adds that it was a good thing he had surgical skills since this enabled him to operate on the animals he was using in his experiments. He then went to study at the University of Southern California in Los Angeles under Magoun. Magoun was an ardent advocate of reticularism, the doctrine that it is from reticular formation in the brain stem that most brain activity arises. As Jouvet explains in the interview, when he returned to France he wanted to test Magoun's claims against those of Pavlov who maintained that it was the cortex that was responsible for all brain activity. With primitive equipment only, Jouvet decided to work on habituation. He decided to see if a cat, with its cortex removed, could habituate. If it did, Pavlov would be wrong and Magoun would be right. It seemed splendidly elegant and simple. It turned out to be much less simple. He never solved the puzzle, as he explains in the interview, since he stumbled on to something quite different.

The way in which he seems to have started work on dreaming is a curious accident. It highlights, again, the extent to which accidents seem to guide careers in psychology. One of the cats whose cortex

Jouvet had removed displayed very peculiar and contradictory signs. To look at, it seemed fast asleep. It was hard to wake. There was no muscle tone in its muscles. But the recording of electrical activity from the brain of this cat which appeared to be in deep sleep showed the animal to be alert, awake and active. It was this phenomenon Jouvet christened 'paradoxical sleep'. 'I did not know then what I was looking at', he points out. But he was sure it was important. Habituation was forgotten for the moment. For the next twenty years that observation that he stumbled on by accident determined what his work was to be.

In Jouvet's case, this is especially ironical since he admits to a certain intensity about being a scientist. 'After all,' he confesses, 'when you invest most of your life in these problems, it becomes very important.' He speaks of this rather withdrawn *vie intérieure* of the scientist or, at any rate, of himself. (I am not sure if 'inner life' is really an adequate translation.) There is something almost spiritual about dedicating oneself so wholeheartedly to the study of something one fell into by chance.

One of the beliefs Jouvet is intense about is that it will be the methods of neurophysiology that will enable us to understand the mind and dreaming. He is at pains to emphasise that he is an experimental neurophysiologist, not a psychologist. He does wonder sometimes why it is that he has been working most of his life on a very psychological problem and, now, that his research has been taking an even more psychological twist. But, as Jouvet confesses, he did not become a physiologist in order to work on the mechanisms by which small cellular organisms manage to live. Interesting as these problems are, he went into neurophysiology to study the brain. He taps his own head and says 'this', with a smile. And, as a neurophysiologist, he is committed to a belief in working experimentally and in making your data public. In a way very different from introspective psychologists, he regrets this. There is, he explained, a peculiar thrill of pleasure in making a discovery and owning it. It is yours. The moment that you publish it, it becomes part of the public domain. You can look back and think that it was yours and, of course, you have some of the credit for it. But that peculiar intimacy between you and the fact no one else knew, the fact that you have established, has gone. This is less true, of course, he smiles, of routine experiments in which you tot up another new technique or another extension of a well-established principle. This work is necessary and important, he stresses. But it's not the same.

And it is now, through the methods of experimental neurophysiology, that Jouvet is trying to work out the secret of dreams. In the interview, he explains his theory at some length and he is careful to point out that it is only a theory at the moment. He has not proved it, though he has made certain observations which seem to him to be very much in its favour.

Although he is a passionate believer in the methods of experimental neurophysiology, Jouvet is afraid of their success. Earlier, he told me he believed that the explanation of why both men and, as he has discovered, animals, dream is one of the last great problems of neurophysiology. We have had an explosion of knowledge in the last fifty years and it may be that we are approaching the actual limits that our knowledge will have. There may be limits, as Chomsky indicated, to what we can comprehend, given our brain structure: Jouvet intends a different limit, I think. Neurophysiology will actually have solved all the major problems it faced. There will be refinements. There will be biochemical work to be done, but neurophysiology will be, grand as it sounds, at an end.

That implies, Jouvet believes, that neurophysiology will be able to offer authorities the means of controlling people. Jouvet argues, in the interview, that animals and men dream in order to retain the personality that they have. In your dreams, your genetic code is replaying itself. The details of Jouvet's position I leave to the interview. But if a person is deprived of dreaming as he can be now by drugs, it may change his personality. Especially, Jouvet believes it will make him more susceptible to conditioning. He cites evidence from mental hospitals where therapy does involve the use of drugs which prevent dreaming. Patients become much more pliable, much more malleable: in the terms of their institution, they become much 'better'. Jouvet sees this as a great and serious danger. He argues that some of his fellow scientists have shown a curious disregard for patients and have, under the cover of science, removed chunks of their brains to 'improve' or 'cure' them. If such an inhuman approach is practised by doctors, it makes him fear the progress of the science which he himself is furthering.

One way in which Jouvet has become conscious of his own motivations and beliefs has been in his attitude to the animals he himself experiments on. He took me into his laboratory and showed me the litters of cats that he would be using and that he would, therefore, be killing in his next set of experiments. He played with them, fondled them and said, 'They're pleasant, aren't they?'

173

Nevertheless, Jouvet told me, he had become infinitely less willing to sacrifice cats or work with monkeys which he knew he would have to kill. He felt a certain respect that had grown on him for all these beasts that dreamed. It was not such a matter of course to slaughter them in the interests of furthering knowledge.

And, equally paradoxical for a man committed to very strong faith in the conventional scientific methods of neurophysiology, Jouvet told me that he had been studying his own dreams. He found himself awakened one night by such strange dreams that he wrote them down. He has now got into the habit of doing so and he has amassed a 'bank' of dreams on which he does some statistical studies. He was a little reluctant, I thought at first, to speak about this work but, though he then expanded on it, he stressed that it would be quite wrong to see this as his major interest or a denial of those physiological methods which had been so fruitful for him. In a way, of course, the fact that he has felt it worthwhile or, perhaps, even been impelled to use introspection to study his own dreams shows the fascination of dreams very clearly. But he resists the idea that this study has enabled him to come to terms with his own personality or that it might allow the development of his own personality. He is not analysing his dreams but recording them. And the facts that he has noticed about his dreams seem to him to confirm the idea that, in his dreams, it is not the conscious experiences or unconscious that is manifest, or latent, that is so important. What is happening is a replaying of the ge. etic programme that makes each individual what he is. He has recorded a proportion of aggressive dreams, erotic dreams and anxiety dreams of his own and the proportion seems to him to tally with his own very conscious estimate of his own personality. The only way in which he can make use of this knowledge is to avoid, say, circumstances that would tend to call for aggressive behaviour after a night in which, it seems to him, he has had aggressive dreams which primed the aggression in his own personality. But he says one can only speak a little vaguely of such things.

His use of introspection in the service of experimental neurophysiology has enabled him, he thinks, to make an observation which goes very much against psychoanalysis. Freud talked at length about the concept of repression. Jouvet cites evidence that, in the cat, there is no connection between the left and the right hemisphere of the brain when they are in paradoxical sleep. Of the usual traffic of messages between the two, there is no evidence. In his own dreams, he has noticed that he will often remember things a person has said in great detail but that, then, he will not be able to remember who has said them. He cannot identify the person. Similarly, he can sometimes see very clearly the person who is speaking, while he cannot specify what they say. In the interview, he gives examples of this. For Jouvet, there is a neurophysiological explanation. He points out that the left hemisphere is responsible for language while the right is responsible for recognition of faces. If the two hemispheres do not connect in dreams or paradoxical sleep, it is not surprising that he can only either understand the words or recognise the faces. In his terms, he has used a mixture of introspection and neurophysiology to explain away the Freudian concept of repression.

I am not sure this is the only way one can take this. It could easily be argued that he has given an explanation at a different level, a neurophysiological level of the concept. One must also recall that there are many dreams – as Jouvet concedes – in which one remembers both the speech and the face, and which therefore do not show this one-sided memory. To me, it seems as much a sign of the different languages which different psychologists will use as of an explanation that refutes one version. One should recall, here, the work in Hudson's laboratory that claims to have shown, also experimentally, repression in the Freudian sense.

In Jouvet's office, there is a sign that says no more interviews, no more symposia, no more conferences. He has felt all the distracting pressures of being a famous scientist. He is invited all over the place. It was fun and flattering, at first. Now, it interferes with his work. There is in France perhaps less of the relentless pressure that American scientists feel. Now he feels the need to carry out the experiments he discusses in the interview which will prove or disprove his theory of dreams. The work of actually administering a department is complex and wearisome. As we walked through, he saw maintenance men fiddling with a deep freeze. 'The less equipment you have,' he pointed out, 'the less it is likely to go wrong.' And while he now has plenty of equipment in his 'labo', as he calls it, he is short of the manpower he needs. He needs to find a PhD student who will take the risk of collaborating on the dreaming and genetic experiments. That is hard to find because it is risky. It is also hard to find because he needs someone who is both a competent technician and has a certain amount of daring. Science is now a career structure in which it pays to play safe. He had just lost an

American student who had worked well on the start of the project but who had had to return to the States. He wanted to do more himself but, for the moment, he had to fly twice weekly up to Paris for the pleasure of helping other scientists to decide how to allocate research funds. It was important and worthy and kept him from his real task. We talked about the need for scientific departments to have administrators, like theatres do, who are not creative scientists themselves. He fretted about the waste of time administration caused.

I suspects he frets a little because in one way he enjoys restlessness. Every time I have talked with him, I think, he has just returned from somewhere. Once it was the USA, which he does not like. Now, it was the Far East which he loves. He had just spent a few weeks in Java and had crossed Java by train. The restlessness contrasts with his secluded, inner life of the scientist. He had just planned a trip to Africa to study the dreams of a tribe where there had been a great deal of cousin marriages – to see if their convoluted heredity expressed itself in dreams.

The last time I saw him, he told me firmly that this was the last interview he was giving. As he walked with me to a cab, put me in it and gave directions so that it would take me to another part of the university all the way across Lyon, it struck me how very friendly of him it was to waste that time walking and seeing me off to my next call. And I suspected that it would in fact be the last interview he gives until he has done the work he muses on in the interview.

What satisfaction do you get out of research?
As I said, when we discovered paradoxical sleep, it was as if one had landed on an island from the ocean. Only slowly one found that it wasn't an island but a continent. At the beginning, all experiments, even simple experiments, yielded golden nuggets. They gave a lot. They were true. They are true. They remain true. There is a lot of joy in that. But now research is less personal. I am like a general. You send troops out to conquer some objective. Some troops get there fast, some not so fast. Sometimes, you think there will be a hold-up and you plan a commando raid to speed things up. But one relies on one's pupils. Now, I have been trying to set up a particular experiment for a while but I have great trouble in finding a PhD student who will take it on. There is a risk that at the end, the experiment will fail and he will have nothing to show for it. The answer may be to hand over the

administration of the laboratory to someone else for six months.
It may be to refuse to attend symposia. At first, it's very flattering
to be invited to all these symposia and you go automatically. But
you should stop going. But it's not easy, just as it isn't easy to
hand over the administration of the laboratory. It's a strange fact
that the more successful a laboratory is, the more there is to
prevent you doing work.

Do you get pleasure from the research of your students?
Naturally, one gets great pleasure if the research of students goes
well. But it's not the same. At the beginning, you see, every result
was major, golden. Now it has become more difficult to get such
golden results. But there is the fact that you get a less major piece
of research that goes well and that is very satisfying.

Why do you think you find that pleasure in research?
It gives me satisfaction, I suppose, because I am programmed to be
curious. Many scientists have showed the importance of curiosity
as a drive in animals and in children. Rats will learn mazes in order
to be allowed to explore a new environment. I am curious and
then, without being pretentious about it, there is a certain pleasure
in making a challenge to the unknown. If you don't know whether
the answer to your question will be found in two years or twenty
years, that is exciting. As I think I mentioned before, much of the
life of a scientist is an inner life. It has to be. You devote
ninety-nine per cent of your life to it. You invest so much in it.
There is bound to be great satisfaction when you discover
something because it is true and it stays true. And, equally, there
is great frustration if it does not work out.

*Is it important to work in a field in which one can make
discoveries?*
The brain undoubtedly is that area of biology where there is most
still to be discovered. If I had a son I would hope he would go
into that field. Compare it with the study of muscles. There,
you can see already what the answers are likely to be. That is not so
with the brain.

*Did you foresee what the answers would be when you started
looking at the reticular formation?*
No, we were looking at this problem I outlined of whether it was

Pavlov or Magoun who was right. Then we came upon paradoxical sleep. We were not the first to see it. It had been seen by a German in 1938 but that had led to nothing. We seemed to be seeing a third state of the nervous system that was neither awake nor asleep. And we then dropped the other question and forged ahead with that.

How did you come to be interested in the problem of dreaming?
I believe I came to it in two stages. Two stages because when I wanted to do neurophysiology, it was not my goal to study the frog's muscle potential, or the lobster, but to study higher nervous functions. So, I was very naive as a medical student and my head was full of Pavlovian ideas. But I realised that the classical conditioning method of Pavlov explained some learning only, and that you had to try and approach problems with more modern methods. I went to the USA to study neurophysiology very seriously and I went to what was at the time considered one of the best departments of neurophysiology, that of Magoun. They had discovered the importance of the reticular activating system of the brain stem. And, as is obligatory in such schools, the balance had tilted so that everything seemed to come from the brain stem. I was in at the golden age of 'reticularism' where the reticular system was the *deus ex machina* of the brain and it seemed to explain everything – wakefulness, transactional mechanisms like learning and so on. And, since it explained wakefulness, it also explained sleep, since at that time sleep was considered the negative part of wakefulness. I learned that the reticular formation was a microcosm which received all information from outside the brain and all information from inside the brain and could mix them. It was, a little bit, the cortex of the cortex.

And what work did this lead you into?
When I came back to Lyon in 1956, I found myself with the following dilemma – either Pavlov is right and it is not the reticular system that makes everything go but the cortex, or Magoun is right and Pavlov has embellished nonsense. I tried to test with a simple experiment which one was right, East or West. It had to be a simple experiment because I had few resources. I had an old EEG machine. The experiment had to be both conceptually simple and practically simple. As I had training as a neurosurgeon and I could operate on animals, I thought that I would choose

what I then thought to be simplest form of learning – habituation.
As you may know, habituation is simple but, even now, it is not
totally explained. And I said to myself, I am going to study
the habituation of the aroused reaction. According to Pavlov,
habituation depended on the cortex so if you could
get habituation of arousal in an animal without a cortex, Pavlov's
theory would be wrong. Indubitably, one would have to admit
this. I thought the experiment should be very simple to perform,
therefore. If, without a cortex, the animal could habituate, then
we would have to admit that the brain stem and the reticular
activating system were capable of the transactional operations we
talked of. If, on the other hand, the animal without a cortex did
not habituate, Pavlov would be right and it would have gone his
way. The principle was simple enough. But when we tried to do
the experiment, things got more complicated, as, in fact, they
always do. If the problem seemed well posed, it was, in fact, much
more complex. We first took out the cortex in the cat and we
noticed, leaving electrodes in the brain, that we could no longer
record the EEG criteria for sleep or for wakefulness. I had lost my
objective, experimental criterion since it was the cortex which
makes the cerebral activity that shows the animal is asleep or
awake. That intrigued me. I looked for the literature on that. Few
people had de-corticated animals with electrical EEG recording
from sub-cortical structures. This made me think Pavlov was right
when he said that sleep was due to some inhibition descending
from the cortex. I thought that myself, since I had shown that
when I took out the cortex, the animal displayed no electrical
signs of sleep. And that was despite the fact I had decided that
Magoun was right. I had my doubts but I found before me the
problem that faces every experimenter. The cat, even though it
had no electrical activity, no muscle tonus, no cortical sign of
sleep, slept in behavioural terms. I was schizophrenic, with a
dissociation between what I saw graphically on the EEG record
and what I saw in behavioural terms.

What did you do to try and resolve this?
In trying to find out in the brain stem other criteria for sleep, we
put electrodes a bit everywhere and put also *au hasard* electrodes
in the muscles. It was then that we came upon the new
phenomenon. Every twenty minutes, the de-corticated cat, or even
the pentile cat from which we had removed all the brain in front

179

of the pons – presented periods of total muscular silence with
general atonie of the muscles, lack of tone. At the same time, we
could record a very peculiar electrical activity from the pons. It
presented a new problem – paradoxical sleep.

*And did you then abandon the question of whether Pavlov or
Magoun was right?*
Yes, the idea of looking between Pavlov and Magoun to see which
was right came second and we fell to examining this new
phenomenon which seemed to us to be a third state of the central
nervous system. I did this work with François Michel. It was in
going back to the literature that we saw this state must be
dreaming. Even if it had been interpreted differently as a light
sleep, we found again and again certain criteria of a deepest stage
of sleep. Suddenly, in 1959, we got objective criteria to work out
dreaming in the animal and, by luck, we knew this was unleashed
in the brain stem. By a bit more luck, we were able to locate it in
the pons. So, *au hasard*, we were in a new continent and we knew
it was a very large one since it was dreaming and we knew that it
was possible to explore it neurophysiologically.

*You have often used that phrase 'au hasard' (or randomly). Was it
just luck that made you put the electrodes in the muscles?*
Oh completely by luck. We said to ourselves that we can see
nothing electrically in the brain. When we wake this cat, it will
move its head so we should see something by putting electrodes in
its neck muscles. We could easily have put them in other muscles
and the experiment could have gone less well. But when you
put electrodes in a cat's muscles, the nearest muscles are the neck
muscles. It was just a matter of commodity. Also, I think there is
the idea which is unconscious in all of us that the neck muscles are
very important. If you ask people which muscles are most
important, if you were going to have all your muscles bar one set
cut, you would probably ask to be left with the neck muscles.

A pretty macabre choice?
Yes, but if you had to make the choice, if you were being put in
Chinese torture.

*So, you established the existence of paradoxical sleep and left the
problems of habituation behind you?*
Yes, we abandoned the habituation experiment. I'm still interested

in it but the habituation problem is now more complex as it has been shown that these very primitive animals – aplysia – who have no cortex or reticular system can be habituated even though they only have very few neurons. I don't regret not having followed this problem because I don't have the training to waddle and wander in problems of potassium and sodium and potentials at these levels of memory among receptors. Nevertheless, when we can explain habituation very well, we shall have taken a major step forward. We spend much of our time getting used to things. (In French, the word is 'à s'habituer' which shows better how closely linked the ideas are.)

But will the way in which an organism with three neurons habituates really throw much light on the way people do? The different scale of complexity is rather fantastic.

Yes, but you argue by reducing, which I have also done, from paradoxical sleep. Now, take the human situation. You live next to a station. On the first night, you will wake for every train. After eight days, you won't hear them, though if your child is asleep and he cries you will hear that noise even though the actual decibels are far fewer. You'll wake. It's a phenomenon that is very simple but also extraordinarily complicated. It supposes that some of your auditory nerve cells recognise the train noise and send a signal not to bother to wake up or the cortex sends to the waking system the same signal – it's not worthwhile bothering. It's a complex schema, but if you want to explain it more logically, more tightly, you have to seek a mechanism, a model that is simpler. As a simple model, I chose the de-corticated cat but it wasn't simple enough. If you can show how a system of a few neurons can habituate, even if that is far from the 'real' phenomenon you are ultimately interested in, it gives a basis on which you can climb back to the more complex.

Have you applied the same principles to your work on dreaming? Going from the cat to Man?

In reality now, the chain that we have established is longer. What holds for the chick seems to hold for the rat. What holds for the rat seems to hold for the cat. What holds for the cat seems to hold for the monkey. And what holds for the monkey seems to hold for Man. I cannot believe that the system in Man is fundamentally different when you establish that long chain. But, for a long time,

Michel Jouvet

ninety per cent of my concern was to sort out the mechanism of
dreaming in the cat. First to show that it was dreaming; I think we
succeeded in that. Then, to work out the neurophysiological
mechanisms and then, to look at what the cat dreams of. The only
essential difference in dreaming between a cat and a man is that
only the man can tell me what he dreams but in this I may claim to
be superior to a psychoanalyst because I can know also what a cat
dreams.

*Which, if it may be said, Freud never tried to do. How did you
manage to do that?*
To know what a cat is dreaming of is, perhaps, best put in quote
marks. Not to upset the psychoanalysts. In paradoxical sleep,
there are two main mechanisms. There is a mechanism that
endogenously excites the brain. According to the theory that I
have formulated, this could be a genetic reprogramming of the
brain - to be what you are as Mr Cohen, so that you are different
from your parents and different from other individuals. There's a
programme that has to be played and replayed, as it were, that
makes you intellectually able, say, which also comes from
education, of course, and a bit extravert and so on. The fact that
you have to programme your neurons, including the motor
neurons and the association neurons, obliges the involvement of a
system of total blockage of motor efference. You may dream you
are flying but the body does not move. There, also by luck, we
managed to destroy this blocking mechanism and it was in this
way that we set up an experiment that allowed us to see what the
cat dreams. It is not an easy experiment to do because it involves
very specific lesions. But, once you have destroyed the neurons
that inhibit most of the motor efference, when the hypothetical
genetic programme is set in action, we shall see it worked out. In
other words, we shall see the cat act out its dreams, perform them.
This is different from sleep-walking, incidentally.

And what does the cat dream of?
What you see in the cat is nearly always aggressive behaviour. Very
stereotyped, extremely monotonous. Certain cats which are very
nice normally become vicious tigers when they are dreaming and
throw themselves at imaginary prey or defend themselves from
imaginary predators. I used to have one in my office which, when
it started dreaming, would terrify people. But, of course, you were

quite safe from it because even though it was only six inches from your leg, it would be busily tearing to pieces some hallucinatory rat it was dreaming of. We had one or two cats that had less aggressive behaviour but which showed feeding behaviour. The few rats in which we managed to carry the operation out also showed a very stereotyped behaviour but in their cases it was flight. And, remember, these animals give every other sign of being deeply asleep, as shown by their pupils.

And the actions seem to you definitely to be an acting out of dreams?
If I can't place a cat on the psychoanalytical couch, I can by neurophysiological means show that what I am studying is the motor expression of dreams. You can always say to me that the cat is a mechanical animal, that the behaviour doesn't show it wants to attack, that it's nothing but a motor system. But if you asked the cat what he's doing, I'm sure he'd say that he's attacking a mouse.

And what do these observations tell you about the function of dreaming?
In predators and cats that have survived through evolution, we see in dreaming innately aggressive behaviour patterns that are perfectly made so that when the cat is faced by prey that system works very well. The experiments that we are now trying to do relate to the hypothesis that in dreaming some genetic reprogramming occurs. We shall take some cats from their mothers at birth and rear them in conditions of total isolation, with very little auditory and visual perception, for a year. We shall see that when these animals are awake they never spontaneously display any aggressive behaviour. That we have shown already in an earlier experiment. But you have to rear the cats for a year because you can only do the lesions that destroy the motor inhibitions when the animal is adult or weighs around two kilos. If when it dreams the cat then shows a perfectly worked out aggressive behaviour, how do you explain it, unless this perfectly aggressive behaviour is part of a genetic programme that is demonstrating itself? This behaviour may not be so well integrated in an animal that has had no practice at killing a few things, because, evidently, there is some interaction between what is genetically coded and what is learned.

183

Michel Jouvet

How far have you succeeded with this study to date?
We've succeeded in doing the first part of it. We brought up
kittens for five to six months in isolation. We observed them and
we saw no spontaneous aggressive behaviour. There was an
epidemic then, even though the animals were vaccinated, and they
died. We have to re-do it. There are many difficult stages to
overcome. The lesion that suppresses the inhibition of motor
efferences in paradoxical sleep is hard to perform selectively,
without causing other motor troubles. So what we are doing in
parallel is to arrive at a perfect siting of these neurons to make
sure that we don't cause other troubles. We hope to prove this
theory, but it is work that may take two to three years

*But your ideas on dreaming do not exclude Freud altogether? If
we need dreams to release innate patterns of behaviour, and society
prevents us expressing these instinctual drives, then maybe one of the
functions of dreams is to fulfil these wishes?*
If you put Freudian ideas at the level of the animal – at the level
of the chick – what can this mean? At the level of Man, maybe.
But I see this as a neurophysiologist. The great problem for
neurophysiology is that Nature invented dreaming when animals
went from homotherms to poikilotherms. Given Freud's
ideas, I don't see any way they fit. That this paradoxical sleep has
kitted itself out in Man in a very rich dreaming activity, I would
not deny. But the small chick also dreams, though his dream is
short. If I went to the depth of my thinking, I would say that we
shall discover the function of dreaming activity in the end in birds'
egg because it's perhaps the best and most convenient model to
work on. In the end, you can perform an experiment more easily
on a thousand birds' chick eggs than on a thousand cats. And, as I
said, what holds for the chick seems in the end to hold for Man
because of all the intervening animals that also show signs of
dreaming.

*Have you made observations on people that support your theory
that when we dream we are enjoying, suffering, I am not sure what, a
replaying of our genetic code?*
It's a little impossible. First, in Man there are many things you can
do but some you can't. Man has the merit of having the richness of
his subjective experience that he can confide to us. Fine. We know
that this subjective experience he will confide to us is given with a

184

split brain sometimes. And that makes things difficult. First, we don't know what is innate in Man though I am persuaded that more things are innate in Man than is usually admitted, and certainly than psychologists like Skinner admit. There is a great stock of innate activities. In a family of five or six, some children will go one way and others go another way. Genetic stocks may differ. A neurophysiologist as I am can't think that this will depend on fundamentally different organisations of the brain – given the plasticity of the system. The environment also has an enormous influence on our brains. Rats who play in rich environments have a more complex cortex than rats brought up in isolation. Twins show identical features. It's easier to explain this whole pattern by a functional but periodic system that comes regularly to bombard . . . I'm not sure if bombard is the right word . . . to reprogramme you to make you what you are – aggressive, choleric or whatever, even if education teaches you to suppress that. In the night, the choleric person will be reprogrammed to be choleric again. In the morning, education may suppress some of that. In that sense, you can find a place for the ideas of Freud. His unconscious, for the neurophysiologist like me, could be part of the genetic code. The brain is not an apple – an observation with which I am sure you will find it possible to agree. An apple is made once and for all to be an apple. The external circumstances will determine if it will ripen, how golden it will be or how green and so on. The central nervous system, for mammals, is programmed *in utero*. But that you and your brother are in some ways alike and in some ways different can only be explained by a periodical genetic programming. It is impossible to believe everything has been programmed *in utero*, once and for all, since the plasticity of the central nervous system is so important. And the brain is the only organ in evolution to have had the privilege to develop the capacity to determine that.

You would, therefore, expect rather serious consequences if animals or people are unable to dream? What happens if you can't dream?

It's the question I expected. Obviously that is the key, but it is a key that has so far opened no doors. First, the experiments on dream deprivation never went beyond ten or fifteen nights. My friend Dement, in his experiments at Stanford, made people go to sleep in his laboratory. When they started to dream, he would shake them to wake them up. First, it was said not surprisingly to increase the paranoid tendencies of people. Then, it seemed to be doing very little. Since the pioneering experiments of Dement, there have been other ways to suppress dreaming. There is an illness of narcolepsy, in which people very easily fall into dreaming. This famous neuron that blocks our motor actions is triggering too easily when people are, in fact, quite wakeful. So, they fall down. Well, thanks to neuropharmacology, we now possess powerful drugs like the inhibitors of monoamine oxides that could suppress paradoxical sleep. These drugs have been used to treat people who suffered from this illness. In four to five cases, patients who have received heavy doses have been kept under reasonable control for five to six months to see that they do not, in fact, dream. No one has seen any specific troubles appear with these patients. That's the problem. If you imagine that dreaming the Man reprogrammes what is innate, you have to ask yourself how often, normally, a person can use his innate capacities in normal life? Our society suppresses our instincts. In the first few months and years of life, paradoxical sleep will constitute the most important part of sleep but, of course, no one has tried to suppress paradoxical sleep for a long time in the child and I hope that no one ever will try. We believe that dreaming is not at all to be toyed with. In an adult, I believe the effects of not dreaming will be subtle but could be dangerous. Let me take an analogy. In *Clockwork Orange*, the boy is subjected to a Skinner-type programme to disgust him with Beethoven. He becomes a good boy. He hates Beethoven's music. Then, he falls from his window and, if you recall, when he wakes up, Kubrick makes him say, 'I had a dream', and he changes suddenly and totally. It is quite ingenious.

Suppose you use drugs to suppress dreams in an individual – you have to do it to cure him. Then, his genetic reprogramming to be aggressive, to be himself, to be free willed, will disappear. It may make it more difficult for people to reject propaganada. If you suppress dreaming, people may become more susceptible to the conditioning that the environment imposes precisely because they have lost touch to some extent with their cerebral genetic programme. Patients treated with strong doses of monoamine oxides who live in hospital do seem to become more susceptible in this way. Nurses say they have become much nicer. When you speak to their wives, they say, 'He's much better than

before', because they are much more able to be sensitive to the
environment and to their wives. In the night, things don't get set
'right' again, right, that is, from the individual's point of view. Let
us say someone is genetically programmed to be insubordinate,
attached to liberty of some kind and has a tendency to reject
authority. If you can refuse him each night the chance to
reprogramme himself into that person, he will be surrounded by
the environment, he will become more suspectible just as patients
become more susceptible and receive psychotherapy better.
Certain schools in the USA and Germany have attempted to work
on depression using precisely this suppression of dreams and in
some cases this does as well as ECT. Now who says that the
tendency to be depressed does not sometimes have a genetic
element? There are families of depressives. Suppose, during the
night, part of the individual's reprogramming does not happen; it
will tend to make him less depressive. It is important to recall that
this genetic programme may set off, at certain key points in life,
important events – menopause, the decline of male sexual activity,
a whole register of actions. If you deprive a person of dreams, you
will take out some of this system. To take a bad analogy of too
simple a mechanical system, if you take out the mini-cassette of
depression, then he will become less susceptible to depression. So
at that level in man, you can understand how the suppression of
dreams could lead to potential dangers. If the dream is a kind of
gyroscope of personality and you have drugs that can easily
suppress dreaming, you will succeed in making the individual more
conditionable. And you can see where it could lead.

*Have you considered using monkeys to work on this theory since
what would be true in the monkey would tend to be more likely to
be true in Man?*
No, partly for reasons of money. Monkeys are dearer than cats.
And, also, ethically, I find myself becoming more and more
annoyed at having to slaughter cats. The cat is near to us. The
monkey is nearer still. One has more and more respect for these
animals that dream. Then, the topography of the neurons
responsible for paradoxical sleep are not known in the monkey.
You would have to sacrifice many monkeys to understand that.
We may develop methods that will allow us to do this work on the
monkey and I believe a group in Paris is working at trying to get
the monkey to act out its dream. If they manage to get that

187

Michel Jouvet

behaviour it will be very important for us. What we are doing is
work on eggs. If the hypothesis that dreaming is linked to innate
behaviour is true, you should be able to show an effect in the
chick. The chick is born with a innate twitter. The twitter
develops in the first day of its life into twenty-two different
twitters which you can distinguish. We are trying to inject drugs to
cut out paradoxical sleep *in ovo*. This is easier to do than in the
foetus. A chick dreams most of the first forty-eight hours of its
life. Some do not dream, but twitter. Others, whose paradoxical
sleep is not suppressed totally, show the twitter but it is of one
type. If we suppress paradoxical sleep, some seem not to survive.
It is a study that is easier to do in the chick. It will take several
years. The methods seem to be OK. But it may turn out to be
impossible.

*Presumably, you might also expect then to find effects in pregnant
women?*

Two groups have studied the dreams of pregnant women and the
movement *in utero* of the foetus. Certain experimenters have gone
so far as to say that the dreams of pregnant women are much like
those of the foetus. In animals my wife succeeded some years ago
in recording the dream of a guinea pig *in utero*. After forty days,
i.e. twenty days before birth, the foetus will spend up to fifty per
cent of its time in paradoxical sleep where the mother may spend
only three per cent of its time in REM sleep.

*In all the time that you have described your approach and work,
you seem to lay great stress on objective, neurophysiological
methods. Do you see any usefulness at all in more introspective
methods?*

For the past two to three years, I must admit that I have been
studying my own dreams, but as a neurophysiological afterthought
or an emphasis in the sense that I'm trying to explain certain odd
phenomena which you find in the recollection of dreams – not so
much in psychological as in physiological terms, a kind of
feedback from neurophysiology to psychology. It's been proven in
the cat that during REM sleep, paradoxical sleep, the *corpus
callosum* connecting the two hemispheres of the brain does not
work. If you put a micro-electrode in its midst, it is totally quiet.
This is rather impressive since in wakefulness, a whole lot of
information is always going from right to left hemisphere and vice

188

versa. This disconnection means that at a certain point in dreaming, you have a split brain like those that Sperry studied in animals and men. Now, you know you recognise a face with the right hemisphere – the absence of recognition is due to a lesion of the right hemisphere. Language, on the other hand, is coded in the left hemisphere. Now I have studied about the first thousand recollections of my own dreams and put into one category all dream memories where I recognise who emitted a message – my wife, Mr So-and-So – and compared these with dreams in which, while I recognise the phrase and can write it down perfectly later, I don't recognise who said it. It's vague. A policeman, a man with an odd face that I can't identify. It seems to me, then, that there are two statistically significant differences between these two kinds of dreams – those where I recognise the message but not the sender and those where I recognise the sender but not the message. It may seem to be in a foreign language. I had a dream recently in which I recognised my sister and I asked her what language she was talking at me. Now, with these significant differences between dreams, if there is a disconnection between the right and left brain, what does it mean? If a psychoanalyst interprets this by saying that there is 'censorship', that I have not recognised who said so and so because of repressions or inhibitions, he will be wrong. I can explain it by saying that in paradoxical sleep, for reasons that escape me, the right and left brain don't speak. And if someone can repeat a message clearly but cannot say who said it, it isn't because of his subconscious or unconscious and it isn't because of any rejection. It is because of that neurophysiological fact. The neurons of the *corpus callosum* are temporarily silent.

Have you found any other differences, for example differences in the contents of your dreams, depending on whether the left or the right hemisphere is working?

Well, in principle, it seems there is one kind of dream when I know who says what, and there is another when I know what is said. Normally, the two brains work in step. It happens often, in fact, that they don't. In a recent dream, as I said, I recognised my sister very well. I recognised her face and her clothes and I said to her, 'What language are you speaking?' At that time, the left hemisphere was not working. If you look at which dreams are of one sort and which dreams of the other, you get a very significantly different distribution.

But are there differences also in the kinds of dream you have?
I have not looked at the differences. I collect my dreams every morning and have done so for the last few years. I have a bank of fourteen hundred dreams and sometimes I make random samples of them to test some hypothesis. If I start to have certain ideas in advance, they may disguise the dream. I prefer to get to two thousand dreams. I have found that I remember, at any rate, 1.4 dreams a night. And also, that there seems to be a period of rapport between events you live through and what you dream. It's well known that dreams are filled with events from the day that has just passed. But one also finds with a frequency that is significant that there is a peak with events that took place seven to eight days before. A great proportion of them, in fact. If you do a histogram of it, you get a big peak the first day, then a hole, and then another peak after eight days, and then it tails off. What that means may be very interesting. It could show that certain processes of memory have a half-life of seven to eight days. This could show, too, how there is interaction in the work one does on cats and men – even introspective work.

Was it difficult for you to get started on this introspective work?
I hadn't thought of it. Then, one night, I had such odd dreams, I woke up and decided to write them down. Then, I got into it. That was in 1970. One day, when I stop work or am retired, I thought I could code them. It is more of a hobby for the future in some ways. I think that if you want to discover the function of dreaming, even, it is very hard, it will be done by experimental neurophysiology and not by introspection in Man. Of that I am profoundly, intimately convinced. Only neurophysiology, maybe in association with neurochemistry, biology and ethology – I think myself that much more will come from the ethologists – will reveal it to us. I think it is one of the most important problems that we face actually in neurobiology because we know why we have a pancreas, why we have temporal lobes. We know why we have a faculty of memory. We know what its use is. Intuitively, we know why we sleep. We sleep to restore certain capacities. That's true even if we have not been able to prove it. But, intuitively, the dream is of no use. Who could have imagined from the start there was a need to dream, in the sense that it's easy enough to imagine a system with two states – wakefulness and sleep. So, it's important to know why we have the third

state – especially in terms of the Western system. The Hindus had a system of three consciousnesses. They had a need in this sense for sleeping and dreaming. In our Western system of thought, everything accords well with mere duality – activity and sleep.

Have you found this introspective study useful to you in a more personal sense, that it has maybe made you more aware of what you are, made you more in touch with yourself?
All research is to a certain extent an inner life. When you devote maybe ninety per cent of your life to this sort of work, it obviously holds a major place. You invest so much in it. You end up by understanding that good results may have reactions in the life of an individual and bad ones also can. I feel I know something about this in the sense that a discovery you make seems to belong to the person who made it only once and for a short time. Take paradoxical sleep. Then, it goes into the public domain and is lost. This kind of sense of frustration is permanent in the scientist and I feel I know it very well.

As for dreams, since I became conscious of dreams in this way and started to study them with this view, after certain depressive dreams I know in the morning that this part of me is in play. It can then affect my behaviour during the day, perhaps so that I avoid certain depressing circumstances or, maybe, so that after an aggressive dream I avoid certain aggressive circumstances. I have the impression that in a certain measure there is a fixed proportion, fairly fixed, of erotic dreams, aggressive dreams, depressive dreams in proportion to the extent that I am erotic, aggressive and depressive – possibly in rapport with my genetic programme. The day that follows an aggressive dream, it may be that my central nervous system is particularly tuned to be aggressive. It is then up to me how I handle it.

And has that knowledge changed you or have you used it so as to change?
I don't think I can change much thereby. But if I understand some of it, I can learn perhaps. I think the ideas are taken much from . . . You can't change that much or that is the impression that I have. The proportion of so much aggression, so much sexuality and so on seems to be fairly fixed. I suppose one could try to learn to change one's behaviour, reducing the importance of the genetic code, but would it be wise during dreaming? In some

191

circumstances it may be useful but it is easy to understand that depending upon the society in which we live, it may be dangerous to alter at will the putative genetic programming which occurs during paradoxical sleep. Individually, this programming makes us dependent upon our genetic code. But for a society it may be a guarantee of freedom . . . I do not believe that there will ever be any authority that will have the right artificially to control the genetic programming of our brain.

8
R. D. Laing

R. D. Laing is not a psychologist by profession. He is a psychiatrist and his insights come from his 'clinical' work. I put the word in quotation marks because, I suspect, he would reject it. He has now opted out of the traditional role of the psychiatrist and clinician: it smacks too much of oppression. His detractors might well say that he has cast off the white coat of the psychiatrist for the more impressive mantle of the guru. A long article in *Esquire* magazine by Peter Mezan (1972) entitled After Freud and Jung comes R. D. Laing', was grounded in this view of Laing. It has recently been supported in many ways by Professor Friedenberg (1973) in his book on Laing in the Modern Masters series. It is, I will try to argue, too facile a view in the light of this interview.

The details of Laing's conventional career are simple. They are briefly put on the cover page of *The Politics of Experience* (1967). Laing was born in Glasgow in 1927. He went to grammar school and then to Glasgow University. He graduated there as a doctor in 1951. Till 1953, he worked as a psychiatrist in the British Army. He then worked at the Glasgow Royal Mental Hospital and in the Department of Psychological Medicine at Glasgow University. From 1957 to 1961, he was at the Tavistock Clinic. Then, from 1962 to 1965, he was director of the Langham Clinic.

Since 1965, Laing has seemed to many people to eschew the path of the scientific medical investigator, he has preferred to become a poet with a political edge. After 1965, he helped found and run a series of hostels in which existential and radical approaches to healing were tried. The most famous of these was Kingsley Hall in the East End of London. Fabulous tales reached the outside world of goings on there. Patients ran wild. They regressed: the psychiatrists regressed with them. Walls were smeared with excrement. Local residents complained. The council eventually forced the hostel to close. By 1968, Laing had

193

acquired the status of a superstar, some kind of elusive folk hero. I remember being asked by the *Times Educational Supplement* to see if I could get an interview with him. They doubted it was possible. As I had made the same suggestion to Granada Television who assured me that they had been trying for six months to persuade Laing to appear on a programme about Kingsley Hall, I also doubted it was possible. The literary editor of the *Times Educational Supplement* knew, however, a man called Zeal. Zeal was, aptly, a disciple of the great man. It was rumoured that he even knew his phone number. Zeal was telephoned. Would he help us to get an interview with Laing? He hesitated: he was not sure such a plan would commend itself to Laing who did not want sensational press comment. He promised, though, to see what he could do after he had been assured that the *Times Educational Supplement* could hardly be considered a frivolous organ of the press. After a few days, Zeal telephoned again with a number. He could not say whether or not Laing would grant the interview but if we were to ring, we would be listened to. I rang. A very efficient medical secretary told me that I could have an interview if I came to an address in Wimpole Street. The time was fixed. It would have all been too easy if I had not lost the address. (Why I did that, however, remains unknown.) I was at a terrible loss. I did not dare ring Zeal up again so I decided to look in the phone directory. (We had all assumed the number was ex-directory.) There, however, it stared me in the face: R. D. Laing. The whole elaborate rigmarole had been unnecessary. Laing, the great critic of mystification, had become so mystified himself that I had thought it impossible to reach him except by the most tortuous means. You do not expect to come easily into the presence of a Master. I offer this story as just an indication of what an extraordinary effect the publicity that surrounded Laing had. Later, it went even further. The gossip on the psychological grapevine buzzed with tales of patients who had gone 'mad' when Laing refused to see them any more. Some said that the guru had himself gone on a voyage into the nether regions of the soul and none knew if he would voyage back, twisting Laing's images to say Laing had finally gone mad himself.

As with Skinner, then, one had to disentangle Laing's work, his studies and his theories, from the image of Laing's work that has been projected and, often, accepted. No contemporary psychologist has the kind of following Laing has. A meeting in 1972 of the Philadelphia association (whose chairman he is) was packed out at Friends' House in NW1 even though that has a very large hall. Disappointed queues waited outside. The interview with Laing shows how aware he is of the fact that his views have been badly represented. He appears especially to resent the implication that he is a guiding light in the extreme left, that his psychological insights somehow support revolution.

The first time I interviewed Laing was in Wimpole Street. It was a very medical setting. He sat facing me. Two chairs were arranged in the room for this kind of confrontation. He chain-smoked Gauloises. I took this as a sign that he looked on the interview as a lecture. He ran quickly, efficiently, through some of his views. The hour came to an end. I was dispatched to make way for a patient, a person whom I presumed he felt was more worthy of his attention.

The second time I interviewed him (in 1974) he was working from a dark green room in his house in Belsize Park. The room was lined with books. A. J. Ayer jostled with Indian mystics on his table. He said that he spent a great deal of his time in this room working with his ideas and with people that he saw. He liked to work in the midst of his family. He stressed the point to emphasise how wrong it was to see him as part of the anti-family lobby. It was David Cooper who wrote *Death of the Family* (1972). The fact that he and David Cooper had once written a book on Sartre together did not mean that he agreed with all that David Cooper said. But the press had seized on him, on Cooper and, to some extent, on Thomas Szasz, the American anti-psychiatrist, as critics of the present state of psychiatry and jumbled all their views together. Just as Laing is at pains to dissociate himself from some of David Cooper's views, Szasz is critical of Laing, and Szasz believes that psychiatrists both in America and in the UK are used to repress people and to deny them legal rights. Szasz has accumulated evidence that the authorities use psychiatrists as intimate spies and that families use psychiatrists to get relatives committed so that their assets may be appropriated. All these faults, Szasz insists, Laing fails to attribute with enough enthusiasm to psychiatrists. The differences among the anti-psychiatry school of psychiatric thought are large and important. This interview suggests that they are especially important in Laing's case.

Laing's work has seen a logical development through a number of books. His first book with Cooper, *Reason and Violence* (1964) is technically an exposition of some ideas of Sartre's philosophy. In *The Divided Self* (1960), Laing tried to make us, the readers, understand what was going on in the mind of a person diagnosed as schizophrenic. At this point, Laing did not hold the view later attributed to him that no one is mad. He was concerned to show that madness, the actions of the mad, are not so incomprehensible. With enough understanding, you can perceive the method behind the madness. An example is the behaviour of a patient of the famous psychiatrist, Kraeplin. In *The Divided Self*, Laing gives the following account (p. 29). He begins by citing Kraeplin:

> The patient sits with his eyes shut, and pays no attention to his surroundings. He does not look up even when he is spoken to but he answers beginning in a low voice and, gradually screaming louder and louder. When asked where he is, he says, 'You want to know that too? I tell you who is being measured and is measured and shall be measured. I know all that and could tell you but do not want to.' When asked his name, he screams 'What is your name?' What does he shut? He shuts his eyes. What does he hear? He does not understand; he understands not. How? Who? Where? When? What does he mean? When I tell him to look he does not look properly. You there, just look! What is it? What is the matter? Attend: he attends not. I say, what is it then? Why do you give me no answer? Are you getting impudent again? How can you be so impudent.

In the book, Laing continues with this example at some length. He also quotes Kraeplin's notes on a young girl patient whom he used to demonstrate some of his ideas in big formal theatres. Kraeplin showed his class that, if he tried to stop her moving about, she would resist very strongly. If he put himself in front of her, his arms outstretched as a barrier, she would duck under his arms. If he tried to take a piece of bread which she held clutched in her hands, she would not let him take it. If he took a firm grip of her body, her usually rigid and impassive expression would change and she would start 'deplorable weeping', as Kraeplin put it. If Kraeplin then pricked her forehead with a needle, she hardly reacted. To any questions the eminent doctor put to her she would only reply: 'O dear God, O dear Mother, O dear Mother.'

Laing's point is very simple: Can you blame her? Can you blame the first patient? If Kraeplin attempted in a street what he was doing to them within the sanctuary of a hospital, he would soon be in jail. The patients are not acting like lunatics: they are resisting. They are using the few means left to them to resist. In *The Divided Self*, Laing gives a detailed analysis of the conversation of the patient in the extract quoted. Laing argues that the patient is carrying on a dialogue between his own parodied version of Kraeplin and his own 'defiant rebelling self'. When the parody Kraeplin asks him where he is, he ripostes, 'You want to know that too. I tell you who is being measured and is measured and shall be measured. I know all that and could tell you but I do not want to.' This is quite sensible when you see it, not as raving, but as defiance backed up by irony. The patient mimics the outrage of the psychiatrist who snaps, 'Are you getting impudent again? How can you be so impudent?' Laing points out that this whole interrogation is being done publicly before a lecture-hall of students. Instead of getting help, the patient is being used as a device to illustrate Kraeplin's definitions of various mental diseases. What is more reasonable than for him to react in the kind of way that Kraeplin labels mad?

It is, Laing argues, a question of perspective. Our usual perspective has been to see such behaviour as a confirmation of insanity. There is, however, a different interpretation. The patient's experience of Kraeplin is of a man who has power over him and is using that power to torment him. Laing asks: 'What is he "about" in speaking and acting in this way. He is objecting to being measured and tested. He wants to be heard' (p. 31).

In his book on Laing, Friedenberg complains that these passages have been, perhaps, used too much. The way Laing analysed them, however, gives a valuable clue to why he has been so persuasive, not only to the psychiatric fringe but to a number of professional colleagues. Laing showed how one could make sense of behaviour that appeared to be unintelligible and, therefore, mad. He used many case histories to illustrate the relationship that existed between the way in which a person went 'mad' and the social or family situation he had found himself in. James, a chemist aged twenty-eight, felt he could not become a person. He lacked a self. Other people mattered and had substance whereas he, he said, was 'only a cork floating on an ocean'. He used two manoeuvres to preserve what Laing calls his ontological security. First, he appeared to comply with what other people said or required of him. That was his outer self. His inner self, however, turned the person he was complying with into an object. In his own eyes, he was destroying the other person as a person. He maintained a paradoxical relationship with his wife. On the one hand, he saw himself as a parasite, ineffectual beside her; on the other hand, he referred to her as 'It'. Laing says that she had become an 'It' to James. He would say things like 'It then started to laugh' and he would then, with due and almost clinical precision, explain how she had been conditioned like a robot to laugh. Laing's use of these case histories was impressive.

During the time that he was writing his next book, *Sanity, Madness and the Family* (with A. Esterson, 1963), Laing was also involved with

David Cooper in a series of experiments that set out to show their kind of family therapy worked as well as, if not better than, the conventional chemical treatments for schizophrenia. The results of these experiments are reported in detail at the end of Cooper's book, *Psychiatry and Anti-Psychiatry* (1967), and Laing strikes in the interview an interesting and paradoxical attitude to this quite traditional scientific approach. He uses it to refute the idea that he is not a scientist but he does not bother to elaborate in any detail on the experimental work. One of his only alterations in the text of the interview dealt with this question. In *Sanity, Madness and the Family*, Laing and Esterson studied twelve cases of schizophrenia. They interviewed the patients who were always in hospital. But they also interviewed the families of the patient. Some interviews were done with individual members of the family; some interviews were done with the family *en bloc* apart from the patient; some interviews were done with the family and patient. In these twelve cases, Laing and Esterson tried to show that a person was diagnosed as schizophrenic because of what was happening in the family nexus. The 'madness' was a means of coping with an impossible situation. Far from being a lunatic escape, it was the only strategy by which a person could salvage any life out of the situation he found himself in.

Laing's work is often examined in a different sequence. It is the general, often the polemic, arguments about the nature of 'madness' that get precedence. A psychiatrist who refutes the idea of madness is in the paradoxical position of a bishop who refutes the idea of God. Both catch our attention easily. Laing warns we are all so alienated that none of us can ever realise our authentic possibilities. The sane are certainly mad: it is just possible that some of the 'mad' are sane. A famous passage occurs at the beginning of *The Politics of Experience*. At one point, Laing accuses: 'We are all murderers and prostitutes – no matter to what culture, class, society, nation one belongs, no matter how normal, moral or mature one takes himself to be.' A few paragraphs later, he mourns: 'We are bemused and crazed creatures, strangers to our true selves, to one another, and to the spiritual and material world – mad, even from an ideal standpoint we can glimpse but not adopt.'

Scientists do not mourn or accuse. They observe, they dissect and, if the facts turn out conclusively, they conclude. They are not supposed to make the kinds of value judgments Laing makes.

In *Sanity, Madness and the Family* Laing made some similar points about the way we label schizophrenics. He and Esterson argued that there were no generally agreed objective criteria for the diagnosis of schizophrenia. They claimed there was no consistency in pre-psychotic personality, course, duration and outcome of the disease. No post-mortem anatomical findings had been discovered. Schizophrenia, Laing and Esterson appeared to argue, was being treated and studied as if it was a known disease. In fact, however, none of the proper medical criteria that define a disease could be applied to 'schizophrenia'. It was a myth.

In this argument, Laing drew a good deal on *The Myth of Mental Illness* by Thomas Szasz (1960). Szasz contented himself with a radical critique of psychiatry as muddled, and psychiatrists are exploitative. They were more jailers than healers. They let themselves become instruments of social control. They did not see that they had no proper medical grounds for claiming schizophrenia was a disease like measles or thrombosis. Schizophrenia had no agreed symptoms, no agreed diagnosis, no recognised form of treatment. Szasz did not create a new kind of therapy though. He remained a fairly orthodox Freudian. He wanted to show up the confusion of modern psychiatry in order to curb its power. Much of his best writing is legal rather than strictly medical. The United States affords great power to its psychiatrists. Szasz was never hailed as a prophet or guru in the way that Laing has been.

Laing's reputation for being more of a prophet and, even, poet than a scientist rests upon two of his most recent books, *Interpersonal Perception* (1966) and *Knots* (1972). *Knots* is set out as a series of poems. They set what Laing wants us to recognise as universal human situations. These are the tangles we get ourselves into; they are typical meshes; they enmesh us. It will be useful here to quote some of these 'knots':

'They are playing a game. They are playing at not
playing a game. If I show them I see they are, I
shall break the rules and they will punish me.
I must play their game, of not seeing I see the game.'

and:

'There must be something the matter with him
because he would not be acting as he does
    unless there was
therefore he is acting as he is
because there is something the matter with him.'

He does not think there is anything the matter with him because

> one of the things that is
> the matter with him
> is that he does not think that there is anything
> the matter with him.'

It is a poem, of course.

It also happens to be, however, a very formal statement of observations. These are axioms of human behaviour. To be satisfactory, it would be necessary to give some idea of the circumstances that force people into such 'knots'. But my point here is only that the gap between Laing, the once scientist, and Laing, the now alleged poet, is not perhaps so very great. It is possible to imagine PhD students using *Knots* to devise hypotheses to test. Laing offers them, of course, as something already true. He has seen it happen. We will recognise it as being within our experience. It is true. It does not need statistics to enshrine it as fact. It is an experiential fact. Many psychologists object violently to such assumptions. They reject not only Laing's assumptions but also the possibility that these 'knots' might be true and are, therefore, worth testing.

Because most psychologists have given up on Laing and Laing has given up on conventional scientific method, it is easy for each side to remain entrenched. However, he was more definite in his allegiance to science in conversation than he appeared willing to be in print. But even so, the interview should, once and for all, dismiss the idea that he is anti-science. He simply does not regard the way that human behaviour is being studied as being particularly scientific. It ignores how we experience people and things and situations. It omits a vital dimension in favour of looking at behaviour. He thinks that is damning. It leaves out what is most essential about being human.

There are two more themes that have been often found in Laing's work. His last two books, especially, seem to be despairing. Having reached the conclusion in *The Politics of Experience* that we are all alienated from our true selves, he seemed to be saying that it was no longer possible for men and women to be whole and free. We were stunted wretches. Critics have seen this strain in Laing as the triumph of Evil. His world has emerged as desolate. We are all hemmed into our particular isolation. We can only touch other people in the most superficial of ways. He seemed to be a purveyor of psychological doom. Our inner world mirrored the darkness of the outer world. Families bred this despair. In the interview, Laing is at pains to correct this impression of total gloom. He claims it stems from the fact that critics of the 'anti-psychiatry' movement seem unable to distinguish the fact that there are various points of view within it. Laing does not see the world, or even the family, as totally evil.

Also, Laing claims that he has been misrepresented as a member of the radical left. He is certainly critical of society as it is. But he seems to be frightened of the radical left opening the way or providing the excuse for a yet more authoritarian society.

Like Skinner, Laing has enjoyed enormous success outside his professional field. His books have become necessary reading for anyone who wants to understand current ideas. Fashionable, they seem to be interpreted in an extreme manner. The gossip that has circulated about Laing's life and about his work like Kingsley Hall has also been exaggerated. More than any of the interviewees (apart from Skinner), he seemed really glad to have an occasion to set the record straight – straight, of course, as it seemed to him.

It is worth noting, too, that in becoming much more interested in expressing his ideas in a poetic and literary way, Laing is only going a little farther than a number of other psychologists who say that the whole science only comes alive for them when they are writing about it.

Why did you become a psychiatrist?
It's a difficult question to answer if one is trying to ferret out one's most radical motivations. I became interested in psychiatry via an interest in how people feel and how people see things and how people act in the light of their different ways of seeing things. And I suppose I became aware of these issues quite early in my childhood. I grew up with a very lively sense of the problematic, as you might call it, of human relationships. So it was a perfectly natural extension of my own untutored interest to get into the domain of the special study of interpersonal relationships. However, when I got into psychiatry a bit, I discovered that that was only a very small part of psychiatric theory and practice. And that psychiatry as it was practised seemed not the unequivocally most advantageous position from which to study how people go on with each other because a great deal of psychiatric theory is, in a way, discounting the relevance of those very matters.

I came to psychiatry from that route and, also, from the

scientific route. In my medical student days, I was particularly interested in embryology and what is now called neuroscience. My first job as a doctor was as an internist in a neurology and neurosurgery unit. I was very interested in those changes of consciousness, those changes of mind, those changes in function and conduct which are related to known organic disorders of the nervous system. Then, again, in the present state of our knowledge, most of the people seen as patients by psychiatrists, when they are examined and tested, are found not to have anything organic the matter with them. These were the problems in that domain of psychiatry that I came to be drawn to.

What were the major influences on you? Sartre, presumably?
I went to a grammar school during the Second World War. There, I came across Sophocles and the Greek tragedians. I read them before I read any modern interpretations of these myths and stories. So I actually read *Oedipus* in Greek before I came across Oedipus in Freud. I would say that Greek drama was one of my most profound influences. Then, when I was fifteen or sixteen, I became interested in finding out what other people had left as records in the written form from the European tradition. I worked my way alphabetically through the shelves of my local public library. And there, at the age of sixteen or seventeen, I came across the complete translated works of Nietzsche. And in chronological order, or rather in alphabetical order, I came across Kierkegaard first and then Nietzsche. These were the major influences that were backed up by Marx and Freud.

Of my nearest contemporaries, Kafka, Sartre and Camus were the main influences. And, in terms of philosophical position, Heidegger, Husserl and Merleau-Ponty. Sartre, I think has never been quite the superordinate influence on my intellectual development that some people take him to be because I did a joint book, *Reason and Violence*, with David Cooper, on some of his untranslated stuff. The main reason for doing that was that it was untranslated. If it had been translated, there would have been no reason. It was a piece of intellectual carpentry to translate a long, involved, complex text which was important for our theoretical background so that English-speaking people could have some idea of what that particular aspect of that background was. But Sartre doesn't stand out to me. He's one of a few major influences but nothing like *the* major one.

Among psychiatrists, was Freud the main influence?
I was influenced by Freud more than by any other psychiatrist or anyone else in psychiatry. I was also very influenced by Jung. The influence of Jung has been less explicit and has been less because of the ideological implications of some of his formulations in the direction of racism. Also, Jung's reputation, particularly at the time when my influences were being formed, was considerably tarnished by the allegation, whether it be justified or not, that he was sympathetic to the Nazi movement at the beginning and by the implication of anti-Semitism. That was reported and you could see it might be a factor. So I've always been a bit chary of Jung in that respect though, at the same time, there is an enormous amount of stuff that Jung went over which still waits to be picked up more generally.

Were you in any way reacting against a religious upbringing in becoming a psychiatrist?
I'm not quite sure what you mean by rebelling.

Professor David McClelland has suggested that people who become interested in psychology and psychiatry often seem to be reacting against rigid moral ideas. They may even have toyed with becoming ministers. Is that true of you in any way?
Not especially – no.

How did the ideas that it was social rather than biological causes that were involved in 'schizophrenia' develop?
When I was in Glasgow, having come out of the British Army in 1955 or so, I worked for eighteen months in a mental hospital. I spent most of my time during the day in the most refractory, so-called refractory ward of the female division of the hospital. This was a ward of about sixty women who, before the days of tranquillisers, were supposed to be stark raving mad, Bedlam. It was the snake-pit scene. These were women who had no dresses, who queued up every morning to have a different dress put on them by whatever nurse was on duty. All these women had been in hospital more than six years, they were the chronics of the place. Most of them, in fact, had only a very tenuous relationship with the outside world. Many of them weren't visited by anyone. Some of them no one knew who they were. I made an arrangement for twelve of these women whom I selected on the

basis that they were most withdrawn, they were the ones that the nurses interacted with least, they were the ones who interacted with people least and, according to a questionnaire I put out to the nurses, they were the ones the nurses felt most hopeless about. So these were the twelve most hopeless chronic women in the hospital. I tried to make more radical changes than turned out to be possible in the end. But what I did arrange was for these twelve to be with two nurses five days a week, from nine to five. The nurses were seconded from other duties and didn't have any ward duties during that time. Well, in the course of it developing, a number of things went on. There were major changes in the hospital. There were ructions all over the place. But these twelve people were able to have the nurses and have the room. And, in under a year, all these twelve people had left the hospital. They had all been given up as completely hopeless and none had been out of hospital for a minimum of six years. Most of them had been in for up to twelve years. All were women between thirty-five and fifty.

Now I left the hospital at the end of that year. Within a year, all twelve were back again. That impressed me. Increasing lobotomy, using lobotomies, using shock treatment seemed beside the point. But increasing the dose, if you like, of a little human personal relationships made far more total change in the whole situation. The other things were beside the point. But it seemed to me that these women had gone out of the hospital and back to the different versions of the same circumstances from which they had come into hospital in the first place. So the study of people in a hospital was completely missing the point. You really had to study people, not in a mental hospital as psychiatrists had done in all their studies of mental patients, but in the ordinary circumstances of their life. It seemed like trying to understand the behaviour of dolphins by studying them in dolphinaria or aquaria instead of in the ocean. If dolphins ever got hold of a human being, put him in a cage in the ocean and got him to do tricks and if, suppose, that guy happened to be Einstein, what would happen? If our brothers and sisters the dolphins who seem to be as intelligent as we are, if not more so, set up Einstein in a human zoo, in a humanarium, I wonder what they could learn about human intelligence by getting Einstein to do tricks and trying to get him to speak dolphin language. It's ridiculous to try and have any understanding if you are studying people who are herded sixty to a ward, and who have been allowed to rot away for years and years and years. If one wants to seriously get any understanding of that situation, then surely one should look at the circumstances in which people live their lives in order to get there in the first place.

It would be as ridiculous as if you had an institution from which doctors never went out. Someone turns up with a black eye. So, doctors examine his eyes and there is damage to the blood vessels and around the eyes and the blood is leaking out, and they say that this is due to some congenital defect of the blood vessels of the eye. If no one had ever gone out of that institution, gone out into the world, they would never, it would seem, know that black eyes were due to the impact of a fist which is a punch. But unless you look at it, you can never tell. But it seems to me that this is quite a mild comparison with what psychiatrists are actually involved in.

After that mental hospital, I decided I wanted to know about what you might call the ecology of mind in its natural habitat. I didn't want to study it under these artificial conditions, and when I looked to see what had been written and what had been investigated in that respect, I found there was practically nothing. All that existed was a few research teams in North America who had started looking into it a few years before and that was only just beginning. Before that, there was nothing.

Would you say that there is any predisposition, any biological predisposition, to schizophrenia?

I can't talk about schizophrenia in that sense, in the same way that Lévi-Strauss refuses to speak about totemism. The history of medicine is full of non-existent illnesses and conditions. The history of medical treatment is, too. Now that we look back on it, I don't think any contemporary doctor would like to be treated by one of his colleagues by the methods employed a hundred years ago. I mean you'd be appalled. If you do a little timeswitch, how would you like to be treated for what we now know to be anaemia by blood-letting or how would you like to be treated for epilepsy by castration or for masturbation by castration. These were standard forms of treatment in nineteenth-century psychiatry and medicine. I'll lay a bet that a hundred years from now, doctors will cringe with horror at the thought of being treated by our methods that are so arrogantly purveyed when they're just scratching in the dark. It's like trying anything.

Instead of an electric shock it is much simpler just to give
people a cosh, a knock on the head and call it 'cosh therapy'.
Electric shock is just an electrical way of producing concussion.
When the brains of rats that have been given electric shock are
compared with the brains of rats that have been hit on the head,
the brain lesions are indistinguishable. It seems a way of producing
an electrical concussion. It's a very simple-minded idea. Someone
is worried about something, he is terribly distracted and agonised,
so you hit him on the head and that helps him.

In The Politics of Experience, *you said that in a hundred cases that
had been diagnosed as schizophrenic and which you, Cooper and
Esterson had studied, there wasn't one where the so-called
'schizophrenia' wasn't, in fact, a strategy for living in an unliveable
situation? Why did you not present these findings in a formal, one
might say acceptably scientific, way?*
Well, I have done so. The book *Sanity, Madness and the Family* is
a study, a research report of an anthropological kind of a number
of families. I also published with them in either the *Lancet* or the
British Medical Journal a report in detail of our family therapy
and compared the statistics we had with what statistics we could
obtain from Medical Research Council sources.

*So the idea that you oppose a scientific presentation of your work
is a misguided one?*
The Politics of Experience is a book that comes out of a number of
lectures I was giving, to professional audiences for the most part,
in the years before it was published. Friedenberg in his book on me
never even mentions my actual scientific writing or the
presentations to learned societies where, in a more technical way, I
present the material that in a non-technical, non-jargon, in some
sense a programmatic manner, I put out in *The Politics of
Experience.* That is not meant to be a scientific report in the
manner of science. There, I'm putting out things from the
background of the work in a way that I hope isn't misleading.
Technically, you have to follow up the references. There are
references given.

*Yes. You were going to say something just then, I didn't mean to
cut you off.*
For the kinds of reasons you talked about, an interview like this is

a valid thing to do, to get at influences, at clarifications. There is a
lot of unclarity about my published work.

What made you write The Divided Self?
As I said at the beginning of *The Divided Self*, I thought that a lot
of the ways in which people carry on that many people find
completely incomprehensible are not, in fact, nearly as incomprehensible or not as incomprehensible as they appear to be.
It was an attempt to give an indication of a way of seeing people
in terms of which comprehensibility could come to light. It also
suggested that if you looked at people in what you might call an
uncomprehending way then no comprehensibility could possibly
arise so one needn't be surprised that it doesn't. But it doesn't
mean to say because you can't find something that it's not where
you're looking for it or that it doesn't exist.

*In that book, you described the false-self system, a sort of
outward face for public viewing many so-called schizophrenics used.
Do you think many normal, quite undisturbed people also use this
because they are alienated?*
Yes, I would say that's true. If I'm to believe what many people
actually tell me, yes, but this isn't a matter where I speak from
any particular position of competency. I think that anyone living
in our society cannot help being aware that a great deal of one's
social interplay uses a sort of mask, a sort of persona, a sort of
front or a sort of set of social stereotypes of actions and
expressions which are not intended and not designed to be
expressions of anything particularly personal. And we all know the
extent to which that mask grows into some people, grows into
their faces so they can't take it off. We are, as it were, stuck with
it. As far as that goes, far more people are stuck with it than are
aware of it and a lot of people are aware of it and find it very
painful because they can't disencumber themselves of it once it's
sort of grown in.

In The Divided Self, *too, you called for an authentic science of
persons. Would that investigate how you could rid yourself of that
mask?*
Oh yes. The practice of what is called therapy has a great deal to
do with the possibility of being able to discard that mask. People
cling to it more out of fear than anything else. It's a mask which is

207

like a castle inside which one can defend oneself from the attacks of what are felt to be other people as one's enemies and, at the same time, it's a prison from which one can't get out. That is the double ambiguity about it. The possibility of being able to function efficiently and competently in our society without actually being a prisoner is something that quite a few people that I meet regard as a rather remote possibility for them. And a lot of people feel so frightened at the prospect of doing without it that the idea seems horrendous to them.

How does one get over that fear?
How does one get over any fear? It's very nice if one can discover that what one was afraid of doesn't exist. If you, as I think many people do, grow up in a childhood in which there's violent pressure and plenty to fear and when you have grown up you haven't incorporated and internalised the person, and you don't carry it around with you continually, then there is some prospect, one can realise with a sigh of relief, that, as far as external circumstances go, one is no longer in prison, in quite the same way at least. It's all very well to say ideologically that our whole society is a prison but there's more breathing space in some sections of it than in others. I don't agree with what might be stated as a possible extreme position – that all possibility of actual open spontaneous behaviour between people is now lost. I think that still happens and still goes on in completely ordinary, unsung, undeclared ways all over the place all the time. It goes on. But it's another world to millions of people.

One position linked to this that you have been seen to hold is that it is society which is ill and the 'schizophrenic' who is sane. Is that a proper statement of your view?
I never said that society was ill. I don't see how one can talk about a society being ill. One could say I was ill if I had the flu. But to talk about society being ill is all right if one is using it *en passant*, as a metaphor, or even as an extended metaphor, as long as one never forgets that it is a metaphor and an analogy. One can compare society, say, to a sick animal. I wouldn't want to say it's anything more than a comparison and I feel that it's a comparison that is made so often now, it's become so trite, that you might as well not make it.

208

I never said that everyone diagnosed as schizophrenic was sane. It's a ridiculous statement to make to say that all people diagnosed as psychotic are sane. That's as stupid as any other fantastic generalisation. What I did say was that all sorts of people get diagnosed as psychotic. Really, all sorts of people do get diagnosed as psychotic. And, sometimes, when people are diagnosed as being mad or psychotic or what not, they are indeed in a state such that they might seem shattered, scattered, bewildered, unable to function, unable to act, unable to move, unable to think, unable to perform the most basic functions. So if we say that is someone who for reasons that we don't immediately know doesn't seem to want to, or to be able to, talk or move or perform many basic functions, someone in whom life is suspended, it's impossible to avoid the conclusion, just looking at the person and not at his social situation, that he or she is definitely in a very disturbed, disordered state – whatever may have brought them to this pass. However, psychiatrists do often diagnose plenty of people as psychotics who don't seem to me to have anything intrinsically the matter with them. In that case, the diagnosis comes to be like the positioning of someone on a social chessboard. Let's say the knight is in a particular position and, the next move, he may be taken. There's nothing wrong with the knight as a piece. Pick up the knight or any of the pieces that have been taken. There's nothing wrong with any of them. It's their positions in relation to the game that determines whether they should be captured. It's that position that determines whether one should be socially helpless. And it falls to other people to decree what should happen to them. That's a position of political weakness. It seems to me that in that kind of small-scale political situation, they lose all power. In our society, zero power, that position belongs not to the convicted criminal but to the committed mental patient because the person who gets put in that position is stripped of everything. They are even stripped of the right to decide if parts of their brain are going to be removed. Almost anything can be done to them, whether they like it or not. And the position is that one is at the mercy of those representatives of society that society has appointed to be in complete control of one's life under those circumstances. I feel that power is at the moment in the West and in Russia completely unmoderated. It can be used all the way to destroy someone totally.

209

If someone had an organic brain condition, would you feel differently about the control over him? Is there a distinction between the medical and the political points in your argument?

If I'm knocked down in the street and I'm rendered unconscious and I'm bleeding from internal injuries, then I am completely at the mercy of how other people are going to act towards me. In those circumstances, I've got no objection at all to other people acting according to the arrangements our society makes under those circumstances. I hope they will do their best for me.

But my own view of how far a doctor can go to give someone help is probably a minority view. For instance, if I'm dying of cancer, I feel it is absolutely abhorrent, as is common medical practice, that the patient isn't told he's dying. Everyone else might know but not him. If I'm dying, I want to be the first person to know. I also feel that it is my absolute right to die in my own way as long as I'm not imposing unfairly on other people. I have a perfect right to die in my own house. If I happen not to want what the doctors say is the best thing for me, if I have cancer and I don't want an operation, I don't feel there should be any question. I'm entitled to refuse treatment, to refuse to go into hospital, I'm entitled to die in my own bed or wherever else I want to. I also feel quite entitled to kill myself, as far as the law of the land is concerned. Whether it's against the law of mankind is another matter. But I don't feel the state has the right to interfere with what's going on inside my body, in health or in sickness. What chemicals I have inside my body, all that, seems to me to be my own business and no one else's. And that goes for everybody else.

In legal theory, people do have all those rights. Do you think they are denied in practice?

Oh yes, not for everyone. But it's a daily, undramatic routine for hundreds of thousands of people in our Western industrial-technological-medical system for them to be denied those rights.

In The Politics of Experience, *you wrote that therapy was extending itself and that a therapist needed to be able to combine great authority with an ability to improvise.*

All sorts of things go on within the general scope of therapy and psychiatry. There are some psychiatrists who see therapy in those terms, but I would say that the majority of psychiatrists aren't interested in therapy of this order.

What are psychiatrists interested in then?
They're interested in the chemical control of mental states
and behaviour. They're interested in exploring ways in which
the different forms of what they'd call mental illness or
psychopathology can be classified. And they're interested in the
way that different syndromes within that classification can be
defined clinically and medically. They're also interested in the way
they can be treated by medical means. They're interested in
pursuing and developing that line of country. In what I've written
and what I've practised, I've found, for me anyway, that that
is an extended metaphor for seeing these things which is
counter-productive for me. And I've given some of the reasons.

*It seems to me that people have a gut reaction to what you say,
it's an emotional thing, yes or no. It's not analysed. Has that been
your experience?*
It seems to be, yes.

Why do you think that is?
Why do *you* think that is?

*I think because it's rather threatening and especially so to
conventional psychiatrists who, if one follows you, should be out of
their jobs and out of their expertise. Don't you think it is a matter of
your work being threatening?*
In a way, yes, and in a way, no. For instance, when I was on the
Dick Cavett Show in America, they also had on Rollo May and
Nathan Klein, who is a director of one of the major drug research
programmes. The question of primal screaming came up and I
said, I was in a way being naive, that I wondered what all the fuss
was about. The great thing that Janov had managed to do, in a
very American style, was to somehow make it respectable, if
you've got enough money, to scream. Not just allowable but
respectable. Anyone who had $3,000 could yell and scream and
groan and writhe and sob and agonise. Even without any particular
guidance, I'm sure that someone would feel better for it at the end
of three weeks. What's wrong with that? Isn't it obvious to anyone
with any common sense that you would feel better if you had had
the chance to do that. But Nathan Klein said, and he looks like a
perfectly healthy guy: 'Well, your patients go to see you to help
them to do things that my patients come to me to stop them

doing because they don't want to do them.' Tranquillisers are quick, cheap and effective. I think there will always be a majority of people who, in our present civilisation, don't want to have any truck with the sort of thing I spend my time doing. They don't want anything to do with it. So I don't feel psychiatrists need feel threatened by it. All I say is, if they let me and my crowd live, we're not going to stop them doing what they're doing except in some of the worst excesses. And I'm certainly entitled to say that something is ethically wrong and, also, a lot of it is sheer stupidity and very bad science, very bad medicine.

If I felt depressed and went to a doctor who gave me a tranquilliser and that made me happy and I felt happy to be made happy like that, would you see anything wrong with that?
Not if that's what you're asking for. I'm thankful for Alka-Seltzer, for aspirin, for coffee and, at different times, for amytal and benzedrine and amphetamine. If I find that for all my meditation, for all my insight, that I get into some sort of downer that a cup of coffee will raise me from – fine. The same thing if I take a tranquilliser.

But you don't want them rammed down your throat?
No, I don't want them rammed down my throat or into my bloodstream or into my mind if I don't want them and haven't asked for them. I also want some measure of honesty as to what I'm getting. These drugs are commodities, they're manufactured. A great deal of money goes into researching them. Between themselves you will find that chemical manufacturers are aware that these drugs are very imprecise blunt instruments. They know there are serious side-effects. But, partly because they are imbued with the sheer sweetness of the technology of getting it sharper and better – and, in a way, I sympathise with it because if you're going to have something, let's pick it off quickly – and partly because they need a lot of money to do the research in these things, in advanced molecular chemistry, they want to sell the stuff to people. Psychiatrists are not chemists, are not pharmacologists. A lot of the people who give these drugs are family doctors who just give, more or less, what is sent through the post. An occasional article might reverberate if it comes out in the major medical journals but the vast amount of stuff that comes out makes it practically impossible for anyone unless they

are very close up to a research field to know just what is going on. If, for instance, someone's pushing it a bit. Conning is going on all the time. So that, within the scientific club at that level, trust is really established only through personal contact. So this guy is really honest, he really wants to find out, he's not using the most complex problems of science just to advance his own firm.

You have been represented, and this perhaps follows from what you have said, as holding a very left-wing revolutionary position politically. Is this right?
Never ever. I'm not anything like that politically and I have never indicated at any time that I was. In the collection that came out of the Roundhouse in 1967, the paper that I delivered was entitled *The Obvious* and, in that company, I made it quite clear in the last two paragraphs what my position was, which was one of extreme scepticism of all sides of the question. At the same time, I wasn't going to shut up if I felt like speaking out on social anomalies and injustices that come my way.

At that time, people like me were aware that the US launched a mass air effort in Vietnam and Cambodia. A year ago, the then US Secretary of Defence said he was unaware of it. I don't know who to believe or what to believe. It's very difficult to tell. I was talking in an atmosphere like that and I still am. The stuff that's going on today is even more . . . zanier.

Have you continued to work with family therapy on the lines suggested in Sanity, Madness and the Family?
Yes. It's almost ten years since that book was being researched and written. I've been working with families and continued to be involved with different sorts of family systems and social systems. I've had a chance to travel a bit and had experience of families in different parts of the world, Indian families, Singhalese families and New Zealand families.

Is the family nexus particularly pernicious in the West or did you find much the same sorts of things going on in India?
Well, this is one of the things I'd be glad to correct. I don't, and some people seem to confuse me with David Cooper and his attitude towards the family particularly as expressed in *The Death of the Family,* condemn the family. His spirit, that spirit, isn't my spirit about the family. You're interviewing me right now in the

midst of my family. I enjoy living in a family. I think the family is the best thing that still exists biologically as a natural thing. I wouldn't like to see it disrupted by state control or interfered with, as could very easily happen if you adopted the slogans of the sixties' psycho-politico anti-psychiatry anti-family left and used that as an excuse to take over. Parents will soon have to have a licence to be allowed to have a child. I have someone who comes to see me who goes along to a psychiatric facility because she's distressed, emotionally disturbed. The first thing they do is to test her. They test her and they find that she's very emotionally disturbed and one of the things that she's disturbed about is the possibility of having a child, whether she's a suitable case for maternity. So, they say, OH NO, NEVER, on no account, never have a child! That just needs a bit more touch on the switch and she'll have to have special permission to have a child. Unless she passes her psychological aptitude test, she won't be one of those who is allowed to have a child. The family is, I think, potentially a great thing, potentially a place where adults can play and be with children and the child can be with some people who are still a bit more human than a lot of those they will run into later. If the kids and the adults who make up a family get it off together well, then it's absolutely great.

My attack on the family is aimed at the way I felt many children are subjected to gross forms of violence and violation of their rights, to humiliation at the hands of adults who don't know what they're doing, and are so arrogant in their ignorance, they're not likely to get the point. Nevertheless, every generation is a new generation. There's no reason basically why these disturbed children of these even more disturbed adults can't remain children with their children and move out from there.

Do you think people can be very different, more human with their own children then?
Yes.

Another position you have appeared to hold is that to become more whole, more complete, one needs some form of religious experience, not God in capital letters. You describe one voyage of a so-called schizophrenic not as an episode of madness but as something spiritual. Is the need for the religious something you hold?
There seem to be spontaneous happenings in the lives of some people, at least they seem to be spontaneous, where these people

become engrossed in some sort of inner psychic state. While in that, they sometimes become completely incompetent socially, unable to carry on and function. I've seen enough of what used to be, and still is called in psychiatric practice, a schizophrenic episode or a schizophrenic form episode or a schizo-affective-reactive state or what might be an acute episode in a progressive schizophrenic process of hebephrenic deterioration or, if you prefer, what not. From my clinical experience, I have come to believe that for many people, if they are not interfered with when they go into that sort of thing, they seem to come out of it again. Sometimes like Jesse Watkins did, in ten days, or sometimes longer. Now in the household environment asylums that we have in London, the successors of Kingsley Hall, this sort of thing happens and goes on. That is the sort of concentrated experience every other week they have in these set-ups. By the person who is going through it, it's often said to be spiritual whatever they mean by spiritual. There's a feeling of profundity very often and a sense of realising all sorts of things that hadn't been realised before, sometimes in such dazzling profusion that the whole thing is impossible to decipher. People who from their point of view are in the midst of that might well appear to others to be incoherent and disorientated. In a way, they are incoherent and disorientated.

What has all the fuss been about? I think it's a matter of impatience and regimentation and the mechanisation of Man, of having no other time-sense than clock time. Whatever is going on is not given any credit for having any method in this apparent madness. There's no sense in it and there's no real readiness to listen to a few people like me when they say that if you don't do this, this will pass because they don't want to know that.

These experiences are, in a way, the flash, the razzle-dazzle. It's compared to acid. It's made into an ideological position. It's a question of Is that a flash of different states of mind? and I'm speaking here of the best of it for the worst of it is absolute hell and no one would ever want to live in the states of mind some people can get into. But my point is that if you look at what psychiatrists do to what seem to me to be pretty normal people, it beggars description what they do when someone is out of their mind. It's like an isometric situation when what is being done is the absolute opposite of what ought to be done, of what clinical tradition and medical sagacity in the Western tradition dictate should be done.

R. D. Laing

But do you think that one must go through some such spiritual experience to become better, become ennobled?
No.

You have been represented as holding that.
I have never ever said that.

What happened to Kingsley Hall? Did it come to a natural end or was it forced to end?
A group calling ourselves the Philadelphia Association was formed in 1964. That group still exists with some different people. I'm still the chairman. We continued to operate in London. Our aim as a group was to develop work in this field along our lines. One of the main things was having households where this sort of thing could be allowed to happen. Kingsley Hall was the largest such place. We had it for five years from 1965 to 1970. We leased the building for five years in 1965 from Muriel Lester and the trustees of the building. They gave us the building for five years and we had it for five years. Now, we have a cluster of buildings in Bayswater and Archway. The work is going on.

Do you do much therapy there yourself?
I'm around but I spend most of my time in this room. I sort of stay here and see people here. I go around to the places. I may go and spend an evening there tonight. But I go around once a week apart from what may happen *ad hoc.*

One of the things that I'm trying to see is what different psychologists and psychiatrists think Man is if 'What is Man?' isn't too vast a question. Do you think we are limited by our physical-chemical make-up?
That depends what you mean by one's total chemical make-up and that depends on what you mean by 'limited by'. Are we limited by those objects of our sight, taste, smell and body perception that we can measure or not? Chemistry belongs to that domain. If we're talking about what we think is the main that is being studied when we look at ourselves, or what is apparently ourselves, in the manner of science then we get a certain picture of things. If you want to weigh this book, it can be measured absolutely precisely. But if you ask me if I feel it as heavy or if you give me the book and ask 'How heavy does it feel to you?', it might feel different

216

depending on the temperature of the room or how my body feels. My body may feel heavier or lighter. But, at the moment, it's impossible to weigh that feeling of heaviness. You can weigh a book but you can't weigh the feeling of the weight of that book. Now that goes for everything else. You can describe in detail the objects in this room that I see and you see but we cannot find a scientific way, at the moment, of getting at the seeing. I'm talking about a really hard natural science way of the most impeccable genuine order, the type of science that astronomy, physics, chemistry is, where any scientist who meets another scientist recognises him as such right away. I think that that is the sort of science, if we're talking about how I feel, not what can be picked up from my EEG, not what can be picked up from my heart as a pump or from any instrument that measures to compare and contrast. Even if you can pick up when I have a feeling, even if you can pick up when I'm dreaming, even if you can put an electrode into my brain and make me dream what is put there by a micro-computer that might set up certain patterns of colour in my cerebral cortex or temporal lobe that could induce me to see a colour or a different shape, it's still not my feeling or dream. We know that very slight changes in enzymes at the molecular level affect it. But, even then, I don't see that if you looked at my brain and my nerves, how you could ever infer this whole world that I see is coming out of there. Suppose you could probe my brain. Now, the eyes aren't like a photographic plate that I can take out so that I can examine the plate. The whole world is the photographic plate. The chemistry is absolutely there all the way and the whole world is there. As William James made clear, you need only the slightest touch of nitrous oxygen, laughing gas, in the way of an acid trip or mescalin or anything can take you far out, through centre point, through the total void and back again in a few seconds. So the whole thing seems to be chemical but it's still the whole thing which isn't chemistry.

It seems to me at the moment to be absolutely mysterious. It seems absurd to say that all it is is the stuff that is in here. [He points to his head.] Yet, in some mysterious way, the slightest changes in here affect what we see out there. If we didn't dream, neuroscientists couldn't take stuff off the brain, couldn't take EEG measures in different stages of sleep to correlate them with dream states. But when we dream, it isn't someone looking down a microscope though we might dream of someone looking down a

217

microscope. We might say that we dream our molecules. The whole thing might be an auto-perception of our brain by our brain. But then, what's our brain? A brain itself is an object of perception. Therefore, it can be classified as all the objects it itself sees are. All the stuff we see is inferred from what is going into the brain. If the brain is itself an object of perception, it's occurring after all the events it has inferred. You can't say the brain is inferring it because the brain has yet to exist. The brain can't see itself, according to the brain, till distal stimuli enter the eyes, go through total transformations in electric wave impulses at the retina, go to optic chiasm, go through two sets of synapses and to the optic cortex. Then, if the rest of the body and its chemistry and its hormones are all right, we suppose we see the visual world. In that case the visual world in occurring after all that and all I have just said is an inference from what is, we are inferring, occurring after. Is the visual brain a part of the set of visual objects? So how can the visual brain which is one of the set of visual objects be used, since it is one of the members of the set that is up for explanation? So, we don't seem to have managed to explain it that way.

There are different intellectual paradoxes too. There's all that science can't begin to get. It's like throwing a net over the surface of the ocean and trying to drag out the ocean.

Do you think science will arrive some day at a fairly total explanation of these mysteries in the end?
No, science is looking in one direction only. Science can only see what it sees down the microscope.

But it can't reintegrate that up the microscope?
A scientist can – and without stopping being a scientist. But he can't have science as a superordinate central position from which he is integrated as a full man. He will have to accept that science is one of the enterprises of the human spirit which is subsumed within that enterprise.

From what you have said, it would seem that you approve the classical scientific tradition and aren't opposed to it as one might think?
It's not possible to answer that in a few words without being misleading because you have to discuss what is really classical

science. I'm here concerned with classical biological science. It's a question of the exact knowledge of biological systems. I think that the way we go about studying biological systems is, unfortunately or not, a consequence of a prior attitude to biological systems which is pre-scientific in the mind of the scientist. Until the scientist studies biological systems he isn't a biological scientist yet. And the way he studies biological systems is not determined scientifically. It can't be. He hasn't yet started to be a scientist. He's got to take a gamble. I think that some of the best credited biological science, Galvani, Volta, Sir Charles Sherrington, is a monumental mistake. Monumental. But my main critique of it, if I ever get it systematised, will have to be made on scientific as well as ethical grounds.

And this pre-scientific attitude leads to bias in scientists?
That goes for all of us. That's where my ground is: that pre-scientific ground that infuses the scientific is my ground, my special subject of study. I can't say object of study.

A much shortened version of this interview appeared in *Psychologie*.

9
Leupold-Löwenthal

The chairman of the Viennese Psychoanalytical Society should be formal and a little stiff. Freud founded the Society and was its first chairman. The present chairman holds a position in direct descent from Freud. Since many critical commentators have sniped at 'the gospel according to Freud', we should find in the current chairman almost a religious figure, a kind of Pope of the Psyche. We have already seen that McClelland has compared the impact of psychoanalysis with the impact, to its founders at least, of early Christianity. Psychoanalysis is often spoken of as a new religion.

Dr Harald Leupold-Löwenthal, the current chairman of the Society, is not at all formal and stiff. He does not seem to seek the mantle of a priest or guru. Throughout the interview, he stresses that he is giving his own personal opinion which may be peculiar, which may be contested by analysts elsewhere. In fact, he says, there must be a definite relaxation. You cannot spend your time analysing your friends, acquaintances or your wife. Divorce lies in that direction. He confessed he found it much harder with his children. Once when his young son showed himself very demonstrative to his mother, he called him 'Oedipus'. More seriously, he says that being an analyst affects the way you bring children up because you are so aware of the consequences that anything you do may have on them. He found it very hard to be tough with them and he wondered if that was not, in fact, bad because children do need some limit beyond which they must not go: he finds it hard to yell at them.

He is a tremendously friendly man. I arrived at eight in the evening for a first interview. I found myself invited to dinner, spent the next day with him, his wife and family and actually only did the interview the following day, after another dinner. His conversation is spiced with jokes. They strike all subjects, paradise and pissoirs,

220

anti-Semites and Jews. He has that curious knack of many non-Jewish Viennese of actually seeming Jewish. He comes himself from a well-established Protestant family. One of his forefathers studied under Melanchthon who was Luther's inspiration. 'When the Nazis came,' he told me, 'all students had to establish their Aryanness so I took this vast pile of family documents and dumped them on their table and told them to take their choice.' They did not care for that attitude at all.

Leupold-Löwenthal lives in a large old flat in the centre of Vienna. He also works from there. As you get to the first-floor landing, one plaque at one entrance tells you it is his home, the other entrance leads to his analysis room. It is the room next to that which I found interesting. It is a study foaming with books. They are stacked everywhere. The shelves are piled up to the tall ceiling and, somewhere in the clutter, we found two chairs to sit on while we talked, dwarfed by these volumes. On the few free walls of this study, Leupold-Löwenthal has some mementoes of Freud, though he is much too young to have known him.

Leupold-Löwenthal expands in the interview on the relationship any analyst must have with Freud and, especially, Freud's work. In 1972, he was responsible for mounting the Goethe Institute exhibition on Freud, an exhibition that travelled all over the world. As a result, he also mounted the permanent exhibition in Freud's old flat at 19 Berggasse. He has become one of the leading authorities about Freud as he had to study him for the exhibition *ad infinitum*. 'It was very interesting for me as an analyst to have to read everything he ever wrote and to be so close to him. It was good too. Finally, there were times when I was really sick of Freud which allowed me to resolve certain problems in myself, problems of the hold of his authority,' he says. He admits that all analysts have to cope with the giant figure of Freud.

Leupold-Löwenthal not only enjoys jokes but says that he does sometimes use them in his actual work. He feels strongly about the ethics involved in being an analyst and the responsibility. The responsibility starts even before you take someone into analysis for more people seek analysis than can get it. The analyst has to choose whom to have. This is a painful choice, confesses Leupold-Löwenthal, but all doctors come up against such choices in dealing with the allocation of kidney machines or iron lungs. The need to make such choices stifles any tendency to cynicism you might have. And so will your patient who will 'hit you on the head'.

Leupold-Löwenthal

Leupold-Löwenthal came to be an analyst by a circuitous route. He studied and practised medicine. After the war in Vienna, you had to work and wait for three years before you made any money as a doctor. 'I was the house doctor and my professor expected me to start at eight in the morning and never to finish. If I was not there at ten at night, he would tell me I wasn't working.' He adds wryly, 'Ah, these young doctors today don't know how easy they have it.' He left Vienna to work in England at the Royal Cancer Hospital on a British Council grant of £35, 'which was much more than the zero I was getting in Vienna'. He worked on implanting tumours in rats to see which tumour tissue would thrive and which would be rejected. When he returned to Vienna, he worked as a hospital doctor specialising in neurology. One day, the head of his department sent him a patient for psychotherapy. He told him he had never done any psychotherapy. His boss obviously did not care for excuses. It was Friday evening and the patient was coming on the Monday morning. 'I went to the library, got a copy of Freud's Introductory Lectures and read them. It seemed to make sense. And my first case worked out wonderfully – a textbook marvel.' The second case was more confusing: the third case was hopeless. 'I decided I had no idea what I was doing and that I would abandon psychotherapy.'

He then went to work as a psychiatrist for the World Health Organisation in Geneva. People were surprised to find a psychiatrist – and maybe a Viennese one especially – who seemed to have no training in psychoanalysis. He became seriously interested in analysis. He also discovered that he did not enjoy 'being a desk doctor. I need patients.' He started a training analysis, returned to Vienna and, for the last ten years, has been earning his living from analysis. He has also written.

His early career makes it clear that he is neither ignorant of nor unimpressed by conventional science which often likes to place psychoanalysis beyond its pale. 'But what you accept as scientific is a matter of convention,' he adds. And what conventional psychology and psychiatry claim in respect of psychoanalysis seems to be to him very superficial and often ludicrously naive.

'For example, critics have a tendency to read a few of the works of Freud written before 1930 and assume that that is where psychoanalysis is now. They seem to ignore ego psychology and work on ego defences. They seem to assume that no one contradicts what Freud laid down. And their attempts to verify

222

some of the theories in terms that they would accept as scientific are marvellously naive.'

He elaborates this in the interview. He tells of a study in which experimental psychologists decided to test Freud's idea of the oral stage in childhood by offering children a choice of chocolates, lollipops and other sweets. The experimenters decided that if the children chose lollipops which were for sucking then it would constitute evidence for an oral stage. 'If you just look at what children do with chocolates and other sweets, you will often see them suck them,' Leupold-Löwenthal acidly commented. But, of course, this piece of observation would contradict the neat assumption of the experimenters and so was never even considered.

He denies the fact that psychoanalysts refuse to let their sessions be taped or their results be evaluated. When Eysenck published his well-known paper in 1952 in which he claimed to show that if a patient had no treatment at all, his chances of recovering were better than if he had analysis, analysts were always being criticised for sheltering themselves behind total privacy, so that the sessions could never be recorded in any way. Nothing must disturb the sanctity of the analytical session. 'I object to the "sanctity",' grinned Dr Leupold-Löwenthal when I made that point. He stresses that things have changed somewhat.

First, psychoanalysts in the USA feel themselves under great pressure to be seen to be scientifically respectable. Many of them are working, therefore, with experimental psychologists on comparing the effects of analysis and other therapies. 'They have also recorded and filmed many analytical sessions', he added. He still dislikes using a tape-recorder. The tape could fall into the wrong hands. The patient may feel what he says will not be totally confidential. The act of taping a session may have a symbolic meaning for the patient which alters the situation. 'I don't know what I am doing necessarily when I tape a session,' he pointed out. And there remains the very practical point that an analysis takes at least 600 hours or so. Who is going to have the time to listen, sift and, indeed, analyse the tapes of the analysis? But he has done it and is not frightened of doing it. It seems to him rather faddish and it does not really help sort out what is at the root of the dispute between psychoanalysts and conventionally scientific psychologists and psychiatrists.

'You must ask what is the goal of an analysis which is a very long process. When Eysenck writes about behaviour therapy, you know what his goal is. It is to get rid of the symptom. In fact, the cases that are the easiest and quickest to deal with in analysis are precisely the kind of phobias that behaviour therapy claims its great successes with.'

But, for him, the goal of analysis is to make the patient autonomous and independent. Behaviour therapy is, at best, very incomplete as it copes only with the most visible of symptoms. Group work seems to him rather dangerous as it substitutes for a person's original dependencies a dependency on the group which may, in order to protect the group, actually decide to sacrifice the individual. He rejects, too, Marcuse's famous argument that the real aim of psychoanalysis is to get the individual to adjust to society, to be realistic and, therefore, malleable. 'Of course an individual may choose to adjust to society in this way, but that is not my aim to get him to do that.' His aim is to make him able freely to choose for himself – not to guide that choice.

The trouble is, of course, that a phrase like 'making a person autonomous and independent' will seem to an experimental psychologist to be so vague as to be meaningless. And, perhaps, worse even than meaningless. For it provides a refuge behind which one can indulge in all kinds of woolly wishful thinking. Moreover, if you elaborate the image of psychoanalysis as a religious activity, you can then find in the long period of training analysis, an initiation into rites and mysteries – precisely the kind of initiation you never get over, whose assumptions you never question. 'But, of course, I can turn this argument against the experimental psychologist who undergoes a similar kind of initiation himself in which he learns to respect certain procedures and statistics, in which he learns what is scientific and what is not scientific', he argues. And it is precisely these convictions on both sides that make it very hard to get proper co-operation between them. He thinks that social psychology has hardly begun to use psychoanalytic ideas. Its use of the idea of 'projection' has been very simple.

'There is, I think, an interesting divergence between an analyst like myself and the experimental psychologist. Few psychologists have had training as doctors and they are oriented towards research. They are able to use people as well, perhaps, as experimental animals. They have created a class of experimental persons. After all, if you deny to a person the kind of therapy you think would help him and if you do this for a number of years, you are not doing your best to help him.'

On the other hand, he admits, there are countless cases in which psychoanalysts have become interested in some particular area or have found that their patients served them up exactly the dreams and interpretations which reflected that interest. The analyst seems to be able to lead the patient in a way that may make it hard to evaluate what is happening objectively. It is more a matter of the patient pleasing the analyst than of anything else. Research and analysis may make bad bedfellows.

No one, of course, feels that experimental psychology is at a stage where it can easily cope with ideas as complex as Freud's. Some psychologists argue, in fact, that Freud's ideas are useless not because they are wrong, but because they cannot be tested. And, however much one may agree with some of the points Leupold-Löwenthal neatly scores at the expense of psychologists, there remains the fact that he does not offer public proof of the Freudian and neo-Freudian hypotheses he works with. He says that he uses, tests, confirms and rejects these hypotheses every day. They are confirmed on the couch. They could be, in principle, confirmed by going through the spools and spools of tape of many analytical sessions. I pressed him to say if he had found areas where psychoanalytic hypotheses needed to be altered. It would be a curious science, after all, in which no ideas were ever falsified. He hesitated and then explained that he thought the libido theory – the heart, indeed, of Freud's work – might need some modification that made sex less important and aggression more important. He thought we had to some extent replaced the taboo on sex with a taboo on aggression. 'If I were to hit you now that would be completely unacceptable,' he pointed out, even though I had been highly critical of psychoanalytic ideas. 'I do not think that we have yet lived through sexual liberation but we have only talked about it,' he added. Still, Freud's Vienna seemed characterised by a taboo on sex or, at least, on open sex. We seem to him often to use our new sexual freedoms to mask aggressive patterns of behaviour. For example, a girl who was once under pressure to remain a virgin may find she comes under pressure from her friends to sleep with all the boys in their group. The pressure still exists but it has become more aggressive, perhaps. He finds these shifts away from sexual taboos and towards aggressive ones in some of his patients. He elaborates in the interview.

He also thinks that analysis has to go on looking for ways of making itself quicker and more accessible. The process still lasts three to four years. Costly, slow, it is needed by far more people than can get it. 'I take the greatest care before I take a patient into analysis. He or she must have a certain degree of intelligence and, if I am not sure, I may use a clinical psychologist to test his IQ. However much you explain to a patient, he does not really know what he is letting himself in for until the analysis starts,' he added; by which time it may be very harmful, indeed, to stop. So, in cases where he does not think analysis is suitable or when he is working for the Austrian National Health Service which does not allow scope for analysis, he uses psychotherapeutic techniques. He finds these can be useful if you have limited, as opposed to analytic, aims.

There have been all kinds of attempts to get analysis to work quicker. In fact, Eysenck got the idea for behaviour therapy from a psychoanalyst, Alexander Herzberg, who made his patients do certain 'tasks' each day after their session. The 'tasks' speeded up recovery, it seemed to Herzberg, and Eysenck argued that it might be these tasks – which led to the extinction of some symptom – rather than analysis itself which cured. Leupold-Löwenthal is sceptical about attempts in the USA to use drugs with analysis or to use group work because in both cases, it is not very clear what the individual is actually receiving. What does the drug mean in the context of an analysis? What does the group do if, at the end of a session, it has made one individual a victim, a focus for hostility? Both situations seem to him to be playing a little too freely with 'deep' material, as he calls it. He remembers once allowing a singer patient to produce some 'deep' material in the last ten minutes of a session before the summer holidays when she was off on an opera tour. The next he heard from her was that her opera had to be cancelled because she was indisposed, as they put it. 'You learn,' he pointed out wryly.

In many ways, his opinions about analysis are very interesting because of the study of Freud that he was involved in to mount the Goethe Exhibition. There are a number of ideas about Freud, one senses, that he is only ready to hint at at present – presumably as he has great respect for Anna Freud, Freud's daughter, who is a distinguished analyst in her own right. Some myths might be questioned.

But, undoubtedly, Leupold-Löwenthal believes that some of the ideas about Freud put forward by Ernest Jones in his massive but far from definitive biography are misleading. Jones was a disciple of Freud.

> 'For instance, you would never know from Jones that Paul Federn who was Freud's president of the Vienna Society for twenty years was an important person. Jones did not like Federn, that's all.
> Also, Jones was an English goy, to put it delicately, and he was not able to really understand Vienna or Viennese Jews which is crucial to understanding Freud.'

Leupold-Löwenthal is also rather critical of certain decisions to protect the Freud archives which will not be opened till the year 2000. He says there is a need to protect the rights of the family – 'and I mean the close family, not analysts' – to preserve their privacy, for Freud was very honest in revealing his inner life but always said 'so far and no farther'. But the lack of material from the archives has led to 'speculations' which he makes sound as distasteful as those of a property spiv. For instance, Paul Roazen's book *Brother Animal* (1970) suggests that Freud wilfully stopped analysing one of his pupils who then committed suicide because of this rejection. At a more ridiculous level, of course, you have, he points out, 'Irving Stone on Freud or the film of Freud. I started laughing there when Freud went to treat a young nobleman who was found embracing a tailor's dummy and calling it mummy.' He was asked to leave the cinema because this was not a film for those who failed to understand such profundities.

But if the archives were opened they might throw new light on two strong ideas we have of Freud. The first is that he found it very hard to get his ideas accepted in Vienna. Leupold-Löwenthal has admitted that it was not till Freud was over sixty that he was made a professor at the University of Vienna but gently hints that his work was not as badly received as history has it. Or not for long. Secondly, the archives could tell us more about Freud's failure, or his refusal, to make a name for himself in other fields. He nearly discovered the bisexuality of the eel in his first research paper but he abandoned that project. His discovery of the potential of cocaine in eye therapy again was a major breakthrough but he did not pursue it. 'To be a psychoanalyst seems to be on the fringe,' Leupold-Löwenthal argues, 'and it may be that Freud wanted to be on the fringe.' He was

227

certainly in an extraordinary position as a young doctor because he refused to wait for a research appointment at the Vienna Hospital and so worked instead as a practising doctor but also pursued scientific work. He was very much an outsider among both the research doctors and the practising doctors. We await both the opening of the archives and the definitive biography of Freud. 'Even my generation of analysts who never knew Freud personally may be too close to him for that.'

Talking to him is fascinating but a little depressing in the end. I had gone to Vienna from Lyon where I had talked to Professor Michel Jouvet whose neurophysiological work on dreaming has helped make many of the mechanisms of dreaming clear. To Leupold-Löwenthal, his ideas about what psychoanalytic ideas of dreaming are seem simplistic. To Jouvet, Leupold-Löwenthal's whole approach would seem to ignore the most basic facts about dreaming such as that animals seem to dream. Both are busy and eminent in their fields. They do not have the time to be more generous in studying what each other is doing. Each specialises in one specialist approach to one specialised problem. All of which must make comprehensive solutions harder to obtain.

Did the war affect psychoanalysis in Vienna disastrously?
Psychoanalysis was a forbidden Jewish science. Most analysts were Jewish and there were only two of those who remained. There was some underground training in psychoanalysis and then, the devastating economic effects of the war after the fall of the Nazi empire meant Austria had to be rebuilt. It was very difficult to start psychoanalysis anew.

But has the Viennese Psychoanalytic Society recovered now and started to flourish?
I would say that the Viennese Society started to become flourishing again because the interest of young doctors and young social workers and psychologists to train in psychoanalysis is very great. So we have now reached, at least in numbers of students, a situation like in the blooming times of pre-1938 which is quite a thing for a small country like Austria.

Has the Viennese Society remained a fairly classical society, not diverging into ideas of group work, encounter work, which seem to have stemmed from psychoanalysis in many other countries?

One could say that the main tendency of Viennese analysts isn't to keep a classical position but an orthodox position. We have quite good contacts with colleagues in France and Germany and Britain and the States so that we are open to influences and to new developments. We sift through them and we take what we find important and necessary. With some developments, we don't go along so easily. It seems to me that this isn't the worst attitude you could have.

But is it an attitude reinforced – to use a word I'm sure you don't care for much – by the fact that the presence of Freud broods over you in Vienna much more than anywhere else?
I wouldn't say so. Every analyst during his training has Freud brooding over him, to some extent, as a gigantic father-figure if you want to use this expression in a naive way. You must come to terms with Freud. Freud is still a very important basis for what we are doing. But analysis has developed farther and, when you read Freud, the complete works, you find that he himself has this tendency not to stay fixed in one position he's taken up. He constantly rechecked his ideas and concepts, constantly remodelled them. This makes it so difficult when we read in texts quotations from Freud because you always have to look carefully at what time Freud has written this. It's a very easy and endless game to play, to read quotations from different periods of his work and with different meanings. This can give a very wrong picture. So, you have to plough further on. You can't remain with the development of psychoanalysis up to 1938.

It's often argued that one of the ways in which analysis has developed is through work on ego psychology, work on ego defences? Could you explain what some of this development has been?
You see, this is structural theory in psychoanalysis – id, ego, super-ego. Analysts became aware of the functions of the ego. Anna Freud herself published a very important book on that, *The Ego and the Mechanisms of Defence*. Hans Hartmann, another analyst, published before 1938 an important book on ego functioning. This was the starting point of the development of ego psychology in psychoanalysis and this also made possible the application of psychoanalysis to a lot of other fields in a different way from before. Applied psychoanalysis, let's say, before the

229

First World War was an attempt to show that the findings you made on the couch were also true in other surroundings, in mythology, in the study of literature and art. But, at least to a reader of my generation, it became a bit tedious to find out that three hundred personages in antiquity had an Oedipus complex. But the new development of ego psychology and object relations means that you can find new and fruitful ways of understanding phenomena of literature and art. This is what a new development makes possible, a starting point for co-operation with the humanities on one side and with the social sciences on the other.

Do you feel that co-operation has begun or is it still to be grasped out of the fog?

It's begun and it's still in the fog, because the language difficulties, especially the language difficulties with scientists, seem to be very great. I find it easiest to collaborate with scientists who have had some form of analytic training or, at least, analytical experience. A lot of misunderstanding of analysis comes from the fact that people think you can treat the body of Freud's work as something from which you can dig up pieces and not look at the whole development that went on and what, specifically, was going on when that piece was published. Marcuse, for instance. I can't imagine how he could overlook the fact that analysis is not trying to adjust people to social reality as the analyst sees it.

But, surely, if you take Civilisation and Its Discontents, *one of the main points seems to be that unless you can move the sexual energies to other fields you simply will not do all these other necessary things?*

You see, *Civilisation and Its Discontents* is one of the works Freud always called 'speculative'. And he says it at the beginning of this particular publication, but it is always overlooked. He did not look on this as strictly scientific but as a work of, more or less, a philosophical character. And it doesn't mean that, as an analyst, one has to take this position, the cultural pessimism of Freud is well known, yes, but out of this work you cannot draw the conclusion that is so often made – that the position of psychoanalysis is reactionary.

But doesn't saying that the work is speculative put you in a difficult position in this way. To a lay reader, the flavour of the book

may be rather like what you would call the strictly scientific corpus.
It feels much the same. You seem to be always teetering on that kind
of rope. That particular work may be speculative but, then, nothing
is really that hard.

Well, that is the feeling you sometimes have. The difficulty for the
non-analyst is to realise that here you have an application of
analytical experiences, experiences from patients to cultural
phenomena. The question is if such an application is legitimate. I,
myself, have done applications of analysis to certain kinds of
literature and I know how dangerous the application can be
because when an analyst applies psychoanalysis to literature he is
an expert in analysis (at least I hope he is) and he is an amateur in
literature. The same applies to the *littérateur* who applies what he
believes to be psychoanalytic concepts. So, you are always in hot
water when you do this kind of work. The only thing you can do
is be careful of what your concepts of the science may be.

But you don't have that kind of feeling when you write technical
analytical papers?

No, because I'm in my home port.

But, of course, the kind of warnings you issue about speculative
work seem very like what experimental psychologists might say of
analysis proper. Yes, the ideas are very interesting but, because of the
conditions under which it was done, I cannot accept it as proof, I
cannot accept it as being objectively valid.

You see, a discussion with experimental psychologists is difficult
because they have a certain position as to what they believe to be
scientific. I personally think that the question of what scientific
means, of what, in the end, is scientific, is a question of
convention. You can't scientifically prove what is scientific. The
English word isn't present for me at the present but the German
word is *Annahme.*

Assumption?

There is an assumption, yes, and for this, it is we who are
completely scientific. So, discussions where one is not criticising
what the other is doing but just telling him that he is not
scientific are not, to my feeling, doing much. Not much comes
out. It sounds like swearing at each other. I think we should try to
understand the concepts we have on both sides better. I think
much of what experimental psychologists do is very fascinating.

Have the attempts some experimental psychologists have made to verify some of Freud's ideas, on orality, on dream symbolism, been of any use to you? Are they valid, do you think?

It depends very much on the design of the experiment. And I must say, even if it offends someone, that the experimental design is often terribly naive, and psychoanalytic concepts of, say, orality are taken in a way which makes an analyst shudder. I don't remember the name of the people who did it but there was an experimental study on orality that used a Choose-A-Candy test in which children had to choose between two or three different sorts of candy, a lollipop, a chocolate and chewing gum and, from that, they made far-reaching conclusions as to whether or not the child was orally-fixated. Now, this is really too simple to be true. It is statistically beautiful, naturally. Now statistics with psychoanalytic concepts are difficult and that is due to the fact that the person-to-person situation, the analytic situation, is something highly complex. You may know that the experimental psychology of highly complex situations is very hard to study because there are so many intervening variables that to cancel them out, to get rid of all of them except the one you want to study, disturbs the situation in such a way that it often is not the same as it was.

Before we go on to the effects that observing a situation is likely to have on the situation, may I ask you why it would not be possible for a group of analysts to observe, say, a group of ten patients? Each patient could be treated individually, unseen, but at the end, each analyst could hand over his patients to the others and say, 'Now is this man all right?' or, 'Has the analysis worked? You could compare that to a group that had not had analysis. Would that not be possible without disturbing the sanctity of the analytic tête-à-tête?

I don't like the word sanctity. [Laughter.]

But still, couldn't that do something towards the doubts of the experimenters?

You see, experiments of that sort are being done by analysts in the United States where it's more keenly felt that psychoanalysis should be scientifically respectable by doing that kind of thing. I, personally, don't have the feeling that I must prove my respectability in experimental ways. These experiments done by analysts in co-operation with psychologists are very interesting.

But there's one thing I find disturbing about it. You see, most of the analysts in Austria come from psychiatry and we are used to working with patients. So the old medical principle, nothing which may do harm, is a bit ingrained in us. I always ask the question, what happens to a patient that I put through the mill of experimentation in the interests of science. And I sometimes have the feeling that this encumbers our possibility for experimental work. If you really want to test you have to start with a certain set of tests and interrogation before you do the treatment. You should, ideally, do it during the treatment and at the end. But the question is, what does this do to the patient. There I have got doubts. This is, to my mind, some of the difficulties we have with experimental psychologists. They have a *Versuchperson*. I don't know if there exists an English word for it – an experimental person. It sounds a bit like experimental animal. And they don't have much care for experimental persons. They can't have. It's not an attack I make now but it's just to explain certain personal difficulties if I have to use a tape-recorder in my sessions.

That could also be taken as a very comfortable belief for you to hold?
Yes, there's no doubt, no doubt. But I think when we try to talk together, we should, at least, give each other the benefit of the doubt that he might be an honest person.

But surely, and this is both rude and dabbling in amateur analysis, might not your reasons for not wanting that situation be precisely reasons that you can't make conscious?
That it might be unconscious reasons? I don't think this danger is very great. You know that the training of an analyst implies a very comprehensive analysis and, during analytic work, continuous self-analysis is going on. To be aware of my own reactions is one of the most important instruments of my daily work. So I must say – and, again, it may sound like an excuse – I would be aware if this was the main reason that I don't want to do this.

But does the tape-recorder have to disturb? I'm thinking of Laing and Esterson's study of families of schizophrenics in which all interviews were taped. Laing hardly comes into the category of obsessional experimenters who have the desire to put everything into neat experimental boxes. But they don't seem to have found there was damage or disturbance done by using tape. Do you have any experience for saying what you are saying?

I have some experience because I used a tape-recorder in psychoanalytic interviews with a certain group of persons, sexual deviators. I found that the most interesting things were told to me only after the tape had been switched off – which was a terrible strain on my memory. I had to write it all down. I think usually the tape-recorder is not such an interference – it could be lived with. But another thing I have to say is this. The situation with a patient is confidential. The patient knows that I keep his confidence and I do not divulge what he tells me. When I make a tape I don't have complete control of what happens to the tape. I might lose the tape. [Laughter. NB, this interview was recorded just after President Nixon had lost yet more tapes.] This could be a terrible happening because it might have unconscious meanings. What happens then? It is an intrusion into a situation where the patient has to be completely honest and it might endanger this honesty.

But you wouldn't have to identify the patient on tape. You would not even have to identify yourself as the analyst, Leupold-Löwenthal.
You could use a number of codes, you are quite right. For instance, when we publish case studies, it is a rule that we change the circumstances – the biography, the profession of the patient and so on – so that he can't possibly be identified. This means in cases where biographical data is very important for the understanding of the case you have to renounce the idea of publishing because you can't waive this in such a case without losing the meaning of it. It's a pity but it is so. I also find that the taking of notes is very often a calamity in that it doesn't cancel out automatically. I, personally, don't take notes. What I have to note, I note afterwards. One of the main instruments we work with is patients' free association giving them free attention. When I start taking notes this attention is focused and this might have an influence on my work. It's a well-known experience that if you are interested in a special scientific problem in psychoanalysis all your patients start telling you things around this theme. Therefore, research work and therapeutic work, I find, don't go well together. At least, the outcome, for the patient, is not quite sure.

But doesn't that mean that for an analyst to do research work is perhaps not irresponsible but, at least, not very caring for his patients?

234

I have to try, as far as possible, to cancel this out. Not to focus on what I am keenly interested in. The rapport between a patient and an analyst is very close, very intimate, and once you have experienced it, it is much easier to understand what I say. And this makes a lot of difficulties with experimental psychologists. What I'm saying is a very personal opinion. There are many analysts who don't have these qualms. They use tape-recorders and even film equipment in analytic session. That leads, too, to another difficulty. If you realise the average analytic treatment might take 600 to 700 hours, how can you work through this amount of tape? You have to listen to this vast amount of stuff, 600 hours, to get an opinion of it – if you have just one observer, that is, but if you have five observers, say, this creates a lot of very practical problems.

And that highlights the fact that analysis still seems to take a long time. Has there been any advance to a way of analysis that would telescope its good effects?

There have been quite a lot of attempts to short-cut analysis. Freud himself in 1918 in a speech to the International Congress at Budapest remarked on that and remarked that the need for psychotherapists was far greater than the number of trained therapists – and that meant analysts at that time. He said that the time might come when the gold of analysis might be amalgamated with the copper of suggestion to provide treatment for the masses.

Most of the attempts to shorten analysis are not very successful in terms of the goal of analysis proper. It can be much more successful in terms of getting rid of symptoms, of crisis intervention. Here the psychoanalytic training of doctors is useful, because then a doctor is much more aware of what is going on and much more aware of what he is doing. The analytically trained psychotherapist has a great advantage over the non-analytically trained therapist in that he understands much better what is going on in the patient even if he doesn't use classical analytic methods. I've had some experience of psychotherapy in the outpatient department of our National Health scheme where it's simply not possible to use analysis proper, but where my analytical knowledge and experience was very helpful in understanding patients much better – even if I couldn't fulfil their expectations. No satisfactory short cut has been found. It's sad because we all feel the pressure of cases that need to be treated very keenly. The opinion that analysts are anti-social and sit in ivory towers with their patients and don't care what happens in the world is very wrong.

There has, of course, been an upsurge in all kinds of group work, encounter work and so on. Do you find much use for these developments?

Well, you see, here you must realise that you have the psychotherapist who does not satisfy the needs of the patient, the unconscious needs but who, in a climate of abstinence, tries to get the patient to confront what he wants and make him find his own solution. These new kinds of therapeutic group work, encounter work, I'm afraid, turn out to be wish-fulfilling, need-satisfying. In my own personal opinion, this is a very dangerous course to take because you then need a very specialised therapist for all the personal needs of people. Also, there is a growing tendency for people to have the feeling that frustration is something bad. To be frustrated is bad itself. One should realise anew that life without the possibility of taking a certain amount of frustration is impossible. And so, for instance, at the May Day Rally in Vienna, this was carried to the absurd with a demand for personal happiness for everybody. This shows this tendency in a well-developed way because personal happiness is not a political question.

Would you then say that the aim of many groups, to help you develop yourself, to help you become the person you really are, is rather different from the aims of analysis and, perhaps, rather unrealistic?

The development of the person you really are is rather a mystical concept. In groups, there happens something – again a personal opinion – which is very doubtful for me. When a patient comes to me, a patient comes to get individual treatment. He knows, at least, he believes he knows, that I will do my best for him. When a person goes to a group, there he knows he will be in a group but he doesn't know, even if he might not be, that in the interests of the integrity of the group, he might be sacrificed. He might even be made a victim of the group because, when he puts too much of his personal problems forward, this might disrupt the group process. This is a point which is very rarely made and I've not found it discussed in the group literature. Yet it's also a point of medical ethics. And what is the feeling of the patient who does not really know he can trust me because it might be in the interests of the group that I sacrifice him?

236

But surely, in groups when you are the victim, you play the victim. It is part of the process, or can be.

What I mean is, I find it expressed specifically in the works of certain group therapists that it is disrupting for the group if you allow this patient to talk too much of his own problems and that you have to stop him and you have to reject him. But what does this rejection mean? He must feel the group rejection, and this rejection is bound to affect his development. My main interest if I am in group work must be the group and not the individual. But, maybe, I am too individualistic about it.

One of the feelings many people have, I think, is that in Freud's day, sex was pretty much forbidden ground and that, as society has changed, as sexual taboos have become less, there must have been changes in what is taboo, in what, in a sense, we do not dare confront. Is that correct?

That's a very difficult question to answer because I don't have the materials a social scientist would have. I can't provide a proper scientific answer but only an impressionistic view of that. First, I am not so sure that we really understand Freud's age and sexual taboos and behaviour strictures that existed. If you read some of his literary contemporaries like Arthur Schnitzler, you find that actual behaviour - hidden sexual behaviour - was not so very different from sexual behaviour nowadays. It is only overt sexual behaviour that is different today. I could say that could have some effect. Sometimes, you have the feeling that an increase in taboos against aggressive behaviour can be noticed. You see, the fact that people speak more freely about sex, that they practise sex more freely, doesn't imply that there are fewer taboos. The group pressures still exist but they are different. The pressure to retain your virginity used to be very important in Victorian times. Now, you have the taboo of having intercourse with everybody in a certain group - there is a taboo not to refrain. So with these pressures it means that there is the possibility of acting neurotic, reacting neurotically to that.

Granted there may be some groups in which you get that pressure, they will surely be rare. Isn't it more important that we cannot just practise sex more freely but think and fantasise about it? This kind of open fantasy you get in Playboy *that is socially acceptable must have affected people's unconscious, surely?*

237

I'm not so sure because I'm not sure it really has changed, that it really means so much. Sexual liberation is really on the margin, what the media can make us believe. The individual patient has not changed much. There are some things in the Kinsey report that seem to point to that. I mean that the lifting of sexual taboos is not as marked as we have believed it might be.

And is the presence of taboos against aggression more marked now?
I would say, this is a feeling that I have, that there are taboos against aggressive behaviour, it is socially disliked if a person behaves aggressively and collective aggressive behaviour is now in some ways as sexual behaviour used to be. But that doesn't mean true sexual behaviour, but sexual behaviour can be used to express aggression because aggression is now taboo.

Does that imply important changes in psychoanalytic theory?
You know, that the theory of aggression and aggressive instinctual drives is in a state of conceptualisation and discovery. Freud's theory of death instincts is not widely accepted by analysts. Most analysts have a feeling that something like an aggressive instinct exists.

When a patient agrees to be analysed, what does he commit himself to? How is it likely to affect his life? One hears so many stories, mythical stories maybe, of patients whose whole time is devoted to being on time for the analytic hour. Could you explain what the commitment is?
What the patient commits himself to he doesn't really know. I must say that in all honesty. Even if you explain it to him in all sincerity and for a long time, his fantasies and his expectations over-ride what he hears rationally so the commitment is always to something very fantastic. What, in fact, he has committed himself to is very hard arduous work to becoming a self-sufficient autonomous person. This I would call the main aim of psychoanalytic therapy. That's a very personal opinion. I don't think we should have hidden agendas or hidden ideologies in our treatment – to make the patient happy or his life worthwhile or things of that sort. I would say that, for me, the main purpose is to make the patient able to choose what he wants to be. If he chooses to be healthy, wealthy and wise that's fine, If he chooses to be something else and that is his real choice without unconscious interferences then it's OK with me.

And you'd hold that against Marcuse, say, who sees what the analyst is doing as teaching the patient to choose what society wants?
Yes, there are many patients who choose to adjust to society, to adjust to reality. But there is also for many the possibility of changing reality and this is what Marcuse has not taken into account. That this possibility exists. So analysts become a kind of bogeyman which I hope we are not.

And what does the analyst commit himself to? What does the process of doing so many analyses each day do to you? Is it very wearing?
It's very hard work because the continuous control of your own reaction is the most important thing. And there is counter-transference. This makes it not just listening, like in the old analysts' joke: 'Who listens?' The patient will very soon realise if you don't listen attentively and will hit you on the head. So you have to listen and you have to listen with your ears and your head and your third ear, as Reich called it once.

And is that a wearing process?
When my working day is finished I can honestly say I am tired.

Is it a problem for you not to become involved with your patients – is it not permissible – or does that become easier?
The longer you are at it. I wouldn't say 'permissible'. It would be plain foolish because it would inhibit my possibility to analyse. I have continuous work, besides what the patient tells me which I can analyse by listening, from what he shows. I have also the constant work of seeing how I react and what does it mean to me. There are some new forms of technique in which you have to use your feelings as a sort of red light that shows you something, but this is even more strenuous work than classical technique and, to some extent, more dangerous for the analyst.

But can you handle all these different streams of observation, observing yourself, observing the patients, observing the interaction? Isn't it too much?
Well, I think if you don't . . . if you don't take too many patients, it can be done.

10
Neal Miller

The first impression I had of Neal Miller was of a busy, boisterous man. He does not like wasting time. He is a large man with a shock of white hair and a slightly ruddy face. He exudes energy, talks quickly and seems to be dealing with at least two things at the same time. The interview itself was hectic. As it turned out, Miller had to deal with some nagging but important academic dispute that afternoon. Academic politics are as political as any others. The phone kept ringing. At one point, he asked me to leave the room while he engaged, or so I suspected, in some sensitive academic haggling. He seemed to enjoy it. And, after each phone call, he would start again very precisely from the point where we had left off.

One of the ways in which Miller uses, and maybe uses up, his energy is in his humour. He likes laughing and making you laugh. The tape of the interview is often punctuated with laughs. He also likes making sure you have got his point. He will lean forward at the end of a sentence and add 'Do you see?' forcefully. If you don't see, his forceful stare must make you feel rather guilty.

Miller is now professor of psychology at Rockefeller University, New York. Miller came to Rockefeller from Yale where he had long ago been a graduate student. He took his first degree at the University of Washington in Seattle. He then followed a graduate career that was much more varied than normal. His teachers included Professor Guthrie, one of the foremost behaviourists of the 1930s and Professor Terman who had some sympathy for Freudian views. Miller went to Vienna, in fact, to study psychoanalysis for a year. He underwent analysis as part of this study with Hans Hartmann, one of Freud's most brilliant pupils.

Miller studied and then became a fellow of the Institute for Human Relations at Yale. The Institute was an interdisciplinary

240

experiment long before interdisciplinary approaches became a conventional experiment. It brought together experimental psychology, anthropology, economics, law and psychotherapy to try and arrive at a more complete view of Man and his behaviour. In the interview, Miller describes some of the work there that led to a number of books, *Frustration and Aggression* (1939), *Personality and Psychotherapy* (1950) and *Social Learning and Imitation* (1941). He wrote them all with John Dollard, an anthropologist. In the books, they tried to use experimental research, often on animals like the rat, to understand human behaviour and to expand on less behaviouristic approaches. Both Miller and Dollard thought it was worthwhile to look at Freudian theories.

The interdisciplinary approach seems to have suited Miller well. He likes to have a number of projects going at the same time. One of the reasons he was attracted into psychology was that he felt it would give him a chance to pursue a wide variety of interests. His first enthusiasm, physics, was more confining. He has moved across a number of fields, social, physiological and biochemical. His energy likes to spread itself around. Now that many people think he is doing nothing but studies of biofeedback and visceral learning, he is still working on topics in the physiology of motivation.

But if he enjoys variety, he is clearly fascinated by the very central problem of how the brain works. In an introduction to a paper (1962), he told his audience:

The more we learn about the brain, the more we appreciate that it is one of the most wonderful miracles in the universe. To try to understand the brain is an infinitely challenging goal worthy of Man's highest humanistic and aesthetic aspirations. This quest does not need to be justified by any practical social consequences, although it certainly has them. None of the people I know who are enamoured with trying to understand the brain are concerned with what to do with their leisure time, or plagued with boredom, a sense of futility or the meaninglessness of their existence.

Eloquent praise indeed from a psychologist who has devoted much of the last fifteen years to problems of motivation and the brain. In another talk in Montevideo, Miller returned briefly to this theme, pointing out that 'psychologists and other scientists study the brain because it is an infinitely challenging mystery which is the most marvellous miracle in our enormous universe'. Few psychologists in

Neal Miller

other fields wax as lyrical; tellingly, Jouvet betrays the same enthusiasm.

Fascination with the brain is a very inner motive. A love of variety sounds perhaps a little frivolous though, again, it is curious to see that Miller also was drawn to psychology because it would give him a chance to write. Miller also clearly sees an important political role for psychology. Where the politicians have failed to bring peace and make a better world, the psychologists may be able to help a little. In 1962, he wrote a long paper in *Science* called 'Strengthening the behavioral sciences'. He argued there that there had been much progress in the behavioural sciences. They needed to be accorded the same kind of status and influence with government as the physical sciences already had. Behavioural scientists needed to be confident enough to ask for really large grants for major projects. And if the government could give this kind of reward and recognition to psychology and the other behavioural sciences, it could call on them to help resolve many conflicts and deal with many needs. From urban planning to international conflict, there was a role for psychology. Miller was careful not to offer panaceas. Psychology had no miracle solutions to problems but psychologists could help, and help, especially, towards better understanding. It is not surprising that a man of Miller's energy should have something of the politician in him. He told a Congress of Psychology in Moscow in 1966:

At this Congress we have seen how scientists from all nations of the world can work together to increase mutual understanding. This inspiring example of mutual respect and co-operation must be extended to other aspects of the national life. Modern science has the potential to give a better life to all peoples of all nations. This enormous power must not be used for war which can only bring destructive misery to everyone but for peace which will bring constructive happiness to all mankind.

Some might argue, of course, that all happiness is constructive.

In the interview, Miller explains how he feels it would be interesting for psychologists to study people who are exceptionally well adjusted and, presumably, happy. The focus of so much work has been on the abnormal and the deficient that we are in danger of not knowing how normal people do function. Miller's interest is a little more rarified. He wants to study the super-normal, the successes who have, maybe, lessons for us all. They certainly seem to

242

have lessons for society because we should not try to learn to prevent failures just from the failures. But the money for such an exercise appears always to have been lacking, as he explains in the interview.

He is very sharp about the fads and fashions in research and funding research. These days, when research tends to be vastly expensive, they tend to be much the same, for the funds follow the fashions all too easily. In the introduction to the 1971 report of the Jackson Laboratory, a major laboratory organisation whose chairman Miller is, he noted that it had become current to ask why money was being spent on basic research when 'we are not delivering to everyone all of the medical services that we already know they need'. Miller refutes this argument. He points out that much more was being spent on the management of polio than on basic research into polio and possibly vaccines. It was always being said that there were not enough funds for iron lungs, for wheelchairs, for other remedial aids. That may have been true. But all the crutches in the world could not cure polio. It was the relatively modest investment in basic research that yielded the vaccine that made the crutches unnecessary for many, many children. Before the vaccine was discovered, the cause of the disease had to be treated as damage to the dorsal roots of the spinal cord. Miller is a great proponent of basic research and is worried by the fact that it is becoming harder and harder to obtain funds for it as against applied research. This seems a very shortsighted approach to him.

One of Miller's other interests is to note the role of luck in science. He himself has been both lucky and unlucky. He feels he had great good luck in identifying areas of the brain which would respond to electrical stimulation and chemical stimulation. He had good luck, initially, with the experiments with biofeedback. Now, finding some of the experiments impossible to repeat, he is experiencing the very opposite. Research is not always the relatively simple success story that appears in learned journals. As he told his Moscow audience in 1966:

Published reports of research are written with the wisdom of hindsight. They leave out the initial groping and fumbling to save journal space (and perhaps also to save face) and exclude almost all of those attempts that are abandoned as failures. Therefore, they present a misleading picture which is far too orderly and simple of the actual process of trying to extend the frontiers of science into unknown territory.

243

Neal Miller

To emphasise the point, Miller gave a history of work that had been attempted since 1958 in his laboratory to see whether there could be instrumental learning or operant conditioning of visceral responses. It took till 1966 to show that rewards given immediately after a response has been performed can be used to control such functions as blood pressure and heart rate. Miller found that if rats were paralysed by curare they learned to make these responses much more easily. He has since found it impossible to repeat the experiment. The work on visceral learning has important human applications. Feedback telling a subject how well he is managing to reduce his blood pressure level seems also to act as a reward. It seems to offer a therapy. Following up the work on rats paralysed with curare, Miller tested selected human subjects with polio and muscular dystrophy or other diseases that paralyse the muscles but leave the autonomic system intact. In a phrase that recalls the influence of Freud, Miller notes that 'the results clearly showed that extensive paralysis was not the royal road to rapid visceral learning'. In the interview, Miller speculates on why biofeedback became so popular as a research field and why he has found it impossible to repeat some of the successful experiments.

In view of the hypothesis suggested in the introduction – that psychologists are motivated by a desire for power – Miller is interesting. He obviously likes the business of running a department. He seems to feel that he can do this and do his own research. The oft-repeated laments about how administration made research impossible were not indulged in. And Miller has taken up a number of political causes or, at least, given a political edge to some of his remarks. He thinks psychology should be used more by government and that psychology has a role to play in all kinds of difficult situations. Unlike colleagues like Hudson and Chomsky and Skinner, he does not seem to take any particular delight in controversy. Perhaps he is merely a quieter politician.

How did you come to be a psychologist?
I'm not perfectly sure. [Phone rings.] The fact that my father was an educational psychologist may have had something to do with it. I was interested in science in general – particularly in physics. Then, as I came to the University of Washington in Seattle, I became more interested in biology. I was also interested in writing. Somehow, it seemed to me in my senior year in college that maybe psychology would give me the widest range of things that fitted my interests.

Just a minute. And so that is how I got into psychology. As I say, it seemed to cover the most things and it gave the chance to do the great variety of things that I was interested in.

Looking at your work, you seem to differ from many psychologists in covering a wide range of topics. Have you always been something of a polymath?

I suppose that tends to be the case. As I said, from when I came into it, looking for something that would give me a chance to pursue a wide range of interests, I presume that made me pursue a wide range of interests in psychology. But there are also probably certain accidents of training. I said I had a good training in the basic sciences and in biology. They had some very stimulating psychologists and teachers at the University of Washington, Professor Guthrie and Professor Stephenson Smith. They got me interested along the lines of the behaviourist type of psychology. I went to Stanford University where Professor Terman got me interested in the psychology of personality. I got a master's at Stanford. He was more sympathetic than many of the psychologists of the day to the Freudian contribution so I got a little interest in that line, in psychoanalysis. Then, I had the chance to go to the Institute of Human Relations as a research assistant to Professor Walter Miles because he was leaving Stanford to go there. He took me along with him. This was during the Depression when any type of an assistantship or position to work while you were studying was very rare.

The Institute of Human Relations was founded at Yale University in an attempt to bring together economics, sociology, anthropology, psychiatry, psychology and law - actually an impossibly wide range. It was trying to bring these various disciplines together that had to do with understanding and dealing with human behaviour so that was a particularly broad setting. There, I was influenced by Professor Hall who was developing learning theory in a very interesting way and was a very inspiring person. He encouraged my interest in psychoanalysis to see to what extent learning theory could be applied to psychoanalysis. Then, after that, I got a fellowship from the Social Science Research Council to spend a year in Vienna studying psychoanalysis which meant being psychoanalysed by Hans Hartmann, one of Freud's pupils. Then, to my surprise and delight, I got invited back to the Yale Institute of Human Relations as one of their younger members. They had found that their older

245

members didn't collaborate very well – an unusually distinguished group of famous people but they went on doing exactly the same kinds of individual work that had made them famous in the first place. So, they thought they'd get some younger people also who had had the advantage of being trained under these people and had a little broader training so they would do more integration of the fields. So the mandate of my position was to work on the integration of the various social disciplines and that encouraged a breadth. And, of course, one of the first things the group of younger people did was a book on frustration and aggression that tried to bring together anthropology, sociology, psychoanalysis, psychology in the sense of learning theory, to try to understand some things about aggression better.

Was this experiment at Yale in bringing these disciplines together something of a rarity then?
It was a rarity at that time. [Phone rings.] Very much of a rarity, trying to bring the disciplines together. But it had been put up by some far-sighted people. Hutchins, who had already left to become president of the University of Chicago, was dean of the Law School. Winternuts was dean of the Medical School and Angel, who had been a psychologist and who, incidentally, had been one of the teachers of my father, was the president of the university and, probably, the moving spirit.

So, I started out with a wide range of interests. Partly by luck, I had the opportunity to go to places that encouraged a wide range of interests. And, as I say, I went into psychology from the side of biology and then, at the Institute of Human Relations, got exposed to sociology and anthropological points of view.

Professor McClelland at Harvard has suggested that many psychologists of your generation went into it as a reaction to a very religious upbringing or to very fundamental moral attitudes. Was that true of you?
Not consciously, I don't think. My parents were more religious than I am by far. My father was reasonably religious but not by any means a fundamentalist in religion.

The first book I encountered of yours was the one you did with Dollard.
That's the second book, actually, I did with Dollard. He was involved

in the book of frustration and aggression. Then, he and I did *Social Learning and Imitation*. Then came the one on personality and psychotherapy, yes.

You were led to try and tie together these two disciplines of learning and psychoanalysis by what was going on at Yale?
Yes.

Could you recapitulate what your main findings were and the arguments you brought forward?
Well, the idea in the book was to bring together the contribution of learning theory, experiments in learning stemming from Pavlov and developed by Thorndike, Hull and many others, the rigour of that, along with some of the dynamics of psychoanalysis. And then, also, to bring in more clearly, we hoped, than had been brought in before the social conditions of the learning as a factor. So you had the situation of psychotherapy as an opportunity to observe people, in more detail than people are ordinarily observed, actually struggling to adapt to the conditions of society with the biological drives they have and, by learning, to adapt. So that was the general idea behind this book. Incidentally, Dollard and I planned to try to study some specially well-adjusted people in as much detail as the neurotics had been studied. But we ran afoul of difficulties in funding and had to start scrambling off in our separate ways to get money to keep our research going.

In that book, it seems to me that you made an assumption that thoughts are somehow like actions.
Yes - that's standard behaviourist practice. It's not quite the Watsonian assumption that thoughts are implicit speech, just speech movements which are too slight to be detectable. That assumption may be true in many cases. But the assumption we are making is that thoughts obey the same laws as actions. And that is a little different assumption.

But, beyond that, you seem to me to be making an assumption about the actual nature of these thoughts. You have an action like hitting the table. Are thoughts that discrete? Did you ever think this was a large assumption and that we may not have these large cellules of thought so that, as you get closer to the terrible one, you may not be able to build your approach/avoidance model in the same way?

Well, like any assumption it may not be true. It seems a good one to me. Actions can be – see [he demonstrates] actions can be rather generalised. You might tense up or wriggle or do something like this. [He demonstrates again.] That would be a sort of generalised action and, later on, you might just press a button like that. Do you see? And, indeed, you do see when a person is learning a motor skill, he'll make a lot of waste motions at first. Finally, his actions will become much more discrete and only the actions that are absolutely necessary to, say, hit the tennis ball will be made. I'm not sure what you're thinking about – that your thoughts may be vague and then become clearer?

Yes.
Well, I just think just the same sort of thing can happen to an action.

I was wondering merely if you could have this progression of thoughts, one neat thought after another, which seems implicit in that?
Well, it is for purpose of description. But it may not be. The actions too, the actions may not be quite one neat, separable action after another. The actions may flow into one another. Or to take another example from athletics and motor skill, when you hit a tennis ball you're told to follow through, though what you do happens when the ball has already been hit. The fact is that if you don't follow through, you may start stopping before you hit the ball actually. Do you get what I mean? The part of the action sequence that occurs after you hit the ball may influence what is happening before you hit it. That is if you're getting set to go like that [he demonstrates] , you may start pulling back before you really do it. You find the same problems and properties with thoughts. You can't just separate them into little rooms.

Were you and Dollard happy about the way you reconciled psychotherapy and learning theory in that book?
Yes, I think we were certainly happy. It was the best we could do anyhow. And I don't think we thought it was perfect by any means but we were happy with the general approach. We felt there was an excellent beginning there but it would need far more rounding out by added investigation following up that general line.

If I understand rightly, you mainly pursued that exploration through work with rats and then developed the approach/avoidance model. Is that right?

248

Actually, the approach/avoidance model was developed before the book. Some of the key experiments and the key theoretical work were done before the book.

In that book, of course, you looked at neurotic behaviour. Do you feel there is a problem that psychology, especially with human beings, is looking so much at abnormal behaviour that one loses sight of what normal behaviour might be and how it's caused?

Yes, I think that is a problem. It's hard to get opportunities to study normal people in the detail that you study abnormal people. That's because the normal people don't have the motivation to talk to you. Go to a Supreme Court judge or to the president of a big corporation and say, 'I would like to talk to you and find out how you solve your problems and I want to do this for an hour a day for two or three years.' [He laughs.] And, you'd probably get thrown out right away. He doesn't have that kind of time to give to anybody.

You don't think it's the psychologists who lack the motivation to study, well, not Supreme Court judges, but rather more ordinary mortals?

No. I don't think psychologists have just a peculiar, unhealthy interest in the abnormal, so to speak, and that that is why they do it. On the one hand, of course, there is some motivation to try and help these people. And on the other hand, you can oftentimes get paid for doing it, which gives you motivation. But I think the really key thing is that the neurotic person who's suffering and in misery has a motivation to talk to the psychologist whereas the normal person . . . well, it's hard to get the same amount of motivation from a normal person. They're likely to be too busy enjoying life to talk to a psychologist.

But I think this could possibly be solved. If there were special grants of funds to do this. And I think it would be well worth while. The problem also is that society is motivated to help and to pay people to investigate problems that are bothering it – like delinquency and mental illness and drug addiction, things of that kind. However, society might really be well advised to pay people to investigate the adjustment of the very well-adjusted people. That might help us to help other people to be better adjusted. You get somewhat the same thing in that society spends a great deal of money on feeble-minded children but tends to spend less special money on the unusually gifted child because he will get along by himself. But he might get along much better.

But isn't there a difference between normal, ordinary people and gifted ones? Gifted kids are a special group. You can analyse what makes them special. But normal people must range so widely that if you studied them, you might be looking for a needle in a haystack?
Might be. But I think one could study people who are especially well adjusted. For instance, in this study that Dollard and I had planned right after the Second World War - it might be a little harder to do now - we thought we might get some family physicians. Family physicians don't exist to the same extent now, but perhaps in small towns you might find some. Anyhow, we would get family physicians who were not specialists but who knew the people they dealt with, knew their parents, knew their children and knew the community. You get such a person to select people whom he thought were unusually well adjusted. And one could study them.

I wouldn't say there is no motivation in itself to study abnormal people for psychologists. It has certain advantages. It brings out certain highlights. But one should also study normal or supernormal people.

After that project with Dollard didn't materialise, how did your work develop?
The work I've done since then has gone off in different directions. I told you we had this project prepared. A foundation encouraged us to prepare a project for studying normal people and then it decided it had to make a policy decision as to whether or not it was going to go into this area of work or not, the general area of psychotherapy. That decision couldn't be made for a year or so. So we were suddenly forced to scramble for funds. And the Institute of Human Relations was concurrently running out of funds so we were suddenly left. And Dollard set up a project on his own for reported psychotherapeutic interviews, to get data from them, a line he has followed since then. And I set up a project for further animal investigations of learning and motivation. This work led me further into the mechanisms of motivation and physiological psychology, away from social psychology and psychotherapy. Actually, we had the drive reduction hypothesis of motivation and, in order to investigate that, I got deeper and deeper into the physiological mechanisms of motivation and ran into some very interesting things

250

to investigate and interesting ways to investigate them. That led me
in a number of different directions, the effects of inserting food
directly into an animal's stomach on its hunger and thirst. And, later
on, into the effects of electrical stimulation of the brain.

So you left fear behind you?
Yes – actually I was still interested in fear along with motives. And
we were looking for places in the brain where electrical stimulation
would induce fe..r or would stop fear. But we had more success at
finding places that would induce eating or drinking. And we
followed the thing that was working.

Is fear, physiologically, very hard to investigate?
Well, there are a lot of different aspects of fear. Your question is a
little bit like asking what the climate of China is compared to that of
the USA, do you see?

Yes.
I had much better luck with hunger and thirst at finding places in the
brain. Actually, in an experiment with Delgado and Roberts, we did
get places in the brain which elicited a pain fear-like response. But it
was difficult to be certain it was fear instead of pain or some other
aversive motivation. It was easier to determine that the points in the
brain that elicited eating seemed to have all the motivational
properties of normal hunger than it was to try and differentiate fear
from pain. So the work went the easier way. But I'm not at all sure
that there's any very fundamental difference there. I have a feeling
that we're getting into a number of sidetracks. Looking at the broad
perspective, the work on psychotherapy and the work on conflict
emphasised the importance of motivation. So I went off into
physiological studies investigating the physiological mechanisms of
motivation. And that led me deeper and deeper into physiological
psychology until, more recently, I came back to an old problem of
whether visceral responses mediated by the autonomic nervous
system could be instrumentally learned as opposed to only
classically conditioned. The equipment and the techniques that were
available in my laboratory for physiological investigation made it
possible to attack this problem in a better way because we could
measure the visceral responses. The work in that chapter I gave you
brought me back nearer to the psychotherapy problem or the
clinical work via a big circle. Do you see?

Neal Miller

One question about fear. It seems to me a lot of work had to do with the measurement of fear and involved difficulties, as you say, of distinguishing between fear and pain. Didn't it ever worry you that the construct of fear you imposed on animals was so anthropomorphic? Or do you think that an irrelevant point?

Well, I haven't been as worried about that as some people. You can say that you want to throw out fear as a concept because that is a concept that has sort of slipped in through human introspection. But then you say we will use *conditioned aversiveness*. And it seems to me that the people who do that use it just about the same way. I don't see an enormous difference. I think you can also define fear rather objectively in humans just as you can in animals. The same goes for hunger, for thirst, for visual stimulation and for almost anything. You can use them in an objective way or you can use them in a subjective way. I think it was awfully important to establish objective techniques for studying things and defining things psychologically and not to get the idea that introspection was a direct window into the mind. Introspection, when you're dealing with another person, is verbal responses, verbal behaviour. But if you can be reasonably clear about that, then I think you can be somewhat relaxed in using your own introspections to guide your research and in using verbal responses from other people. The old sort of behaviourist battle was fought and won and we don't have to keep worrying about that so much.

Do you think there is still a tendency among psychologists to deny any usefulness to introspection?

Oh yes. There are those who deny any usefulness to it. I haven't been bothering to, I haven't interviewed other people on it. But you're going to be talking to Skinner tomorrow.

Yes.

I won't venture to say what he's going to say but it'll be interesting to see what he's going to say to that.

How securely do you think the work on fear, on approach and avoidance that you did with animals, could be applied to human beings?

There are two questions wrapped up in that. I'm glad one is to do with the subjective and objective with respect to fear and the animal and human point.

I think with respect to things like hunger and fear there is a very great transfer from other mammals to people, especially with respect to the physiological mechanisms, because these are rather primitive functions that seem to be quite a bit controlled in their most primitive manifestations by the hypothalamus which is a rather primitive part of the mammalian brain anyhow. Now that isn't to say that there wouldn't be aspects that would be differently set up in people. I might sum it up thus. That I think that the things lower mammals have, people also have. That doesn't mean to say that everything that people have the lower mammals have also. Do you see? It doesn't work backwards. So I think the things you discover about hunger or thirst in rats, dogs, monkeys and so on are quite likely to apply to people but you won't discover everything solely by investigating dogs, rats and lower mammals. Do you see?

I follow, yes. Is that why behaviour in conflict neurosis is so appealing to study because you have then stripped your human subject of some of that added extra that sets them apart?

Yes, somewhat, but I think that's an oversimplification. Too. But I think there may be something to that. The other side of the coin is that if you're studying something like short-term memory, for instance, you can do experiments on people that are perfectly ethical and it's also easier to do them on people than on lower mammals. But if you're working on fear and conflict and trying to dissect out the physiological mechanisms of motivation by putting electrodes into the brain, by making lesions, by operating, by putting chemicals into the brain, you can't do this kind of work on people so you have to work with animals. You also have much more rigorous experimental controls. I had the experience in the Second World War of being given a task which I finally defined for myself as devising situations that would frighten eager young aviation cadets who were trying to be pilots without terrifying generals and congressmen. This turned out to be impossible. Which shows the difficulty of experimental studies of fear on people.

Now, there is a possible way out of that which I pointed out to some graduate students and which some of them have followed up. That is to find situations such as in a hospital or like that where people are, by experiments of nature so to speak, exposed to really frightening situations. Otherwise you're limited to saying 'Boo' to a person and the person knows you couldn't possibly be going to hurt him in any way because you'd be in deep trouble if you did. So he can't really have that much fear. If you're interested in this problem of stress and neurosis you're driven to work with animals and animals are appealing to you rather than vice versa because you're interested at the human level in these problems and you think that the work is applicable.

So, what you're saying is that you have no alternative but to work with animals if you want to investigate the physiology?
Yes – and also if you do experiments on it. What you then try to do is to check your animal observations against the clinical experience or experiments of Nature or cross-cultural observations or something of that kind on people which can't have the rigour of your experimental work but do have the virtue of being directly applicable to people. There is a very small chance that the experimental work on animals and the clinical work on the other kind of observations on people may seem to agree with one another although they're different. That is, you get something that looks the same but there are quite different reasons for it. Although you have to bear that in mind as a possibility, it's very unlikely in most cases so that if you have the experimental work on the animals fitting in with the clinical work on the people, then you can think it probably is correct. Do you see?

Yes.
Then, your conclusions about the people are correct.

Did physiological psychology remain your main field till you went into the study of visceral learning?
Oh well, it was never my exclusive interest. And now that I'm in visceral learning, that isn't my exclusive interest either. I'm still working in physiological psychology. I've got an assistant here who is trying to do electrical recording from certain cells in the reticular formation which I have some good hopes may be a good index of fear or, at least, of a state of arousal. That's physiological. If so, I'll go back and fill in more detail with experiments on conflict and avoidance learning.

How did you come to the study of visceral learning?
[A long pause.] Well, as you know, two of the bright students of learning in the earlier days were Pavlov with his work on conditioned responses and Thorndike with his trial-and-error learning and the

effects of rewards and punishments. Now, one of the points of
Professor Hull was to take some of the detailed laws that had been
discovered in classical conditioning and show they applied to
Thorndike-type situations that you got running down a runway
when, for instance, you got a gradient of reinforcement with the
strongest responses being nearest the goal which was like Pavlov's
effect that more delayed rewards were more efficient than
immediate ones and that if you removed the reward you got
experimental extinction but if you waited a while, you got a certain
amount of spontaneous recovery. I was greatly impressed by the
similarity of laws describing learning in these two types of situation.
Hence, in the book *Social Learning and Imitation* (1941) and in
Personality and Psychotherapy (1950), it was stated explicitly there
was just one type of learning and this obeyed the same laws. If that is
true, you would expect the glandular and visceral responses that are
able to be classically conditioned also to be able to be learned by trial
and error, or operant conditioning, or instrumental learning, or
whatever you want to call it. That followed directly from the
position that there is only one type of learning. And, indeed, the idea
that you couldn't instrumentally learn these things was used as one
of the greatest arguments for two different types of learning, the
autonomic and the somatic. This was on my mind for quite some
long time but I never got to the point of testing it. Perhaps – one
doesn't always know these things – there is a slight unconscious fear
that the test might turn out to be negative so one didn't sharpen it.
Certainly, it's the type of thing that if you did have sharpened up
would tend to have people dismiss your theory. If you put it clearly,
it's arguing against it it seems. Also, there were other things to do and
it was a difficult problem to approach. When Bycoff's book was
translated into English, it became clear that a large number of
different visceral responses in addition to salivation and heart rate
and blood pressure could be modified. Intestinal contractions could
be classically conditioned. Contraction of the uterus could be
classically conditioned. Contraction of the spleen could be
classically conditioned. Even the rate of formation of urine by the
kidney could be classically conditioned. With evidence that more of
these internal responses could be subject to learning in the terms of
classical conditioning, the whole problem of whether they could
be also subjected to influence by instrumental learning became
much more important. It had also great relevance to psycho-
somatic symptoms. And that tied in with the earlier interest in

255

psychotherapy and psychopathology. At the same time, we were in a better position in the laboratory, in having the skills available for operating on animals and in having more recording equipment.

We got apparent success. We had success. Then the work heaved along great. Then, we have run more recently into difficulties with curarised animals. Paradoxically, some of the human work has been coming along a bit better though there has been an enormous exaggeration in the public press. We have to worry about placebo effects a lot in clinical applications. I still think it's going to have valuable clinical applications.

A Dr Patel in England has just published a paper in The Lancet *that she used yoga to relax patients, gave them feedback and managed to lower high blood pressure pretty consistently.*
Yes, I think she was the person who used galvanic skin response for feedback. I don't think she measured blood pressure on a minute-to-minute basis. That's a case, too, where one would have to worry a bit about placebo effects.

What were the main findings with animals that you made with respect to visceral learning?
I summed them up in *Science*. I summarised them there as succinctly as I can and I don't want to give a less good verbal report than the one I sweated over. So, if you don't mind . . .

But you have had difficulty in repeating the experiments? Have you any idea why? Were they exact repetitions?
We've made as exact repetitions as we could. I don't have any idea why. That's a great puzzle.

Are you trying to investigate why?
We're still trying to investigate it. I think maybe the next thing we're going to do is - I've heard that Paslovski in the Soviet Union has repeated on paralysed rabbits both with heart rate and with blood pressure. One possibility [for not repeating the results] is that there's something peculiar about the rat. Another possibility is that there's something peculiar about the drug curare. But oftentimes, there's one or two ways to do things right and a million ways to do things wrong. And, if you've got off the right track, you may not know exactly what you are doing wrong and to canvas all those million or so things is an extraordinarily difficult problem.

I know from Professor J. B. Rhine, he said he had found it interesting that you had trouble repeating the results. At certain periods in his research, he had similar trouble and he formed the theory that if you deal with difficult areas your chances of getting repeatability are lower. Do you find that an inadmissible thought?

No. I suppose, though, it may be a bit circular. If you have these troubles, you say it was a difficult problem. Whereas, if everything is going nicely and you get everthing to repeat, you say it was a nice easy simple problem. And, again, you may not know in advance if it's going to be difficult or easy.

This may not be a line you would like to pursue. But if you never managed to repeat those results, what would you conclude happened when you did get positive results?

You could think of different possible explanations. For example, you could imagine there had been a mutation in the strain of rats you dealt with that favoured that type of learning. Then, you could imagine that mutation died out in the strain of rats you were getting so it's gone. But that kind of speculation would not be very useful because there would be no way of testing it. So if you cannot repeat it, it sort of removes it as a scientific problem because the very essence of science is that you discover ways you can repeat things. That doesn't mean it didn't happen. It means you can't investigate how it happened so you might as well forget about it. There are other possibilities. You might be able to repeat and show it was a mistake or an artefact or the result of some uncontrolled factor. It was real but it wasn't what you thought it was. But you can't decide that until you can repeat it.

Did you meet a lot of criticism when you went into the field of visceral learning? Were people completely startled by your results?

They seemed to be – yes. Well, the problem first was when it was very difficult to get students or paid assistants to work on the problem at all. Now, it has flipped over too far in the other direction, with the whole theory of visceral learning and biofeedback being too much of a fad and people making too wild claims and people having too much enthusiasm about it. Not enough thought now. It flipped over from one extreme to the other too rapidly. I think it must be general cultural things that are behind this. The kinds of things that have led a number of young people to be interested in Eastern religion, for instance. It's not just my experimental work that has flipped it over. It just came at a time when the thing was ready to flip. Some of the people who picked it up have been the woolly people your British colleagues worry about.

Does your work on the voluntary control of visceral responses mean one can reinstate the 'will' in psychology? Does it have implications there?

Certainly psychology has to do with the phenomenon of voluntary control or what used to be described as the will. I believe that one can make a behaviouristic or, in other words, objective approach to such phenomena and indeed that this is the approach we must use since we do not have any direct window into the minds of people other than ourselves and, as Freud has shown, we may not be aware (in other words, able to give a correct verbal report) of all the factors that are determining our own behaviour. Certainly, the will is not a separate faculty of the mind as used to be thought by faculty psychology. It is an intervening variable or a hypothetical construct.

Briefly, a response is under voluntary control when a co-operative and well-motivated subject can perform it when we ask him to do so either by a verbal command or a signal and can stop it upon a similar request. The problem is to discover the laws of how such responses come under such control. One approach to this problem is to study how behaviour comes under such control during the development of children but here the changes produced by maturation confuse those produced by learning. The problem of voluntary control is posed acutely when we try to teach adult subjects to control responses such as blood pressure and heart rate that they have not already learned how to control. And I am hoping that the fact that rapid maturational changes are not involved with such subjects may make teaching them to control their visceral responses an especially good situation for the study of voluntary control.

I realise that I have touched on only one aspect of the problem and that there are many others, such as the conditions that enable a person to persist on a line of behaviour that seems to be mediated by his own cue-producing responses in spite of social pressures to do something else - called strong willpower or stubbornness, depending on one's attitude towards the behaviour.

I believe that such problems can, and should, be studied by objective methods.

There seems to be some growing doubts about the objective behaviouristic methods. Do you feel worried by a sudden resurgence of a certain kind of woolly psychology?

Yes, I am worried by that. I think there is a danger of some people getting unduly woolly. Everyone thinks the position they are at is the right position. If you didn't, you'd be in some other position. So, some people are too woolly and some people are too hidebound. I think I'm just right. But I wouldn't maintain dogmatically that I'm just right.

Once or twice in this discussion, you've touched upon the part that good luck and intuition play in research. Do you have intuitions?

No, I don't think it's intuition like that. Certainly, one does have a certain amount of intuition. I think there is more of an element of chance than we like to admit in research. You're moving into the unknown; particularly, the more original work is, the more unknown you're moving into. You can't tell in advance whether this is the right choice or that is. It's only after you've made the choice that you know whether it was a mistake or not a mistake. Of course, there is quite a large element of judgment. You try to use everything you can to determine a choice but I think that oftentimes the more you're moving into the unknown, into something that's original, you can't tell if it's going to work out or not. And there may be equally good reasons for trying A, B, C, D, E, F, G, but the person who happens to choose D is lucky, because it works and the other people who happen to choose the others are just unlucky. I don't want to give you the idea that it's all a matter of luck but I think it's more a matter of luck than one likes to think. Particularly if one watches students. If one happens to hit on a PhD dissertation that works very well then one gets a better job and one has the chance to do better things. If one happens to pick one that doesn't work very well then one may get a poorer job later and so on. You get either a vicious circle down or a benign circle up.

Do you think there is a great temptation now in academic life if you do hit something that works to settle in it, explore it, rigidify in

it? Do you have to fight to be as varied as you've been?
I suppose you do somewhat. The thing that I see as a danger
now is that as funds for basic research are tightening up,
interdisciplinary research may fall by the wayside more than it
should. It's a little bit like Stephen Leacock said of himself:
'Among the humorists I am viewed as a famous political scientist
and among the political scientists, I am viewed as a famous
humorist.' Well, so this is the thing that has always been a
problem. It was a problem at the Institute for Human Relations.
Take a department of psychology. If it came to the crunch, it
would say we want to spend our money on a pure psychologist. A
department of anthropology, when it came to the crunch, would
want to spend it on a pure anthropologist and say let the
psychology department give the promotion to the guy who is
between anthropology and psychology. John Dollard had a good
deal of trouble that way between psychology and anthropology
and sociology. Let the other one take him, each department said. I
see difficulties of that kind. In order to do interdisciplinary
research, you may not be doing the things that are most
interesting to the specialist person in each discipline.

*Finally, you seem to have trodden a narrow balance between a
behaviourist approach in your methods but you don't seem to have
been committed to the sort of narrowness of much behaviourism.*
Yes.

Does that seem a fair position to ascribe to you?
Yes – and I think you can say that, perhaps, being interested in
clinical phenomena and in social behaviour maybe forces one out
of too narrow a behaviouristic mould. And one tries to deal with
these phenomena that are more complex and can't be handled
quite as easily in a narrow framework, and yet try to remain as
rigorous as you can and to make your assumptions clear. You
could make the assumption that all thought is really action, to go
back to what we were discussing, that all thought is really action
in the muscular sense. We actually leave open the possibility that it
could be all imagery inside the brain and the important thing is
that it does obey the same laws as the actions you can go out and
analyse and study. And you make the assumption and you try to
see what the consequences of that assumption are. And you see
how well that is applicable to observations on thought, how well

your deductions check out. Now, that assumption may be wrong. It certainly might be wrong. At least, you can hopefully be clear about it. So that someone knows what assumption you're making and can see what you're doing about it and they can then challenge you.

11
Burrhus Skinner

Whatever psychologists think of Professor Burrhus Skinner's work, he has become something of a legend. His less technical books such as *Walden Two* (1948), *Science and Human Behaviour* (1953) and *Beyond Freedom and Dignity* (1972) have caught the popular and journalistic imagination. Few psychologists get the ultimate American accolade, being featured on the cover of *Time* magazine. Skinner achieved this. His work includes the development of a number of techniques of 'behaviour modication'. 'Behaviour modification', based on sound principles of Skinnerian conditioning, has become nearly as popular in the USA as psychoanalysis. It is being used with delinquents, with the mentally handicapped, with autistic children and with other people whose behaviour is considered in some way inadequate. Even weight watchers use it. In *Walden Two*, Skinner described a perfect and harmonious community. In order to achieve this new Utopia, one had to use the kind of conditioning and reinforcement that Skinner has now made famous. He has always had something of the social reformer in him. He is now a very influential one.

It is this very evangelical vein that angers many psychologists. They see him as a man who is more interested in publicity than in experiments. He prefers speculation, they say. To be a propagandist is not academically respectable; to be a successful propagandist is even worse. Skinner's most recent book, *Beyond Freedom and Dignity*, was an instant best-seller. Could one ask for a more powerful condemnation? His autobiography, *Particulars of My Life* (1976), has attracted much attention.

Because of all the publicity, Skinner has acquired an image and risks becoming its prisoner. He looks a small man. His head seems a little large for his body. It looms out of it so that he has the aspect of an

Elder, one of the Wise in some science-fiction epic. He looks intently through you at times. This detached intensity suits the image that has developed of him as a man who is seeking to change the way we think of ourselves. He headed one of the sections in *Science and Human Behaviour*, 'Man a Machine'. He went on to say: 'Behaviour is a primary characteristic of living things. We almost identify it with life itself' (p. 45). The polemical heading 'Man a Machine' suggests, of course, that many psychologists will deny such a mechanical view. They cower, Skinner implies, behind the myths of free will. But what is controversial about Skinner is not so much his view that man is a very superior machine but his views as to what runs that machine – or makes it run. Skinner dismisses all the baggage of consciousness, all feelings, all motives, all intentions as, at best, by-products. We attribute to the mysterious inner man the reasons for behaviour that we are unable to explain otherwise. Skinner offers us these elusive explanations purely in terms of the past history of the organism. Where Freud argued that one's motives are central to what one is, Skinner dismisses as irrelevant anything except actions. For there can be no behaviour without action. In Skinner's view it is, of course, fitting that such a psychology should come out of America, the country of action.

Since most of us think of ourselves as being somehow rooted in the stream of our consciousness, Skinner's views seem dehumanising. In fact, he seems to want to supersede what we think of as our unique human qualities. To be free to choose what one wants to do, to act because of our feelings, to be intimately aware of ourselves through our consciousness seem essential to being human. Skinner says that this is an illusion and a dangerous illusion. It threatens our future. We have to learn to control ourselves better, by which he means to control our behaviour better.

Skinner's great discovery was a new kind of conditioning which allows him to shape behaviour just as a sculptor shapes clay. In the 1930s, he found that if he placed a rat or a pigeon in a cage, he could train that animal to do any number of things. The process was simple though it must have needed enormous patience till the requisite machines to carry it through were built. If, for instance, Skinner saw that the pigeon raised his head high sometimes, he would reward it each time that it did raise its head. He would then only reward the pigeon with a pellet of food if the bird managed to get its head above a particular height. Skinner found he could nudge the animal along in this way till it frequently raised its head above its 'natural' level. With rats, Skinner did the same kind of things. A rat was placed in a cage with a lever and a slot through which a pellet could fall. It is this apparatus that has come to be called a Skinner box. At first, Skinner rewarded the rat every time it made the least movement towards the lever. Then the rat had to get to within a foot of the lever to get a reward. Then the rat had to come within six inches to get its reward. Eventually, the only time Skinner would reward the animal was when it stood just by the lever. Finally, the rat had to press the lever to get food. Skinner's 'shaping' of behaviour is a precise and meticulous process. You reward each bit, each segment of behaviour that brings the animal nearer to the final action you want it to accomplish. It is like an elaborate but very precisely measured dance.

By such means, Skinner has taught pigeons to peck at keys and at balls so that they can even play a primitive form of table tennis with two birds pecking passes at one another. He has also trained a dog to open a door and three pigeons to guide a missile. This may sound incredible. Skinner devised, in fact, a plan known as Project Pigeon. The Pentagon thought it essential to counter the V1s and V2s Hitler was developing. The trouble was that the guidance systems for the primitive missiles that existed were yet more primitive. Skinner believed he had the answer with his pigeons. If they could be taught to play table tennis they could be taught to guide a missile. All you had to do was to teach them to peck at something like a map strapped into the nose of the missile. The pigeons pecked at a symbol that stayed in the centre of the map as long as the missile stayed on course. If it veered off course, the symbol moved to the left or the right. The pigeon's peck also then moved. This provided information to the servo-mechanism which enabled the missile to steer itself back on course. By using certain schedules of reinforcement, Skinner could guarantee these pigeons would go on pecking till they dropped dead. Various tests showed that this was a practicable scheme. Though at first Skinner was annoyed by the ignorant scepticism of defence administrators – they asked him, among other things, if he didn't love animals – he got backing in the end. Project Pigeon, however, was abandoned in favour of the development of the atom bomb. When the Manhattan Project got going, the pigeon missiles were grounded.

Bizarre as this tale might seem, it shows how exquisitely accurate the control that Skinner achieves can be. He is doing in a very analytical way what good animal trainers have done for centuries. It is this that lends him the slightly sinister air that many writers have attributed to him. For Skinner's psychology makes it possible to control not just animals but also people.

Skinner feels quite angry about a few small details that have been misused, he claims, to reinforce this idea of him as a macabre, power-hungry individual. It was rumoured that he and his wife brought up their daughter in a Skinner box. It was not remotely the kind of cage the Skinner box is. He built a special crib for his baby daughter. He has always been fond of building gadgets. Second, critics often blamed him for the techniques of persuasion used in the film *Clockwork Orange*. Those techniques depended on vicious punishments. In the film, every time the boy hero had a thought, a desire, an urge that was forbidden because it was anti-social, he was punished. Electrodes had been implanted in his brain. They could, leaping across decades of research no one has managed to do yet, tell when the boy was thinking forbidden thoughts. They then activated the pain centres of his brain. He soon learned that it was better not to be punished. To be unpunished, he had to think no evil thoughts. And so, he didn't. Skinner says that people think that he advocates more and more refined punishments, even though he has spent his whole career since *Walden Two* attempting to use science to make punishments unnecessary. It is an interesting misrepresentation. R. D. Laing, who is the most publicised of the 'humanist' psychologists, perhaps, claims that he has been misrepresented too.

For a man supposedly so hard and mechanistic, it is ironic to come across him pottering on his lawn in a beautifully wooded and select suburb of Boston. In his Bermuda shorts and tennis shoes, he seems the model of the relaxed, successful American living the good materialist life. A harpsichord dominates the living room. The walls are crammed with etchings and colourful doodles. Sipping Scotch by his swimming pool, the problems of 1971 America seemed miles away. In 1971, he seemed leisurely, unpressed for time. He talked gladly about why he thought American society was breaking down. By 1974, Skinner was in a much less talkative frame of mind. He politely explained that he had nearly not given me the interview because he felt he only had the time left to him to do so much. He could no longer fritter away time. He insisted on an interview much shorter than I would have wished. It was only when he talked about what he was believed to believe and believed to argue that he seemed eager to make points. If you discover you have written a gospel, you want people to interpret it correctly. In 1971, Skinner was bothered because he felt he was not properly understood. 'I have made constant efforts to clarify my position', he said then, 'over the last thirty-two years but I am still dismissed as a Watsonian behaviourist.' He feels as annoyed now by that.

When Skinner came to Harvard in 1929, he had already read Pavlov and J. B. Watson. And though it was Watson who influenced the thinking behind the experiments, it was Pavlov who had the more immediate influence. Skinner went to work on the reflex. In the interview, he explains how he became dissatisfied with it. His concept of the *operant* comes from his critique of the *reflex*. The distinction between Skinner's operant and the reflex is easily glossed over, especially if one is interested in the social applications of his work. The main difference is that in operant conditioning you examine and utilise the consequences that a particular behaviour generates. In *Science and Human Behaviour,* Skinner explained this as follows (pp. 64–5):

> We may make an event contingent upon the behaviour without identifying or being able to identify, a prior stimulus. We did not alter the environments of the pigeon to *elicit* the upward movement of the head. It is probably impossible to show that any single stimulus invariably precedes this movement. Behaviour of this sort may come under the control of stimuli but the relation is not one of elicitation. The term 'response' is, therefore, not wholly appropriate but is so well established that we shall use it in the following discussion.
>
> A response which has already occurred cannot, of course, be predicted or controlled. We can only predict that similar responses will occur in the future. The unit of a predictive science is, therefore, not a response but a class of responses. The word 'operant' will be used to describe that class. The term emphasises the fact that the behaviour operates upon the environment to generate consequences. The consequences define the properties with respect to which the responses are called similar.

Many of the key points in Skinner's psychology stem from this definition. First, it is behaviour and its consequences that matter. Unless there is an action or a response that 'operates' on the environment there is nothing worth studying. Some people have thought that Skinner actually denies the existence of thoughts and feelings which are not made public and which cannot be publicly verified. In fact, he does not deny we have feelings or thoughts. He denies to these feelings and thoughts any central role. Once, men were so arrogant as to believe the Earth was the centre of the universe. They resisted fiercely the ideas of Copernicus that displaced them from this central spot. It is equally human arrogance to insist we have feelings, intentions and purposes which we know through introspection and which make us do things. In *Beyond Freedom and Dignity*, Skinner uses a quotation from Voltaire to summarise the folly of such arrogance. 'When I can do what I want to do,' said the author of *Candide*, 'there's my liberty for me but I can't help wanting what I do want.' There's the rub.

As far as Skinner goes, it is the key point. His work shows that you can explain actions not in terms of inner feelings and intentions but in terms of past history – and this history is one of external actions. I can't help what I do want because of what has happened to me in the past. The consequences of my past actions have shaped and, in fact, determined the pattern of my response now. I have no choice. It would be inaccurate to say that I did this because I felt such and such or thought such and such. Skinner accepts that our actions may be accompanied by these inner rituals but they are merely epiphenomena, by-products. The stream of consciousness, that supremely human flow and rush of ideas, impressions and moods, has nothing to do with what life is really about – behaviour.

In *Beyond Freedom and Dignity*, Skinner set out to analyse the resistance to his ideas. 'The mentalists', as he called them in 1971, refuse to see how circular their ideas are. If you say that a person ran away because he was afraid, you are not saying anything useful about why he ran away. If he had not run away, you would not have known fear was his state of mind. If a person says that he hit you because he was angry what Skinner would do is look at the context in which he hit you. Suppose you had, in fact, just hit him. The fact for Skinner is that he hit you because you hit him or because, an hour ago, he had been insulted by his boss. Inner events do not provide causes of actions. Looking for the answers to motivation inside the head is looking in quite the wrong place.

Some fairly radical consequences follow from this and, in *Beyond Freedom and Dignity*, Skinner looked at them. If I have no choice, I am not free. I can deserve no blame if I happen to be anti-social: I can take no credit if I happen to be a genius. It is the environment that did it to me. Skinner claims that it is this insight that has made him such a critic of punishment. It is not merited and, also, it seems too often to be ineffective. But much of that book is devoted to an attack on 'the literature of freedom'. Since the Greeks, men have in their arrogance cherished the dream, the illusion, that they are free. They have defined this freedom as something mysterious, uniquely human. At its most poignant, it is perhaps the freedom to die with a certain dignity. Viktor E. Frankl in his account of life in Nazi concentration camps goes so far as to rebuke many inmates there for failing to assert their freedom by the manner of their death. But many did succeed.

Skinner contends that we have deluded ourselves as to what it means to 'feel free'. This isn't some ecstatic, mysterious inner state. You feel free when you have escaped from conditions you wanted to avoid. Freedom is the avoidance of painful conditions. In *Beyond Freedom and Dignity*, he writes (p. 37):

> Almost all living things act to free themselves from harmful contacts. A kind of freedom is achieved by the relatively simple forms of behaviour called reflexes. A person sneezes and frees his respiratory passages from irritating substances . . . . More elaborate forms of behaviour have similar effects. When confined, people struggle ('in rage') and break free. When in danger, they flee from or attack its source. Behaviour of this sort presumably evolved because of its survival value: it is as much part of what we call the human genetic endowment as breathing, sweating or digesting food. And, through conditioning similar behaviour may be acquired with respect to novel objects which could have played no part in evolution. These are no doubt minor instances of the struggle to be free but they are significant. We do not attribute them to any love of freedom; they are simply forms of behaviour which have proved useful in reducing various threats to the individual and hence to the species in the course of evolution.

The mistaken view is that freedom is a possession. 'A person escapes from or destroys the power of a controller in order to feel free and once he feels free and can do what he desires, no further action is recommended,' Skinner adds (p. 37).

He goes on to accuse those who are responsible – if, of course, they can be fairly said to be responsible for anything – for 'the literature of freedom'. It is not quite clear what this literature is. It sounds political. Recall Rousseau: 'Man is born free, yet everywhere he is in chains.' But, when one thinks, it is more than political. *Hamlet* without free will is as worthless a dramatic proposition as *Hamlet* without the prince. Macbeth becomes ridiculous if he does not have the choice to kill or not to kill. The whole of literature almost is the literature of freedom. Skinner's anger at literature

268

strikes one as interesting, especially as he seems once to have had literary ambitions of his own.

Skinner singles out for special blame those who have used the slogans of freedom as a means to obstruct reform. His work makes it possible to change many penal practices for the better. It offers practical solutions to educational and remedial problems. But all these benefits are contested all the way in the name of freedom – a freedom, Skinner always hastens to point out, that is quite illusory, for no one is free in the glorious literary way. The desire to feel free has impeded the kinds of reform that would free people from some of the more noxious forms of control and punishment they have to suffer. But, of course, those who practise the 'literature of freedom' prefer to suckle their illusions. They hope to prevent the kinds of reforms Skinnerian techniques could offer in education and penology and they do so because they claim such improvements would be new and sinister forms of control, 1984 made flesh.

It is apt that Skinner attacks Noam Chomsky, the linguist. Chomsky has made a reputation in two quite separate fields. He is regarded as one of the greatest linguists of the century: he also happens to be a radical political activist. Chomsky also does not believe that the environment, and the history of a child, account for the fact that children in all cultures have learned how to speak by the age of five. By then, any child who is not handicapped will have mastered an incredibly complex set of rules. He will be able to generate original sentences and to understand sentences he has never heard before. Chomsky argues (as we saw in the interview) that only some inherited organisation in the brain that is specifically destined to acquire language can explain how the infant learns to speak. It doesn't depend on what happens in the environment. Skinner regards such a view as anathema. In *Science and Human Behaviour*, he anticipated the view that he was to set out in full in *Verbal Behaviour*. He wrote: 'Verbal behaviour always involves social reinforcement and derives its characteristic properties from this fact.' For Chomsky, verbal behaviour – and he would shudder at the way Skinner felt obliged to pin the label of some kind of behaviour on language – derives its characteristics from the fact that it is part of our biological specialisation. It is unique to man. It seems to require some inherited schema, something akin to the rationalist philosophers' theory of innate ideas. The history of a particular organism may marginally affect how well it speaks but this environmental effect is minute. When Skinner published *Verbal*

Behaviour, Chomsky gave it a murderous review. Skinner believes the book is his most important, as he says, because it bridges the gap between explaining relatively simple behaviours and complex ones. But in the book, Skinner attempts to explain the child's learning of language purely in terms of what language it is exposed to and what language behaviour is reinforced. Skinner feels the book has never been adequately appreciated. Perhaps, of course, its thesis just does not hold. In the interview with Chomsky, the criticisms are fairly damning.

Apart from these psychological disputes, Chomsky and Skinner disagree about issues of social control. Chomsky sees Skinner as a man whose ideas are making it easier, and more respectable, for the state to exercise power over individuals. Skinner denies that it is his aim. His opponents always elevate the ghost of the totally free man. No such being exists. All men are controlled but we prefer the controls to be less conspicuous. If a man has a burning desire that stems from his childhood history, he is not really choosing to have it. There is no inner man who has the choice to decide not to succeed. Childhood history, childhood reinforcements, have determined the man. We prefer, however, to endow him with this mythical freedom. Skinner believes that one of the reasons for this is that if a society were intelligently designed, men could take neither the credit nor the blame for their actions. They would not deserve anything. Or, in the sense that we now praise people for great deeds and great souls, there would be nothing to praise. The deeds and the souls would be the product of contingencies of reinforcement within the culture. Skinner does not mind the fact that this sounds soulless. He argues, quite tellingly, that this free and autonomous man has ravaged the planet, massacred his fellow man and shows no sign of being able to live in constructive peace.

But radical thinkers like Chomsky suspect Skinner of really finding ways to enshrine the status quo. There are many dire warnings against permissiveness. Though Skinner has often said he is opposed to punishment, he often inveighs against dropping out and coming to see sex and drugs as an alternative to a fruitful social life. He writes, in *Beyond Freedom and Dignity* (p. 117):

> When the control exercised by others is thus evaded or destroyed only the personal reinforcers are left. The individual turns to immediate gratification, possibly through sex or drugs. If he does not need to find food, shelter and safety, little behaviour will be

generated. His condition is then described by saying that he is suffering from a lack of values.

Two assumptions here are worth noting. Without the need to make money – for what else are finding food, shelter and safety about in a capitalist society? – there will be little behaviour. It is not difficult to see one could add something like 'that is socially acceptable or useful'. For those who rebelled against the whole ethos of America in the late sixties did not suddenly stop doing things; they stopped behaving themselves. The authoritarian 'Behave yourself' is very apt here. The rebels of films like *The Graduate* and *Easy Rider* could still think, feel and act. But, according to Skinner, it would seem they were generating only little behaviour. Little behaviour, it might be thought, means little behaviour of the kind American society as established now would like to see. Second, Skinner calls this state one that has been described as a 'lack of values'. He goes on to explain why the word 'values' is inappropriate. But he clearly does not even consider the possibility that the protest of the late sixties stemmed from a rejection of existing values for better ones. Unless the values are those of America, there seem to be no such things as values. A critique of the existing values seems out of the question. 'Permissiveness', Skinner writes, 'is not however a policy. It is the abandonment of policy and its apparent advantages are illusory' (1972 p. 85). Permissiveness is the soft option.

Skinner argues the emptiness of protest, and the reasons behind protest. It is not surprising, therefore, that his techniques of 'behaviour modification' should arouse the suspicions of the left or liberal-minded people in general. Sometimes, they can see the usefulness of using behaviour modification in very limited ways. A social worker in New Jersey explained to me that she detested Skinner till she came across a patient who could not urinate or defecate except in his own home. As the man was in business, this quirk was a threat to his career: American business thrives on motion. The client went to a 'behaviour modification' therapist after a psychoanalyst had told him that it would take at least a year to get to the root of his problem. Skinnerian conditioning cured the man in three weeks. Skinner would argue that this is a typical instance of where the 'technology of behaviour', as he likes to call it, is of real benefit. His opponents would argue that such a case was too simple and too comic. The client wanted to be cured of his peripatetic constipation. He was not being forced to conform to society's ideas of what he should be like in any serious way. Such a case would not, for them, begin to justify the risk to liberty they see in Skinner's work.

It must be said, however, that Skinner has personally argued for reform since *Walden Two*. He has argued for penal reform and for educational reform. He claims that people suffer unnecessarily because such ideas for reform are received with hostility. Professor Eysenck, in his interview, makes a similar point. The science of behaviour has to come to grips with the fact that many people do not want to use science to remedy their behaviour.

The interview goes some way to explain what a precise position Skinner holds on some of these issues. It seems to me that he has more grounds for claiming that he has been misunderstood on the issue of feelings than on the issue of control. He seems to shift his ground considerably on feelings. It is not always clear if he says that feelings are not causes, and therefore do not need to be studied at all, or that we need to study feelings from a behaviouristic point of view and that it is mistaken to regard them as causes.

On the issue of control, he reiterates that he is not after an authoritarian society. Skinner argues he has been misinterpreted. He does not want rigid control to maintain the present system: he wants his work to be used to design a better culture. He claims that no one person, no one body would create the rules of the operant society. I have no reason to doubt his sincerity. But he can offer no guarantee that his work cannot be put to uses very different from those that he would welcome. History suggests this is likely. It will need a lot of evidence to convince many liberal-minded psychologists that behaviour modification is not dangerous. And, certainly, it can be argued it will need much vigilance to ensure that behaviour modification techniques are not used so as to modify behaviour to make us more easy to control.

Why did you become a psychologist?
That's a long story. When I was in college, I wanted to be a writer. I majored in English. I had no psychology. And, between my junior and my senior years, I went to a small school of English in Vermont. One of the figures backing that school was Robert Frost. He came there for a day or two and I was introduced to him. We had lunch together and he asked me to send him some of my stuff. The next fall I sent him three short stories and he wrote me a very encouraging letter which appears in *The Collected Letters of Robert Frost*,

although the editor was not able to identify the Mr Skinner involved.
This decided me. I was going to be a writer.

I took a year living at home which was a miserable failure. I didn't
produce anything of any value whatsoever. And then, some friend of
mine said: 'Well, after all, science is the art of the twentieth century.'
So I thought I'd be a scientist. What scientific background had I had?
I had thought of biology at college but I decided I was going to be a
psychologist. I had read Watson and then I got hold of Pavlov and I
came to Harvard fully expecting to find a department which was
completely behaviouristic. But, of course, I found nothing of the
sort.

But that was how I got into it. I turned from the kind of interest in
human behaviour that the novelist has to the kind that the scientist
would have. I turned bitterly against literature. I heard that
Chesterton had said of a character of Thackeray's, 'Thackeray didn't
know it but she drank.' In other words, Thackeray had managed to
portray an alcoholic woman without knowing she was alcoholic. It
seemed to me that was true of someone like Dostoevsky who could
portray marvellous people because they were all parts of Dostoevsky
really without his understanding it at all. I was very bitter about my
failure in literature and I was sure that writers never really
understood anything. And that was why I turned to psychology.

*Professor McClelland suggested to me that many psychologists of
your generation went into the field as a reaction against religion and
fundamentalist moral positions. Was that true for you?*
He's got me in the wrong generation. It was a generation or two
before. The people who in the 1890s went into psychology had
often been ministers or studied for the ministry. I think that is true.
There was some of that, I suppose, in Watson and there was some of
it in me. I was raised a Presbyterian but I gave that up before I went
to college. I don't believe I was following Jeremy Bentham in trying
to get over my fear of spooks which he acquired from the nursemaid
who told him ghost stories. No, I don't think that would be true of
me.

What were the major early influences on your work?
Accident primarily. I've developed that theme in a paper. I had read
Watson and Pavlov before coming to Harvard. Then, I met a graduate
student, Fred Keller. He knew standard behaviourist arguments and
lingo. I had some contact with Walter Hunter, one of the original

behaviourists, who came to give a seminar. I don't believe I got much from Hunter. I got some general physiology from Crozier who had an influence on me of sorts. He left me to do my own thing but he turned my attention to the organism as a whole. I started off being interested in reflexes, in Pavlov, Sherrington, in Magnus and postural reflexes. But Jacques Loeb had developed the concept of the organism as a whole. If you deal with the organism as a whole, you can't deal with organs in isolation. What is the organism as a whole doing? He's behaving in space, in an outside world. You're no longer interested in what's going on inside, in a gland or in a muscle. Loeb could only find a tropism as orienting behaviour in space. I turned to the reflex but I moved from a section of the leg and a Sherrington preparation to the whole organism. The first apparatuses I developed which were very close to ethology were concerned with the reflex behaviour of the total organism.

Did you ever meet Watson?
No, and I don't know anyone who did. He had already left the field by that time. He had been kicked out of Johns Hopkins for moral turpitude. Today, no one would think twice about it but he had an affair with his assistant and married her eventually when his wife divorced him. For a year or two, he was reduced, I think, to selling rubber boots in Louisiana. Then he got into advertising and emerged as a very important executive. The only psychologist that I know who kept contact with Watson was Lashley. He came to Harvard in the middle thirties and I believe that he only came after consulting with Watson.

What organisms did you work with first on the reflex, animals or humans?
The first animal was the squirrel, three baby squirrels. I had already done experiments with the squirrels in Harvard Yard, hanging peanuts on a string from a branch and watching a squirrel pull on the string to get the peanuts up. I was thinking of Kohler's *Mentality of Apes*: I was going to do *The Mentality of Squirrels*. I kept those squirrels around as pets for a long time but I went to work with rats. And baby rats at first because they showed all the postural reflexes in Magnus's book. I studied the behaviour of a rat that was running down a straightway on a very delicate platform. I would sound a click and the rat would come to a dead stop. I would get a very good measure of that stop, very much like Sherrington's torsion wire

myograph in responding to a single muscle. I was trying to get the response of the whole rat as Sherrington had got the response of a muscle. That was my thinking at the time. From that, just by accident, I got into reinforcement and the operant area.

What particular accident was it that led to that?
I had my rats running down this alley and I would reinforce them with food. They would then go up a back alley before coming down again. I noticed that they would wait before starting and I began to time that wait and I found it was changing. So here was a change in the probability that a rat would go around that loop, so I set up a special apparatus to follow that change. In other words, I was looking at the rate at which a rat would respond under direct reinforcement and then, by accident, I got it on a cumulative curve and I found I was scheduling. I found that I was in.

How did you find you had to modify Pavlov to accommodate the findings you made?
Pavlov remained a physiologist dealing with organs, not the organism as a whole. Moreover, he was dealing with the autonomous nervous system and with just about the only gland that would have worked. It's an amazing accident that he hit on it. It's very hard to find another gland that could be used. I did not think that efforts to use muscle preparations as with flexion of the leg, for example, were Pavlovian and I don't think so today either. You can't use tears. You probably could have used some other gastric secretions if you could get at them more easily. But I doubt that you could use urine or sweat. Salivation was it. As a matter of fact, though I've only just thought of it now, you might say that Pavlov was a specialist in conditioned salivation.

When you began your research, was there still much controversy about a behavioural approach or had that battle been fought and won in the 1920s?
Well, I can't say it was won. My colleagues among the graduate students at Harvard, with the exception of Keller and, possibly, of Charles Trueblood who dropped out of psychology shortly afterwards, were all interested in Titchenerian psychology. They studied lifted weights, thermal sensitivity, absolute judgment and so on. One of them had spent a year in Germany with the Gestalt psychologists studying the phenomenon. They were all mentalists of

275

the first order. I wouldn't say that behaviourism won its place at that time at all.

How did you come to develop the concept of the operant?
I was very strongly moved at first to think in terms of the reflex. I separated it from physiology in my thesis, in accord with the burgeoning positivistic movement of the time. I read Bridgman. (I was the second psychologist to cite Bridgman. Harry M. Johnson was ahead of me on that.) I read Mach, Poincaré and the people who led up to the Vienna Circle. I never followed them. I don't think they were on the right track but I was looking for the observations upon which one bases concepts. My thesis contended that the reflex was not a physiological device. Sherrington never saw a synapse. The reflex was a statement of the relationship between stimulus and response. That was the beginning.

I developed this further in another paper on the generic nature of stimulus and response. I was moving in the direction of the operant. But it was Konorsky and Miller who, when I first published my papers on lever pressing in the rat, sent me a copy of a paper they were submitting to the *Journal of General Psychology*. Preparing a reply, I realised how I had moved away from a reflex formulation and, also, how I differed from Konorsky and Miller. They had taken an ordinary reflex and added a consequence. You shock a foot, the leg flexes and the flexion produces food. This was in addition to a Pavlovian formula and they felt it was similar to what I had done. My objection was that, by using a reflex, shock-flexion, they killed the whole thing. You would have to find in nature stimuli which were correlated with consequences whether the reflex occurred or not, since the flexion was producing the food.

It occurred to me that you have to have relative freedom from stimulus control in an operant to get the effect of reinforcement. That was our difference then and that is the difference now. It was in my reply to Konorsky and Miller that I first used the word 'operant'. By the time I came to write *The Behaviour of Organisms* the concept was fairly clear. Most people feel that I distinguish between the autonomic and the skeletal nervous systems and assign the autonomic to respondent or Pavlovian conditioning. When I tried myself to condition an autonomic response as an operant I failed. I got what looked like it but there turned out to be a mediating response, as there almost always is, unless you knock a man out with curare – which you can't do!

Much of your work started out as animal work. How securely do you think it can be applied to human beings?

Well, by the end of the war, it had not been applied at all, with one or two exceptions. I think Fred Keller did something with one of his children. But then I wrote *Walden Two* which was a wild guess about how this could be applied to the design of a culture and, slowly, the research moved into the human field.

By 1953, I had published a book, *Science and Human Behaviour*, in which I talked about the place of the operant in religion, government, education, economics, psychotherapy and so on. Then the whole programmed instruction movement came along very quickly. Then behaviour therapy developed. Ogden Lindsay and I were, in fact, the first to use the term 'behaviour therapy'. We did the first work using operant conditioning with psychotics at the Metropolitan State Hospital. Behaviour modification also came in and, meanwhile, a great deal of laboratory work was being done with human subjects. There's no question in my mind that it works well with any species, any vertebrate species at least.

Some of your critics have argued that while you can control the contingencies of reinforcement for an animal very exactly the same doesn't go for Man. Though you are showing something that can be made to happen, it isn't how those things normally do happen. Do you see any justice in such criticism?

You have a similar problem in medicine. If you have a really sick person, you take him to a hospital because there you can handle things properly and make sure he gets the medicine at the time he wants it. You're not quite sure he'll take it when he is out in the world at large. Of course, you can arrange conditions much more precisely in the laboratory. On the other hand, it will work in the world at large, if it is being applied. The achievements of behaviour modification to date are quite dramatic.

But presumably you don't just want to modify behaviour. I understand your work to be trying to explain how we have come to do certain things and, even, to feel certain feelings.

Yes, I would say there are three things that can be done in the world at large through an understanding of behavioural processes. One, we can use them to predict what people will do in given circumstances. Two, if we can arrange the circumstances, we can control behaviour. Three, we can use it to *interpret* behaviour.

277

This is very important and it is an aspect of it that is easily misjudged.

In what way?
Interpolation isn't guesswork, it isn't theory, it isn't metascience. It's what the astronomer does when he interprets information from outer space as, say, a black hole. He doesn't know. But from what he knows about the behaviour of matter, when it is under his control, he can make some guesses about what is going on when it is not. We can make some guesses about what is happening in, let us say, a family where there is a behaviour problem with a child. We can make better guesses by looking at the contingencies of reinforcement that are visible than the psychoanalyst who turns to theory and starts talking about the relation of the son to his mother. We can point to more relevant things and we're more likely to suggest effective changes.

Do you foresee a study that will map the whole reinforcement history of a person?
That's out of the question for anyone. Psychoanalysts themselves sometimes try to reconstruct a life history. And a good psychoanalyst doesn't, of course. No, I think you have to accept the fact that human behaviour is extremely complicated and you do what you can. I have never claimed that I have solutions to all the problems in the world. I have solutions to very few, alas.

You seem to have a very ambivalent opinion of Freud, if I may say so. You're obviously critical but you seem to me to be far kinder about him than many other psychologists. Can you explain why?
I think Freud made some very important discoveries and, also, that he brought attention to discoveries which had been made by other people. We have changed as a result. We no longer believe in accident, in whim, in caprice. There are reasons why you forget appointments, for instance. I don't think he always gave the right reasons but I accept his determinism. I think his great mistake was to invent the mental apparatus, as he called it, a fantastic creation out of German will psychology. It was a tragedy. If he had organised his facts without reference to three personalities of ego, super-ego and id, without reference to the topography or geo-graphy of the mind, the conscious, pre-conscious and uncon-scious, he would have made much greater progress but he

wouldn't have attracted so much attention. There's no question that there is fascination in this theoretical stuff. It gives a sense of profundity, of depth. Psychoanalysts love the word depth. It also means that Skinner is on the surface. They're more profound. I don't think his therapy has been the success psychoanalysts think it has. Eysenck is perhaps a little extreme on this but not too much so.

Your rejection of the mental apparatus leads me to another criticism, certainly of European psychologists, and that is that your work is the ultimate in the tendency of American psychology to study action rather than thought. Is that fair?

It's probably a by-product of the peculiar environment that Americans came into in moving here from Europe. You could act here. You could go places. There were all sorts of things you could do, as I am realising as I write in my autobiography about my childhood days. And Americans have been men of action rather than of contemplation. It is largely an environmental difference, I'm sure. It's certainly not due to character – whatever that may mean. But it is important because, to my mind, cognitive psychology is an appeal to ignorance. It is putting explanatory entities of one kind or another inside the organism – things associated with thinking, reasoning, intuition. I want to get at the environmental manifestation of the behaviour which is attributed to these inner thought processes. When you do that, you take a step forward because if you explain behaviour in terms of what a person is thinking, you then have to explain that thinking. You have a whole new problem.

If you ever achieve a final explanation of behaviour, as it were, would you then feel you should attack thinking or do you believe it is just an unimportant by-product?

I'm very much concerned with the problem of thinking. I have a book coming out in the spring which has a great deal about the problem of thinking. I think that behaviourism makes the greatest possible contribution to an analysis of thinking.

I must confess I find that surprising.

The reason is that we are trying to get at the external manifestations of that behaviour attributed to thinking. I make a distinction between behaviour which is shaped by contingencies,

and behaviour which is generated when people follow rules
extracted from those contingencies. And rational behaviour
involves the giving of reasons where the reasons are statements
about contingencies. I can deal with rational behaviour very well.
It's very different from contingency-shaped behaviour. Rational
behaviour is also contingency-shaped but it is so at one remove.
We learn to extract rules and we have to be given reasons for
following them.

Can you also deal with creativity on this model?
That is another one of those 'soporific virtues'. How do you
account for the fact that a child can utter sentences it has never
heard? Why? Because it possesses some cognitive rules of grammar.
And how do you know that? Because it emits sentences it has
never heard before. That passes for solid thinking nowadays
among linguists.

Do you think then that creativity is an artificial concept?
No, creativity is simply the production of novelty, of original
forms. You have precisely the same problems with operant
behaviour that Darwin faced in evolution. Natural selection and
operant conditioning are very similar. Both move the concept of a
prior design to an *a posteriori ex post facto* selection. Both move
purpose from before to after. This explains origination. The key
word of *The Origin of Species* is 'origin'. The environment of the
child who is learning to speak selects behaviour and it has the same
creative function as the environment in natural selection. The
child comes up with novel combinations. There are reasons for this
which I set out in my book *Verbal Behaviour*. As a result, the
child will emit novel verbal responses. You say it is due to
creativity. I say that is creativity.

Your book Verbal Behaviour, *in fact, stirred up tremendous controversy. Why do you think that was?*
I think it is my most important book. It's the missing link between
the animal research and the human field. But its importance is one
thing. The linguists have missed it so long now because they do
not understand an operant analysis. They don't feel at home in it.
They can't get into the book and it frightens them. But there is
now some growing interest in the book even though it is so far
away from traditional linguistics (which is almost totally

mentalistic) that it doesn't appeal. (As a matter of fact, it hardly is linguistics.) Verbal behaviour is not what linguists talk about, they talk about verbal communities. I have a small appendix at the end of my book on linguistics and I think that's where it belongs. There are no specialists in verbal behaviour now. There are a few courses being given using my book but there is no person calling himself a linguist or a psycholinguist who specialises in the field, important though it is.

To what extent did Chomsky's famous and hostile review contribute to this neglect?

Linguists have taken it very seriously. They take Chomsky very seriously. I didn't even read that review for ten years. Then, my students told me that I should and I did. I have never read his long attack on *Beyond Freedom and Dignity.* He's an emotional person who, for some reason, is outraged by whatever I write. I don't know how to explain it. When I'm often asked: 'Why is Chomsky mad at you?' I don't know why. Well, if he's right, I'm wrong and if I'm right, he's wrong, but I can view that with equanimity. It seems he can't.

Another field of some controversy has been ethology. You have said that some of your first work was along ethological lines and that you are puzzled by how people react to some of your work, arguing that you deny an importance to genetic endowment.

I don't know where they get that. There is, of course, Watson's famous remark that he could take any child and make him any kind of person. But he said that he was exaggerating and he certainly was. I have never known any behaviourist, with one exception, who has denied the very considerable role of genetic endowment. I do question what it is. The work done on imprinting by a student of mine, Neal Petersen, showed that what was inherited was not the duckling's tendency to follow the mother but a tendency to be reinforced by reducing the distance between it and the mother or mother-object. It is not behaviour that is inherited but a capacity to be made aware of it by the verbal community that says, 'Why did you do that?' 'What are you going to do next?' Consciousness is imposed on the unconscious rather than the unconscious being produced by driving conscious material to the repressed depths.

281

Do you see any value in second-level needs, like for achievement and affiliation. Are they motivating in any way?

I don't like the word motivating. You feel the need for something and there is a need in the sense of a want. You need food in the sense that food is wanting. But that is a condition in which, because of the history of the species, some kinds of things are likely to be reinforcing. I don't think people 'need to be reinforced'. They *are* reinforced. That is all you can say.

You make a firm distinction between what psychologists and what physiologists should do. Why?

It's again the question of the organism as a whole. The behaviour of the individual in the environment in which he lives is not going to be analysed by instruments that get inside that organism. It's on the outside that the behaviour takes place. Changes occur inside, and the omniscient physiologist may eventually tell us what they are. At the moment he can't tell us very much. I said in 1938 that I knew of no physiological fact that threw any light on behaviour, and I still don't. Take hormones. What do we know about hormones and behaviour. We know we can change the extent to which sexual contact is reinforcing by giving hormones. That doesn't tell us about the deprivations that build normal sexual behaviour, or about satiation, about generalisation to other behaviours. We still have the problems we had in the first place – about the extent to which a person is reinforced by sexual contact and what it does to him.

Because of this stand you have come to be regarded as a psychologist of the empty organism. Is that fair?

That's not my phrase. I've always acknowledged the importance of what goes on inside the organism. You would have to be a fool not to. But I leave that to the physiologist. I don't want to meddle. I want to help, and a good clear statement of behaviour gives the physiologist his assignment.

You have also not been well understood in that many people think you advocate more punishment.

I would like to see no punishment at all. I have never had anything to do with aversion therapy, though when I was in England, a year ago, I saw they were blaming *Clockwork Orange* on me. I have been so bitterly against punishment that some of my colleagues

have been trying to psychoanalyse me to find out why. Did my
father beat me? (Actually he didn't.) I don't think you can get rid
of punishing contingencies. You can suddenly become permissive.
We have to find alternatives to punishment.

If we may turn to Beyond Freedom and Dignity. *There, you turn
your attention to what you call 'autonomous man', that rather
dangerous homunculus within us who thinks himself free to act. Do
you think we cling to that idea of ourselves?*

We certainly do. The whole history of the struggle for freedom, and I
accept that struggle as having made great strides in human progress,
has led us to believe we are masters of all we survey. But that's not
true. We are what we are because of our history. We like to believe we
can choose, we can act, and it's true that we can if we overlook what
determines how we act in our past history. We believe we are
responsible for our past achievements though we like it less when
we're held responsible if we do something wrong. Then society is at
fault. In the long run, I don't believe a person is either free or
responsible. However, I want a world where people feel free as they
have never felt before. I want a world in which people are under
positive reinforcement instead of aversive control, in which people
achieve more than ever before. I want people to feel tremendously
worthy. (The word 'dignity' isn't quite what I want. The French
word *'digne'*, is closer perhaps.) But that doesn't mean they originate
anything. The awful thing about the present obsession with the
individual and his immediate gratification is that we are paying no
attention to the future. That's the theme of *Beyond Freedom and
Dignity*. By all means let's have freedom and achievement but they
mustn't over-ride the need to plan for the future.

*But doesn't that leave you in a contradictory position? You want
people to feel free and yet you say freedom doesn't exist. Aren't you
offering an illusion of freedom?*

I don't call it an illusion. It's a feeling. If I'm holding a gun at your
head and I say give me ten dollars, you're not free. But if I just say
give me ten dollars and you're a nice guy and give them to me, you
say you're free to do so. There are reasons why you give me ten
dollars. Possibly you hope to get something from me in return, or
you may have been given a large sum of money, a thousand dollars,
and you don't know what to do with it. So you give me ten dollars.
There are reasons why you give them to me even if I'm not holding a

gun to your head, and you feel free in doing it. You don't feel free when I'm holding a gun at your head. This is a very important difference and I'm as much concerned as anyone to free people from punitive coercion. I wouldn't call that an illusion. You feel free. You have a feeling which is associated with positive reinforcement which is very different from a feeling associated with coercive control. And you call it freedom. That's OK.

But what, on your model, is that feeling, that feeling of freedom? That seems a very crucial question, as you deny the validity of feelings...

I don't deny that. That's another misunderstanding. I think the behaviourists are ahead of the field in analysing feelings. I wrote a paper just before I wrote *Walden Two* that is, I think, extremely important. It explains how a person can be taught to describe private events within his body. It is something that Wittgenstein missed completely. He could never see how you could describe a private event. For him, the statement 'I am in pain' was nothing but a cry of pain. In that paper, I described how the verbal environment can teach a person to describe the state of his own body. We will call it feelings or introspections, in spite of the fact that the verbal community has no information about it.

I have no hesitation in saying I feel my own body, I feel happy, I feel tired, I feel exhausted, I feel cheerful. But I don't behave in any way *because* of my feelings. That's the main point. Feelings are by-products of behaviour. The mistake people make is to take them as causes.

So feelings are epiphenomena?

I wouldn't say that either. Feelings are not causes but that doesn't mean they're ephiphenomena. If I kick you on the shins, you may be inclined to hit me and you will also feel angry. Now the kick on the shins creates the probability that you will hit me and also creates that state of your body you call anger. You feel angry. Now what's epiphenomenal about that? But suppose I then ask you, 'Why did you hit me?' and you say, 'Well, I felt mad at you.' That's not right. You hit me because I kicked you on the shins. You didn't hit me because you felt mad. But both, the anger and the hitting, are the products of a single cause.

Would it be fair to say then that feelings can be consequences but not causes?

That's exactly it. They are collateral products. They are states of the body associated with behaviour, some of which can be felt. I make the point in the paper I recently gave at Oxford. Feelings are bad evidence and not very important to the physiologist for they don't get at the important mediating mechanisms.

Just as feelings are by-products, you seem to argue that consciousness is a by-product. You have said that awareness is imposed on us by society.

All behaviour is unconscious to begin with. You behave even though you aren't aware of why you're behaving. But you can be made aware of it by the verbal community that says, 'Why did you do that?', 'What are you going to do next?' That is imposed on the unconscious rather than the unconscious being produced by driving conscious material to the repressed depths.

Your work is being put into practice in many ways in this country. Isn't there a danger that, if you design the culture you want, control will be exercised over people's lives but they won't be aware of it?

There's certainly a danger and that's why I spend so much of my time explaining how people can be controlled. If you sequestered it, if you said let's not talk about it, there would be 'controllers' who'd snap it up and have a field day. No, I want everyone to be aware of how he is controlled. We are all controlled now. A friend of mine returned from China and said: 'You'd love it there, people are so controlled.' What do you think happens here? People are just as much controlled in America as they are in China but the control isn't as conspicuous, that's all. We are absolutely one hundred per cent controlled in America.

But who will design the culture? What will you reinforce? What will you not reinforce?

A great many people will be designing it. Teachers will be teaching better. Psychotherapists will be helping people more effectively. Industry will be arranging more effective incentive systems which make people not only work better but also enjoy what they are doing. Governments will be able to govern without having too many policemen about. These are the changes that will be made. No one person will emerge as the controller.

Burrhus Skinner

In your writings you have quoted both Hull and La Mettrie, saying that Man is a machine. At the same time, I believe, one of the reasons why you express an occasional doubt over being called a behaviourist is that it seems to imply not only that Man is a machine but that he should be treated mechanically.

It depends on what you think a machine is. If you're thinking of a nineteenth-century machine, a push-pull collection of levers, that's not what I think Man is. A man is a mechanism at the molecular level, a biochemical machine. That's all it comes down to. Miniaturisation should have given us some idea of how far down a machine may go. When I say that Man is a machine, I mean that, as far as I know, the whole thing is an orderly physical system. It's certainly not a nineteenth-century machine with push-pull causality and that is an important difference.

It would be presumptuous to attempt a complete critique of Skinner's position in a few pages. Some interesting points, however, emerge from this interview.

First, Skinner clearly believes that he is a pioneer waging a lonely battle against the autonomous man. He insists that we cling to this inner homunculus out of arrogance and ignorance. In *Beyond Freedom and Dignity*, he wrote: 'Unable to understand how or why the person we see behaves the way he does, we attribute his behaviour to a person we cannot see, whose behaviour we cannot explain either but about whom we are not inclined to ask questions' (p. 19).

Ruthlessly, Skinner pursues his condemnation of the autonomous man, a creation of Greek psychology. He goes on: 'He [autonomous man] initiates, originates and creates and, in doing so he remains, as he was for the Greeks, divine. We say that he is autonomous and so far as the science of behaviour is concerned, that means miraculous' (loc. cit.).

It seems important to set these insights into context. Skinner's autonomous man does not differ much from Gilbert Ryle's 'ghost in the machine'. In *The Concept of Mind* (1949), Ryle elegantly bundled this ghost into oblivion. As a philosopher, Ryle wanted to show how misleading it was to talk about feelings, intentions, motives and purposes as private states accessible only to the individual who possessed them. As a psychologist, Skinner starts out from such a base but goes much farther, though, in a series of directions that are perhaps more confusing than is generally realised.

Skinner moves all causes outside the body and outside the organism. It is what has happened to you, the external consequences of what you have done in the past, that make you behave the way you do now. Man is what he has done and what has been done to him. In the interview, Skinner rejects the view that he is a psychologist of the empty organism. He points out many defects in physiological psychology. But to point these out does not indicate what role there is in his own thinking for what goes on inside the organism. To say that the stream of consciousness is an irrelevance is one thing; to say the bloodstream is, is very different. Many internal factors affect behaviour. Why is one person angry one day when faced with a certain situation and not angry another day? There is evidence from Eysenck that people inherit different susceptibilities to the processes of conditioning. A philosopher like Ryle can ignore these factors for they do not affect the way we talk about things. But they certainly affect the ideas that should guide our research.

One result of Skinner's popularity has been to continue denying much importance in psychological research to feelings and intentions. Skinner chuckled when he said it would surprise people to discover he had feelings and admitted it. He had been misrepresented. His point was that his feelings, the flotsam of his mind, did not make him act the way he did. If he had no feelings, he would act the same way. This seems a gross assumption. Skinner's revelation that he is at work on an analysis of thinking does little to reassure one. One presumes his analysis of thought will be closely connected to his analysis of verbal behaviour. Will it be called *Thinking Behaviour*?

Moreover Skinner has admitted that the history of any human being is so complex that it would be impossible to trace the incredible chain of reinforcements that made him behave the way that he did. Although the principles Skinner argued applied to situations as intimate as falling in love, choosing one's friends and relating with one's children, it was beyond the wit of man actually to account in detail for the reinforcements that led to a particular event. This is unsatisfactory. It leaves Skinner in this position. He has shown that, by conditioning, he can make certain things happen in very structured and artificial situations. He uses this to prove that, in fact, behaviour in all situations is caused in a similar way. Yet, he cannot account in detail for real-life behaviour in many such situations because real life is too complex, the chain of events is too long. It is arguable that Skinner forces behaviour to happen and to be caused in particular ways which may not be the way they normally do occur. It is a criticism that he does not really meet in the interview.

Skinner's precise position on feelings is, actually, harder to pin down than one might expect. In *Beyond Freedom and Dignity* (p. 19), he writes of William James's theory that it is our actions that cause our feelings and not, as is usually assumed, the other way round:

> In other words, what we feel when we feel afraid is our behaviour – the very behaviour which in the traditional view expresses the feeling and is explained by it. But how many of those who have considered James's argument have noted that no antecedent event has in fact been pointed out? . . . No explanation has been given as to why we run away *and* feel afraid.

The interesting point here is that he comes close to saying that psychology should look at why we feel afraid as well as at why we run away. If he did not stress the relative triviality of feelings, their lack of real importance in the scheme of behaviour, he might have encouraged a more complete analysis of what happens when we do run away and feel afraid. He might also have made it reasonable to look at why, sometimes, we feel afraid but do not run away. We behave quite often, after all, in a way that clashes with our feelings and intentions. This seems to support Skinner's analysis in some cases. We do not do the things that we think we want to do. But various factors are probably involved in this. The situation, the way we perceive the situation, what we want to get out of it, what we want to show ourselves as, are as likely involved as not. If these things sound vague, I can, at least, reply that Skinner also is vague. For, as we have seen, he admits that it is not usually possible to trace out the history that has led a person to a particular action at a particular time. By his concentration on overt behaviour, he is not taking all the data into account. He writes, at times, of 'inconspicuous behaviours'. These also need to be understood.

In the behaviourist approach, there is also little room for pretending. In the introduction, it was argued that we often behave in a way that conceals our feelings. Our feelings seem to be neither by-products nor causes in such a situation. Skinner fails to come to ask such questions. He is not alone in this. But in his psychology, such questions appear to be ruled out as unimportant.

The second main criticism of Skinner is that he fails to appreciate the dangers of behaviour modification. He says that since *Walden Two* he has tried to educate people so that they can see what techniques are being used to control them. It is curious that *Walden Two* is the one book that he wrote at great haste under pressure, and perhaps fervour, of inspiration. He has no sinister aims. He does not want to become Big Brother. To be fair, he does not sound as if he is longing for the opportunity to redesign the world personally. He stresses that no one person, no one institution, will lay down the desirable things that are to be reinforced. But the essence of the kind of culture that Skinner seems to want is that it has to be created in some definite image. His plans will not work if parents are reinforcing one thing, schools are reinforcing another and government yet another. If the culture is to be designed, the design of the culture has to be co-ordinated. There is the danger, at the very least, that the image of the culture will be designed by those in power. The ominous sentence 'Good things are things that are positively reinforced' (1972) itself reinforces the idea that there will be a complete moral vacuum. It sounds like a blueprint for an authoritarian and conformist culture. Skinner's strictures against permissiveness suggest that he, personally, would tend that way too. That emphasis, of course, makes the idea very appealing to some and repulsive to others. Like all technologies, the technology of behaviour is neutral in principle. But few technologies have been used neutrally. Radical thinkers, like Chomsky, do not believe the technology of behaviour would be. Since it could be even more devastating for Man and his precarious liberties than military technology, it is not surprising that many people see Skinner as sinister. He seems to me to share the political naïveté of many scientists. He argues that science is bound to go on making discoveries. They may always fall into the hands of the wrong people. But there is nothing the scientist should do, or could do, about this. Muzzling him is no answer.

It would be certainly wrong to attempt to end work in behaviour modification. In limited situations, it has often been beneficial. But one should be aware of its dangers and, perhaps, too, of why many people in the USA find it so attractive. Skinner certainly seems too little aware of its dangers. The interview suggests that he believes he has found out something whose benefits infinitely outweigh its dangers.

In his autobiography Skinner lists virtually every event that seems to have happened to him. Despite this comprehensiveness and despite the fact that he admits to having feelings, Skinner seems to hesitate to record what these events made him feel, even on such occasions as when his mother washed out his mouth with soap and water to punish him. At least Skinner is consistent in his portrait of himself: *Particulars of My Life* smuggles in little ordinary emotion or consciousness – it is a list and little else.

Skinner remains a psychologist who sees life in terms of action, not of reflection. It is no accident that it is in America, the land that extols action, the man of action, that he has been the most influential. His own environment has certainly helped and affected his own success.

12
Henri Tajfel

Henri Tajfel came late into psychology. He was born and brought up in Poland between the two wars. From Poland, he went to live in France. He was taken prisoner when the French Army had its 'great débâcle' in June 1940 and he spent the next five years in a prisoner-of-war camp. When Tajfel was liberated, he went to work for various international organisations on the rehabilitation of children. He spent some six years in this kind of work, dashing between Paris, Brussels and north-west Germany. In 1951, he came to England expressly for the purpose of studying psychology. He had to do this in the evenings while he worked during the day and, when he got his first degree, he was already thirty-five years old.

It would be odd, of course, if Tajfel's experiences before he became a psychologist had not affected him. He thinks that they did in two specific ways. The experience of being brought up in semi-fascist Poland between the wars made him feel, as a Jew, that he was very much part of a discriminated-against minority. This feeling made him a likely candidate for social psychology. It is also reflected in his particular interest at present – intergroup behaviour. For one of the curious facts about anti-Semitism is its ability to flourish even when it seems to fulfil no simple need like finding an economic scapegoat. Tajfel believes that work on other intergroup situations will yield insights into such phenomena. He sees a renewal now of anti-Semitism and, also, of various nationalisms throughout the world.

The second effect of his European background and his early work for international bodies has been to leave with him a certain dedication to international co-operation. Tajfel has been deeply involved with the foundation of the European Association of Social Psychology. He was its president for a number of years and on the

291

committee of the association for some ten years. There are two aspects to this kind of work. One is scientific. Tajfel has worked to get European psychologists together to know what they are doing. He edited, with J. Israel, a collection of papers called *The Context of Social Psychology: a Critical Assessment* (1973) in which various criticisms of American domination of social psychology were expressed. In the interview, Tajfel is careful to insist that he is not hostile to American social psychology and that some of the criticisms made in the book have been misunderstood. The second aspect of this work is much more political. Social psychology does bear on various social policies and even political problems. As well as being involved in international scientific administration, Tajfel has also done many stints on various international committees. He recently was, with three other professors, part of an OECD team that studied national social policy in France, a task that he enjoyed though he found it a great strain on his memory. You could not take in a tape-recorder when interviewing Giscard d'Estaing, even before his elevation to the presidency.

This international influence is reflected in Tajfel's office. There are certificates of membership of psychological associations from all over the place, including one from Uruguay. Tajfel says that he thinks interesting psychological developments will soon take place in Latin America. He hopes to be involved with them.

Tajfel came to England in 1951 to study at Birkbeck. He got one of the two best firsts in the University of London in his graduation year and so found it easy to get a job. He was appointed a research assistant at Durham, Durham being the only university that did not have assistant lecturers. He began by working on quite technical perceptual problems, looking at the fact that people tended to overestimate the sizes of stimuli that were positively valued by them. Tajfel divides his intellectual life into three distinct periods. The first was this technical period in which he looked at certain specific problems in perception and judgment. The second, which led to a theory about social perception in general, was when he discovered that what he had to say about his social perception had even wider implications than he had thought. The third phase of his work, his current phase, has lasted for about five years. In this, he has been involved in work on intergroup behaviour developing a new theory of intergroup relations – a field which has always been very weak in psychology according to him.

The essential philosophy behind Tajfel's work is that social psychology has been far too much concerned with individuals and inter-individual relations. It has accepted from experimental psychology the idea that you can study a person without looking at the context in which he lives. Tajfel in his early days as a psychologist was much influenced by Bruner's work, the so-called New Look in perception, which made it clear that motivation affects perception. We see what we expect to see: we tend not to see things we dislike as easily as things we like. There was, and to some extent continues to be, a whole area of controversy around the field of perceptual defence. From accepting that motivation could affect perception, Tajfel went on to study a much more complex area – that of social perception. And he became convinced of the importance of the social context, of seeing people not just as individuals but as members of groups. His theory of intergroup behaviour starts out from this premiss set out in the Katz–Newcomb lectures at the University of Michigan (1974).

> Social psychology is supposed to be about the behaviour of individuals in a variety of social contexts, much of it about their behaviour in groups. There is no doubt that relations between individuals belonging to different groups display certain uniformities which can be distinguished from uniformities in intragroup behaviour. There is also no doubt that these intergroup uniformities are as common and pervasive as those which are found *within* human groups. And therefore, the question of the relative theoretical neglect [of them] is both intriguing and potentially important.

Tajfel does not believe that this neglect is due to the fact that it is hard to devise experiments to look at these problems. The essential point is that most of social psychology has, to date, been American. America was created and has been sustained by the idea, among others, that a bright kid with the right Get Up and Go could, in fact, go and get up the social ladder. It is a society where the belief in social mobility is high. Therefore, it is possible for a person who dislikes the particular group or class he is born into or finds himself in, to move on out of it by hard work or luck or whatever. Such a belief is very different from one in *social change*, as Tajfel puts it. In societies that are based on social change, an individual cannot redress his own position by himself. He has to change the position of his group as a whole. It would be interesting to test the hypothesis

293

that British miners see British society very much in this kind of way and that is what gives them both the determination and the conviction to strike for their own and their group's benefit. Social change, as Tajfel argues, has been neglected by social psychology, both in America and outside it. This strikes him as a very dangerous omission for if we are to understand the world, which is rapidly changing, we surely need a social psychology of social change.

In feudal society, he points out, every distinction between class and class was God-given. You had been ordained to the station you were in. People low down on the scale would not dare to compare themselves with the barons. This may be partly why the lords found it so easy to crush revolts like the peasants' revolt. But today, people, however down-trodden, however disadvantaged, feel they can, and are beginning to, compare themselves with others. How has this come about? There is the question of how it becomes perceived to be legitimate to compare one's group with other groups. There is also the question of the perceived legitimacy of the perceived relationship between the groups. Is it right we are down here and you are up there?

There are certain social psychological conditions that have made possible this switch from large-scale acceptance to large-scale questioning. Social psychology needs to look at them neither in terms of individual processes nor in terms of economic or social analysis. One of the areas that Tajfel wishes to explore and see explored is how a person becomes a member of a group. For before the members of an ingroup can act together, can hate or dislike or discriminate or act against an outgroup, they must have first acquired a sense of belonging to an ingroup. Social psychology has looked at this problem but, according to Tajfel, in too one-sided a manner. It has usually been argued that people draw together in ingroups in response to threats, fear of an outgroup. A direct 'objective' conflict of interests between groups creates the groups. Tajfel is not so sure. Any individual is born into a society full of groups, some of which he must fit himself into. As Tajfel said in the Katz–Newcomb lectures:

> One of the most important and durable problems that is posed to an individual by his insertion into society is to find, create and define his place in these networks. It is reasonable to assume that both his ingroup and his outgroup behaviour must be determined, to some extent at least, by this continuing process of self-definition.

Tajfel is, of course, aware that such a movement to look at social psychology in terms of relationships between large-scale groups is a new direction to research. He has been criticised in America for succumbing to that old European sin of empty speculation. He rebuts this in two ways. He argues, first, that any discipline that does not question the direction of its own research is very incomplete. Second, he says he can point to research based on this new kind of thinking, research both in Bristol and in Europe.

In 1970, Tajfel started a series of experiments that seemed to reveal a great need on the part of people to see themselves as members of groups and a willingness to act on this group membership. The situations appear, at first, ludicrous – a classical case of laboratory work so artificial that its bearing on real life one feels, intuitively, must be nil. Subjects first performed a relatively trivial task. They had to guess the number of dots in a rapidly projected cluster or to express a preference for the paintings of two fairly abstract artists, Kandisky or Klee. They then worked separately. They had to decide, on a number of payment matrices, about the division of points worth money between two *other* subjects. They knew to which group they belonged and to which group those they were dividing money between belonged. Tajfel found very highly significant results in the direction of awarding most money to members of the ingroup. Moreover, the subjects tended to make choices of payments that would assure there would be the maximum difference in favour of the ingroup, rather than giving both equally large sums of money or dividing fairly.

In the interview, Tajfel explains how he believes that it is essential for psychology to look at these problems and how he feels that it is useless, as radical psychologists do, to reject experiments totally. He wants a constant flux between experimental and field studies.

Like a number of other psychologists, Tajfel places a great deal of emphasis on writing up his work. It is there where he is truly creative, he feels. It is, unlike for Hudson, not an unmixed joy for it costs him a great deal of effort to write even two pages and he often falls prey to the feeling that what he has written is worthless. But it does remain for him the acid test of doing psychology.

Why did you become a psychologist?
It's a very long story. I knew nothing about psychology until the end of the war. Then, in a number of ways, I became involved in rehabilitation work with children and young people immediately

after the war. I worked for international organisations, finally for the United Nations in France, in Belgium, in West Germany. I envisaged psychology mainly as an applied field of endeavour to do with helping people, the usual kind of thing you hear from an undergraduate who comes for an interview today. I came back from West Germany after having been there one and a half years and I decided to do psychology as a degree. I went to Birkbeck College which meant working full-time in the day and doing studies in the evening. Then I had a series of unexpected academic successes at Birkbeck, including getting a very good degree, and before I knew where I was I had my first academic job. So it happened in a fit of absent-mindedness like the British Empire. As an undergraduate I became interested in problems of cognition and perception; from there I became interested in problems of social cognition and social perception; and from there, in general, social psychology. So it all happened by chance.

Had you thought of becoming something else? Were you trained as something else for the rehabilitation you did?
Hardly. I was just over twenty when the war started. Before I knew where I was I was in the army in France when it had its great débâcle in June 1940. The only definite advantage that came out of the war, it seems to me sometimes, is that it prevented me doing chemistry. I was a prisoner of war and spent the next five years mainly in Germany and Austria. And then I came out in 1945, unchained and hopeful, and I spent the next five years doing the kind of international work I mentioned, almost by chance. I got interested in psychology soon after and I remember, as I was shoved from place to place, Paris, Brussels, I did what I could about psychology. I had just the time to get one *certificat* at the Sorbonne. You needed four to get a *licence en psychologie*. Then I was sent to Brussels to a bigger job and I did a diploma in educational sciences, as there was no psychology at the time in Brussels. Then I went off to north-west Germany, then occupied by the Allies, where there wasn't much chance of doing anything. I came to England in 1951 for the purpose of doing psychology.

Was chemistry a serious interest?
I was sent to study from my native Poland to France in 1936. My parents thought that whatever I did had to be 'practical' – the prospect of getting a job was then as gloomy as it is going to be

now, as it is now. And chemistry seemed practical. It was as
indifferent to me as anything. I remember I failed then the only
exam I ever failed because I was interested in three things, one, the
contemporary American novel, heaven knows why, two, the civil
war in Spain, you can imagine on which side, and three, in playing
poker. Well, I've done a lot of all those three things.

*So, though you couldn't study psychology formally, you did try
to learn some psychology?*
Yes but not until 1948/9 when I took it up, so that by the time I
became interested I was thirty and over. By the time I got my first
degree I was thirty-five or over. That was when I finished at
Birkbeck in 1954. And I was more or less pushed into a job in
Durham. I was frightened out of my wits to go and live in the
north-east of England where I had never been. But they had a job
as research assistant – Durham did not have a post of assistant
lecturer – and I went for an interview before finals. Then I got one
of the two best firsts in the university in my year so we packed up
and went to Durham.

What were the main influences on you?
Early on, Bruner and the kind of approach that he represented. I
can, perhaps, describe it best by saying that once we were walking
down one of the streets of Cambridge, Massachusetts, when I was
at Harvard in 1958/9, and I suddenly asked him, 'Jerry, what is it
you really are interested in?' and he said he was interested in the
way in which a human being comes to develop his full cognitive
and intellectual potential and that, of course, is reflected in his
latest work. I remember I said I was interested in the effects of
social and cultural milieu in which an individual lives on the way
in which he looks at the world. But these statements reflect a
desire to get away even from the more narrow framework of
cognitive psychology, which has been dominant, in order to go
into more complex problems. I became more and more interested
in bringing the little ideas we had to be tested into a large-scale
context. Bruner was one important influence. Indirectly, though I
have not met him more than one or two times, Piaget must have
been quite important. I'm not really conscious of it. But there is
his influence. I haven't really asked myself this question, who was I
influenced by? It's difficult. I remember I was very much impressed by

Richard Peters's lectures when I was an undergraduate. I don't really know.

Festinger, to the extent that I disagree with him more than I agree with him. As a friend said, why is it when you two meet it is always like a war in the Balkans?

I think what has been more important is that I have never really been a 'scientist'. My genuine interests have always been, well, in political phenomena, social history, cultural history. As I became more and more of a social psychologist – explicitly, as distinct from being a psychologist – I think I was seeking how to marry these various interests. Add to this a general dissatisfaction . . . . What I am saying is that really the influences were cultural influences. I've also been interested in the history of art and the history of political movements. What is coming now is some attempt to bring it all together, some attempt at convergence even at the expense of what some people might think as respectable.

McClelland has suggested that psychologists go into the field in order to get away from a very religious or fundamentalist upbringing? Was that in any way true in your case?
No. I had my only religious crisis at the age of four or five. I never had a 'proper' religious crisis, which I suppose is very bad. I've always been happy to be an agnostic. Why do you want to know that? But, the fact that I am a Jew, not as a matter of religion, but that I am a Jew, may well have determined me to go into social psychology.

How?
Having been brought up in Poland, I've always been felt a member of an extremely discriminated-against minority which was the case with Jews in semi-fascist Poland before the war. It's nothing to do with religion but it is to do with my social background. Everyone's social background is relevant to what they do. That's trivial.

When you went to Durham, how did your work first develop?
At that time I was interested in what was then called social perception and, more specifically, the relationship between motivation and perception. This was at the time of the big New Look in psychology in the fifties. I was then very influenced by Bruner's work on autochronous and behavioural effects on perception. I became specifically interested in the issue of

perceptual overestimation, i.e. why do objects or stimuli which have a positive value to a subject appear as larger – and, of course, there's a whole host of difficulties in 'appear as' – to the subject than neutral objects. I ran a number of experiments on the relation between the value to the subject of the stimulus and the judgment of size. Then, with the encouragement of Bruner who became a life-long friend, I stuck my neck out and wrote a theoretical paper for the *Psychological Review* which, lo and behold, was published. This paper has, I believe, remained something of a classic in this field. After two years in Durham, I was appointed at Oxford in 1956. My interests widened. From my work in this relatively unimportant field of motivation and perception, I drew what I thought was a more general schema of biases in social perception which has led to a fairly wide theory of social judgment. I went on working on this kind of thing for the seven to ten years. Then came the crisis. [He laughs.] One became less and less satisfied both intellectually and socially with what social psychology was doing.

At the time, Oxford was very behaviouristic in its approach to psychology?
No, not behaviouristic. If you think of Carolus Oldfield, who was professor then, he was not a behaviourist, in any sense, certainly. I respected him, I liked him, he was a man of great integrity but I think it is true to say that he tended to be afraid (or that is how I interpreted it) that psychology would not be scientifically acceptable in Oxford which tended, perhaps, to make him cautious. But this wasn't behaviouristic but physiologistic.

At one time, there were there Harry Kay, Stuart Sutherland, Tony Deutsch, Michael Treismann, Anne Treismann, myself, Michael Argyle, Marcel Kinsbourne, Jeffrey Grey and Roy Davis, and everyone was really going in their own direction. There was no pressure to be one thing or another except pressure to show people we were as good scientists as anybody else was which, anyhow, was unsuccessful in Oxford then. Now that is over. This kind of pressure, there's no doubt, created serious handicaps for the development of social psychology. This is still true in Cambridge. In Oxford, social psychology has developed though not, perhaps, in directions I find particularly interesting.

In the book you edited, The Context of Social Psychology: a Critical Assessment, *you seemed to me to argue that the American domination in social psychology had been harmful. Is that a correct interpretation?*

Harmful is the wrong word. This was related to something else which was one of the most important things to come in the book and still is. And this is that it is useless to pretend social psychology could be culture free, much more useless than any other branch of the subject . . . but social psychology is certainly much more dependent on the social and political and cultural context from which it arises than experimental psychology. Therefore, it seemed to me crucial that a second intellectual centre of social psychology, along with America, had to be developed, because as long as we had only one centre we should be blind to our own blindnesses. So a group of us in the early sixties started to work to create a European Association of Social Psychology. As a result, over the years a number of us got to know each other well, created a network, by now an old boys' network, mainly in Western Europe. First, we discovered that though in many countries we knew what was happening in the United States, no one in Holland knew what was happening in England, or no one in France knew what was happening in Norway and vice versa. When we got together we discovered how strongly our work had been influenced by work in America. In a sense we had taken over hook, line and sinker, assumptions from a very powerful culture that was in some ways different from our own. If we were really serious about creating a second intellectual centre, we had to re-create our own tradition. Now this is easily said but it can't be done by programmatic statements. It has to be done by hard work. There's little doubt over the years it has begun to acquire a certain identity so that now we are beginning to influence America. Anyhow, because we are known as a group we became known in America, so that although some of us were also well known as individuals becoming known as a group was more important.

How was your Critical Assessment *received?*
First, the book had some rather good reviews. But recently a rather bad one came out in *Contemporary Psychology* which is, of course, the leading journal of reviews of psychological books in the States, by a young social psychologist called Philip Shaver who is at Columbia. The review was mainly that this is the old

European sin of speculation and asked, where are your research designs? I wrote back saying that there are two kinds of activities essential to the well-being of any discipline. One is to do further research and the other is to question the direction in which you are going. And this has always been rather anaemic in social psychology and it is important that it should also exist. Then, in addition, I was able to quote four areas of research by contributors to the book, the general approach of which was very much in consonance with the book – research done in Paris by Moscovici on social influence which adopts a new point of view, research by Flamment at the University of Provence on social representation, research done in Scandinavia by people like Rommetveit on the social context of psycholinguistics, and research we're doing at Bristol on the social psychology of intergroup relations. All are consonant with this approach.

So you feel it is too strong to call the American influence harmful?
I think not harmful. It's easy to go wrong here. Not only was it not harmful, but without American social psychology there would be no social psychology whatever. What one can try to do – and they are just as aware of the need to find new directions – is, well, perhaps a concrete example serves best. I recently met at Harvard Albert Hirschmann who used to be professor of political economy there and has just been invited to become a permanent member of the Institute for Advanced Studies at Princeton. We discussed a number of things and we suddenly discovered a convergence of ideas which came without either of us having read what the other had written. In *Exit, Voice and Loyalty* written in 1970, Hirschmann used certain concepts from economics which he partly translated into concepts in political science. In these lectures at Ann Arbor, I was trying to say one can distinguish between two extremes of structures of belief about the society in which one lives. One extreme is the structure of belief in social mobility. By social mobility I mean the belief that you live in a society in which you can move if you don't like the conditions in which you live, it's possible by whatever means – hard work, luck – to move out into another group, i.e. free-floating mobility. A structure of belief in social change would inhere in a society perceived by its members as being very stratified so that if you want to change your conditions of life you can't do it by moving

freely out of one social group into another, but you must change
the position of that group as a whole in relation to the rest of
society, not as a member of it. When you look at the history of
work in intergroup relations in social psychology, you see that all
the theories we have had were theories arising from the structure
of belief in social mobility and very few, if any, arise from
considering the structure of belief of social change. We've always
done work on individuals and inter-individual relations when we
were concerned with racial, social class or religious groups. And
this is a good example of what one might call the restrictive
aspects of the American influence because, of course, as
Hirschmann wrote, the belief in social mobility is one of the most
powerful images of the American myth. This was part of the idea
of America. And this is reflected in the kind of social psychology
we've been doing when it is concerned with small groups,
individual processes, but social psychology also needs to be
concerned with the psychological aspects of large-scale social
processes. We have for practical purposes never looked at that.
Even if we have looked at them, it has been restricted to so-called
applied social psychology with little or no theory. In this sense, I
feel what we are trying to do now is 'European' because it is closer
to a European cultural tradition than to the American tradition.
But already Hofstadter, in his *Social Darwinism in American
Thought* (1945), referred to the same myth of social mobility. In
that sense I feel we can do something not just for ourselves but for
social psychology in general, including American social
psychology.

*In what other ways do you think the American tradition needs to
be shifted?*
This is not just American, it's also European. I don't want it to
appear as some kind of . . . look, what the Americans are doing . . .
I think it is all over the place. The whole thing is falsified if one
talks about American and not American. I really insist on this.
This misunderstanding appears in the *Contemporary Psychology*
review. It is simply the fact that we've all known for a long time
that the social behaviour of the individual or of categories of
individuals, is an interaction between social context, social
expectations and social evalutions on the one hand and what one
can call 'general basic processes' on the individual level. Yet most
of us have always done our experiments not taking into account

the social context of the experimental situation. There has been a move now, starting with work on the experimenter effect, by Rosenthal, when suddenly everyone discovered that what happened in an experiment very often depended on the subjects' expectation of what the experimenter expected them to do. All right, but this had become a methodological issue when, in fact, it is a theoretical issue. It's a question here of one's general example of the functioning of social influence and social expectations. If these were not shared in the culture by the experimenter and subject there could be no experiment at all. Really the issue is a theoretical issue but, typically, it has been treated as a methodological one.

To some extent, of course, there seems to be a distrust of theorising in much psychology. You started working on relatively small, technical problems. Has your concern with theories developed gradually?

Let's be careful. I don't believe in something which to me has always been very mysterious – a 'global' theory of social behaviour. I don't understand what it means. The more global it is, the more trivial it becomes. (An example is social exchange theory which is useless when you try to apply it to specific situations.) On the other hand, I am not wedded to prediction, I am also wedded to 'understanding'. I'm not sure we've been able to predict anything much, I don't think we ever shall be. 'Understanding' is more important. Therefore, what I mean by theory is not theory with a capital T but a coherent – don't let's be pretentious – a coherent set of interrelated ideas that have to do with a specific problem – large or small – that you are concerned with. In some of my past work I was concerned with discovering what would provide a coherent set of ideas about certain biases in social judgment, and in moving from biases about other individuals to biases about all human groups. I started from the way people judge the length of lines in certain experimental conditions and was able to extrapolate to a number of social phenomena in the late fifties. I had a theory of certain aspects of social and cognitive judgments that could be and was tested – at that time, experimentally. Today I'd be more happy if it was tested at the same time experimentally and through field work. At least experimental testing made me understand this whole field of problems better than before. The same is true now. To begin with,

Henri Tajfel

I am concerned with the fact there are crude extrapolations, reductionism of various sorts. Take something like the frustration/aggression hypothesis. You start to argue from individuals who frustrate other individuals who then aggress against other individuals but from this you suddenly get extrapolation to large groups who are frustrated by other groups and then aggress against other groups. Well, it always seemed to me there are assumptions in these direct extrapolations which don't take into account the crucial problems of diffusion of ideas and communication processes and these extrapolations are bound to a certain extent to be both correct and completely trivial. I'm not saying they're invalid. I'm saying this is the wrong level of approach, never mind explanation. From that point of view there has to be a certain autonomy of social psychology from psychology, from putting it all down to personality differences, which is absurd, or to cognitive dissonance.

Why do so many people do the same thing over a period of time? Maybe the Germans were frustrated between 1919 and 1933 but that hardly explains what happened. So one needs social psychology to find its own level to some extent independent of general psychology and, on the other hand, it has to be autonomous from, of all things, the Skinnerian model of sociology, crude versions of Marxism which assume economic input on one side and the behavioural output on the other. It's a new black box. What we should be concerned with as social psychologists are the large-scale social processes in between. One of the many problems we have never looked at is how come, in so many social and political conditions, so many people behave in a uniform manner. This is the kind of problem we've never looked at.

Could you, perhaps, expand on that?
A similar example I had in mind was Milgram's book *Obedience to Authority*. There was a review of it by Eysenck in the *Guardian* in which he said that Milgram was not paying enough attention to what is the central problem, personality differences between those who obeyed and those who did not obey the instructions. Well, I think this is pure nonsense. In the experiment, it was enough for the experimenter to leave the room and give his instructions by phone for the rate of obedience to fall by two-thirds. This can hardly be due to personality differences. It has to do much more

powerfully with the social context of the situation. A much more tragic example is Vietnam. Why did only *one* soldier refuse to shoot and kill during the Mai Lai massacre? The answer is not in personality differences but in the social pressures on American soldiers in Vietnam. I'm not saying there were not possibly some personality differences in the Milgram experiments, I'm trying to say that by asking the 'personality' question you completely divert theoretical attention from what is the major problem, which is why so many people are ready to do this kind of thing under such and such conditions. I'm not saying questions about personality are not valid questions in this context, but that the other questions should be more important to a social psychologist – and also to others. What does determine this kind of uniformity, or relative uniformity so that people do something they would not normally have done? Instead what you have is diversion to another problem which is also genuine in some contexts but is not a problem for *social* psychology. Social psychology has suffered this kind of diversion for a very long time.

And you see the answer to that problem of uniform action as being a social psychological one?
Well, what else? No, no, a social psychological answer with whatever is the analysis of the social context. In this case, I would assume you would have to have an almost social anthropological description of what were the pressures on the average American soldier in Vietnam and what was the diffusion of these pressures so that you had this horrifying uniformity of killing. There are the Zimbardo studies on prisoners and guards where, after all, volunteer subjects were randomly assigned to be prisoners or guards but Zimbardo had to stop the whole damn caboodle after eleven days – although it was planned to run it for three weeks – because people began to behave so much like real guards and prisoners. Yet they were randomly assigned to their roles.

Now we are hardly beginning to understand these issues and then, suddenly, we are told that we should be concerned about personality differences? It's of course a matter of emphasis and the only thing I'm trying to say is that this kind of emphasis on social behaviour has been seriously under-represented in social psychology for the last thirty to forty years.

Do you, then, see yourself as a social psychologist as being rather different from psychologists in general?

No, I think not at all. Let me give you an example. Over the last few years I've discovered that, as I become more interested in certain aspects of social psychology which approach political science, social anthropology and social history, I have, in a sense, become less and less interested in reading things in 'pure' psychology. I've now got on my desk at home four books that I want to read next. One is by a political economist, one is by a social philosopher, one is by Anatol Rapoport, what do you call him . . . a polymath, and one is by a modern historian. I use these books as a psychologist. I have not lost my identity as a psychologist but, at the same time, I feel these books provide me with more food for thought concerning the problems I'm interested in. They give me more stimulation for new ideas than most of conventional psychology literature. The result is that I have been out of the mainstream of what is conventional psychology, not deliberately but quite willingly. It doesn't worry me. If I go to a British Psychological Society meeting I am very lucky to find one paper out of so many per day in which I am really interested. Which is why I haven't gone very often in recent years. This does not mean I question the quality or the validity of this work. It is a question of interests. In this sense, I like to think that I am, perhaps, part of the wave of the future, at least, in social psychology.

How do you see the future? Do you see your kind of approach winning ground?

I think it is winning ground. I don't know where it's going to go. If, twenty years from now, someone is interested enough to write that Tajfel was writing nonsense, that's fine. I think it is necessary to stir these issues up because I think they are important. To make this clearer I have to come back to the intergroup work. It is not just because I am interested in it now but there is no doubt that, however you wish to define social change and it may be undefinable, there is a great deal of change in the world at large, due to changes in relations between large-scale human groups. Once you've said that, you've almost defined social conflict and we've never had an adequate social psychology of social conflict. And social conflict is ever so slightly visible here and there nowadays. That is why I think what we are doing is relevant,

if we can contribute to create a social psychology of social
conflict. In this sense I am quite optimistic that things have
to go in our direction.

*Do you see that as a way of getting past the accusation that social
psychology is trivial?*
Yes, but . . . .

Is it fair, in the first place, to call much of it trivial?
To begin with, I don't think it is fair. I don't think it's true. I
think you made this the main point of your review of our book in
the *Times Higher Education Supplement*. It's not true and I
resented it actually. The point of the book was not just that what
was done was trivial. But more than that. We tried to do
something positive. I don't think social psychology is as trivial as
one thinks. Much of it has undoubtedly been trivial but once again
this was, I think, because most of it remained on the level of
inter-individual relations (unless you do a micro-analysis which
does yield interesting results) but all the remainder, however much
disguised as a theory, is not much more than a transcription of a
shared social experience – an extension from common sense, much
of which may be obvious to anyone who has thought a bit about
his social life and this is where the triviality resides. If, however, as
I think strongly necessary, we go into those aspects of social life
and behaviour in which we all take part with the sense 'this is me',
'I do this', and suddenly realise thousands of other people also do
the same thing, then suddenly it all becomes much less obvious
and trivial. And it's worthwhile looking for the underlying causes.
I have much more hope and faith in the subject than ten years ago.

*If you look at textbooks of social psychology, you often get the
impression that social psychologists are seeking the invariant laws of
human behaviour. Do you think it is, in fact, possible to find such
laws?*
It's an important point which, fortunately, I've never found
relevant to my work. I don't see why it should be asked unless you
are a philosopher of science. Invariant, eternal, permanent laws.
No, I think not. I'm going to stick my neck out, I think, for one
reason: this is, to use a fashionable word, dialectics. By reacting to
his environment, man has always changed his environment. By
changing his environment, he has changed himself. You have a

spiral there which would make me very sceptical about permanent universal laws, in the sense of infinite as well as of everybody. There are always mutual and interactive changes between individuals, groups of individuals and the social environment that continuously act back on one another. Let me give you an example from the race, heredity and intelligence debate in which I'm not an expert. It sounds a bit like science fiction. We've presumably in the past fifty years tapped the full range of human genetic variability. But we cannot have tapped the full range of environments in the sense that if, for example, we make new discoveries about human cognitive development, we may be able to create milieux that will quadruple environmental influences (if you can measure such a thing), at any rate to increase them enormously. We may have new methods of education we can't even imagine today. So, it is not possible to be invariant about it. What the relationship is today does not predict the future relationship. There is another example from an idea not sufficiently explored by social psychology, but which can be found in Marx, though some Marxists say there can be no such thing as social psychology. The idea is that there is a very close-knit relation between man's methods of production and his social behaviour. Now methods of production have changed, are changing and will continue to change. There will be other important changes in behaviour, I have no idea what they will be but I must, at least, admit theoretically the possiblity of such a thing. No, I don't believe in universal laws.

My impression is that for many this search for invariant laws is psychology.
I think they think it or they don't ask themselves the question.

The kind of approach you take is very different from the traditional empirical approach. Did the fact that you came to psychology late and after a grounding in European culture different from Anglo-Saxon psychologists affect that?
Undoubtedly. Several things helped. That was one of them. By the time I came here I'd lived in several cultures, I was by no means a naive undergraduate. That helped. Another thing is more personal. Once I started, success to put it crudely, came quickly. Very quickly, for simple objective reasons, I didn't feel I had to worry about things very much. The more I became aware of this, the

more I just went ahead and did what I wanted. That was true not only of my time in Bristol but also applies to most of my time in Oxford.

If I can turn to some methodological problems, do you think that one of the reasons why the impact of the social context, of cultural influences on psychology have been small, is that this can't be quantified?

I don't know what you mean by quantified. I don't think scales are of the first, second, third or fourth importance here. I think what is important is to provide, in the old sense of the term, *Verstehende*, understanding, of the phenomena which you can use as a basis from which to run a number of empirical studies. If you begin to have eight or nine or ten studies which are not perfect in their own right but which all tend in the same direction, you have acquired new knowledge. I don't feel that quantification, in this case premature quantification for the sake of respectability, is in any case a requisite for valid empirical knowledge which might contribute to a theory.

When you say understanding, how do you distinguish that from prediction? To some, the word 'understanding' seems to conjure up a kind of romantic, even mystical kind of psychology in which you are absorbed, almost, by the subject. Is that your kind of understanding?

I think to say you should be able to predict is entirely justifiable if you are running an experiment. To run an experiment without predictions is nonsense. To devise experiments, unless you have predictions to test which come from a wider framework, is nonsense too. On the other hand, and this has been the cause of much heart-searching, it is rather difficult to ask anyone who is doing any form of general work to predict for any particular situation. As social psychologists, if we are concerned with any real-life' situation, we are being like clinicians, and you have to study, in great detail, that particular situation. I don't believe that, however much I do in intergroup relations in the next ten years, it will enable me to predict what will happen in race relations in Britain in the next ten years. I'd have to study race relations.

And yet I can come to certain more general kinds of understanding which may or may not lead to predictions. Let me give you an example. A few days ago I was in West Germany and I talked to a fairly aged lawyer who had just been in South Africa.

He said, 'You are a social psychologist, tell me, what can be done there?' Predict what may happen. Well, I have a prediction which in a sense is trivial but in another sense is not so trivial, if it arises from a general body of ideas. The prediction is this – the more concessions that are made by whites, the more likely it is there will be social unrest. This is based on certain theoretical ideas and is not necessarily obvious. You don't have to be a psychologist to make this prediction, and you certainly don't have to be a wizard. On the other hand, if it does come, logically come, from a certain wider body of ideas, it makes you think you are getting somewhere. Psychologists usually make experimental predictions on the basis of general psychological processes. Other social scientists in terms of economic situation, political situation and so on. There is one type of phenomenon in between these two – the extent to which any social group, small or large, acquires its identity only through comparing itself with other social groups. By definition, what you are doesn't exist unless it's compared to other people. We are what we are because 'they' are not what we are. Then the question arises, what is the range of comparison as it relates to various forms of social action?

So your sense of understanding has none of this air of the mystical about it?

I don't see anything mystical in it. It is, if you wish, at the same time an intellectual curiosity but it is also more than that. It is also being curious about the real world. I am, incidentally, extremely sceptical about any influence, positive or negative, we have as social scientists. Take a problem that may be important to both of us, perhaps. There is no doubt a reawakening of anti-Semitism. It happens I am a Jew although I have never been an active Zionist or religious. I am strongly a Jew. Here is a phenomenon that seems to exist through history, irrespective of social conditions. It is somehow not fully explained or understood through an economic or other form of social analysis. Today we have left-wing anti-Semitism as well as right-wing anti-Semitism. There is anti-Semitism in some East European countries although it is difficult to see what interest it serves. Another phenomenon is the development of dozens of different nationalisms around the world. It seems to me there is a need of some kind of a bridge for us to understand what happens between the economic and social input and the behavioural output. This cannot be done on the

basis of everyone is frustrated and, therefore, they aggress. But we
have to look at this as a social phenomenon or movement. For
some reason, people who have a common identification, and
decide and act in common, feel in common, think in common
– which is very much a problem for social psychologists and
very much less of a problem for anyone else. Therefore, what I
mean by understanding – and I cannot put it any better, it is no
use trying for formal definitions – is if I can achieve a better
insight into what happens without denying validity of either the
more individual explanation or the more social one, if I can
achieve a greater insight, I think I can be useful.

For these kinds of problems, do you think experiments are useful?
I disagree with those 'radical' psychologists who tell us what a bad
thing experiments are without saying that what is needed is
neither not good or bad experiments nor experiments or no
experiments but good theories – don't let's be pompous about the
term – good coherent sets of ideas related to certain problems.

*But, presumably, the prior notions you have will guide you, both
to how you study problems and to what problems you choose to
study?*
I can put it this way, simply. Social psychology is not value free in
one way, and in another way it is. I don't believe for one moment
that the selection of one's problems is value free. You select
problems you think important. However, I do believe, and this is
where I disagree with the majority of the so-called radical
psychologists, that once this is admitted, clearly, to oneself and to
others, that we do have to fit in with certain basic criteria of
evidence. Otherwise, we become charlatans.

And what are these criteria?
Rational inferences drawn from reliable evidence.

Could you expand a little on that?
I believe experiments do still have a place. I believe it much less
than I did twenty years ago. I believe that in social psychology – and particularly in social psychology – the best way
is to have a *va et vient* from experiment to field research, from
hypothesis through testing of hypothesis and so on. I am not
prepared, however, because experiments have certain limits which

are so obvious it is almost trivial to discuss them, to say that they
should be dropped. I think they can be used and should be used,
as a supplementary and important tool. Perhaps the best answer I
can give is an example. We now have two small teams on a research
project. One team is doing field research and the other team is
doing experiments. These can be used in relation to each other. I
have been supervising a student at Leyden who was looking at the
relationship between a group of students at a higher institute of
technology training to be engineers and students of a technical
college training for the same skill who were of 'lower' status. We
were able to design ways of looking at this that were in some sense
controlled and still kept all their natural relevance. It was
half an experiment, half not an experiment. Out of that we were
able to collect an enormous amount of interesting data on
attitudes and behaviour in two groups of different status relation
to each other. It can be done. It needs some imagination. It has
been done before – but not enough.

*Does observation, I was going to say pure observation, if there is
such a thing, have a place to play?*
I don't believe in what I should call, paradoxically, blind
observation. I do not believe either in observation or experiments
that start out saying 'let's find out what happens'. If you have no
better question, you'll end up with a mass of useless data. That's
basic. Whether you are a person who likes or does not like the
word 'hypothesis', you obviously start with some idea of what
you're looking for. You might as well make it explicit and call it a
hypothesis. I must have a question and must know how it relates
to the wider field. Otherwise, I think, we shall become even more
diffuse than we are.

*In your work, you seem to have been little influenced by the need
to dress it, no, to present it, scientifically, which seems to weigh
heavily on most psychologists? Have you felt that pressure?*
I think this may have been so when I was a green psychologist. I
can say now honestly that this issue hasn't existed for as long as I
can remember. I don't give a damn. I think it so happens my work
is 'respectable' but that is not because I am concerned to fit in
with any criteria but because I happen to believe that whatever
you do you must fit in with those kinds of criteria I mentioned for
evidence, to draw rational inferences from reliable evidence – that

was, is, as far as I am aware of any pressure to do one thing or another. I don't feel, don't have, any other pressure.

From a number of things you have said, you seem to be rather critical of the movement towards radical humanistic psychology as well as of more traditional psychology. Is that true?
I examined an enormous PhD thesis written by a radical psychologist recently and the last thing he expected was to have me call him, as I did at the *viva*, a reactionary. But I did. It is not enough to go in the direction of encounter groups, to go in the direction of studying the whole person (whatever that may mean . . . how do you do it? James Joyce did it better than we can ever do and so have a lot of others). The essential idea is that if only you can find a way of making people individually nicer to one another, our problems will be solved. This is pure nonsense, obvious nonsense and reactionary nonsense. Which is why I am amused when I see those 'radical' psychologists coming along with these kinds of ideas. You do not change people's behaviour to one another in large varieties of social situations, however much you have achieved in small groups or individuals becoming nicer to each other. What has got to be looked at is the general social context. As long as you go around saying you need the whole person, the stream of human experience or encounter groups for people to understand how badly they have treated others and been treated by others, you will get nowhere. I have no doubt it is useful for the individuals concerned but I think it is nonsense to say it has any large-scale social significance.
   The 'radicals' are at least as wrong as those they criticise, though they are right in some of their criticisms of the old. They are doing just as much good as if you drop out of college and live a happy life in a commune. It's very nice for you but it does nothing for anyone else.

Communes tend to break up anyway.
That's a different story. [He laughs.]
   You said you wanted to ask more personal questions. Is it my sex life?

No, no, I was wondering more if now that you ran a department . . .
I don't run a department. I became professor in Bristol on

condition that the university should appoint a head of department. We have a very good head of department, Professor John Brown . . . I'm responsible overall for social psychology but I don't run a department.

Does that leave you free to do a lot of research? Did you make that condition so that you would have that freedom?
Yes, but mainly there was a reason of health. It would have been irresponsible to refuse when Bristol modified the terms of its invitation in asking me to become professor of *social* psychology. There are only three chairs in the country – LSE, Sussex and here.

Do you do your research now in a less personal way?
No, I do not. Yes, it is less personal. Nonsense. I am lucky to have people who are working with me who are both independent and whom I can trust. This is the best combination. In a sense I am more removed from it than twenty years ago. And this is in part due not to so much local administration as to the fact that I have always had this bug about international co-operation since the war, for obvious reasons. And I've done an awful lot of administration on the international level which is why I tend to travel more than most – which usually means hard work and not glamour. Somehow, you don't know how you accumulate these responsibilities. You forget to say 'no' for two weeks and you suffer two years later. I feel one should do things like the OECD thing I mentioned.

How does it feel when a piece of research goes well or you have understood something?
You remind me of one of those television interviewers. How did you feel? What was it like when the fire started? What do I say? Nice. Awful. I don't find it an answerable question. How does it feel like?

What kind of pleasure do you get from it?
The pleasure in my case is a very mixed affair with as much agony as pleasure. The point where I think I tend to become creative, if I ever become creative, the only time I am ever creative, is when I sit down at my desk and write the damn thing up. To write it up – the research results come in and they're interesting and it is a great thrill – but I've found it an even greater thrill, independently

of any specific situation of research, if I feel I have got by the tail
a set of ideas which I find promising. Of course, you think you
have them, and then you start writing and, of course, that is really
the acid test, because you come up against contradictions,
weaknesses and so on which you haven't noticed before. So I
could sit down at home for five hours, say. I tend to write at home
and mainly in the morning when I can get a free morning, and I
discover after five hours I have two pages covered. That's all. Well,
if you can do two pages in five hours, you can do twenty pages in
fifty hours so it's not too bad. This is where the pleasure and the
frustration come in. This is also the time when I really think. I
really think when I write. That is why it is not so crucially
important to have direct intellectual contacts, day to day, with
other people, because I really know that I only think when I sit
down on my own and write. But then, suppose I wrote yesterday,
I would wake up at 6.30 in the morning and the first thing I think
is, what is this nonsense I wrote yesterday? Really, it feels terrible.
And, finally, after breakfast, I come back to my desk and it's not so bad
as I thought it was when I woke up. But it's up and down, up and down,
a difficult business.

13
Niko Tinbergen

With undergraduate memories of his work, I expected Niko Tinbergen's house to be filled with birds and fishes, gulls and sticklebacks that he would be observing at all times of the day and night. The birds wouldn't be in the house, of course, for he has always been interested in observing animals in their natural habitat in the garden.

It was in the 1930s, at the University of Leyden, and after the war, at Oxford, that Tinbergen established a reputation as one of the first ethologists, a pioneer (together with his close friend Konrad Lorenz) of a new approach to the study of animal behaviour. This new approach was not the result of any theoretical preconceptions but simply, he explains, 'started as a revolt by young zoologists against the dead animal. We felt no guidance and returned to psychological texts but found little relevance to the things we saw. We turned to McDougall and felt that's not the scientific way of looking at animal movements.'

There is no menagerie in his house. No greylag geese flap around after him like you picture they always do after Lorenz. He is not a flamboyant man, but deeply gentle and courteous. He sits in his living room which is decorated with primitive art heads and an Arctic photograph, in an anorak, and he looks rather as if he is all kitted out to go bird-watching. But he is not, in fact, at all divorced from reality. His pursuits, like bird-watching, may be solitary, and he sometimes displays a rather distant and elusive smile, but then he snaps back with a wry point or sharp remark. Despite his long stay in the English academic idyll that Oxford claims to be, he has remained very Dutch. He says 'ya' (not like a German, please note) rather more often than yes. He shares the amazement that most Dutchmen have at finding themselves hailed as such tolerant and permissive citizens.

His home country clearly seems rather staid to him. His tolerance extends to his own work. Once or twice, having flayed an academic adversary in conversation, he retracts. 'No, that's rather unkind.' One gets the feeling that he sees himself as slightly beyond the stage of demolishing opponents with relish.

'The early ethologists were often bird watchers and aquarists. We found forerunners in Charles Otis Whitman and Julian Huxley who looked, as Darwin did, at behavioural patterns that were common to species.' He quotes Lorenz to the effect that ethologists should consider behaviour like one looks at organs – it is an organ. 'The exercise has been to deal with animals' behaviour like the more concrete topics in biology were dealt with, asking the normal questions in biology, but about animals' behaviour.'

It is easy to forget how novel the approach of the ethologists was in the 1930s and 1940s. In the USA, psychology was dominated by the study of laboratory animals, mainly rats. There were not observed: they were experimented on. One of the most fundamental points the ethologists raised was that studies should be made of the whole life-cycle of species – a fine one was done on Cichlid fish – which implied, of course, that observation should precede experiment. At the time it was not doing so. Further, in the 1930s it was held that nothing was innate, everything was learnt. Creatures were a *tabula rasa* for learning theories to dazzle and impose upon. The ethologists, Tinbergen and Lorenz foremost, maintained much was innate. 'We were a bit rash, I think, in the emphasis we placed on the innate but it was part of our reaction to psychologists then,' Tinbergen explains. But this strong anti-nurture, anti-environment line did bring Continental ethologists, starved of Anglo-Saxon contacts, into critical rapport with many American psychologists.

In 1936, Lorenz came to Holland and invited Tinbergen back to Austria to spend a couple of months with him. He is remarkably frank about his relationship with Lorenz. 'We supplemented each other. I was more a verifier, an experimenter, whereas he had a ray of light at first sight.' He was inspirational to Tinbergen while, on the other hand, 'he held experimentation in high regard.' There is an echo in Tinbergen's voice that suggests almost too high regard. But, until the war forced Lorenz into the German Army and Tinbergen into (eventually) a hostage camp in Holland, they collaborated and corresponded enormously.

After the war, Tinbergen decided that they would not have any success in introducing their observational approach into the

317

English-speaking world unless one of them settled there. Professor Hardy at Oxford had a job going; so he came and settled, being allowed by the Dutch government to take only £35 out of the country – plus his family. He discovered that there was already some hint of equivalent British work. 'Thorpe was already working at Cambridge on birds, for example.' But his presence in the English-speaking academic world did provide a great impetus.

Ethology suggested a number of very important concepts like imprinting, displacement activities (which occur when two incompatible behaviour systems are aroused in an animal) and innate releasing mechanisms. These mechanisms have to be triggered in an animal by outside stimuli, often another's behaviour pattern, like the right wiggles in a stickleback's mating dance. Tinbergen's own work on gulls and sticklebacks is one of the classics of that period for it broke down the elements of behaviour that had to occur, in their proper sequence, so that a full behaviour pattern could take place. It was akin to breaking down a *pas de deux*, showing how animals did communicate.

'But now you can't really talk about ethologists any more. We learnt a great deal from the American psychologists who criticised us and they also came to see the value of the sort of evidence we had. Now, for example, you have two zoologists teaching here at the Institute of Experimental Psychology and plenty of psychologists have developed an interest in animals other than the white rat. There's been mutual traffic.'

In the traffic, ethology has lost its ideological frontiers, its pioneer aloofness that it needed to survive when Lorenz, Tinbergen and the others were just a tiny group of 'insiders', as he terms it.

Clearly, the most important contribution made by the ethologists was that they rediscovered observation in the life sciences.

'We placed a tremendous emphasis on observation. Observation is a creative act and we have been in danger of skipping the whole observational phase. When you observe, when we observe, we are hypothesising all the time. We think in terms of evolution, in terms of natural selection. Those behaviours, those animals, that failed . . . well . . . they're not with us any more.'

A man had recently asked him what were the rules when he

observed, what was the grammar. And he found he couldn't answer. He compared the situation to a primitive tribe that can speak its language perfectly well but couldn't begin to analyse its grammar, the rules abstracted out of the way they speak. The same goes for observation. Good ethologists know how to do it but they can't self-consciously dissect how or why. 'You can't, for example, teach all pupils how to observe. You could almost say, either they've got it or they haven't.' It surprises him, too, how easy it is to miss things. 'I've been observing gulls for forty years and, last year, I went with a student and he pointed something out to me that I'd missed. Suddenly I said, "Yes, you're right Joe, gulls always do that." But I'd never noticed it.' Observation is an individual thing, more individual perhaps than many life scientists would like to admit. It's ironic, too, how little study has been made of observation. Observing observation does sound a little like one of Russell's paradoxes but it isn't paradoxical at all. It could be argued that any philosophy of the behavioural sciences is going to have to face the problem of what actually happens when scientists do observe – what they bring to observation, what they select from it – not assume it's a replication of the impersonal (allegedly) observation of the physical sciences.

The past few years have seen many applications of ethological concepts to man. Desmond Morris's *Naked Ape* (1967), Lorenz's *On Aggression* (1966), Ardrey's *The Territorial Imperative* (1967) set a trend which has been both fruitful and imitated. Tinbergen has also begun to be interested in humans but in a much more specific, much less grand way. He and his wife have become interested in the subject of autistic children and how they can communicate.

> 'I have begun to feel that maybe I was a little asocial through my life with my animals. And then Oxford started a new faculty of human sciences and so I have had to try and teach animal behaviour in a way that it can be used in the study of Man.
> Then – another accident – I was roped in a few years ago by a couple who were studying autistic children. I didn't feel I could help them much, but then it dawned on my wife and me that everything we've heard described about autistic children we have seen, at some time, in normal children. As autistic children don't speak, understanding them must be based on expression and movement. These sorts of movement and expressions had been seen in animals. Many of these children live in perpetual conflict between hyper-anxiety and frustrated social longing.'

He and his wife have developed a new hypothesis which emphasises the environmental causes of autism. This is at odds with the often orthodox opinion that autism is wholly genetic or organic in its causation. Tinbergen is reticent about the theory because he is afraid that it may raise false hopes and, also, that some parents may feel that they have been to blame (although their intentions were good) for their child's condition.

His work on autism is the research that he feels most involved with now. Much of our talk dwelt rather on the past because he feels that, at his stage, a scientist must resign himself to the fact that he has to carry on research by proxy, by suggesting new fields to students and then making sure he doesn't interfere too much. 'I say to a student, and I know enough to say it with conviction, that here is a wonderful subject, but then I must leave the development of the subject to him.' He day-dreamed about how he would use ten years without a single administrative chore. But while he frets clearly at the amount of effort that administration takes, he has become deeply interested in popularising the study of animal behaviour.

'I couldn't make up my mind whether to be a photographer or a biologist when I was young', he explains. And so it is no surprise that he enjoys filming – and has been very successful at it. His film, made with Hugh Falkus, *Signals for Survival,* won an Italia Prize film award and he has supervised the making of thirteen animal films which were shown on the BBC and other TV networks round the world. 'We've seen that people are interested not just in pretty-pretty pictures but in a story. They want to know how the African elephant lives and, to the limited extent that we know, why it lives in tne way that it does.'

He has had somewhat of a hard time with TV, with final cuts of films being shown without consultation, and he has become a little cynical about TV. He doesn't make the films principally for TV because he believes that, together with reading material, they are going to be vital for the teaching of animal behaviour. 'So the TV pays for it', he smiles.

It is easy now for a scientist to latch on to one issue, one speciality, and carve his career and livelihood out of the one nook. You expect Tinbergen to be the ethologist, less flamboyant than Lorenz but stubborn towards that one approach. 'Lorenz', he says, 'freely admits that he is a preacher now. He has been rather disappointed because he feels many psychologists and psychiatrists haven't understood really what he is getting at.' Tinbergen, less flamboyant, seems not at all one-dimensional. He has gone beyond ethology, not yet having satisfied himself that it has been fully incorporated in the behavioural sciences. Now, Tinbergen looks forward both to popularising animal behaviour studies and to applying them in very specific human areas. Will he be writing his own *Naked Ape?* (What about *The Naked Zoologist* as a title?)

He says he feels that a weakness of both Morris and Lorenz, whose works he admires, was that they didn't reveal what kinds of methods they used. 'They didn't expose either the power or the limitation of their methods.' And that, he thinks, might be worth doing.

In his life, he has had occasion to adapt animal knowledge to human behaviour in a light way.

Having meandered through many topics before, during and after lunch, you ask if there's anything else he wants to say. He smiles again: 'An interview, to use a grand word, is your creation.' He won't impose. His wife, though, says with a quite surprising insistence that he should tell what happened to him in Canada recently.

He was on a lecture tour, apparently, and was trailed by Maoist students who heckled him all the way from Montreal to Vancouver, breaking up a lecture. They brought out a pamphlet suggesting he was a fascist, because he published one article in a German periodical at the beginning of the war. 'They never said, of course, that he, like all the other staff at Leyden, resigned because the Germans sacked the Jewish professors and that he spent two years as a hostage in a German camp, not a concentration camp but bad enough.' There is a moment's silence for the whole pleasantly quiet interview has been changed. She apologises in a kind of way for her intensity. So does he. I really don't see why. Few things can be nastier than to be called a fascist who co-operated with Germans during the war. But the display of passion, of personal passion about himself as a person, is obviously not something Tinbergen likes. For he is a tolerant man who doesn't want to dominate – a rare enough thing.

Shortly after giving me these interviews, Professor Tinbergen shared the Nobel Prize with Lorenz and von Frisch. I approached him, as I was writing this book, to ask if I could round out this second interview raising some additional points which had occurred precisely as a result of writing the book. The effect of sharing the Nobel Prize, Professor Tinbergen explained, had been to make it impossible for him to do any work for the subsequent year. He had had so much to do in connection with becoming a laureate that he had not done a stroke of ethological work for a year. He regretted, therefore, the fact that the time had come to call a halt to giving

Niko Tinbergen

interviews. But it had. He was very apologetic – and very firm.

As a result, there are some questions which I would have liked to put to him which I could not. Nevertheless, I felt it extremely important to include an ethologist in this book and one of the most interesting things about Tinbergen is the way that he has developed ideas on observation which might usefully be studied, at least, by psychologists. His work on autism in children has involved the use of observational techniques taken from ethology and applied to human situations.

How did you become interested in the study of animal behaviour?
Having as a boy taken delight in observing wild animals – along my native seashores, in the rich Dutch sand dunes and coastal marshes, in the little aquaria I kept in the back garden – I was not happy with simply dissecting dead animals, or showing that my spit, in a test tube, did something to starch. I was interested, just as a hunter is, in what intact animals did. To get professional advice, I turned to psychology textbooks, but found that they offered little help – the things I saw were just not discussed there.

When you looked to the psychology textbooks, what did you find there and how did it affect you?
At first I went to what was then modern American psychology – a less dogmatic but more method-obsessed form of behaviourism. It was only much later that I discovered the early papers of Watson and Lashley, who together did some quite interesting field work on birds. McDougall did for a time appeal to us, but although he discussed behaviour in a wide context, we soon became disillusioned with his essentially vitalistic attitude. We had a strong urge to observe closely what animals did when coping with their natural environment. I dare say there was a great deal of intuitive projection of self in these early studies, and we were vaguely aware of that, and tried desperately to be 'objective' about animal behaviour. This made us react over-violently against such pioneers as Portielje, Buytendijk and Bierens de Haan. Nowadays we are less ashamed to admit that a certain amount of identifying oneself with the animal, of 'creeping into its skin', does often guide one's intuition. It's at the verifying stage that one has to be wary of relying too much on one's intuition.

What were the major influences on you and who did the group of ethologists in the 1930s consist of?

322

The early ethologists – Darwin of course, later Heinroth, Huxley, and then the great reviver of ethology, Konrad Lorenz – were all naturalists. After I had published some of my early studies, on the homing of wasps, on the everyday life of the hobby, on the mutual signalling of sticklebacks, I got in touch with Lorenz. Lorenz considered Heinroth as his revered teacher. But Heinroth had a curious attitude of refusing to theorise; in his papers, one can read a great deal between the lines, but even when giving a beautifully organised lecture, packed with new facts, he would end by saying, 'Well, the moral you can of course draw yourselves.' Lorenz – psychiatrist, zoologist, philosopher – was the man who designed a theoretical framework; one can now hardly imagine what a tremendous impact his early papers made. The translations of his papers have come too late to bring this out. Lorenz invited me to come and work for a time with him, and the four months spent with him in Altenberg have been of decisive importance for me. He showed me the value of observation as a method (and *he* felt an undue admiration for my knack of experimenting). After my return to Holland we kept up a busy correspondence, but I also had stimulating contact with Dutch friends, whose names are hardly known to our young ethologists today: Makkink, Verwey and, in spite of all our basic differences, Portielje.

Does observation play a crucial role?
Yes – although, as I said, we did experiment a great deal, we spent most of our time patiently watching, interfering as little as possible with what the animals did. The watching was so fascinating because one *interpreted* all the time; and one also compared the animals' behaviour with what went on in the environment, either as likely causes of behaviour, or as likely effects – such as the effects of their 'displays' on conspecifics. Medawar, and also Lorenz himself, have since broken a lance in favour of such 'creative observation' as a legitimate, indeed indispensable, scientific method. I myself have also learned a great deal from what I like to call 'natural experiments' – seeing for instance what events in the environment 'set off' a reaction in an animal. Strictly speaking no more than a correlation, but one on which one could build a little hypothesis. It has often been said – most clearly by Frank Beach in America – that 'in its haste to step into the twentieth century, psychology has skipped the observational phase.' To have made 'inspired observation'

323

respectable again in the behavioural sciences is, I believe, a positive achievement of ethology.

Did the early ethologists attempt to describe the whole life-cycle of particular species?

That is true – at least we attempted it. In the thirties a number of 'ethograms' were published. We realise now how schematic they were, but they helped us in seeing the wood and not merely the trees.

After all these years devoted to observation of animals, do you have a clear idea of what you are doing when you observe?

That is an interesting point. When my wife and I recently applied some of the observational and interpretative methods of animal ethology to the behaviour of children, we came in contact with many psychiatrists, to whom our approach was entirely alien. And one of them asked at a given moment, 'What is the *grammar* of what you do?' I could not really answer him, and realised that we had paid too little attention to analysing our own procedures. Of course the use of the word 'grammar' was not quite helpful – it made one think of the rules of language which linguists *extract* from their study of language, not of the (unconscious) rules which people apply when they speak. The fact that even now so much in our selective observation is intuitive makes this type of observing so difficult to teach. And since our teaching has not yet developed very far, one has to rely in educating one's students very much on their gifts, and one finds it very difficult to develop good observational powers in a student who is not a 'born observer'. One can provide a few rules of course, such as: 'describe movements rather than use catchwords', 'ask yourself what made him do this or that?', 'ask what could be the survival value – if any – of this or that?', but how very personal one is in unconsciously attaching value to certain aspects of behaviour becomes clear every time one observes the same scene jointly with a graduate. Two persons see quite different things. Often, of course, I can call a pupil's attention to events he has overlooked, but quite often a new collaborator calls *my* attention to quite obvious things, of which I have to admit at once: 'You're right – I've seen it time and again, but I have not *registered*.' Very humiliating, but a very salutary experience.

Niko Tinbergen

Do you think that the process of observation itself might be worth studying?

I certainly do. And in a primitive way, we all are trying to do it all the time. But it offers all the difficulties of a system (the brain) studying itself – and the system is, of course, incredibly complicated. What is particularly worrying is to experience in oneself how strongly one's own expectations, even one's non-rational moods, can colour and even distort what the senses report – quite a long way towards hallucination. That's why we must record on film, on tape, etc., so that one can submit the material to a number of observers.

Does observation depend on experience?

Yes and no. I have found that very often pupils come up with a profusion of ideas, of which they cannot quite assess the validity because lack of experience prevents them from knowing evidence that refutes many of them. The role of the experienced man is then to marshal this evidence, and to demolish. But also to jump up on some occasions and say enthusiastically, *'That's* it! *That* you must follow up. It fits with this and this and this – a splendid idea!' It was in this way that Martin Moynihan 'discovered', and I helped working out, the important concept of 'appeasement signals'.

What were the main problems of the early ethologists?

Apart from putting the emphasis on observation, there was the emphasis on 'innateness' of much behaviour – more correctly (as we often put it now) the considerable genetic contribution to the 'programming' of an animal's behaviour machinery. Early ethology also broadened our insight into social behaviour. Perhaps one could put it most generally by saying that we learned to see behaviour as the outcome of natural selection. That's where we owe so much to the pioneering work of Julian Huxley, who as a young man showed, in his famous paper on grebes, the courage of his convictions when these were not at all popular.

Much of your work has been experimental, has it not?

Yes, and that is still the work I love most. I am sure that Lorenz is right when he says that I am a hunter at heart – my interest in an animal intensifies at once when I see it in its own environment, whereas in a zoo it bores me stiff. And I am irresistibly drawn to

325

Niko Tinbergen

animals that elude one, that one has to outwit. Yet, I don't regret at all the time spent in laboratory studies, nor the time spent with birds that are easy to study, such as the gulls. There the challenge comes from a more subtle way of 'outwitting' – something of the nature of: 'I know what you are up to, and why – better than you know it yourself.' It was one of the great experiences in my life when I could help putting the Serengeti Research Institute on its feet, join my pupils there in their work, marvel at what then seemed the Garden of Eden, now a most gruelling demonstration of 'nature red in tooth and claw'. Apart from all that, it's the beauty of unspoilt habitats that fascinates me.

Was it difficult to find a receptive audience for your theories in the 1930s?

Yes and no. To make clear to psychologists what we were after was very difficult – partly because they were themselves busy with fascinating problems, and because our techniques were in many respects very crude and unsophisticated compared with theirs; partly because we were still working so intuitively, and finally because we were abysmally ignorant of what they did. Zoologists responded much more readily, although our early 'physiologising' (in some respects naive, in others too wild) put off most neurophysiologists. On the whole it has been an uphill struggle, and this I think explains our aggressiveness, mixed with arrogance, in those early days. My younger friends still say that I am far too much of a missionary. Gradually I have learnt some tact and, I hope, some humility, but once a missionary, always a missionary.

What were your relations with Lorenz like?

One in which we mutually supplemented and stimulated each other. He was and still is the man with vision; I am the more pedestrian verifier. And because we are such close friends, we always gave our best when we disagreed with each other. Naturally, when we both became involved with increasing responsibilities, locally, nationally and internationally, there simply was no time any more for correspondence, and hardly any for a relaxed half-day a year.

How did the Second World War affect the development of ethology?

At once, after the invasion of the Low Countries, contact between German and Dutch scientists began to suffer – with censorship

326

operating it was impossible to correspond fruitfully. At first we could continue with research and could write up (and many scientists on both sides tried to keep scientific contact going – a few years ago I was bitterly reproached by some Canadian Maoists for having published in the *Zeitschrift für Tierpsychologie* in 1942). But Lorenz was drafted; my university clashed with the German authorities and I ended up in a hostage camp. Not as bad as a concentration camp, but not exactly a picnic. Unknown to me, Lorenz was 'reported missing, presumed killed' at the battle of Witebsk, and was not released until 1947. Neither of us will ever forget our meeting at Bill Thorpe's house in Cambridge. Friendships with many Germans have weathered the Nazi storm. Research ground to a halt halfway through the war, but a surprising number of gifted youngsters joined us soon afterwards. Living under Nazi occupation taught us a great deal about human behaviour – normal, sick and heroic.

Is it still possible to speak of the ethologists as one group?
Not really – national trends have developed so that German ethology is now rather different from Anglo-American ethology; and many borderline fields, between ethology and neurophysiology, genetics, ecology, animal and human psychology, are being, so to speak, invaded from both sides. Some of our closest colleagues are psychologists by original training, and many psychology departments now employ zoologists on their staff. Here in Oxford zoology and psychology share the same building. And of course ethologists now begin to look seriously at human behaviour – think of Lorenz himself, and of course of my very gifted pupil, Desmond Morris. It was a source of great satisfaction to me when he decided to return to Oxford as his base.

Are you following in Lorenz's footsteps in seeking to study Man?
To a certain extent, yes. I have been late in taking the plunge, but my social conscience finally caught up with me. But I am doing it my own way – I can't claim to have the vision, or the flamboyance, of Lorenz and Morris. Although I admire their work very much, there is something missing in their more widely known works *On Aggression* and *The Naked Ape.* I feel that we will have to explain the methods more fully that we consider of potential value to the study of Man, including their limitations. And this is

327

where I believe I can still make a useful contribution. And since I joined Professor Pringle and Dr Halsey in their work on behalf of the newly founded finals course on the human sciences, I had, of course, an extra spur to think about ethology's potential.

Then, by accident, my wife and I joined forces in one particular area where ethological methods could be fruitfully employed. Many years ago, Drs John and Corinne Hutt had asked me for advice with their studies of autistic children. For a long time I felt I could not be of much use to them. But when, a few years ago, they pointed to similarities in the behaviour of autistic children, and of normal children under certain conditions, my wife – who has an enormous fund of knowledge of children – made me look at the whole problem more closely. We found that we could 'cash in' on our lifelong studies of social behaviour in animals and by careful study of the situations in which normal children showed, let us say, 'autistoid' behaviour, we arrived at a hypothesis, a dual hypothesis really: we concluded that many autists suffer from a severe emotional conflict, in which fear blocked affiliation and later socialisation, and also exploratory learning; and we were forced to conclude that the social environment, including parents, often has much more to do with causing the disturbance than is generally acknowledged. Having the sad fate of these severely damaged children in mind, we decided to publish our ideas, with a description of our methods, before we could marshal as much evidence as we could have wished. Our entry into the world of psychiatric research and psychotherapy gave us many cold showers, but also a surprising amount of support. It is still too early to say to what extent we are right, but research and therapy are profiting from this exercise, if only by being forced to have another look.

Can one easily apply ethological ideas to the study of Man?
To certain areas, yes. For instance to problems of non-verbal communication; and to children's behaviour. Here the application of ethological methods, by Corinne Hutt, and by Nick Blurton Jones in London (who recently edited a very valuable collection of studies by a variety of workers), seems to me to have great promise. But I do think that psychiatry, and those responsible for medical research, still vastly underrate what ethology can contribute. But the application of primarily ethological methods can't be stopped – 'ideas have no frontiers' – and although I shall

not be able to do much of this kind of research myself, I am looking forward greatly to the planned close collaboration with Professor Jerome Bruner, who has just joined us.

Of course in a minor, incidental way I could not help looking at my own children with the eyes of an ethologist. When one of my children began to yawn compulsively when our family doctor came to see her, he said, 'She seems to be very tired' and I had to explain to him that she was merely scared stiff – it is a very common 'displacement activity' such as scratching, or biting your nails when under slight stress. And speaking of nail biting: one of our children started biting his nails when he was still not quite a toddler. I remembered that female birds often eat anything hard and white when they have just laid eggs, and that my wife was a bad 'processor' of calcium, a defect that he might well have inherited, and (with the puzzled approval of our very research-minded doctor) we smuggled extra calcium into his diet. A wild gamble, but it paid off: the nail biting stopped promptly and never came back. Most doctors will even now laugh this kind of thing off, but then the medical training is not, of course, tailored to research, and certainly not to genuine biological thinking.

Does that mean that you have abandoned research with animals?
At my age, and with so many different types of involvements, one inevitably does research increasingly 'by proxy' – by interacting with students and colleagues, by suggesting, criticising, enthusing, creating opportunities and so on. What I shall do when I retire I still don't quite know. It will certainly involve a kind of reappraisal, of finding my priorities. Some of my old books badly need a face-lifting; I should also like to continue my work on behalf of educational and documentary films – a fascinating new method of mass communication which is still evolving very rapidly.

What kinds of films?
Making good films that tell a story – rather than 'wildlife spectaculars' which drown the viewer with ever flashier, even more dramatic 'glimpses' – has become possible for us teachers since the explosion of TV. The BBC have given Hugh Falkus and myself some fine opportunities. But we find, with several TV companies here and abroad, that they still lag behind the rapid evolution of

public interest. 'Pretty-pretty' pictures have their place, but an increasing number of people want a film to tell a real story, and to tell it clearly. One often meets with a very opinionated attitude in producers or with people who dare not experiment for fear of losing out in the rat-race for promotion, and such TV producers interfere much more with the integrity of the man who makes the film than a publisher ever does with the author's integrity. To make our type of film successfully one also needs more time than is given to the usual documentary, and one needs a closely integrated team of cameraman, scientific expert and script writer, not to speak of a director. So now, after having completed a series of films on animal behaviour that will appear on TV soon, we have decided to be a little more independent. This became possible when we received outside support without strings attached.

And what we are, of course, really after is not the occasional TV showing, but full and regular use of our films in teaching and entertainment, and of reading material as well. We want to continue 'multi-media publication', as we achieved it with *Signals for Survival*: TV programme, film copies and a little book.

Do you think that ethology has been successful enough to allow it to go out of business, as it were?
As an isolated discipline it may go 'out of business' the way a small shopkeeper may be swallowed up by a supermarket. But as an integral facet of the behavioural sciences it's only just coming into its own. I am more optimistic than Lorenz, who sometimes feels that outsiders and colleagues in other disciplines somehow always manage to get hold of the wrong end of the stick, and misapply our work. The main reason why I think that ethology will become very influential even in the study of Man is that ethology puts the amazing phenomenon of 'adaptedness' – the characteristic of living things – in the centre of its attention, and that what threatens mankind at the moment, and will threaten it for a long time to come, is disadaptation – a loss of adaptedness. Most people still think of the evolution of human society as 'progress', and have no idea at all of the frightening precariousness of living – which for our species is *more* precarious than for animals. And with a surprising blend of optimism, complacency and arrogance, even many biologists still believe that our behavioural adjustability can easily match the rapid changes that are taking place in our society. But this is very doubtful.

What is the solution?
Whoever claims to know that is either a crank or a scoundrel. We
shall have to mobilise all our intellectual resources to even begin a
proper study of Man as an animal species – as a unique species
who is the guinea pig in what one could call an experiment of
Nature. For our type of evolution, the 'cultural' or 'psycho-social'
evolution, there simply is no precedent in the history of life; we
have not a single example to go by – not even one that tells us
how *not* to proceed.

Is Man in danger of forgetting his biological make-up?
You could put it like that, but it's a rather negative statement.
Man should take a 'cold look' at himself, and brace himself for
some unpleasant discoveries. We shall need all the optimism we are
capable of, lest we throw up our hands in despair. And a desperate
man loses what little understanding he may have had, and can't
explore.

*How has your role as a man who teaches about animal behaviour
affected your career?*
It has, if only because our field is now so popular that one can't
confine oneself to teaching one's specialist students. One has to
write and communicate in other ways, such as through TV and
educational films. And of course for every teacher there comes a
time when he has to hand over; when he has to admit that he can't
quite follow any more what a very bright new generation is doing.
And the present generation of young behaviour students are a
bright lot. Just as well, for society will soon be clamouring for
them.

This chapter is based on material originally published in the French
magazine *Psychologie* and in *New Scientist*

Tentative Conclusions

There can be, of course, no conclusive conclusions from a study like this. Any interesting trends need to be treated with caution since this sample of psychologists (i) was very eminent, (ii) was approached by me who am, no doubt, bogged down with my own prejudices and (iii) agreed to do it, with the exception of Professor Tinbergen whom I had interviewed before this book was mooted. The methodologically fastidious will easily find plenty of other reasons for suggesting these tentative conclusions should be treated with kid gloves. Nevertheless . . .

Many psychologists said they had taken up the career at least partly, by accident. This was a very common reply that, in some form, was made by many of the thirteen. Only one, Liam Hudson, appeared to suggest that he had been destined to become a psychologist: Tajfel argued that the fact that he had been brought up as a Jew in semi-fascist Poland made him, undoubtedly, a likely social psychologist. But accident appeared to predominate.

In spite of this apparent excess of chance, there are some psychologists whose work clearly reflects interests they had before they were psychologists. It does not seem coincidental that Eysenck, who came to London to study physics but found he had taken the wrong examinations to satisfy the all-powerful bureaucrats of the University of London, should want to instil in psychologists more of the scientific method. Hudson, one of the chief critics of the experimental method as it has been practised, first read history and then was interested in philosophy. Broadbent who has argued so charmingly for behaviourism was going to read natural sciences if he had gone up to university before the war. Tinbergen, much of whose work depends on the observation of animals, was tempted to be a photographer and has, during the whole of his career, taken pictures to illustrate his work. There is, obviously, some kind of relationship between what a person wanted to be or might have been if he had not been a psychologist and the emphasis (or some of the emphases) his psychology has taken. But any optimism I might have had that this relationship was clear-cut or ideologically simple was facile.

It is obvious there is no very clear pattern. But it is surprising how many of these psychologists wanted to be either natural scientists or writers or began their careers as doctors. Only three (McClelland, Tinbergen and Chomsky) lie totally outside the pattern and McClelland made some mention of liking psychology because it gave him a chance to write.

It would have been pleasing to find that all those who wanted to be natural scientists turned out to be 'hard' psychologists. It is not true, however. Festinger straddles the middle ground though his latest work in physiological psychology is definitely 'hard'. Moreover, both Laing and Leupold-Löwenthal in their early medical work do not seem to have been particularly pastoral or patient-oriented, or interested in people. Laing was fascinated by the way the brain worked and did some neurology; Leupold-Löwenthal worked in cancer research and implanted tissue tumours in the brains of many rats. Both might say the experience made them less receptive to conventional ideas of science, especially in psychology, but it does disrupt a nice pattern. It remains true: those who wanted to be or were interested in physics or chemistry have tended to be much more 'hard' in their approach – for this sample, at least.

But more curious and, perhaps, unexpected than this is the relative poverty of other careers psychologists might have followed. There are no visual artists or mathematicians or lawyers or teachers *manqués:* there are no politicians or civil servants or drop-outs here. Tinbergen's temptation – to be a photographer – marks him out, almost, as exotic.

When Hudson said that one might have predicted he would be a psychologist by looking at how interested he was in people at the age of fifteen, he said something that might strike one as being utterly obvious. Only those interested in people, surely, would bother going into psychology. Looking at this sample, one might well wonder. Almost none of the professions mentioned involved contact with people. Writers, physicists, chess players are all involved in rather solitary pursuits. The writer is concerned with persons or, at any rate, one person, him or herself, the rest of the flux of humanity being merely the background against which the artist asserts himself.

Those psychologists who were doctors were not attracted into particularly pastoral or patient-oriented branches of medicine. Jouvet was a neurosurgeon; Leupold-Löwenthal was a research doctor working on cancer and a desk doctor at WHO before he made the discovery that he 'needed patients'. This is a curious fact. Psychologists should gravitate towards people. It is, against this, interesting and paradoxical to note that though many psychologists regretted the fact that administration kept them away from research, almost none said that it kept them away from people or their subjects. Professor Tajfel, who had gone to great lengths to have freedom from administrative chores to have time for his research, was still quite content to use research collaborators to see people and collect data. Hudson, who makes such play of the need for more reality and relevance, admits, cheerfully, that for every day collecting data at least eighty days should be spent in analysis: of the data – not the psychologist. Hudson, too, says that he now does his research in a less personal way. I am tempted to propose the first paradox of the psychologists.

The more successful a psychologist is, the less he needs to actually see, observe or collect data on people himself.

He does not need to run experiments on persons. Assistants can perform this lowly task. Since, intuitively, one might expect people went into psychology because they were interested in people, one might expect them to miss this contact. To echo Leupold-Löwenthal, psychologists might be assumed to 'need subjects', and therefore, to lament this lack of contact with the basic stuff of their science. But no psychologist seemed to suggest he needed or missed contact with people (as subjects) as the chores of success, administration, committees, interviews (like mine) sapped away precious time. There is an interesting parallel that suggests itself here with Hudson's work on doctors who were found to work on different areas of the body depending on their social class (1972). Perhaps the most status in psychology lies as far away from any human contact as possible. Certainly industrial and educational psychology are low-status fields of psychology. Why, if psychology is remotely connected with persons? Even those most committed to humanistic psychology, like Laing, Chomsky and Hudson, seemed to follow this trend. Tinbergen is, on the other hand, an interesting exception. He spent 1972 studying autistic children with his wife and the two of them did all the observing themselves.

In his interview, McClelland argued that psychologists seek two things by going into psychology. First, the subject allows them to express their need for power. They can have an impact on people. Second, many psychologists studied wanted to react against a fairly strict religious upbringing. By doing psychology, they could study the scientific version of Man, a study which has often given the impression, and sometimes fulfilled the expectation, that it could reduce religious ideas about the nature of Man to irrelevance. McClelland recalled how he had hoped, by having a few facts marshalled after years of training, to be able to persuade his father.

Many of the interviews here recorded seem to offer confirmation of McClelland's argument about the need for power. Skinner, for example, clearly wants to make an impact on how people and society plan their lives; Chomsky became a radical political hero during the Vietnam war and sees in Skinnerian ideas and methods a means society can use to control people with methods that do not appear to be brutal. These are clearly arguments about the impact of psychology and science on people. Chomsky and Skinner in their dispute are not the only psychologists to revel in such disputes. Laing, for example, has clearly used his ideas so as to get the maximum possible impact. In his interview, Eysenck often returned to the sad theme of how it seemed to him that people preferred not to know the truth about certain things which he thought it was very necessary that they did know.

There are, certainly, many references in the different interviews to the fact that psychologists enjoy the more direct exercise of power. Miller, for example, seemed to be relishing giving an interview and carrying on some skirmish in academic politics at the same time. Hudson referred to the fact that he enjoyed the business of wheedling money out of committees that allocated research grants. Tajfel said that he had for many years been interested in establishing links between psychologists in different countries and had been heavily involved with the international administration of psychology to this end. There were those who reacted quite differently. Both Tinbergen and Jouvet seemed to be annoyed by administration because it kept them away from their work. Others, like Festinger (who clearly wants his old ideas, even, to influence people), admitted they had no interest in administration. In this perhaps lesser manifestation of the need for power, that of enjoying running departments, psychologists were pretty much divided.

In the area, however, of fighting about what psychology should be about, psychologists seem to release much of their need for power.

Many of the arguments in the interviews, the many controversies related, do not have to be retold. Often, of course, the controversies are important though sometimes, as McClelland indicated, they seem to have expanded mainly for the purpose of giving psychologists something to argue about. But even when they are important, they are marked by a particular intransigence. It is as if one brand of psychology has to triumph over the others. Eysenck's account of how people want to suppress serious research into race, heredity and IQ is telling. I want to return to this point at the very end.

McClelland's arguments about religion seem to be much less clearly sustained. Many psychologists said they had no religious training or that the religious training they had was very far from strict. Broadbent suggested that American psychologists tend to be much more vituperative against religion than British ones. Some psychologists certainly seemed to be indignant at the idea that they could ever have been so naive as to believe in God. Festinger, for example, asserted that even if he had faith to tell him God existed, he would have to reject the hypothesis on the grounds of insufficient evidence. He suggested McClelland was trying to project his own 'hang-ups' on the rest of the profession. Tajfel, Laing, Hudson all made it clear they had no particular interest in religion when they had been young. Miller indicated that although his parents had been quite religious, they could hardly have been said to have given him a religious upbringing. Skinner seems to have been brought up in quite a religious home. The influence of religion in making psychologists psychologists must, on this showing, remain very variegated. The only three psychologists who seem to have been seriously affected by it are Skinner, McClelland and Broadbent. Moreover, whether or not a psychologist had a religious upbringing does not seem to affect the kind of psychological position he has reached.

There are two other main interesting suggestions that emerge from this biographical data.

The first is that the three men who trained as doctors all seem to have doubts about the extent and the way in which people should be manipulated as subjects. In the interviews with Laing and Leopold Loewenthal, this stress is fairly clear but it is all the more interesting in Jouvet who is committed to the conventional methods of science and of neurophysiology as much as, say, Skinner. Jouvet is afraid that the progress of science will enable the authorities to use new techniques against people. He is, especially, concerned about the abuse of drugs that can inhibit dreaming which appears to make those who experience this lack of dreaming much more malleable. He is himself working, more and more, on lower animals. Where, at one time, he would cheerfully sacrifice cats in order to gain knowledge, he is now much less content to do so. His concern reminds one of the creature that Leupold-Löwenthal criticises experimental psychologists for having created – the experimental person. Jouvet was in a long tradition of using cats as experimental animals but he now doubts its propriety. He adds that he will not do work on adults, let alone children, which involves dream deprivation – once a very popular kind of experimentation – even though it could be scientifically fruitful and, given his views, is theoretically imperative.

The other area is much more complicated. It is to do with the part that writing plays in psychology.

It is curious, indeed, how little mention of the role of writing, of the use of the imagination, is usually made in books on psychology. These usually have a few introductory pages in which it is stressed that now, at last, the twentieth century brings you the possibility of a scientific study of man where previous ages, steeped in their superstitions, could offer nothing but speculation and prejudice. Grandiloquence in the service of psychology reaches, from time to time, dizzy heights.

But, nowhere, among the bewildering variety of activities these purveyors of future salvation engage in, do we find writing mentioned. The science of psychology is entirely a matter of collecting data, designing experiments, checking results and, by these conventional means, seeking those elusive laws of human behaviour. The material collected in these interviews suggests that the actual creation of psychology is quite different and takes place when the psychologists are doing none of these things, but when they are writing. Paradoxically, Popper, while he argues for hypothetico-deductive proofs, makes some apt comments in a section titled 'The Elimination of Psychologism', a provocative title surely. Popper refuses to see it as his task to understand how scientists get new theoretical ideas (1972, p. 31):

> Such processes are the concern of empirical psychology but hardly
> of logic. It is another matter if what we want is to reconstruct
> rationally the *subsequent tests* whereby the inspiration may be
> discovered to be a discovery or become known to be knowledge. In
> so far as the scientist critically judges, alters or rejects his own
> inspiration we may, if we like, regard the methodological analysis
> undertaken here as a kind of 'rational reconstruction' of the

corresponding thought processes. But this kind of reconstruction would not describe these processes as they actually happen.

Popper argues that logic has nothing to do with the process of having a new idea. He disclaims any expertise in this muddy field but adds: 'However, my view of this matter for what it is worth, is that there is no such thing as a logical method of having new ideas, or a logical reconstruction of this process.'

Popper sees these flashes of irrational creativity as preceding experiments. They set up the problem: they work out the ideas that lead to the crucial test. Psychologists, if one bases oneself on this sample, appear to work in a quite opposite way. Their creativity takes place after they have the results of their experiments. If they no longer presume to study mankind sitting in an armchair, they tend to elaborate their studies sitting at a typewriter. Setting up a study, collecting the data, marshalling the results are not where the psychological action is. It is, for many at least, in the writing up. And the dangers of this emphasis are clear. In writing something one rarely remains dispassionate. One tends to work the material up into more than there was originally. This is, after all, part of the skill of writing. But from a scientific point of view, this elaboration of ideas is risky for it must be rather personal. As a science, psychology is supposed to transcend the personal quirks and prejudices of its practitioners. But if psychologists psychologise most when they write, then it is arguable that they enjoy it most then precisely because they are finally free of the manacles of the scientific method and can, in Hudson's graphic phrase, 'utter' themselves. Unfortunately, or fortunately if you seek to argue the impossibility of a scientific psychology, these passages into the personal are not clearly labelled 'And this is where I become personal' but, instead, 'Discussion', or sometimes, 'Conclusions'.

I suspect this is made more acute by the fact that the ideas about Man a psychologist has, and uses in his work, must at least partially affect him or her as a person. Many psychologists have criticised behaviourists on the grounds that the behaviourist psychologist must feel himself to be an agent: he cannot feel himself to be the determined puppet his theory appears to require. Psychologists are beginning to discuss the extent to which subjects give data that will please psychologists but they are still shying away from looking at the way in which the theories they adopt fulfil their own personal needs. It was odd to notice how comfortable each psychologist was with his own brand of humanity and psychology. This is, again, very difficult ground but it is a kind of perspective that needs to be taken into account, especially in view of the fact that much psychology is taken up with competitions between different theories for the main area of the discipline.

In the textbooks, however, there is no mention of the importance of writing to psychology. If this study can claim to have shown anything unexpected, it is the importance of writing to psychologists.

Skinner had wanted to be a writer and, in his youth, sent some short stories to Robert Frost. Frost was encouraging. After a year spent at home, Skinner had published nothing and he turned to psychology. He writes well and with enormous care, taking at least five or six drafts to get a book. Hudson writes poetry and would like to write a novel. Miller, McClelland and Tajfel all mentioned the fact that they like writing psychology. For Miller it was a crucial reason in making him choose psychology. In his later work, Laing has started to write in what critics refer to as the poetic mode. The critics usually refer to this critically; it is an aberration for one who was once some kind of scientist. If scientists must write, they should separate their writing from their career and turn to pure fiction. Tinbergen also mentions the fact that he enjoys writing and, if he does not write poems, makes films. For scientists these are curious emphases.

Two of the psychologists go farther. Both Hudson and Tajfel say that it is in the process of writing that they are actually creative, that they make psychology. Like Skinner, both refer to the fact that writing is a very slow business for them. They work, painstakingly, through many drafts. It cost Hudson a million words to write *The Cult of the Fact*; it cost Skinner much the same to write *Beyond Freedom and Dignity*. Both are short books. It could be argued that, though Skinner does not say so, the process of writing is also for him the process by which he creates psychology. He insisted on how strange it was that *Walden Two*, describing his utopia, was the only book he ever wrote quickly. It is his only work of fiction. Tajfel also says of writing:

The only time I am ever creative is when I sit down at my desk and write the damn thing up . . . Writing is, of course, the acid test because you come up against contradictions, weaknesses and so on you haven't noticed before . . . This is also the time when I really think, when I write.

Hudson said, similarly: 'I find I cross something of a gulf in trying to express myself. It's fluent enough when it comes, often quite

339

vivid. But patterns of words come from a part of mind I have little conscious access to. They seem to appear by some sleight of hand, and the most vivid appear unbidden.'

Many scientists have written of the unconscious element in scientific creativity. But the literature on creativity in science says almost nothing about writing, which is supposed to be an art after all. In other sciences, creativity seems to happen more at the point where a new problem is posed, an experiment is designed or, perhaps, when the results come out. Writing up the results is much more a chore. The French mathematician, Henri Poincaré, described how he was trying to prove there could not be any functions like those that are called Fuchsian functions. He struggled with this problem for a long period; he had little success. Then, one night, he went to sleep after having tried to put the problem out of his mind. He spent a restless night but when he woke up, almost in spite of any effort he had made, the solution appeared in his mind. It took him just two hours to write out the necessary proofs.

This seems very different from the way in which those psychologists who stressed the importance of writing seemed to get their insights. The kind of intuition that great physical scientists seem to be blessed with for part of their lives, at least, seems to have no counterpart in psychology. Some psychologists who model themselves on orthodox science distrust intuition, of course, as it is unscientific. And those psychologists like Hudson who are happy to use their intuitions appear to use them in a quite different way. It is interesting that Freud, who is often considered to have been one of the most intuitive of psychologists, one of those wise men who really know how mankind works, should never have reached the kind of certainty either Einstein or Newton reached in the early twenties. As Leupold-Löwenthal points out, Freud constantly checked and modified his ideas.

I am not saying that one kind of intuition such as that displayed by Einstein and Newton is right and that, therefore, psychologists should cultivate it. And, after all, few physicists are Einstein or Newton. But it is surely peculiar for many psychologists to seek to model themselves on how physical scientists have worked when it is clear that the way the greatest of these have made their most fundamental discoveries, by introspections about the nature of the universe, cannot apply to psychology. Psychologists work differently. That is why the emphasis on writing as part of the process of psychological discovery seems so interesting and needs study. It also suggests that one of the reasons why so many psychologists have been so avid to be scientifically respectable is that they wanted to ape proper scientists while they also felt a great need to repress artistic, literary and generally unscientific urges. It was not just a matter of building up a career; it was not just a matter of acquiring the trappings of science; it is a question of inner tension between the psychologist-as-scientist and the psychologist-as-artist. Each man kills, or more prosaically represses, the thing he loves. It is surely striking that a number of psychologists compared the pleasure they got from doing good research to the feeling they had when they read or listened to some artistic masterpiece. There were many references to the aesthetic pleasure that doing good research offered. How you prove these ideas is another matter, of course. They do suggest, though, that it may be fundamentally wrong for psychologists to seek to imitate other scientists. It would also be worthwhile to explore further, and seriously, the differences between the sort of intuitions that physical scientists have about nature and the intuitions that psychologists use. Psychologists do not seem to be blessed with intuition before a mystery but with a much more partial, *post hoc* intuition as they attempt to make sense of results they have already obtained. Not even Freud ever had the kind of confidence Newton or Einstein had that what they had thought and had seen must be right.

Although he drew no direct comparisons, Jouvet also spoke of how his research was very much an inner life and, when it went well, satisfied some inner need. Some psychologists were also, it must be admitted, much more simple. McClelland said that he got 'fun' out of doing research and, also, the feeling sometimes that he might have helped somebody. Again, these ideas are ideas and not conclusions. One is also tempted to reflect on the not inconsiderable vanity of psychologists who are prepared to compare the satisfaction they get from their work with that which they get from Brahms or Eliot.

I have, so far, only dealt with such tentative conclusions about psychologists as I have derived from this study. They are offered with all due reservations. It was a small sample of eminent psychologists. There are many other eminent psychologists: there are many many other psychologists. Hopefully this will offer food for thought.

The other point is, of course, that during these interviews it has become clearer what questions or problems of methodology can acquire not so much a paradigm as a set of paradigms which are acceptable to most of those working in the subject. At the present time there is a series of sometimes overlapping, sometimes frankly incompatible paradigms competing for the centre of the psychological stage. And one of the destructive trends in contemporary psychology is that one paradigm will be immediately hacked to pieces by its opponents. One man's paradigm is another man's untruth. Such a situation is aggravated by the tendency of psychologists to enjoy polarising the disputes in the subject. Examples of the love of invective are scattered too often through the interviews to need repeating. I have, therefore, presumed to offer a list of those problems which it seems to me must be resolved before there can be a general advance in psychology. There have, clearly, been lots of local advances and some psychologists are, for all they might polemically say, remarkably eclectic in the way they do research. But the image of what research should be like remains powerful for many - and blinding. Many of the psychologists in this book adhere very strictly to one kind of research. What follows delineates problems rather than suggests answers. It makes no claim to be comprehensive but stems very much from the process of thinking about and editing these interviews.

1. Field Studies

For a long time there have been pleas for more research to be done outside the laboratory, so that psychologists should look at real-life situations, that most complex of phrases. When Bickman and Henchy (1972) looked at the articles published in the *Journal of Personality and Social Psychology,* they found only 3 per cent involved field research, Fried, Crumpper and Allen (1973) looked at two other major journals, the *Journal of Social Psychology* and the *Journal of Social and Abnormal Psychology* and came to findings equally depressing for those who advocate more field research in psychology. They classed studies as being field, laboratory, survey or interview studies. They counted papers published between 1961 and 1970 as shown in Table 1:

TABLE 1

	Field	Laboratory	Survey	Interview
1961	5	120	87	2
1965	6	182	55	3
1970	6	130	35	2

Source: *American Psychologist,* February 1973

Though there has been a decline in the number of studies using surveys, studies using field research or interview material have hardly increased in the light of the critiques of writers like Jordan and Chein.

A number of psychologists will, of course, say that data must be reduced in the laboratory to fit into the conventions of experimental design. Broadbent is particularly strong on this. But unless there is some field research done, some observation prior to the experimental stage, then how can one be sure that the situation bears any resemblance to anything in real life? Ethologists, Tinbergen especially, have arrived at a happy compromise for they would first observe animals in the wild and then run experiments on them, as Tinbergen did with the stickleback and herring gull and various of their behaviour sequences. But if psychologists reject field studies as being too vague, too impressionistic in themselves, should they not work out in some detail the relationships between prior observation in the real-life situation and their eventual experiments? In his interview, Broadbent explained that he spent much time observing air traffic controllers at work on site in air traffic control towers before devising experiments to test their abilities. But Broadbent was under contract to perform a specific task – easing the lot of air traffic controllers for the RAF. He had to observe them to see what problems they were having. He could hardly approach this task in a pure theoretical way. He had to go out and look and then had to convert his impressions into experimental designs.

Many psychologists adopt a much less reasonable stance. They oppose any sort of mentalism or intuitive knowledge. Therefore, they argue, psychology must be done scientifically, in the laboratory. Yet they often perform experiments which appear to have some relation to real life, without any prior observation of what happens in real life. They act as if they had special, almost intuitive, knowledge of what the experiments should be about without checking, first, by observing real-life situations to see if the design they are using does have basis in reality.

Observation is never neutral observation. As Tinbergen says, you nearly always observe with some idea in mind. But should psychologists allow themselves to have an idea in mind without the prior observation? It has dangers, surely.

It has been argued that, in its hurry to become part of the twentieth-century scientific scene, psychology skipped the observational phase. But the reason for this skip is usually supposed to be professional status-seeking on the part of psychologists who are presumed to have a certain naive eagerness to don white coats and be scientists. I suspect the reasons are more complex. First, as I have already suggested, there appears to be a paradoxical unwillingness on the part of psychologists to come to grips with their subjects directly. Often the psychologist who is directing a piece of research seems quite willing, like an armchair general, to send his captains all over the place gathering the data while he, free from wearisome contact with subjects, can pull together all the subtle strings of analysis. Nearly all the psychologists here interviewed pointed out that they did research in a less and less personal way as time went on. Anne Roe (1953) in her study of eminent psychologists found that many of them had had very difficult childhoods. As a result, they had not withdrawn from personal relations but invested a great deal of importance in them. At the same time, they were very bad at them. Roe studied a quite different set of psychologists, of course, and I did not, as she did, attempt a set of 'clinical' interviews. But she found, as I suggest I have, a very paradoxical relationship among many psychologists in their relation to people. And the part of the paradox that suggests psychologists may prefer to keep away from subjects in the raw and handle them as data may contribute to the generally unfavourable light in which so-called 'pure' observation is held.

Another factor is that we all think we know what people do. We are surrounded by behaviour. And, since we all live in a world that is positively awash with behaviour, we tend to think we know much of what needs to be known about how people behave. Psychologists bring these assumptions to their work in, at least, the general sense that they will mock anyone who proposes an experiment that says, 'Let's see what happens if . . . .' That kind of experiment is acceptable if you are dealing with an abnormal group – with monkeys, with children, with the mentally deficient.

It is surely curious that while an ethologist like Tinbergen feels it vital to ground his students in techniques of observation, few human psychologists would suggest that students need to learn how to observe people. We take it for granted that we can do that. We treat what is familiar with, if not contempt, at least complacency. So psychologists do experiments often without the prior observation that might help them to know what they are looking for. They rely, perhaps excessively, on those situations in which subjects are closely observed (animal primate studies, studies of the mentally deficient or 'sick') for ideas as to what to look at in normal behaviour. In his interview, Professor Tajfel argued that he could see no sense in observation which

344

starts out from the simple question 'Let's see what happens if . . .' One needed a much more precise hypothesis in mind. The kind of hypothesis that Tajfel seemed to be referring to would be a much more detailed and complex one than one formulated by Tinbergen who admits, cheerfully, to observing always with some question in his mind. But often the questions are vague, perhaps fruitfully vague, such as what event made the animal do that or what is the survival value of that particular pattern of behaviour for the animal. But we don't necessarily feel we know what animals are likely to do and much research is driven by the need to see 'how human' they are. We presume we know how, and in what ways, we are human, so we don't need to observe ourselves.

It seems necessary to develop ideas and practices about the relationship between observations in the field and the design of experiments so that one might, first, do some observations, then test these hunches in an experimental situation and, thirdly, take the findings of the experiment back to the field situation to see how useful and valid they appear to be in that situation. Sometimes using such an approach, though costly and slow, might help reconcile two main methodological positions – one, that observation is too vague to be useful and, two, that experiments are too artificial and that psychology ought to happen in the laboratory. Some psychologists may already work sometimes along these lines but these are not procedures that are recognised as usual. One rarely sees articles in learned journals whose introduction is taken up with detailing the actual observations that led to the framing of the hypothesis.

2. The Normal and the Abnormal

Both Miller and Hudson argued that psychology is too much concerned with the study of 'freaks'. Miller would like to see a study of people who have adjusted extremely well rather than of those who have failed to come up to society's scratch. The extent to which so much psychology has been done on non-volunteer and abnormal subjects – children, students and patients – is really quite worrying, especially for a discipline that has avoided the detailed observation of 'normal' behaviour. Ignorance about what is 'normal' has also been combined with a quite justifiable ethical endeavour. Psychologists want to 'help' the abnormal so they study them more. Moreover, ever since Freud, psychologists have been proving that there are no clear-cut distinctions between either the normal and the neurotic or the normal and the abnormal. The whole thrust of the anti-psychiatry 'school' of Laing and David Cooper has, in part, been similar. But in almost all of these cases, the accent has been, not on showing what normal behaviour is, but on showing that those who have been labelled by someone or by some institution as abnormal very often behave normally or, to be more exact, as it has been presumed normal people behave when they behave normally. In fact, the whole issue of looking at people who are behaving in such a way as to escape attention has been shelved, partly because the question of 'what is normal' has seemed to be such a reactionary question. But one still needs to look at how, and why, people who manage, cope and live 'average' lives do so. There must be limits to what abnormal behaviour can tell us about normal behaviour. Those limits need to be clarified.

It is also useful to link this argument with Hudson's plea that small samples should be studied in some depth – often using interviews. But if the interview method is so rejected by psychologists working in the field of personality, one hardly expects to find it favoured in other fields. As Hudson argues, there is growing interest in a methodology for dealing with small samples.

There is another point here also. Normally, a psychologist comes to a sample with a precise set of questions. If of an experimental frame of mind, he will have formally set forth predictions. It does not do, for example, to ask a sample of ten people what they think the most important issues in their lives happen to be. Such an approach, bringing psychology to the people to coin a slogan for it, might seem clumsy and is clumsy. But there is some need for this kind of approach. Even humanistic psychologists like Maslow seem to fight shy of giving their subjects such control over the subject matter of psychology. He quotes, with approval, a test that will tell people whether or not they have become self-actualisers or, in his less technical phrase, reached 'full humanness'. It must be worrying, indeed, if your answers to the *Personal Orientation Inventory* reveal you as a stunted, uncreative, not quite full human being. It is surely time that people tell psychologists what mattered in their lives as, at least, a springboard for further research. But again, the apparent knowledge we have about why and how people tick makes it hard to ask these sorts of questions.

The fact that such talking to subjects smacks of introspection is, of course, very helpful for those who want to avoid doing it. Introspection led to chaos in psychology before J. B. Watson rescued us all from the slough of studying consciousness. In fact, the kind of introspection that was pursued when people tried to study the contents of consciousness has little to do with asking someone to describe what he feels or say what he thinks. What a person says as a result of his own introspections need not be true. Freud often assumed his patients lied or distorted the truth. Every time a psychologist asks you to fill in a questionnaire that asks such questions as 'Do you sometimes feel sad for no apparent reason' he is asking you to introspect. Fear of introspection has been used as a reason for rejecting more humanistic approaches to psychology for far too long. It is one kind of very useful evidence. Every psychologist uses it to some extent without, perhaps, realising that he, *horribile dictu*, is asking his subjects to do introspections. If they were 'answering questionnaires' it would seem so much safer. And the kind of inquiry that would get normal people to talk about their lives, the things that mattered in them, in conjunction with a due battery of tests, would at least provide a mine of rich data to seam.

3. Prediction

The whole subject of prediction has become very vexed. To some psychologists, it seems improper to attempt a scientific study of man and not try to predict. To others, any attempt at predicting human behaviour lessens man. Again, the trend towards polarising positions may have helped simplify the issues but it has not helped to clarify them.

Popper in 'Problems, aims and responsibilities in science' (1963) wrote:

> Agreement between theory and observation should count for nothing unless the theory is a testable theory, and unless the agreement is the result of attempts to test the theory. But testing a theory means trying to find its weak spots; it means trying to refute it. And a theory is testable if it is refutable.

A theory can be tested if its hypothesis can be stated so as to lead to predictions which may be tested empirically. The results of an experiment will either falsify the theory or give it conditional support. The hypothesis must precede the experiment. It is no good looking at a mass of data and extracting conclusions from them: it is no good devising *ad hoc* explanations for facts which turn up. The only serious progress can be made by a *pas de deux* in which hypothesis precedes

347

experiments. Popper's examples in *The Logic of Scientific Discovery* are drawn from physics, largely.

Yet this model of how science should be has captured much of the ground in psychology. Holt, in a paper in which he argued against the ideographic approach in the study of personality, wrote: 'In science when we say we understand something, we mean we can predict and control it' (1962). He contrasted this serious scientific attitude with that of the Romantic Movement in science which aims at some kind of emphathetic understanding rather than knowledge. This kind of understanding seems to have something terribly self-indulgent about it.

Without the use of prediction one cannot hope to devise those laws of human behaviour which is what, after all, psychologists are in business for.

This tyranny of prediction can be found if one looks in most psychology journals where it has become obligatory, almost, for the author to set down a list of hypotheses which are to be tested. How often, one wonders, are the hypotheses written up after the results? This applies even to such once-'freer' fields as educational psychology.

Two psychologists who are not afraid of showing hostility to lack of rigour are Broadbent and Eysenck. Yet each in his different way has criticised this fetish for prediction. Broadbent wrote in *Decision and Stress* (1971, p. 5):

Amongst psychologists, the fashionable mode of reporting results has for about thirty years been the hypothetico-deductive form, and the journals consist of a steady stream of papers giving hypothesis, prediction and verification. This stream is punctuated by occasional protests from those who feel the balance has swung too much the other way . . . [Broadbent's] argument can be fairly described as a rationalisation of a felt distaste for the amount of theory current in psychology; he located the source of this distaste in the deductive method. Many complex theories were verified by experiments which were so simple that alternative theories would predict the same result; when predictions as specific and detailed as the theory were tried, they were usually disproved, and in that case the research led to no advance.

Eysenck, for his part, attacks the simple-minded notion of the scientific method that he feels most psychologists have. He writes (1970a, p. 404):

In psychology, and indeed in most sciences where research is carried on at the edge of the unknown, weak rather than strong theories are the rule, and successful prediction is of greater importance than unsuccessful prediction; the former suggests important follow-up investigations and leads to the conclusions that the theory, though not necessarily correct, may be leading in a promising direction, while the latter is open to many divergent explanations which do not necessarily imply a failure of the theory as implied by the major premiss.

Eysenck goes on to say (ibid., p. 405):

> Psychologists sometimes seem in danger of throwing out promising ideas of wide applicability through premature insistence on a degree of deductive and experimental rigour which is quite out of place in a young science just beginning the hard task of building up its foundations.

And, of course, psychologists usually seem to think that when a prediction works out this is a new fact. But it is one thing to make a prediction, such as that if the theory of relativity is true, then if you fly a clock round the world it will go slower being in motion than a clock that remains earthbound. This prediction was tested using an atomic clock and was found to be verified. It is quite another thing to argue that delinquent boys have a weak self-concept and to show that delinquent boys at a level of probability of $p < 0.05$ tend to have 'weaker' self-concepts. In the case of relativity, the prediction is both clear and absolute. It refers to a particular set of events. Predictions in psychological literature are rarely borne out so well. For example, a study on delinquent boys would not hope to conclude that all the delinquent boys in the sample had weaker self-concepts. The editor of a learned psychological journal at least would be content if the evidence indicated that on some measures of 'weak' self-concept, delinquent boys tended to have a higher rating. The precise measurements would always be expressed in the way in which the scores differed from what would be expected by chance. It is common, of course, to accept a trend that could only have occurred by chance one time in twenty as being significant. If a trend could only have occurred by chance one time in a hundred, it is highly significant. If a trend could only have occurred one time in a thousand, it is a kind of conceptual jackpot. On the side of diminishing probability there has been a tendency in recent years to cite results which might have happened by chance one time in ten as 'tending' towards significance. Moreover, in a psychological experiment, one is also very rarely dealing with a situation that is so 'pure' you can be absolutely sure that what caused the variations in results was what you thought, and hypothesised, should. In spite, however, of these very different levels of significance, by the time you reach the 'Conclusion' part of most papers, all bar the one-in-ten are treated pretty much equally as facts that have been established. Yet the predictions as to each have not been equally borne out. Surely a fact at 100 to 1 is more than a fact at 20 to 1. And at 1,000 to 1, it is a superfact.

It is arguable that psychologists should predict at what level of significance their hypotheses will be confirmed. Let us assume your theory requires prediction A to be true and that prediction A is a key notion in it, it is surely not the most splendid vindication if it just scrapes into a level of significance at $p < 0.05$ or at 20 to 1. Yet how many papers will note the fact that the author was disappointed by the level of significance that was achieved.

It could be argued, like Eysenck suggests, that I am here requiring a quite unrealistic degree of rigour. But many psychologists believe that they are furnishing precisely this kind of rigour. The use of more and more complex statistics seems to fuel this impression although it could be argued that the better statistics you have the more possible it is to display some interesting correlations according to some figures. Again, it would be interesting to know if there have been cases where psychologists using one test of significance have found their results insufficiently significant while on another test, the data have passed statistical muster. I have never seen that reported. Can it never have happened?

It is also usual for any predictions, if confirmed, to be applied as widely as possible. It is rare for a theory to be defined so that it only applies to the kind of subjects it was tested on. If an experiment with students shows that what they hear is very much influenced by some information that has just been given them, it is usually argued that this applies to all human beings. Psychology is after the laws of human behaviour irrespective of the people, almost. But could one assume, on the basis of these experiments, that the same would hold true of middle-aged people?

Moreover, if predictions are falsified, the traditional response of psychologists seems to be not to cast away the theory but either to

350

point out that there may have been mistakes in putting together the sample of subjects or to point to actual difficulties in the experimental situation or to suggest that what we are seeing at work are various variables, so subtle and unexpected as not to have been taken into account. None of the psychologists I interviewed hinted that over the ten to thirty-five years that their ideas had been tested they had, in any major part, been found to have been wrong. Festinger left cognitive dissonance because he was bored with it; and it was no error, he said, in his theory, but in himself. He could get no new ideas; he left the field. All the others felt time had vindicated their work. Their work had, of course, progressed and there had been important (but essentially minor) criticisms but nothing major. Recall Broadbent's claim: 'Experimenters don't disagree that much.' Recall Skinner's point that he knew early in his career the things he wanted to discover. Hudson, though his work has been severely criticised, feels it has stood the test of time; Eysenck, too, is equally criticised and equally convinced: so is Festinger. Tinbergen came, perhaps, the closest of any psychologist in admitting that there had been serious errors when he said that ethology in the 1930s had been aggressively against American psychology. I am not saying, of course, that psychologists do not allow minor revisions in their theories but that, by and large, the idea that a major theory was wrong does not seem to have been much admitted. Although they often conflict, all the main theoretical ideas of the psychologists in this book have, in the estimation of those who created them, stood the test of time.

Such attitudes cannot help the development of psychology. If you don't accept my fact, since my fact invalidates your fact, we can hardly be said to be doing our best to lay the foundations of knowledge. As McClelland pointed out, psychologists do not usually place their new brick of knowledge on someone's well-established brick: they want so much to be original they start a new brick pile instead. There remains confusion as to what is a fact in psychology. So though there is the model of predictive science, when predictions fail or when critiques are launched, that tends to be forgotten. It is surely telling that Skinner for many years could not be bothered to read Chomsky's critique of *Verbal Behaviour.*

4. Humanistic Psychology

It is surely paradoxical that there should be a controversy as to whether psychology should be humanistic or not. That said, the task of those

351

who want to scoff at humanistic psychology has been made significantly easier by humanist psychologists who often reject not just behaviourism but also science, society and the modern way of life as well. Or appear to. It will be recalled that Laing felt it necessary to point out that he did not belong to what he labelled the psychedelic left as everyone appeared to suppose he did. In the name of humanism, some dreadful psychology is done. And by pointing to the lack of rigour that is often found among humanistic psychologists – and I mean here intellectual rigour as well as experimental rigour – traditional psychologists can have a field day. But what is one to make of statements like this:

> The first overarching Big Problem is to make the Good Person. We must have better human beings or else it is quite possible that we may all be wiped out and, even if not wiped out, certainly live in tension and anxiety as a species . . . . This Good Person can be equally called the self-evolving person, the responsible-for-himself-and-his-own-evolution person, the fully illuminated or awakened or perspicuous man, the fully human person, the self-actualised person . . . etc.

The author was Abraham Maslow, the father of humanistic psychology, writing in 1968. Maslow also listed criteria for this superb specimen, the self-actualised person. In a different paper, 'Self actualisation and beyond' (1971), Maslow made some other points: 'Self-actualisation means experiencing fully, vividly, selflessly, with full concentration and total absorption. It means experiencing without the self-consciousness of the adolescent' (p. 47).

Later Maslow writes (ibid., p. 49):

> We have talked so far of experiencing without self-awareness, of making the growth choice rather than the fear choice, of listening to the impulse voices and of being honest and taking responsibility. All these are steps toward self-actualisation and all of them *guarantee* better life choices. One cannot choose for a life unless he dares to listen to himself, *his own self,* at each moment in life, and to say calmly, 'No, I don't like such and such.'

This surely is no more than the reappearance of Polonius who instructed Laertes 'to thine own self be true'. Maslow is so totally vague in what he means by self-actualising which also involves becoming more sensitive to things like truth, beauty and goodness that it is quite unclear what he is about although it sounds rather good. Maslow, who started off by studying monkey societies had, at least, to the end some of the reservations scientists hedge round difficult ideas and data. He often seems to have forgotten, or transcended, these reservations, but he kept some awareness of them. Those who have followed his line of thinking have often suggested that the solution to human problems lies in just those techniques they are advocating. The Encounter Group movement has led to many spin-offs, some weirder than others. There are many of these movements that are much more linked to religion than to psychology. Oscar Ichazo's ARICA movement is, frankly, concerned with turning out a better individual and uses all kinds of religious exercises and frills culled from all sorts of religious traditions to this end. These developments play right into the hands of those who want to see psychology as a fairly rigid science since they seem to show that a humanistic psychology has to be so self-indulgent.

And one concept, especially, which it allows to be made ridiculous is that of understanding. Holt argued that understanding in science means to be able to predict and to control. This is manifestly false. Geology, for example, has been much concerned with continental drift. There is no way in which geologists can either predict or control this event. Astronomers cannot control the behaviour of the stars, let alone the Universe. But against the background of many of the vagaries of humanistic psychology, it has been easy to suggest that understanding is a romantic, even mystical concept, in which the psychologist feels understanding, sympathy, empathy with his subject, in which he grows to love, care, understand and even to be absorbed in him, her or it. This is a very polemic use of the word to 'understand'. Understanding is seeing the reasons why something happened or some of them, perhaps. It is also being able to make connections between the event X and other events. Why did John drop out of college? Why do many people like reading romantic novels? In neither of these cases does it seem necessary to be able to predict what will happen in another event for us to understand why the first event happened. Nor is it necessary to have been able to predict that John's dropping out of college would happen. That does not mean, however, that one needs to sink in a pit of varagies such as exemplified by the editorial of the opening issue of *Self and Society,* the Journal of the Association of Humanistic Psychology. It ran:

Live more fully. Enjoy more. Suffer more. See more. Feel more. Get away from talk, talk, talk. Love generously. Hate heartily. Say what you feel: feel what you say. Be more human and remind me of my humanity.

Inside me there is a young child and a wise old man. They know each other. The child plays a lot on his own. The old man does not talk much. They are both a bit frightened of other people and most of the time they wear the cloak of the adult me to meet others. With special people at special times, the cloak is dropped: my little boy romps with yours, my old man responds to your wise person.

Such a level of debate guarantees the success of behaviourism. I hope that the interviews with Hudson, Chomsky and Laing will do something to suggest that it is quite possible to argue and practise, or attempt to practise, a more humanistic psychology without lapsing into this kind of ego-coddling stuff. For it allows psychologists who want to think that if you try to study complex, real problems, if you do become involved with your subjects, you are bound to become a victim of this kind of psychological revivalism that preaches freedom with the same kind of authoritarianism as the Victorians preached discipline. Humanistic psychology does not have to become a religion of the ego. But while it can be parodied as such, the behaviourists and experimenters will use it as a dreadful example of what happens when you drop your scientific standards. A more rational, less enthusiastic approach to a humanistic psychology is possible and should be explored.

5. The Paradigm of Psychology

Recently, much philosophy of science has been concerned with the relationships between having a paradigm that all workers in a certain field accept and progress in that field. If these interviews have shown anything, it is surely that there is no widely accepted paradigm in psychology. We have a series of conflicting paradigms not so much as to the nature of Man (though here there are clear differences) but as to the nature of the kind of research that should be done. Nearly all the psychologists here are evangelists for their own particular point of view which is usually either embattled or under-represented. It fits in well with McClelland's ideas on power motive in psychologists, surely, to find that psychologists seem to want their approach to become all-powerful. There are a number of serious results that come from this sense of battle.

Research in psychology does not seem to lead to results that are widely accepted and can be built on. Within a particular field where a particular paradigm appears to guide research, there may be progress. Broadbent's *Decision and Stress* (1971) sets out how over the ten years between 1958 and 1968 the information theory approach to certain problems of perception and memory was modified by experiment upon experiment. It led to new knowledge. It was, however, only a local advance. For the paradigm that underlies this whole field of inquiry – that Man may be regarded as a kind of cybernetic communication channel – would not be regarded as true or useful by Laing or Chomsky or Leupold-Löwenthal. This does not affect just the future of research but also the past knowledge we are supposed to have acquired. For what is a fact, and an important one, for one psychologist will not be a fact, let alone important, for another one. The easiest way to show this is with reference to Freud. The Freudian model has been of importance to Laing, McClelland and, in some ways, both Hudson and Miller as well as to Leupold-Löwenthal. The latter picked with polemic skill on those experimental psychologists who attempted to identify the oral personality by seeing which children preferred to suck lollipops. Eysenck, Broadbent and Skinner, on the other hand, all reject Freud and cite experiments to show that he was wrong when you could actually produce an experiment to test one of his ideas. In other words, the hope of arriving at a paradigm of psychology seems slim.

Mahoney's study (1976) which showed that psychologists tended not to recommend papers that went against their personal positions shows how very hard it is to be truly objective. Psychologists are people who are obliged to pretend they can suspend all prejudices. It will be interesting to see what reaction Mahoney gets to his study and if he extends it by asking the psychologists involved what they thought of the outcome.

It is also made worse by the fact that psychologists seem compelled not just to promote their own ideas but to do it at the expense of any other theories. Theories in psychology compete not only for the local battlefield of any speciality – let us say, how we learn motor skills – but they also compete for the whole image and larger ground of what psychology is about. Psychologists are normative although they usually seek to deny the fact. They want to impose their particular view of the science on others. There is a strange tendency echoed in these

355

interviews for psychologists to strike an attitude of 'those who are not for me are against me'.

There is no answer to these problems, though I hope it will have been useful to try and set them out. They are not the only problems that psychology must resolve if it is to patch up its wounds. There are problems about the role of the psychologist in society, about experimenter effects and about the cultural milieu. To some extent, these have been touched on in the interviews. No book like this can ever be complete because there is no sense in which it can be complete, but at least an awareness of some problems and issues which are tearing and slowing psychology may prove of some use for the future. If, as Pope said, 'the proper study of mankind is Man', it is perhaps rather crucial that different approaches to psychology should begin to make more than partisan progress, accepted more or less only by those who started out thinking much the same. How one achieves a solution, as opposed to analysing the problem, is a very different matter. Psychology touches on what the psychologist sees himself to be and the kind of psychology one espouses must reflect the sort of person one is, the background one has and who one is becoming. So the problem is not just a methodological one, but apart from uttering pieties about goodwill, tolerance, more interdisciplinary research and such like, it is difficult to see what the solution is, although part of the solution lies in psychologists learning to see the angle from which they approach the problem they are interested in *as being one angle* and not, necessarily, the only valid angle. As Tajfel said of building up European social psychology, it is not something which can be done by programmatic statements, let alone pious ones. But it is a perspective on research that might well help.

Bibliography

Ardrey, R. (1967), *The Territorial Imperative*, Collins.

Austin, M. (1971), 'Dream recall and the bias of intellectual ability', *Nature*, 231, p. 59.

Bannister, D. (1970), 'Comment', in *Explanation in the Behavioural Sciences*, ed. R. Borger and F. Cioffi, Cambridge University Press.

Bartlett, F. C. (1932), *Remembering: A Study in Experimental and Social Psychology*, Cambridge University Press.

Bem, D. (1967), 'Self-perception—an alternative explanation of cognitive dissonance phenomena', *Psychological Review*, 74, p. 183.

Bickman, L. and, Henchy T. (1972), *Beyond the Laboratory: Field Research in Social Psychology*, McGraw-Hill.

Borger, R. and Cioffi, F. (eds) (1970), *Explanation in the Behavioural Sciences*, Cambridge University Press.

Brehm, J. W. and Cohen, A. R. (1962), *Explorations in Cognitive Dissonance*, Wiley.

Broadbent, D. (1958), *Perception and Communications*, Pergamon.

(1961), *Behaviour*, Eyre & Spottiswoode.

(1971), *Decision and Stress*, Academic Press.

(1974), *In Defence of Empirical Psychology*, Methuen.

Chapanis, N. P. and Chapanis, A. (1964), 'Cognitive dissonance—five years later', *Psychology Bulletin*, 61, pp. 1–22.

Chein, I. (1972), *The Science of Behaviour and the Image of Man*, Tavistock.

Chomsky, N. (1957), *Syntactic Structures*, Mouton.

(1959), Review of *Verbal Behaviour* by B. F. Skinner, *Language*, 35, pp. 26–58.

(1965), *Aspects of the Theory of Syntax*, MIT Press.

(1966), *Cartesian Linguistics*, Harper & Row.

(1968), *Language and Mind*, Harcourt, Brace & World.

(1970), 'Comment', in *Explanation in the Behaviour Sciences*, ed. R. Borger and F. Cioffi, Cambridge University Press.

Cohen, D. (1973), Interview with Michel Jouvet, *New Scientist*, March.

Cooper, D. (1972), *Death of the Family*, Penguin.

357

Bibliography

Dollard, J. and Miller, N. (1939), *Frustration and Aggression*, New York University Press.

(1950), *Personality and Psychotherapy*, McGraw-Hill.

Eysenck, H. J. (1953), *The Structure of Human Personality*, Methuen.

(1952), 'The effects of psychotherapy and evaluation', *Journal of Consulting Psychology*, vol. 16, no. 5, pp. 319-24.

(1957), *Sense and Nonsense in Psychology*, Penguin.

(1967), *The Biological Basis of Personality*, University of Chicago Press.

(1969), *Know Your Own IQ*, Penguin.

(1970a), 'Comment', in *Explanation in the Behavioural Sciences*, ed. R. Borger and F. Cioffi, Cambridge University Press.

(1970b), *Uses and Abuses of Psychology*, Penguin.

(1971), *Race, Intelligence and Behaviour*, Maurice Temple Smith.

Festinger, L. (1957), *Theory of Cognitive Dissonance*, Row & Peterson and Carlsmith, L. (1959), 'Cognitive consequences of forced compliance', *Journal of Abnormal and Social Psychology*, 58, pp. 203-10.

Riecken, H. W., Jnr and Schachter, S. (1957), *When Prophecy Fails*, University of Minnesota Press.

Fried, S. B., Crumpper, D. C. and Allen, J. C. (1973), 'Ten years of social psychology' is there a growing commitment to field research?', *America Psychologist*, 28, pp. 155-7.

Friedenberg, E. Z. (1973), *Laing*, Fontana.

Harris, Z. (1949), *Structural Linguistics*, University of Chicago Press.

Hick, W. E. (??????), 'On the rate of gain of information', *Quarterly Journal of Experimental Psychology*, vol. 4, pp. 11-26.

Hirschmann, A. O. (1970), *Exit, Voice and Loyalty*, Harvard University Press.

Hofstadter, R. (1945), *Social Darwinism in American Thought*, Beacon Press.

Holt, R. R. (1962), 'Individuality and generalisation in the psychology of personality', *Journal of Personality*, 30, pp. 377-404.

Hudson, L. (1966), *Contrary Imaginations*, Methuen.

(1968), *Frames of Mind*, Methuen.

(1972), *The Cult of the Fact*, Cape.

(1975), *Human Beings*, Cape.

and Jacot, B. (1971), 'Marriage and fertility in academic life', *Nature*, 229, p. 31.

Hull, Clark (1933), *Hypnosis and Suggestibility*, Irvington.

Immergluck, L. (1964), 'Determinism—freedom in contemporary psychology', *American Psychology*, 19, pp. 270-81.

Jordan, N. (1968), *Themes in Speculative Psychology*, Tavistock.

Kuhn, T. (1962), *The Structure of Scientific Revolutions*, University of Chicago Press.

Laing, R. D. (1960), *The Divided Self*, Tavistock.

(1966), *Interpersonal Perception*, Tavistock.

(1967), *The Politics of Experience*, Penguin.

(1972), *Knots*, Penguin.

and Cooper, D. (1964), *Reason and Violence*, Tavistock.

and Esterson, A. (1963), *Sanity, Madness and the Family; Families of Schizophrenics*, Penguin.

Lorenz, K. (1966), *On Aggression*, Methuen.

McClelland, D. (1951), *Personality*, Sloane,

(1953), *The Achievement Motive*, Appleton Century,

(1961), *The Achieving Society*, Princeton University Press.

(1964), *The Roots of Consciousness*, Van Nostrand.

(1965), 'Achievement and entrepreneurship: a longitudinal study', *Journal of Personality and Social Psychology*, 1, pp. 321-92.

(1973a), 'The two faces of power', in *Readings in Human Motivation*, edited by D. McClelland and R. S. Steele, General Learning Press.

(1973b), 'Testing for competence', *American Psychologist*, 28, pp. 1-14.

Mahoney, M. (1976), 'Seekers after truth', *Psychology Today*, April.

Maslow, A. H. (1971), 'Self-actualisation and beyond', in *Farther Reaches of Human Nature*, Viking Press.

(1973), *Farther Reaches of Human Nature*, Penguin.

Mezan, Peter (1972), 'After Freud and Jung comes R. D. Laing', *Esquire*, January.

Milgram, S. (1974), *Obedience to Authority*, Tavistock.

Miller, N. E. (1962), 'Strengthening the behavioural sciences', *Science*, 136, vol. 2, p. 327.

and Dollard, J. (1941), *Social Learning and Imitation*, Yale University Press.

Morris, D. (1967), *The Naked Ape*, Cape.

Polanyi, M. (1971), *Knowing and Being*, Routledge & Kegan Paul.

Popper, K. (1972), *The Logic of Scientific Discovery*, Hutchinson. Originally published in Germany, 1934.

(1963), 'Problems, aims and responsibilities in science', in *Conjectures and Refutations*, Oxford University Press.

Roazen, P. (1970), *Brother Animal*, Allen Lane.

Roe, A. (1953), 'A comparative psychological study of eminent psychologists and anthropologists and a comparison with biological and physical scientists', *Genetic Psychology Monographs*, vol, 67, no. 352.

Rosenberg, M. (1965), 'When dissonance fails', *Journal of Personality and Social Psychology*, 1, p. 28.

Ryle, G. (1949), *The Concept of Mind*, Hutchinson.

Self and Society (1972), Journal of the Association of Humanistic Psychology, no. 1.

Skinner, B. F. (1948), *Walden Two*, Macmillan.

(1953), *Science and Human Behaviour*, Macmillan.

(1957), *Verbal Behaviour*, Methuen.

(1972), *Beyond Freedom and Dignity*, Cape.

Szasz, T. (1960), 'The myth of mental illness', *American Psychologist*, 15, pp. 113-18.

Tajfel, H. and Israel, J. (eds) (1973), *The Context of Social Psychology: a Critical Assessment*, Academic Press.

Bibliography

Taylor, C. (1964), *The Explanation of Behaviour*, Routledge & Kegan Paul.

Tinbergen, N. (1965), *Social Behaviour in Animals*, Chapman & Hall.

Wallach, M. and Kogan, N. (1965), *Modes of Thinking in Young Children*, Holt, Rinehart & Winston.

Watson, J. B. (1913), 'Psychology as the behaviourist views it', *Psychological Review*, 20, p. 158.

Winterbottom, M. R. (1953), *The Relation of Childhood Training in Independence to Achievement Motivation*, PhD thesis, University of Michigan.

Zimbardo, P. (1969), *The Cognitive Control of Motivation: The Consequences of Choice and Dissonance*, Scott Foresman.

and Ebbesen, E. B. (1969), *Influencing Attitudes and Changing Behaviour*, Addison-Wesley.